STRATEGIC MANAGEMENT PRACTICE

READINGS IN STRATEGIC

MANAGEMENT

25¢ 76

STRATEGIC
MANAGEMENT
PRACTICE

READINGS IN STRATEGIC
MANAGEMENT

JOHN A. PEARCE II

School of Business Administration

George Mason University

RICHARD B. ROBINSON, JR.

College of Business Administration

University of South Carolina

IRWIN

Homewood, IL 60430   Boston, MA 02116

Sponsoring editor: Craig S. Beytien
Developmental editor: Kama Brockmann
Project editor: Jean Lou Hess
Production manager: Bette K. Ittersagen
Designer: Diane Beasley Design
Artist: Benoit Design
Compositor: Alexander Typesetting, Inc.
Typeface: 10/12 Century Schoolbook
Printer: R. R. Donnelley & Sons Company

Library of Congress Cataloging-in-Publication Data

Strategic management practice: readings in strategic management/
    John A. Pearce II, Richard B. Robinson, Jr.
        p.   cm.
    ISBN 0-256-09452-7
    1. Strategic planning.   I. Pearce, John A.   II. Robinson, Richard
B. (Richard Braden), date
    HD30.28.S73345   1991
    658.4′012—dc20   90-41309

Printed in the United States of America
1 2 3 4 5 6 7 8 9 0   DOC   7 6 5 4 3 2 1 0

Preface

The study of strategic management and business policy demands that we understand how the art and science of managing strategically is actually accomplished. Textbooks focus on a theory that provides a critically important basis by which the experiences of individual companies can be generalized to new situations faced by strategists. Often, however, the business examples that are briefly abstracted in textbooks are so shallow in content and vague in meaning that we are left uncertain and suspicious as to their value. Additionally, textbook authors are typically perceived as removed from the practice of strategic management, or at best, reporters of current business actions. While this perception is rarely a fact, it may well be the case that practicing managers are also an important source of information from whom we can learn about the realities of strategy formulation, implementation, and control.

The conclusion that we have reached is simply that despite their inestimable value as instructional tools, textbooks need to be supplemented with input by and about the actual behaviors, experiences, attitudes, and preferences of company executives. In response to this need, we have assembled *Strategic Management Practice*.

This book is no random assembly of loosely connected readings. Rather, it is a carefully selected and coordinated set of 29 articles that provides an up-to-date overview of strategic management in action from the perspective of practicing executives. While most authors would be justifiably reluctant to try to provide "how-to" dictates in an article, the selections in this book were chosen in part because they contain useful observations about how strategic planning and action can be productively managed.

The articles are arranged in four sections around four themes: the strategic management process, competitive environment analysis,

v

alternative company strategies, and strategy implementation. We believe that these themes represent key issues of investigation under any of several varied pedagogical approaches to the study of strategic management.

The articles themselves were written by some of the most prominent and insightful executives and scholars in the field of strategic management. The works were carefully reviewed for quality and interest level by 13 successful and popular journals that target executive readership. The original publishers of the articles that you will read are the *Academy of Management EXECUTIVE, Business, Business Horizons, California Management Review, Consultation, Journal of Business Strategy, Journal of Engineering Technology Management, Journal of Small Business Management, Management Review, Managerial Planning, Planning Review, Sloan Management Review,* and *Small Business Reports.*

Abstracts of the articles have been positioned in front of the book's four sections. These abstracts provide incisive overviews of the theme and key points of each article. While these are not article summaries and thus cannot substitute for the actual study of the articles themselves, the abstracts will help readers to anticipate the kinds of knowledge and insights that each article is likely to yield.

As consultants and practitioners ourselves, we rely on the information that is contained in the articles that we selected for this book. We hope that they provide you with similar kinds of valuable insights and, by so doing, that they contribute to your strategic management practice.

In using this book, we hope that you share our enthusiasm both for the rich subject matter of strategic management and for the articles that we have selected. We value your recommendations and appreciate hearing from you. Jack can be reached at the School of Business Administration, George Mason University, Fairfax, VA 22030, or by telephone at (703) 323-4361. Richard's address is College of Business Administration, University of South Carolina, Columbia, SC 29208; his telephone number is (803) 777-5961.

Jack Pearce
Richard Robinson

Contents

PART I
The Strategic Management Process

1 An Executive-Level Perspective on the Strategic
   Management Process *John A. Pearce II*   7

2 The Strategic Management Process: A Model and
   Terminology *Lloyd L. Byars*   24

3 The New Strategic Planning Boom: Hope for the Future
   or a Bureaucratic Exercise? *Sidney C. Sufrin and
   George S. Odiorne*   36

4 Tough Questions for Developing Strategies
   George S. Day   55

5 The Strategy Audit *Milton Lauenstein*   70

6 Principles of Strategic Planning Applied to International
   Corporations *Ellen C. Fingerhut and Daryl G. Hatano*   79

7 Corporate Mission Statements: The Bottom Line
   John A. Pearce II and Fred David   98

8 Objectives and Alternatives in the Context of Systems
   Analysis and MBO *Gil R. Mosard*   110

PART II
Analysis of the Competitive Environment

9 Competitive Analysis from a Strategic Planning
   Perspective *Syyed T. Mahmood and M. Munir Moon*   135

10 Developing an Effective Environmental Assessment
   Function *Allen H. Mesch*   146

11 International Competitor Analysis *Diane J. Garsombke*   158

12 A Manager's Guide for Evaluating Competitive Analysis
   Techniques *John E. Prescott and John H. Grant*   171

13   Environmental Forecasting: Key to Strategic
     Management   *John A. Pearce II and
     Richard B. Robinson, Jr.*   186
14   Analyzing the Competition   *James E. Svatko*   203
15   Environmental Scanning for Small and Growing
     Firms   *John A. Pearce II, Bruce L. Chapman, and
     Fred R. David*   212

PART III
Alternative Company Strategies

16   Selecting among Alternative Grand Strategies   *John A.
     Pearce II*   227
17   Concentrated Growth Strategies   *John A. Pearce II and
     James W. Harvey*   241
18   Quick Change Strategies for Vertical
     Integration   *Kathryn R. Harrigan*   251
19   Joint Ventures in the Face of Global
     Competition   *Benjamin Gomes-Casseres*   262
20   Corporate Divestiture: Pruning for Higher
     Profits   *Richard J. Schmidt*   279
21   Divestiture: Antidote to Merger Mania
     Clark E. Chastain   289
22   From Warning to Crisis: A Turnaround Primer
     P. Scott Scherrer   301
23   Customized Strategies for Service Sector
     Businesses   *John A. Pearce II and Lanny Herron*   313

PART IV
Strategy Implementation

24   Five Steps to Strategic Action   *David R. Brodwin and
     L. J. Bourgeois III*   337
25   Problems Encountered in Operationalizing a Company's
     Strategic Plans   *Robert E. Seiler and Kamal E. Said* 355
26   How to Implement Strategic Plans   *Don Collier*   365
27   Considerations in Implementing Strategic Control
     Peter Lorange and Declan Murphy   373
28   Growth Industries: Here Today, Gone Tomorrow
     Claire Starry and Nick McGaughey   390
29   Small Manufacturers—When Going outside Makes
     Sense   *Richard B. Robinson and Patricia P. McDougall* 401

PART I

The Strategic Management Process

Strategic management is the set of decisions and actions that result in the formulation, implementation, and control of strategies designed to achieve the objectives of an organization. Thus, strategic management involves a process by which major planning activities are undertaken and coordinated. Among these activities are the determination of the company mission; assessment of the firm's resources and capabilities; analysis of the firm's external competitive environment; assessment of the company's strategic options; and determination of the firm's long-term objectives and master strategy. Other activities involve: the development of short-term objectives, annual and functional strategies, and operational policies; design of implementation strategies involving budgeted resource allocations; matching of tasks, people, technologies, and reward systems; and development of monitoring and control systems to gauge strategic performance. Strategic management processes also involve the activation of all of the activities.

The focus of this first set of eight articles is to provide you with alternative ways of viewing and integrating the activities of strategic management into a carefully coordinated process. Having completed the readings, you will be in an excellent position to decide which approach is best for the situation that you are studying or even to generate a slightly modified process to address special planning needs that your strategic management situation has created.

The final two articles in this section address major tasks that characterize all perspectives on the strategic management process: specification of the company mission and development of the firm's objectives.

Abstracts

AN EXECUTIVE-LEVEL PERSPECTIVE ON THE STRATEGIC MANAGEMENT PROCESS

Strategic management is acknowledged by corporate executives as their principal approach to determining and directing the efforts of their firms for the long term. The problem for most planning executives who are as yet uncommitted to a strategic management system is that of determining the ways by which this "new" approach differs from their current framework for planning.

The focus of this article is to provide an executive-level perspective on the management process of strategy formulation and implementation. The emphasis is on the major components of the process and their interrelationships, followed by a critical evaluation of the system's strengths and limitations.

Because of the similarity among general models of the strategic management process, it is possible to develop one eclectic model which is representative of the foremost thought in the area. The basic components of almost all strategic management models are very similar: company mission, company profile, external environment, interactive opportunity analysis and strategic choice decision making, long-term objectives, grand strategy, annual objectives, operating strategies, implementation of strategy, and review and evaluation. The objective of the process pertains to the formulation and implementation of strategies which result in a long-term achievement of the company's mission and a near-term achievement of its aims.

There are several important implications of strategic management as a process. First, it means that a change in any components of the system will affect several or all other components. A second implication is the sequential nature of strategy formulation and evaluation. A third implication of strategic management as a process is the necessity for feedback from implementation, review, and evaluation to the early stage components of the process. A final implication is the need to view the process as a dynamic system.

It is also important to understand the limitations of strategic management models so as not to diminish their overall impact by overlooking their weaknesses. In this article, three such limitations will be stressed; namely, that most models are wholistic, descriptive, and nonpolitical.

THE STRATEGIC MANAGEMENT PROCESS: A MODEL AND TERMINOLOGY

The purpose of this article is to present a model for the terms and expressions used in describing it.

Strategic management is concerned with making and implementing decisions about an organization's future direction. Basically, strategic management can be broken down into two phases: strategic planning and strategy implementation. Strategic planning involves making decisions with regard to:

1. Determining the organization's mission, which includes a statement of both philosophy and purpose.
2. Formulating policies to guide in establishing objectives, choosing a strategy, and implementing the chosen strategy.
3. Establishing long- and short-term objectives to meet the organization's mission.
4. Determining the strategy or strategies to pursue in achieving the organization's objectives.

Strategy implementation is concerned with making decisions related to developing an organizational structure to achieve the strategy, ensuring effective performance of activities necessary to accomplish the strategy, and monitoring the effectiveness of the strategy in achieving organizational objectives.

The organization's mission statements, policies, objectives, and strategy are not mutually exclusive components of the strategic planning process. Rather they are highly interdependent and inseparable. Because of their interdependence, all of the steps in the strategic management process need to be examined when a strategy fails. Likewise, all of the steps need to be examined when a strategy is successful in order to ensure future successes.

THE NEW STRATEGIC PLANNING BOOM: HOPE FOR THE FUTURE OR A BUREAUCRATIC EXERCISE?

Strategic planning is an increasingly important part of the business world. It functions not as a means of tactical development, but as an attempt to assess and prepare for likely changes in technology, ideology, politics, and environment. For strategic planning to succeed, preknowledge and preinformation concerning the future must be an integral part of the planning. Regardless of the model or system used, strategic planning involves:

1. Adjustment to the inevitable by anticipation or a refusal to accept inevitability.
2. Consideration of society.
3. A choice of goals and means to those goals.
4. Prediction of unintended side effects.
5. Management of risk and uncertainty.

Strategic planners need to develop a theory of change by using accounting, statistics, economics, and social psychology. Strategic planners also need to act responsibly and ethically with a clear perception of the impact that planning has on society and labor. Last, planners should learn to take advantage of available power, resources, and information.

TOUGH QUESTIONS FOR DEVELOPING STRATEGIES

The real cost of an unfocused strategy dialogue between corporate and operating management is felt when the strategy fails to deliver the promised outcomes. Most problems are eventually traced to unrealistic assumptions, distorted resource allocations, or a lack of management commitment. At the heart of all efforts at improvement is the development of robust and mutually acceptable criteria for testing and refining business strategies.

While the impulse to make unrealistic assumptions colors all forecasts, the real reasons are more deeply rooted in the way managers cope with ambiguity. The author identifies three sources of bias: anchoring, selective perception, and illusion of control. These three problems are compounded when top management has unrealistic expectations and requires operating management to make commitments that may not be possible.

Corporate allocations of resources for maximum impact are often thwarted by the "gamesmanship" of operating managers manipulating the planning process to serve their own ends. The resulting distortions are magnified when the measures of prospective performance used to compare strategies are themselves misleading. The result is a bias toward short-run payoffs from investment in mature businesses.

Strategy failures often boil down to a lack of cohesion and commitment by management. A lack of cohesion is often evident in strategies that have evolved over time and are held together by shaky alliances among functional departments. However, the consequences of a lack of cohesion and resulting absence of commitment to integrated action are greatest when the business embarks on a new strategy.

To avoid the predictable reasons for strategy failure, the author provides a series of evaluation criteria for corporate and operating managers. These criteria are cast in the form of seven "tough" questions that are understood and accepted as appropriate ground rules by all participants in the strategic dialogue. These criteria pertain to suitability, validity, feasibility, consistency, vulnerability, adaptability, and financial desirability. Strategies that do not meet these criteria are unlikely to succeed.

THE STRATEGY AUDIT

Strategic errors can be most costly, even threatening the survival of the affected enterprise. One potentially useful approach to avoid this problem is to conduct an annual audit of corporate strategy. Such a strategy audit should not take the form of a backward-looking critique of what has been done. Rather, it should be designed to take full advantage of the experience and expertise of the board of directors in determining the best strategy for guiding the corporation in the future.

Companies encounter a number of pitfalls in developing a sound strategy, such as habit and paper entrepreneurialism, or they may undertake dangerous cure-alls such as unwise portfolio management and diversification. Executives are hindered in strategy formulation by such factors as lack of objectivity, pressures for performance, and inexperience. A regular systematic strategy audit by the board can reveal inconsistencies and weaknesses and, thus, provide a stimulus for corrective action.

The well-planned audit will address such issues as whether the firm is adequately informed about its markets, what resources will be required to implement a chosen strategy, and whether provision has been made for employing the strategy as a guide for operating decisions. In auditing over-all corporate strategy, directors must also be sensitive to broader corporate issues. These include objectives, finance, scope of operations, and organization.

PRINCIPLES OF STRATEGIC PLANNING APPLIED TO INTERNATIONAL CORPORATIONS

Much of the information on strategic planning models ignores the unique problems of firms engaged in international business. In this article the authors examine strategic planning models in an international arena by analyzing the conceptual difficulties the models encounter when applied to international firms and by noting issues multinational corporations need to include in their plans.

The authors explore the problems of strategic planning in the global marketplace by first examining the firm's external situation for opportunities and threats, then performing an internal analysis to determine the firm's strengths and weaknesses, and finally developing strategies to capitalize on the strengths, pursue the opportunities, and thwart the threats.

Among the issues discussed are foreign government industrial policies (including nationalization and protectionism); international finance; joint ventures; and the impact of global operations on the experience curve, market segmentation, and portfolio planning.

CORPORATE MISSION STATEMENTS: THE BOTTOM LINE

Developing a mission statement is an important first step in the strategic planning process. Nevertheless, the components of mission statements are among the least empirically examined issues in strategic management. Thus, the research reported in this paper focuses on the nature and role of mission statements in organizational processes; its goal is to improve our understanding of the link between strategic planning and firm performance.

The findings of this study support the idea that the inclusion of eight desired components in a mission statement is positively associated with a firm's financial performance. Furthermore, the findings suggest that corporate philosophy, self-concept, and public image are especially important components to include in an organizational mission statement. A comprehensive mission statement should provide a basis for making better strategic decisions which, in turn, should contribute to improved organizational performance.

The authors further argue that organizations that differ dramatically in such areas as profit motive, stakeholders, and geographic marketplaces will differ in the components included in their mission statement. For optimal effectiveness, mission statements need to be as distinctive as the relatively unique competitive situations in which organizations conduct their strategic planning.

OBJECTIVES AND ALTERNATIVES IN THE CONTEXT OF SYSTEMS ANALYSIS AND MBO

Setting objectives and developing alternatives are essential steps in the systems analysis framework for problem solving. This paper considers tasks and techniques designed to improve analysis and communication in systems analysis and also management by objectives (MBO) planning. Fundamental tasks are proposed with respect to setting objectives and developing alternatives.

The identification of major needs or goals, objectives, and subobjectives is a complex process whereby broad needs or goals are explicitly developed and then broken down into more specific objectives and subobjectives. After identifying needs, objectives, and subobjectives, and developing a hierarchical structure, the alternative ways of achieving the objectives must be developed and evaluated. These alternative ways can be specified explicitly as sets of activities or tasks in order to specify each alternative set of activities more completely and precisely for management planning and control purposes.

The significance of the tasks is discussed in both the context of the systems analysis framework and in the context of the management by objectives approach to planning. In addition, managerial techniques to accomplish the fundamentals are described and demonstrated. A short case study is presented in order to clarify the proposed system of tasks and techniques.

An Executive-Level Perspective on the Strategic Management Process

John A. Pearce II

Strategic management is increasingly being acknowledged by corporate executives as their principal approach to determining and directing the efforts of their firms for the long term. One recent study found that 49 percent of the predominately *Fortune* 500 firms that responded to a mail questionnaire were engaged in "complete" strategic planning. These firms had written long-range plans covering at least three years which were rated as comprehensive, systematic, and future oriented. An additional 35 percent of the respondents were classified as involved in some, but not all, major phases of strategic management planning.[1] However, the approach has not experienced similar adoption rates across the wide spectrum of American businesses. This is particularly true among firms which do not employ permanent personnel with responsibilities exclusively in planning, among smaller firms, and within certain industries. A recent survey of banking institutions with total assets in excess of $10 million found that only 33 percent of the respondents had long-range plans with at least a two-year time horizon. The research also found the expected positive relationship between bank size and involvement in strategic management planning. Sixty percent of the banks reporting over $500 million in total assets prepared long-range plans, while less than 27 percent of the banks with $10 to $50 million took similar action.[2]

However, the trend favoring a strategic management orientation is clear and accelerating, particularly as evidence mounts attesting to its

Source: © [1981] by the Regents of the University of California. Reprinted/Condensed from the *California Management Review* 24, no. 1, pp. 39–48. By permission of The Regents.

favorable bottom-line impact.[3] The problem for most planning executives who are as of yet uncommitted to a strategic management system is that of determining the ways by which this "new" approach differs from their current framework for planning.[4] There is an understandable reluctance to restructure existing systems, with the associated inherent cost, before the pros and cons of the proposed method are clear. The focus of this article is to provide an executive-level perspective on the management process of strategy formulation and implementation. The emphasis will be on the major components of the process and their interrelationships, followed by a critical evaluation of the system's strengths and limitations.

THE STRATEGIC MANAGEMENT PROCESS

The processes which businesses use as a means to formulate and direct their strategic management activities vary among companies. Sophisticated planning organizations, like General Electric, Procter & Gamble, and IBM, have developed more detailed processes than similarly sized, less formal planners. Small businesses which rely on the strategy formulation skills and limited time of an entrepreneur typically exhibit very basic planning concerns when contrasted with larger firms in their industries. Understandably, firms with diverse operations due to their reliance on multiple products, markets, or technologies also tend to utilize more complex strategic management systems. Nevertheless, the basic components of almost all strategic management models are very similar.[5]

Because of the similarity among general models of the strategic management processes, it is possible to develop one eclectic model which is representative of the foremost thought in the area. One such effort, the Strategic Management Model, is shown in Figure 1. It provides a visual display of the major components of the entire strategic management process. The model also shows conceptually how the components are related and their sequence throughout the process.

COMPONENTS OF THE STRATEGIC MANAGEMENT MODEL

In this section the components of the Strategic Management Model will be defined and briefly described. The majority of the components will be familiar, but the discussion which accompanies them will indicate the new scope, priorities, relationships, and imperatives of strategic management.

FIGURE 1   Strategic Management Model

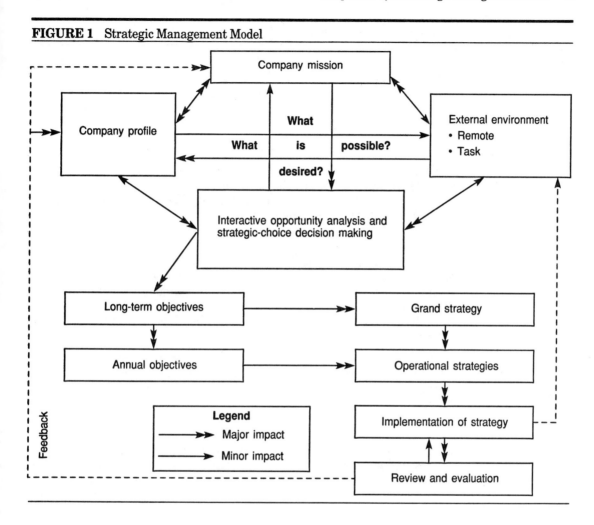

Company Mission

The mission of a business is the fundamental, unique purpose that sets it apart from other firms of its type and that identifies the scope of its operations in product and market terms. The mission is a general, enduring statement of company intent. It embodies the strategic decision makers' business philosophy; it implies the image the company seeks to project; it reflects the firm's self-concept; and it indicates the principal product or service areas and the primary customer needs which the company will attempt to satisfy. Further, it suggests the prioritized goals of the firm in terms of survival, growth, and profitability. In short, the mission describes the product, market, and technological

---

TABLE 1   Mission Statement of NICOR, Inc.

Preamble

We, the management of NICOR, Inc., here set forth our belief as to the purpose for which the Company is established and the principles under which it should operate. We pledge our effort to the accomplishment of these purposes within these principles.

Basic Purpose

The basic purpose of NICOR, Inc. is to perpetuate an investor-owned company, engaging in various phases of the energy business, striving for balance among those phases so as to render needed, satisfactory products and services and earn optimum, long-range profits.

What We Do

The principal business of the Company, through its utility subsidiary, is the provision of energy through a pipe system to meet the needs of ultimate consumers. In order to accomplish its basic purpose, and to assure its strength, the Company will engage in other energy-related activities, directly or through subsidiaries or in participation with other persons, corporations, firms, or entities.

All activities of the Company shall be consistent with its responsibilities to investors, customers, employees and the public and its concern for the optimum development and utilization of natural resources and for environmental needs.

Where We Do It

The Company's operations shall be primarily in the United States, but no self-imposed or regulatory geographical limitations are placed upon the acquisition, development, processing, transportation or storage of energy resources, nor upon other energy-related ventures in which the Company may engage. The Company will engage in such activities in any location where, after careful review, it has determined that such activity is in the best interest of its stockholders.

Utility service will be offered in the service territory of the Company's utility subsidiary to the best of its ability, in accordance with the requirements of regulatory agencies and pursuant of the subsidiary's Purposes and Principles.

---

areas of emphasis for the business in a way that reflects the values and priorities of the strategic decision makers.

Because the conceptualization of company mission can be difficult to grasp, an excellent example is shown in Table 1: the mission statement of NICOR, Inc., as abstracted from an annual report to its stockholders.

Company Profile

A company profile is the product of a firm's internal analysis which determined its performance capabilities based on existing or attainable resources. It depicts the quantity and quality of financial, human, and physical resources available to the firm. It assesses the inherent strengths and weaknesses of the firm's management and organizational structure. The profile contrasts the historical successes of the firm and the traditional values and concerns of its management with the firm's current capabilities in an attempt to identify the future capabilities of the business.

An example of one kind of analysis that contributes to the overall development of a company profile is the functional-area, resource-development matrix. This analysis provides a yearly record for the firm of its level of commitment of each functional area. This approach enables the firm to quickly calculate the total investment which it has made to each functional area over time as a basis for better understanding its comparative and competitive strengths and weaknesses. (See Table 2.)

External Environment

A firm's external environment consists of the sum total of all conditions and forces which affect the strategic options of a business but which are typically beyond its ability to control. The Strategic Management Model shows the external environment of a firm as consisting of two interactive segments, the remote environment and the task environment.

The remote environment consists of the forces and conditions which originate beyond and usually irrespective of any single firm's immediate operating environment and which provide the general economic, political, social, and technological framework within which competing organizations operate. Spiralling inflation, import restrictions on raw materials, demographic swings in the populations of the geographic areas served, and revolutionary technological innovations which make production systems unexpectedly obsolete are examples.

The task environment refers to forces and conditions in a specific competitive operating situation, external to the firm, which influences the selection and attainment of alternative objective/strategy combinations. Unlike changes in the remote environment, changes in the task environment are often the result of strategic actions taken by the firm or its competitors, consumers, users, suppliers, and creditors, or by appropriate regulatory groups. A consumer shift toward greater price consciousness, a loosening of local bank credit restrictions, a change of

TABLE 2   A Functional-Area Resource-Deployment Matrix

Functional areas	Resource-deployment emphasis	5 Years ago	4 Years ago	3 Years ago	2 Years ago	1 Year ago	This year
R&D and engineering	% strategic development dollars						
	Focus of efforts						
Manufacturing	% strategic development dollars						
	Focus of efforts						
Marketing	% strategic development dollars						
	Focus of efforts						
Finance	% strategic development dollars						
	Focus of efforts						
Management	% strategic development dollars						
	Focus of efforts						

Source: William F. Glueck, *Business Policy and Strategic Management* (New York: McGraw-Hill, 1980), p. 169.

administrators in the regional OSHA office, or the opening of a new wholesale outlet by a competitor are all likely to have a direct and intentional positive or negative impact on a firm.

Interactive Opportunity Analysis and Strategic-Choice Decision Making

The simultaneous assessment of the firm's forecasted environment and its company profile enables a firm to determine the range of interactive opportunities which it might find attractive. These opportunities represent the alternatives which are possible avenues for investment. However, the full list must be screened through the criterion of the company mission before a set of possible and *desired* opportunities can emerge. The latter process is called strategic-choice decision making. Its purpose is to provide the combination of long-term objectives and grand strategy, which will optimally position the total firm in the external environment as the means to achieving the company mission.

Consider a firm whose strategic managers feel that it is overly dependent on a single customer group, such as a chain of record shops whose principal customers are ten to twenty years old. The firm's interactive opportunities might include expanding the product line, heavily emphasizing related products, accepting the status quo, or selling out profitably to a competitor. While each of these options might be possible, a firm whose mission stressed a commitment to continued existence as a growth-oriented, autonomous organization might find only the first two opportunities desirable. In that case, the two options would be evaluated on the basis of payoff and risk potential, compatibility with or capability for becoming the firm's competitive advantage, and other critical selection criteria.

The subprocess by which strategic choice is determined is complicated. Figure 2 magnifies interactive opportunities analysis and strategic-choice decision making. As the figure shows, strategic-choice decision making involves a process of matching each of the possible and desirable interactive opportunity options with reasonable long-term objectives and targets, and with the most promising grand strategies. Each of the resulting sets of alternatives is then evaluated individually and comparatively to determine the single set or group of sets which is expected to best achieve the company mission.

The critical assessment of strategic-choice alternatives initially involves the development of evaluative criteria which will serve as the basis for comparing one set of alternatives with all others. As is the case in making any selection, the company's strategic-choice process involves the evaluation of alternatives which are rarely wholly acceptable or wholly unacceptable. The alternatives are compared to determine which option will have the most favorable overall, long-run impact on the firm.

Among the evaluative criteria used by businesses in assessing strategic-choice alternatives are strategic managers' attitudes toward risk, flexibility, stability, growth, profitability, and diversification. Other factors which are included in the decision-making process are the volatility of the external environment, the life-cycle stages of the evaluated products, the company's current level of commitment to its organizational structure, its access to needed resources, its traditional competitive advantages, and the potential reaction of influential external or internal interest groups.

FIGURE 2   Detailed Component: Interactive Opportunities Analysis and Strategic-Choice
Decision Making

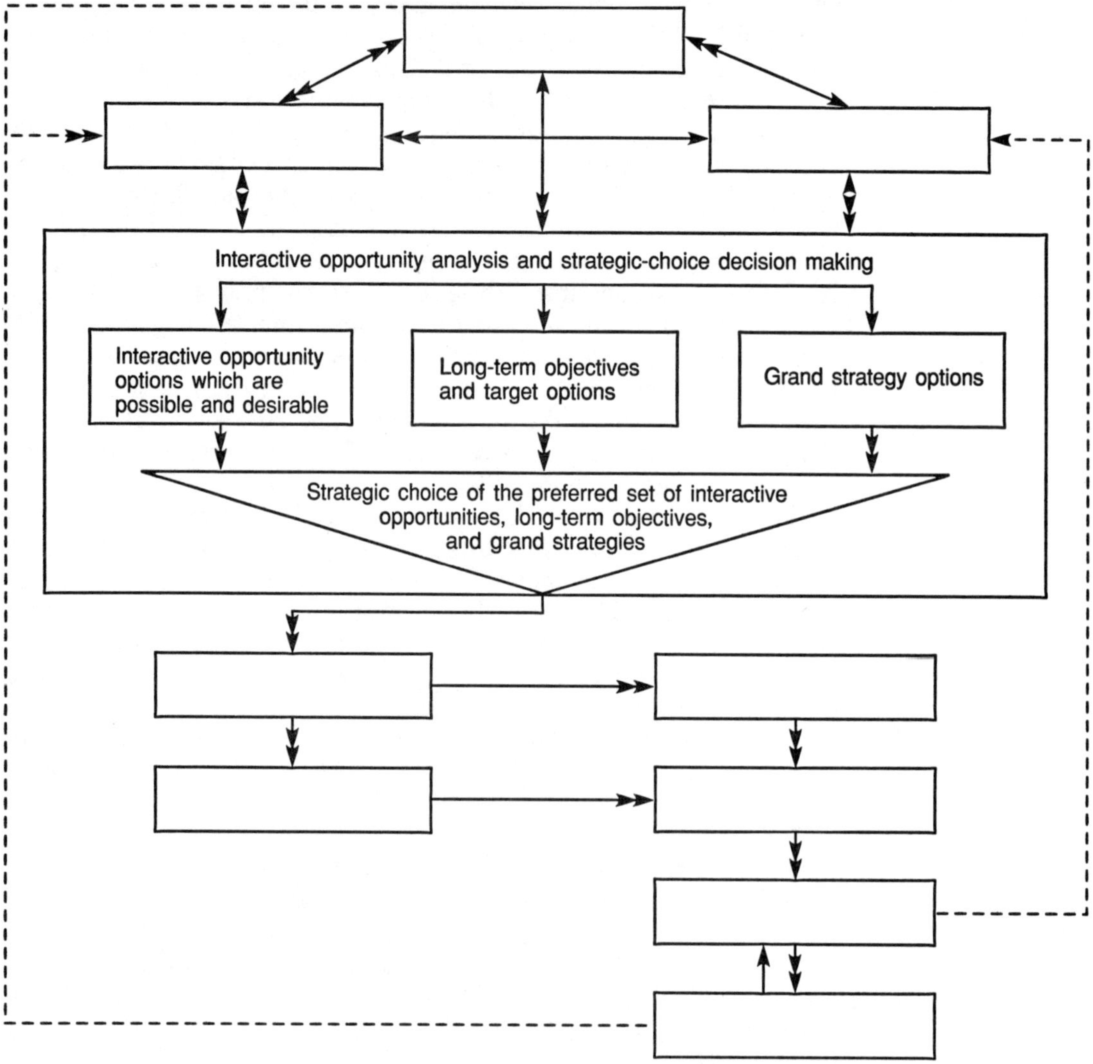

Long-Term Objectives

The results which an organization seeks to achieve over a five-year
period are known as its long-term objectives.[6] Such objectives are typically developed in some or all of the following areas: profitability,
return on investment, competitive position, technological leadership,
productivity, employee relations, public responsibility, and employee

development. To be of greatest value, each objective should be motivating, measurable, achievable, and consistent with other objectives of the firm. Objectives state what is expected from pursuing a given set of business activities. Examples of company objectives include: a doubling of earnings per share within five years with increases in each interim year; a move from the rank of third to second as a seller of commercial electrical fixtures in Oregon; and a decrease of 10 percent a year in undesirable employee turnover over the next five years.

Grand Strategy

The comprehensive, general plan of major actions by which a firm intends to achieve its long-term objectives within its dynamic environment is called the grand strategy. This statement of means indicates how the objectives or ends of business activity are to be achieved. Although every grand strategy is in fact a fairly unique package of long-term strategies, twelve basic approaches can be identified. They include concentric and conglomerate diversification, product and market development, concentration on current activities, joint ventures, horizontal and vertical integration, innovation, retrenchment, liquidation, and divestiture. The purpose of any of these grand, or master, strategies is to guide the acquisition and allocation of resources over a period of time, typically five years. Admittedly, no single grand strategy, or even several in combination, can adequately detail the strategic actions which a business will undertake over so long a period. However, the commitment of a firm's strategic managers to a fundamental approach for positioning the business in the competitive marketplace provides a galvanizing central focal point for subsequent decision making.

Annual Objectives

The results which an organization seeks to achieve within a one-year period are referred to as annual objectives. The topic areas for short-run or annual objectives are similar to those for long-term objectives. The difference between the two types of objectives stems principally from the greater specificity which is possible and necessary to guide short-term strategies. For example, a long-term objective of increasing companywide sales volume by 20 percent in five years might be translated into a 4 percent growth objective in year one. It is reasonable that this companywide short-run objective should be reflected in the planning activities of all major functional or divisional components of the firm. The research and development department might be expected to suggest one major addition to the product line in the first and each following year; the finance department might set a complementary objective of obtaining the necessary $300,000 in funds for an immediate expansion of production facilities; and the marketing department might establish an objective of reducing turnover among sales representatives by 5 percent per year.

Operating Strategies

Within the general framework of the grand strategy, a specific and integrative plan of actions is needed for each distinctive business unit in the firm. Most strategic managers attempt to develop an operating strategy for each related set of annual objectives (one for the marketing department, the production department, and so on). Operating strategies are detailed statements of the means that will be used to achieve objectives within the following year. The company's budgeting process is usually coordinated with the development of the operating strategies to insure specificity, practicality, and accountability in the planning process.

Implementation of Strategy

Implementation involves the management activity of acquiring and allocating financial resources in conjunction with the development of structures and procedures necessary to put a strategy into operation. Prior to implementation, strategies are only ideas. Principally, implementation involves the assignment of responsibility for the success of all or part of a strategy to appropriate employees, along with the allocation of required resources. Implementation means putting strategies into action.

Five variables are commonly considered to be critical factors in the implementation of a strategy: tasks, people, structures, technologies, and reward systems. Successful implementation of company strategies requires that methods be effectively designed and managed to efficiently integrate these factors. A major priority of implementation efforts involves synchronizing the key resource components of the planning process.

Review and Evaluation

An implemented strategy needs to be monitored in order to determine the extent to which it is resulting in the achievement of its objectives. The process of formulating a strategy is largely subjective, despite often extensive efforts to reduce it to objective decision making. The first substantial reality test of the value of a strategy comes only after implementation has begun. Strategic managers must watch for early signs of the responsiveness of the marketplace to their strategies. They must also provide the means for monitoring and controlling to insure that their strategic plan is followed correctly.

Although the early review and evaluation of the strategic process concentrates on market-responsive modifications of the strategy, the underlying and ultimate test of a strategy is its proven ability to achieve its ends—the annual objectives, long-term objectives, and mission. In the final analysis, a firm is only successful when its strategy achieves its objectives.

STRATEGIC MANAGEMENT AS A PROCESS

The Strategic Management Model shown in Figure 1 depicts a process. The term *process* refers to an identifiable flow of information through interrelated stages of analysis directed toward the achievement of an objective. In the strategic management process the flow of information pertains to the historical, current, and forecasted data on the business, its operations and environment, which is evaluated in light of stakeholder values and priorities. The interrelated stages of the process are the ten components discussed in the last section. The objective of the process pertains to the formulation and implementation of strategies which result in long-term achievement of the company's mission, and near-term achievement of its aims.

There are several important implications of strategic management as a process. First, it means that a change in any components of the system will affect several or all other components. The majority of arrows in the model point both ways, suggesting that the flow of information or the impact is usually reciprocal among components. For example, forces in the external environment influence the nature of the mission which a company's strategic managers and stakeholders design for the firm. Reciprocally, the existence of that company with that mission legitimizes the environmental forces and implicitly heightens competition in the firm's realm of operation. An example is that of a business that is persuaded, in part by governmental incentives, that its mission statement should include a commitment to energy-efficient products, and that promises to extend its research and development efforts in the area of solar photovoltaics. Obviously, the external environment has affected the firm's definition of its mission, and the existence of the revised mission alters a competitive condition in the environment.

A second implication of strategic management as a process is the sequential nature of strategy formulation and evaluation. The strategic management process begins with the development or reevaluation of the company mission. This step is associated with, but essentially followed by, the simultaneous development of a company profile and an assessment of the external environments. Then come strategic-choice decision making (which results in the definition of long-term objectives and the design of grand strategy), definition of short-term objectives, design of operation strategies, implementation of strategy, and review and evaluation. The apparent rigidity of the process needs to be tempered by two qualifications:

• The need for a reevaluation of the strategic posture of a firm on any of the principal factors which determine or affect company performances. Entry into the market of a major new competitor, death of a prominent board member, replacement of the chief executive officer, or a downturn in positive market responsiveness are among the thousands of changes which can prompt the need to reassess a company's strategic plan. However, irrespective of where the interest in a reassessment originates, the strategic management process begins with the mission statement.

• Not every component of the strategic management process deserves equal attention each time a planning activity takes place. Firms in an extremely stable environment may find that an in-depth assessment is not required on a five-year schedule.[7] Often, companies are satisfied with their original mission statements, even after decades of operation, and need to spend only a minimal amount of time in addressing that factor. Additionally, while a formal strategic-planning process may be undertaken only on a five-year basis, yearly updating of objectives and strategies is usually undertaken. At these times, rigorous reassessments of the initial stages of the process are rarely necessary.

A third implication of strategic management as a process is the necessity for feedback from implementation, review, and evaluation to the early-stage components of the process. *Feedback* can be defined as the post-implementation results of a strategy which are collected as inputs for the enhancement of future decision making through the strategic management process. As shown in Figure 1, it is important for strategic managers to attempt to assess the impact of their implemented strategies on their external environments so that future planning can reflect any changes which were precipitated by their actions. They should also carefully measure and analyze the impact upon the need for possible modifications for the company mission.

A fourth and final implication of strategic management as a process is the need to view it as a dynamic system. *Dynamic* is a term used to describe the constantly changing nature of conditions which affect interrelated and interdependent strategic activities. Managers need to recognize the components of the strategic process as constantly evolving. They must remember that formal planning artificially "freezes" the changing conditions and forces in the company's internal and external environments, much as a photograph freezes the movement of a swimmer. In actuality, change is continuous and the dynamic strategic planning process must be constantly monitored to detect significant changes in any of its components as a realistic precaution against implementing a strategy which is obsolete.

PRACTICAL LIMITATIONS OF A MODEL

It is important to understand the limitations of models such as the Strategic Management Model so as not to diminish their overall impact by overlooking their weaknesses. An awareness of how the models can be properly used will help to ensure effective strategic management. In this section, three points will be stressed; namely, that most models are "wholistic," descriptive, and nonpolitical.

Most prominent strategic management models are "wholistic." This means that users of these models believe that strategic planning should be initiated by a company's top management. Because of the broad perspective of these executives, the strategy process works from general to specific. The business is first studied as a whole within the context of its competitive environment; then individual functions or divisions, and eventually specific operations of the firm, are involved in the strategic management process.

Some researchers have argued that in certain circumstances the wholistic approach is inferior to a tactical approach to strategic planning. With the tactical approach, strategic managers work up through the firm in their study of its potential. Then, with a strongly operational view of the firm's strengths and weaknesses, the managers assess their firm's compatibility with its external environment.

The risk of using the wholistic approach, which is implicitly advocated by models like the Strategic Management Model, is that executives might be unrealistic in their planning because of a potential tendency to minimize the difficulties of implementing a plan. The wholistic approach can sometimes lead managers to gloss over details that may eventually be critical to putting into operation the firm's strategies.

The tactical approach poses far greater risks to strategic managers. First, the tactical approach tends to create inflexibility in planning. Managers risk placing such a great priority on operational details that they can come to overstate the extent to which the firm is locked into the status quo. It is difficult to envision new interactive opportunities when initial planning activities stress narrow operational concerns. Second, the integration of planning activities is more difficult with the tactical approach. Lacking the kind of overall framework for planning which is characteristic of the wholistic method, the initial phases of planning are often disjointed, leading to complications in developing a unified strategic plan. Third, and most damaging, the tactical approach concentrates on the present rather than on the future of the firm as strategic planning does. The emphasis is too often on improving current capabilities to satisfy historical rather than anticipated needs.

In the final analysis, it appears that the wholistic approach is superior to tactical alternatives. However, users of a wholistic model should be alert to the shortcomings in planning which it fosters and should guard against their development. Specifically, users of wholistic models should continually challenge themselves on issues pertaining to the data-gathering and implementation phases of their firm's strategic activities. In this context it is important to remember that although middle- and lower-level managers seldom vote in the strategic-choice process, they are a principal source of the operational data on which the ultimate decisions are largely based. These managers' advice and critiques should be actively sought and carefully considered in all phases of the strategic management process.

A second major issue of concern in the use of strategic management models is that they are analytical or descriptive rather than prescriptive in nature. The models typically either suggest a conceptual framework for the evaluation of strategic situations or describe in a general sense an approach that businesses have actually used in conducting their strategic activities. However, while there is considerable evidence that firms which undertake formal strategic planning outperform nonplanners, somewhat different planning models were used by every business that has been studied.[8] There is no known best wholistic model, and no model should be seen as the prescription for strategic planning. In using the Strategic Management Model or any similar model, it should be remembered that the model builders are recommending the general approach they believe will provide a sound basis for strategic planning, not a model which they are certain will lead to the best results. It is important that users of such models are continually alert to the need for occasional additions to or deletions from overall planning activities. Strategic management models will be most valuable if they are treated as dependable outlines upon which strategizers must construct individualized planning systems.

The third major limitation of the models is that they are nonpolitical in constitution. A new planner could be misled to perceive the strategic management process as largely devoid of subjective assessments, biased interpretations, human error, self-serving voting by individual managers, intuitive decision making, favoritism, and other forms of political activity. In reality, most strategic planning experts believe the opposite. Strategic planning is a behavioral activity and as such is vulnerable to the same shortcomings as other people processes. It is truly a management process. People involved in all phases of the strategy formulation and implementation must be skillfully organized, led, planned about, and controlled. The limitation of the strategic management planning models is that they explicitly ignore the political considerations. The principal reason for this intentional omission is that managers cannot dictate rationality, objectivity, or altruism. The models presume that strategic planners are skilled managers, and that they are sensitive to the people-related issues that continuously arise in every phase of the strategic planning process.

Owing to the incalculable variations in political activity which can take place during the strategy process, it is not particularly valuable to include this factor as a component in the process models. However, the effects of political activity on the planning process are critical to its effective functioning and are a principal determinant of the plan's final composition. Strategic planners who are attentive to this political realization, and who skillfully manage the inevitable people-related concerns, will have overcome the limitations of the nonpolitical models.

CONCLUSION

The strategic management process can be seen now to represent a logical integration and extension of established planning systems. The task facing most potential adopters is one of revising rather than replacing their existing approach. The adjustments for most companies center in the process used in planning rather than in the content of the information needed in order to design and put into operation the plan itself. This is because the major differences between traditional and strategic management processes are found less in terms of what the inputs should be and more in terms of how the inputs should be prioritized and integrated in an organization's comprehensive planning and implementation efforts.

While the strategic management process is not without its limitations, it offers a promising approach whose proponents have experienced generally improved success in positioning their firms profitably in increasingly turbulent environments.

REFERENCES

1. Ronald J. Kudla, "The Effects of Strategic Planning on Common Stock Returns." *Academy of Management Journal* (March 1980), pp. 5–20.
2. Richard W. Sapp, "Banks Look Ahead: A Survey of Bank Planning," *Bank Administration* (July 1980), pp. 33–40.

3. Thomas H. Naylor and Horst Schanland. "A Survey of Users of Corporate Planning Models," *Management Science* (May 1976); D. Robley Wood, Jr. and R. Lawrence La Forge, "The Impact of Comprehensive Planning on Financial Performance." *Academy of Management Journal*, Vol. 22. No. 3 (1979). pp. 516–26.
4. For an excellent historical perspective on the evolution of planning systems, see H. Igor Ansoff, "The State of Practice in Planning Systems," *Sloan Management Review* (Winter 1977), pp. 1–24.
5. Models by academics, typically developed from consulting experience and intended either for business or educational use, which reflect such similarity include those of Howard Stevenson, David Rogers, and William King and David Cleland. Models recommended for use by small businesses, almost identical to those recommended for larger firms, include Frank Gilmore's and George Steiner's (1967). Finally, models which describe approaches for accomplishing strategic options contain similar elements to those of general models: see Millard Pryor on mergers and Steiner on diversification (1964). Frank Gilmore. "Formulating Strategy in Smaller Companies," *Harvard Business Review* (May-June 1973); William R. King and David I. Cleland, *Strategic Planning and Policy* (New York, New York Van Nostrand Reinhold Co., 1978); Millard H. Pryor, Jr., "Anatomy of a Merger," *Michigan Business Review* (July 1964), pp. 28–34; David C.D. Rogers. *Essentials of Business Policy* (New York, New York: Harper & Row Publishers, 1975); George A. Steiner. "Why and How to Diversify," *California Management Review* (Summer 1964), pp. 11–18: idem, "Approaches to Long-Range Planning for Small Business." *California Management Review* (Fall 1967); Howard H. Stevenson, "Defining Corporate Strengths and Weaknesses," *Sloan Management Review* (Spring 1976), pp. 51–68.
6. Five years is the normal, but largely arbitrary, period of time identified as the "long term."
7. Formal strategic planning is not necessarily done as a rigid five-year schedule, although this is the most common period of time. In fact, some planners advocate planning on an irregular timing basis to keep the activity from being overly routine.
8. See, for examples, H. Igor Ansoff, Richard G. Brandenburg, Fred E. Porter, and Raymond Radosevich. *Acquisition Behavior of U.S. Manufacturing Firms, 1946–65* (Nashville, Tenn.: Vanderbilt, 1971); David Burt, "Planning and Performance in Australian Retailing." *Long Range Planning* (June 1978), pp. 62–66; Joseph Eastlack, Jr. and Philip McDonald, "CEO's Role in Corporate Growth." *Harvard Business Review* (May-June 1970), pp. 150–163; David Herold, "Long Range Planning and Organizational Performance: A Cross Validating Study," *Academy of Management Review* (March 1972), pp. 91–102; Delmar Karger and Zafar Malik. "Long Range Planning and Organization Performance," *Long Range Planning* (December 1975); Zafar Malik and Delmar Karger, "Does Long Range Planning Improve Company Performance?" *Management Review* (September 1975), pp. 27–31; Leslie Rue and Robert Fulmer. "Is Long Range Planning Profitable?" *Proceedings Academy of Management* (1972); Sidney Schoeffler, R.D. Buzzell, and D.F. Heany. "Impact of Strategic Planning on Profit Performance," *Harvard Business Review* (March-April 1974), pp. 137–45; Stanley Thune

and Robert House, "Where Long Range Planning Pays Off," *Business Horizons* (August 1970). pp. 81–87; Ross Stagner. "Corporate Decision Making." *Journal of Applied Psychology,* Vol. 53. No. 1 (February 1969), pp. 1–13; William F. Glueck, *Business Policy and Strategic Management,* 3rd edition (New York, New York: McGraw-Hill Book Co. 1980); and Wood and LaForge, op cit.

The Strategic Management Process: A Model and Terminology

Lloyd L. Byars

Various terms and expressions are used in describing the strategic management process. These terms often have a variety of meanings and interpretations depending on the author and source. For instance, some of the terms that are used interchangeably with strategic management are strategy and policy formulation, long-range planning and business policy. The purpose of this article is to present a model for analyzing the strategic management process and to propose definitions for the terms and expressions used in describing the strategic management process.

Strategic management is concerned with making and implementing decisions about an organization's future direction. Basically, strategic management can be broken down into two phases: strategic planning and strategy implementation. Strategic planning is concerned with making decisions with regard to:

1. Determining the organization's mission.
2. Formulating policies to guide the organization in establishing objectives, choosing a strategy, and implementing the chosen strategy.
3. Establishing long- and short-range objectives to achieve the organization's mission.
4. Determining the strategy that is to be used in achieving the organization's objectives.

Strategy implementation is concerned with making decisions with regard to:

1. Developing an organizational structure to achieve the strategy.

Source: Lloyd L. Byars, "The Strategic Management Process: A Model and Terminology," *Managerial Planning* 32, no. 6 (1984), pp. 38–44.

2. Ensuring that the activities necessary to accomplish the strategy are performed effectively.
3. Monitoring the effectiveness of the strategy in achieving the organization's objectives.

Figure 1 illustrates the steps in the strategic management process. Although the steps in this process are shown to be separate and consecutive, it is important to note that considerable overlap among the steps exists. For instance, the setting of long- and short-range objectives may be done simultaneously. Likewise, policies can evolve simultaneously with the objective setting process. Additionally, considerable feedback must occur throughout the strategic management process. To illustrate, suppose that a particular strategy has not been achieving the objectives of the organization. Among other reasons this could be a result of having established unrealistic objectives or having selected the wrong strategy. Because of their interdependence, all of the steps in the strategic management process need to be examined when a strategy fails. Likewise, all of the steps need to be examined when a strategy is successful in order to help insure future successes.

DEFINING THE ORGANIZATION'S MISSION

An organization's mission includes both a statement of organizational philosophy and purpose. An organizational philosophy establishes the values, beliefs, and guidelines for the manner in which the organization is going to conduct its business. The importance of having an organizational philosophy was stated by Thomas J. Watson, Jr., former Chairman of the Board of IBM, as follows:

> This, then, is my thesis: I firmly believe that any organization, in order to survive and achieve success, must have a sound set of beliefs on which it premises all its policies and actions.
>
> Next, I believe that the most important single factor in corporate success is faithful adherence to those beliefs.
>
> And finally, I believe that if an organization is to meet the challenges of a changing world, it must be prepared to change everything about itself except those beliefs as it moves through corporate life.[1]

Watson went to describe IBM's philosophy to be:

1. *Respect for the Individual.* This is a simple concept, but at IBM it occupies a major portion of management time. We devote more effort to it than anything else.

2. We want to give the best customer service of any company in the world.

3. We believe that an organization should pursue all tasks with the idea that they can be accomplished in a superior fashion.[2]

FIGURE 1   The Strategic Management Process

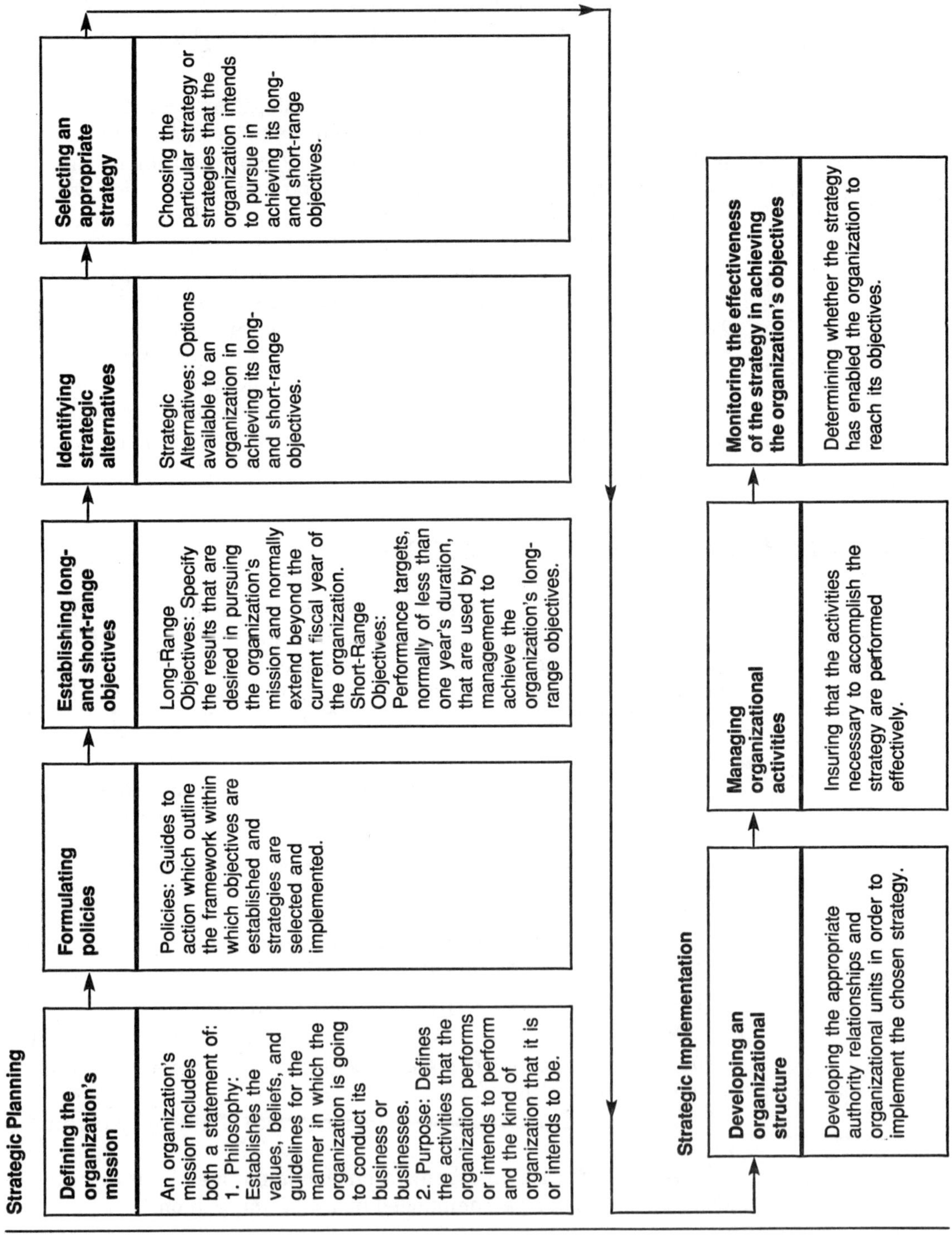

Strategic Planning

Defining the organization's mission

An organization's mission includes both a statement of:
1. Philosophy: Establishes the values, beliefs, and guidelines for the manner in which the organization is going to conduct its business or businesses.
2. Purpose: Defines the activities that the organization performs or intends to perform and the kind of organization that it is or intends to be.

Formulating policies

Policies: Guides to action which outline the framework within which objectives are established and strategies are selected and implemented.

Establishing long- and short-range objectives

Long-Range Objectives: Specify the results that are desired in pursuing the organization's mission and normally extend beyond the current fiscal year of the organization. Short-Range Objectives: Performance targets, normally of less than one year's duration, that are used by management to achieve the organization's long-range objectives.

Identifying strategic alternatives

Strategic Alternatives: Options available to an organization in achieving its long- and short-range objectives.

Selecting an appropriate strategy

Choosing the particular strategy or strategies that the organization intends to pursue in achieving its long- and short-range objectives.

Strategic Implementation

Developing an organizational structure

Developing the appropriate authority relationships and organizational units in order to implement the chosen strategy.

Managing organizational activities

Insuring that the activities necessary to accomplish the strategy are performed effectively.

Monitoring the effectiveness of the strategy in achieving the organization's objectives

Determining whether the strategy has enabled the organization to reach its objectives.

It is interesting to note that almost 20 years after Watson stated these three basic beliefs, IBM Board Chairman Frank Cary stated: "We've changed our technology, changed our organization, changed our marketing and manufacturing techniques many times, and we expect to go on changing. But through all this change, those three basic beliefs remain. We steer our course by those stars."[3]

The organizational purpose defines the activities that the organization performs or intends to perform and the kind of organization that it is or intends to be. The establishment of an organization's purpose is critical; for, without a concrete statement of purpose it is virtually impossible to develop clear objectives and strategies. Furthermore, an organization's purpose must be defined not only at its inception but also must be redefined regularly during both difficult and successful periods. For example, if the railroad companies had defined their purpose to be developing a firm position in the transportation business rather than limiting themselves strictly to the rail business they might not be in the economic situation that they find themselves today. In fact, the Southern Railway Company has defined its corporate purpose to be transportation services, and today it has the highest earnings per share of any company in the railroad industry. Southern achieved this position through careful acquisition of other railroads and maintaining its stated purpose of providing useful transportation services to its customers.

Robert Townsend stated the purpose of Avis Rent-A-Car to be: We want to become the fastest-growing company with the highest profit margins in the business of renting and leasing vehicles without drivers.[4] Notice how this statement of purpose defines the business of Avis and would preclude considering acquisitions of motels, airlines, and travel agencies.

When John D. Rockefeller conceived the idea of the Standard Oil Trust, his purpose was to develop a monopoly in the oil refining business. Rockefeller came close to achieving his purpose largely by using whatever methods he could to drive out his competitors. Of course, his actions and the actions of others with similar purposes and methods contributed to the establishment of the Sherman Anti-Trust Act of 1890.

An organization's purpose is defined by its customers. In this regard, Peter Drucker has stated:

> To know what a business is we have to start with its purpose. Its purpose must be outside of the business itself. In fact, it must lie in society since business enterprise is an organ of society. There is only one definition of business purpose: to create a customer.[5]

Thus, defining an organization's purpose starts with defining its present and potential customers. Questions that need to be answered in defining the present customers are:

1. Who is the customer?
   a. Where is the customer located?
   b. How does the customer buy?
   c. How can the customer be reached?
2. What does the customer buy?
3. What does the customer consider value [i.e., what does the customer look for when he or she buys the product[6]]?

In defining an organization's potential customers, the following questions need to be answered:
1. What are the market trends and market potential?
2. What changes in market structure might occur as a result of economic developments, changes in styles, fashions, or moves by the competition?
3. What innovations will alter the customer's buying habits?
4. What needs does the customer presently have that are not being adequately met by available products and services?[7]

One final question needs to be addressed in determining an organization's purpose. Is the organization in the right business or should it change its business?[8]

Answers to many of these questions can be seen in the reasons given by Philip Morris for acquiring the Miller Brewing Company.

> Inevitably our (Philip Morris) domestic cigarette business will level off as our market share increases and growth in consumption stabilizes around one-two percent per year. Our cash flow will increase dramatically at that time and we need growth businesses in which to invest this cash flow . . . (however) it's hard to find another business that is as good as this one. . . . Beer probably comes closest to matching our skills with a market opportunity.
>
> Both are low priced, pleasurable products made from agricultural commodities that are processed and packaged on high-speed machinery. Both are advertised the same way and are sold to many of the same end use customers through similar distribution channels. Your beer drinker and your cigarette smoker are often the same guy.[9]

In small organizations, the owner or chief executive officer (CEO) often establishes the mission of the organization without consultation with others. In some organizations, the founder of the business establishes the mission, and this mission is often maintained throughout the life of the organization. For example, Thomas Watson, Sr. of IBM and James Lincoln of the Lincoln Electric Company established missions for their organizations that are still in existence today. Furthermore, some CEOs with strong wills or personalities influence their organization's mission throughout their tenure at the organization.

However, in many larger organizations, consultation and participation by a large group of top managers is the normal process used in formulating philosophy and purpose. For example, James McFarland, shortly after he became CEO of General Mills, stated as follows:

> I asked myself what was expected of me as CEO. I decided that my role was really to build General Mills from a good company into a great company. But I realized this was not just up to me. I wanted a collective viewpoint as to what makes a company great. Consequently, we took some thirty-five top people away for three days to decide what it took to move the company from "goodness" to "greatness." Working in groups of six to eight, we defined the characteristics of a great company from various points of view, what our short-comings were, and how we might overcome these.[10]

Ideally, an organization's philosophy should rarely change. However, an organization's purpose should be analyzed periodically to determine if changes need to be made. Changes in competitive position, changes in top level management personnel, new technologies, changing availability and increasing costs of available resources, demographic changes, changes in government regulation and shifts in consumer demand can result in the need to change an organization's purpose.

Changes in an organization's purpose can lead to major changes in an organization's operations. A study which involved interviewing 100 top managers in 10 companies over a period of several years, outlined how the need for a change in corporate purpose is recognized and implemented.[11] First, the need for change is often sensed by top management in quite vague or undefined terms (i.e., things just don't seem to be going right). Declining profits or market share often serve as a signal for the need to reexamine an organization's purpose. Next, an awareness of the need for change is often built by hiring study groups, staff, or consultants to consider problems, options, contingencies, or opportunities posed by the need. Broadened support for the need to change is developed by unstructured discussions and probing of top management positions. A clear focus can be gained by having an ad-hoc committee formulate a position on the changed purpose or by having the CEO express either in writing or verbally the changed position of the organization. The whole process of formulating an organization's purpose is "a delicate art, requiring a subtle balance of vision, entrepreneurship, and politics."[12]

FORMULATING POLICIES

Policies are defined as broad, general guides to action that outline the framework within which objectives are established and strategies are selected and implemented. Policies should flow logically from the organization's philosophy. For example, after describing

IBM's philosophy Thomas Watson, Jr. outlined just one of IBM's corporate policies as follows:

> Open-door policy—Every employee has the right to talk to whomever they wish including any member of top management concerning problems, or concerns they have about management actions or decisions.[13]

Policies help to ensure that all units of an organization operate under the same ground rules. They also facilitate coordination and communication between various organizational units.

Several factors influence the formulation of policies. One important factor has been the federal, state, and local governments. Government regulates organizations in areas such as competition (antitrust and monopoly), product standards (safety and quality), pricing (utilities), hiring practices (civil rights), working conditions (OSHA), wages (minimum wages), accounting practices (income tax regulation), and insurance of stock (SEC). Policies need to be developed in order to guide an organization's employees in meeting each of these regulations. For example, as a result of government regulation many organizations have developed a policy statement which declares the organization's unqualified opposition to all forms of discrimination.

Policies of competitors also influence an organization's policies. This is especially true with personnel policies such as employee wages and benefits and working conditions.

An extremely important consideration in policy formulation is that policies should facilitate the successful accomplishment of organizational objectives and implementation of strategy. All too frequently policies emerge from history, tradition, and earlier events. Changing environmental conditions and changed organizational objectives trigger an evaluation of organizational policies to ascertain if they are still appropriate or should be changed.

LONG- AND SHORT-RANGE OBJECTIVE

Long-range objectives specify the results that are desired in pursuing the organization's purpose and normally extend beyond the current fiscal year of the organization. They are not vague and abstract but are specific, concrete, and measurable results that must be achieved if the organization is to be successful in attaining its mission.

An organization's objectives depend on the particular organization and its mission. Although objectives can vary widely from organization to organization, normally they can be categorized as follows: (1) profitability, (2) service to customers, clients, or other recipients, (3) employee needs and well-being, and (4) social responsibility. The following items provide potential areas for establishing long-range objectives for most organizations.[14]

1. *Profitability*. Expressed in terms of profits, return on investment, earnings per share, or profit-to-sales ratios.

   Examples: To increase return on investment to 15 percent after taxes within four years.

   To increase profits to $15 million within three years.

2. *Markets*. Expressed in terms of share of the market or dollar or unit volume of sales.

   Examples: To increase commercial sales to 85 percent of our total sales and reduce military sales to 15 percent of our total sales over the next three years.

   To increase the number of units of Product X sold by 500,000 units within four years.

3. *Productivity*. Expressed in terms of a ratio of input to output, cost per unit of production, and others.

   Example: To increase the number of units produced per worker by 10 percent per eight-hour day over the next three years.

4. *Product*. Expressed in terms of sales and profitability by product line or product, target dates for development of new products, and others.

   Example: To phase out our product with the lowest profit margin within two years.

5. *Financial Resources*. Expressed in terms of the capital structure, new issues of common stock, cash flow, working capital, dividend payments, and collection periods.

   Examples: To increase working capital to $10 million within five years.

   To reduce long-term debt to $8 million within three years.

6. *Physical Facilities*. Expressed in terms of square feet, fixed costs, units of production and other measures.

   Examples: To increase storage capacity by 15 million units over the next three years.

   To decrease production capacity in the West Coast plant by 20 percent within three years.

7. *Research and Innovation*. Expressed in terms of amount of money to be spent and in other terms.

   Example: To develop an engine in the medium-price range, with an emission rate of less than 10 percent, within five years at a cost not to exceed $3 million.

8. *Organization Structure and Activities*. Expressed in terms of changes to be made or projects to be undertaken.

   Example: To establish a decentralized organizational structure within three years.

9. *Human Resources.* Expressed in terms of rates of absenteeism, tardiness, turnover, or number of grievances. Also can be expressed in terms of number of people to be trained or number of training programs that are to be taught.

   Examples: To reduce absenteeism by 8 percent within three years.

   To conduct a 40 hour supervisory development program for 300 supervisors at a cost not to exceed $400 per participant over the next four years.
10. *Customer Service.* Expressed in terms of delivery times, customer complaints, and others.

    Example: To reduce the number of customer complaints by 40 percent over the next three years.
11. *Social Responsibility.* Expressed in terms of types of activities, number of days of service, or financial contributions.

    Example: To increase our contribution to United Way by 30 percent over the next three years.

All organizations do not have objectives in all of these areas. Religious and other not-for-profit organizations obviously need a different set of objectives from private enterprise organizations. Generally, long-range objectives need to be established for every area of the organization where performance and results directly influence the survival and prosperity of the organization.[15]

Long-range objectives must support and not be in conflict with the organization's mission. They should be clear, concise, and quantified whenever possible and should be detailed enough so that the organization's personnel can clearly understand what the organization intends to achieve. They should span all significant units or areas of the organization and not just concentrate on one area. Objectives for different areas of the organization can serve as checks on each other, but should be reasonably consistent with each other. Finally, objectives should be dynamic in that they need to be reevaluated in light of changing conditions.

Short-range objectives are performance targets, normally of less than one year's duration, that are used by management to achieve the organization's long-range objectives. Short-range objectives should be derived from an in-depth evaluation of the organization's long-range objectives. Such an evaluation should result in a listing of priorities of the objectives. Once the priorities have been determined, short-range objectives can be set to achieve the long-range objectives.

Long- and short-range objectives for departments, units, and subunits of an organization are based on the long- and short-range objectives of the total organization. Long- and short-range objectives at any level of the organization must be coordinated with and subordinated to the long- and short-range objectives of the next higher level. Such a system ensures that all objectives are consistent and not working against each other.

Some example goal statements might be:

1. To increase profits by 5 percent during the next year.
2. To open a district office in Dallas, Texas, during the third quarter of this year.
3. To increase our church membership by 10 percent this year.
4. To open 10 new retail outlets during the next year.

Both long- and short-range objectives serve to give direction to the organization in achieving its mission.

STRATEGY

The word *strategy* came from the Greek word—*strategos*—which means a general. At that time, strategy literally meant the art and science of directing military forces. Today, the term *strategy* is used in business to describe how an organization is going to achieve its objectives and mission. Most organizations have several options for accomplishing their objectives and mission. Strategy is concerned with deciding which option is going to be used. Strategy includes the determination and evaluation of alternative paths to achieve an organization's objectives and mission and, eventually, a choice of the alternative that is to be adopted.

INTEGRATING MISSION STATEMENTS, POLICIES, OBJECTIVES AND STRATEGY

Organizational mission statements, policies, objectives, and strategy are *not* mutually exclusive components of the strategic planning process. Rather they are highly interdependent and inseparable. One cannot talk about attaining objectives without knowing the policies that must be followed. Similarly, a strategy cannot be determined without first knowing the objectives that are to be pursued and the policies that are to be followed. Furthermore, strategy implementation impacts upon the strategic planning process. Figure 1, which shows the entire strategic management process as a series of sequential steps, should be considered merely as a method for analyzing the entire process and not as a step-by-step process that should be sequentially followed. Because this article defines a large number of terms Table 1 is presented in order to summmarize these terms. It is also hoped that this article has provided insight into resolving many of the definitional problems in the study and analysis of the strategic management process.

TABLE 1   Definition of Terms

Long-Range Objectives specify the results that are desired in pursuing the organization's mission and normally extend beyond the current fiscal year of the organization.

Short-Range Objectives are performance targets, normally of less than one year's duration, that are used by management to achieve the organization's long-range objectives.

Strategic management is concerned with making decisions about an organization's future direction and implementing those decisions. It is composed of two phases: strategic planning and strategy implementation.

Strategic planning is concerned with making decisions with regard to determining the organization's mission, formulating policies, establishing objectives, and determining the strategy that is to be used in achieving the organization's objectives.

Strategic implementation is concerned with making decisions with regard to developing an organizational structure to achieve the strategy, staffing the structure, providing leadership and motivation to the staff, and monitoring the effectiveness of the strategy in achieving the organization's objectives.

Organizational mission involves establishing a statement of organizational philosophy and purpose.

Organizational philosophy establishes the values, beliefs, and guidelines for the manner in which the organization is going to conduct its business.

Organizational purpose defines the activities that the organization performs or intends to perform and the kind of organization it is or intends to be.

Strategy describes how an organization intends to achieve its objectives and mission. It includes the determination and evaluation of alternative paths to achieve an organization's objectives and mission and, eventually, a choice of the alternative that is to be adopted.

Policies are broad, general guides to action that outline the framework within which objectives are established and strategies are selected and implemented.

NOTES

1. Thomas J. Watson, Jr., *A Business and Its Beliefs* (New York: McGraw-Hill Book Company, 1963), p. 5.
2. *Ibid.* pp. 13, 29, 34.
3. Frank T. Cary, "The Remaking of American Business Leadership," *Think Magazine*, vol. 47, no. 6 (November/December 1981), p. 24.
4. Robert Townsend, *Up the Organization* (New York: Alfred A. Knopf, 1970), p. 129.
5. Peter Drucker, *Management: Tasks, Responsibilities, Practices* (New York: Harper & Row Publishers, 1974), p. 61.

6. Peter Drucker, *The Practice of Management* (New York: Harper & Row, Publishers, 1954), pp. 52–54.
7. *Ibid.,* p. 56
8. *Ibid.,* p. 57.
9. Financial statements and public statements by executives of Philip Morris.
10. James B. Quinn, "Strategic Goals: Process and Politics," *Sloan Management Review,* vol. 19, no. 1. (Fall 1977), p. 22.
11. *Ibid.,* pp. 34–36.
12. *Ibid.,* p. 36.
13. Watson, *A Business and Its Beliefs,* p. 19–21.
14. Anthony Raia, *Managing by Objectives* (Glenview, Ill: Scott, Foresman and Company, 1974), p. 38.
15. Drucker, *Management: Tasks, Responsibilities, Practices,* p. 100.

The New Strategic Planning Boom: Hope for the Future or a Bureaucratic Exercise?

Sidney C. Sufrin and George S. Odiorne

STRATEGIC PLANNING—HOPE OR ILLUSION?

Strategic planning is partly a misnomer. Strategy has to do with broad gauged reflection and policy. It is concerned with mapping the future. In this sense it is opposed to tactical planning or operations. Planning may involve the control over strategic areas; i.e., the future, or it may merely mean assessing the future. As used in the military and in business, planning means both. Probably due to the nature of the realities greater emphasis assessing the future is more common because control is often too difficult to imagine in detail.

In business strategic planning represents a shifting of focus from those forces which are within the firm; e.g., organization, product lines and personnel, or immediately outside the firm as the markets of sale and purchase to broader perspectives. The shape of the future as evidenced by likely technological, ideological, and political changes, the various opportunities likely to be available to the firm and such broad probable impingements are the usual stuff of Strategic Planning. The future is not so much to be controlled as understood. Pre-knowledge and pre-information are the goals.

Government too would benefit if it had a better idea of what to expect. The tentative future budgets prepared each year by each

Source: Sidney C. Sufrin and George S. Odiorne, "The New Strategic Planning Boom: Hope for the Future or a Bureaucratic Exercise?" *Managerial Planning* 33, no. 4 (1985), pp. 4–13, 46.

administration is a partial attempt. But these documents are heavy with the bias of each administration.

There are three major confusions of strategic planning:

1. The Idea of Strategy Is Sometimes Confused with Tactics.

The goals of enterprise and the choice of goals are understandably confused with the means to attain the goals. We say understandably because the distinction between means and ends, in an ongoing situation, is often vague. Means are seen as ends, and in their turn, the ends become means to other ends. In this discussion we shall treat means and ends in conceptual fashions. Our concern is with the idea of strategic planning, not with its application. Let it suffice to report that such companies as General Electric, TRW, IBM, AT&T, and Texas Instrument are increasingly involved with the aspect of Strategic Planning.

2. More Form than Content

Does the idea of Strategic Planning differ from the traditional planning efforts of enterprise? Probably less in content than form. Strategic Planning rests on the truth that a micro unit, any micro unit, is affected in varying degrees, by its macro setting. Put another way, Strategic Planning not only accepts but stresses the idea that the setting of enterprise (including government), the relevant parts of the world change and in changing (may) affect the enterprise. Therefore to plan for the future without a regard for the parameters of the future is dangerous.

What is involved is an attempt by the most prepared, most powerful of enterprises, to think in terms of a "philosophy of history," to use a pretentious academic phrase, or a "theory of social change," to employ a slightly less pretentious phrase. As overblown as these two expressions are, they do suggest the ultimate implication of strategic planning. Most planners are not up to that.

3. The Young against the Old

Nevertheless Strategic Planning, if it is to be strategic and planning, must be concerned with how, and possibly why social change, within a reasonable horizon, will or may have a measurable bearing on the present decision process. The whole of the future is of less managerial concern than the part of the future which will become the relevant setting of the institution. The young people of the world, innocent of experience, cling together in their newly acquired techniques. The old with history and memory cramming their minds look to a longer span of a future replicating the past. The conflicting drives distort and weaken the process of Strategic Planning, and generate confusion as to its purpose, and hence the proper ways of going about it.

ENTER THE MANAGEMENT OF CHANGE

Social change, generally speaking, occurs on a spectrum. At the one extreme are changes of varying degrees of triviality. A new way to make tennis balls is of small importance. A better tennis game may bring pleasure to millions but has only negligible influence on the social and business orders. At the other extreme are changes which do influence and affect behavior far beyond the areas of immediate application. The development of the Pill caused a plethora of moral and religious issues and changes as well as institutional adjustments in the family market. It had political implications for legislature and public administration, and it indeed affected the prevailing ideologies. Great effects of innovation are, by all odds, less likely than modest effects. We can see five elements which are the essence of Strategic Planning regardless of the model or system used.

1. The Process of Adjustment by Anticipation

To be sure, all social change is not caused by technology. Other factors in politics, ideology and in Nature itself (e.g., abundance or shortage of natural resources) may cause major or minor social adjustments. Technology, however, seems to be involved whenever social change is of serious proportions.

If knowledge about changes which can affect an enterprise are secured prior to the event coming to fruition, the institution can play accordingly and use the inevitable development for its own (micro) benefit. If the future promises to bear the seeds of managerial failure, the planners can also avoid undertaking forward commitments, and look for alternative opportunities in traditional economic fashion. Or, and this is the risky alternative, the planners may seek ways and means to alter the future. In such a situation the enterprise, in its own self interest, would literally try to change the world.

What, then, is ultimately suggested by Strategic Planning is the adjustment of an institution to the inevitable, or the refusal to accept the future as inevitable. The latter heroic action is not unknown; e.g., the introduction of new products or new political programs. Point four and the Marshall Plan of President Truman are cases in point. But, on a market scale, frozen foods and synthetic fabrics also changed the future.

2. Planning Involves Society

In general, social fears engendered by the creativity of a single firm are probably groundless. Most entrepreneurial novelty is minor or even negligible insofar as social development is concerned. If the novelty of enterprise does change the world, that is the price a free society pays for its liberty. Untoward results can, supposedly at least, be corrected by market or legal action. Beneficial results enhance the quality of life.

So Strategic Planning is, as a concept, quite in accord with the premise of a free, open society. The gist of the whole matter is the growing conscious attempt of enterprise to relate itself, its future, and its alternative operations to the setting in which it operates. As we suggested, this is not a brand new idea. It is an idea more organized and carefully crafted than its precursors.

3. Strategic Planning Requires Choices of Goals

The essence of planning, strategic or other, is to set goals to determine what an administration should be and do, and to suggest ways and means of getting from resource to goal. Since the way is not likely to be smooth, since all sorts of contingencies and unexpected circumstances, events, and possible alternatives of means as well as ends are likely to present themselves, the ideal of planning includes the need to take advantage of, avoid, or overcome contingencies. In other words, risk avoidance is implicit as a purpose. Over time risk avoidance, or at least minimization, may well result in changes in the means employed by enterprise and the ends sought. Hence the very nature of the enterprise is involved. The Minnesota Mining Company of earlier in the century became the 3M Company (Minnesota Mining and Manufacturing) with the enterprise becoming, by 1980, quite different from what it planned for itself 50 years earlier. The opportunities, challenges and direction of thinking attendant upon the patent of an adhesive tape transposed what essentially was a mining and abrasive manufacturing company to the present multioriented 3M Company.

4. Strategy Means Predicting Unintended Side Effects

Looking at the societal-enterprise relationship from another angle, the oil embargo and price-quantity controls of the 1970s made coal, gas, and solar energy more attractive to investors and also as fields for technological and scientific investigation. Enormous political and investment changes will continue to flow from pollution control effects and by the high price of oil.

5. Strategic Planning Means Managing Risk and Uncertainty

Risks, we assert, are always present in action, but uncertainties too are a function of action. And if risks and uncertainties cannot be avoided, at least they can be minimized, or used. Strategic Planning cannot lead an undertaking to complete security and safety. It can, however, make an enterprise more cognizant of the implications of its choices so that opportunities are not totally unknown and lost.

Failure to grasp market opportunities may well be implied in a current criticism of American business. According to that criticism business tends to make short run decisions, eschewing long run commitment, and so restricts employment and output growth because the short run commitments tend to be more speculative than productive. The results are seen in declining investment and productivity.

WHAT IS THE BUSINESS OF STRATEGIC PLANNERS?

The tools and technical apparatus available to strategic planners are many. Economists, accountants, sociologists, cultural anthropologists, engineers, futurists, and all the other clans, tribes, and nations of the disciplines can bring their expertise and techniques to the task. In practice, however, since cost is a consideration, a small team of insightful persons with varying technical training is usually set to define the task. Inevitably they confront, consciously or otherwise, certain key items in their agenda. The directions given the team's members cannot be explicity and elegantly defined, for then the choices would be unduly limited to the means at hand and to current knowledge. Leeway must be given in the first instance to permit the consideration of alternative ends as well as alternative means.

To limit the discussion to means would reduce the planning to the tactical rather than raising it to the strategic. The art of tactical planning is similar to the usual problems of management science or managerial economics. The setting of the enterprise is assumed static, with the goals of enterprise fairly well defined; e.g., to increase market share to 2/3 from 1/3, or to acquire one or two other enterprises with these certain characteristics, or to secure X$ in funding. Such tasks are essential but they have not the breadth of Strategic Planning. They may be included as part of Strategic Planning.

In essence, Strategic Planning is concerned with change. For example: "What is involved for the enterprise, and what are the implications of changing from generating electricity by oil to generating and distributing electricity or energy by other techniques which are or may become available?" "How will business and government interact in the near and more distant future, given certain political or ideological changes?" "What are the alternatives and their implications of further automating large manufacturing firms which have major competitors abroad?" The method and speed of robotization, the political, technological, labor, personnel and investment aspects are all relevant. The United States and the Western world are groping their way through the realities of such examples.

1. We Need a Theory of Change

There is no discipline of change. There is, for example, no accepted theory of why women's fashions behave as they do. Or on a grander scale there is neither revealed nor received truth about the sociology of business, even though business touches the lives of more people, more continuously, perhaps than any social institution, excepting the family. This is strange for a society which has been called a Business Society. To be sure there are studies of firms, industries, business leaders, and markets, but there is no general discipline, a sociology, with general propositions comparable to urban or rural sociology, or even to the sociology of war or politics.[1] It may be that the several divisions of the business disciplines as Real Estate, Finance or Marketing are, in reality, the sociology of real property, financial instruments and selling. In great part such studies are technical exercises concerned with how constrained markets operate and are not much concerned with the interconnectedness of the subject at hand with other social and entrepreneurial activities.

2. Which Tools Should We Use?

This leads us to examine the elemental analytic means and techniques available to study, directly, enterprise behavior. In our opinion they are:

1. *Accounting.* The oldest formal analysis. It is quantified, analytical and limited to a historical framework.
2. *Statistics.* The manipulation of quantity to investigate and expose quantitative relations. It is conceptual in its theoretical aspects, but is directly applicable to micro and macro data. In its application it does not readily lend itself to circumstances outside the confined data set.

---

[1]The work of Parsons and Smelser represent extremely interesting efforts. But in general business has not provided a base for social investigation equal to, for example, criminal behavior or the family.

3. *Economics.* The concern with allocation of scarce resources and relative prices. By itself economics has no substance, it is essentially an exercise in logic. However it has proved to be applicable to real, historical situations and quantification. Its great strength is its ability to be integrated into the data to specific situations; e.g., marketing, production, labor.

4. *Social Psychology.* The relation of groups to other groups and of individuals to groups. It is akin to sociology, but unlike that discipline makes little attempt to integrate or synthesize other social disciplines into a gestalt or unity so as to explain given social situations or issues. Social psychology seems content to study social structure abstractly and apply the principles of the abstractions in concrete situations.

Practitioners in all four areas tend to extend their interests beyond the borders of their own fields. The integration of some of the above is managerial economics. That synthetic discipline, in essence, tends to combine accounting data and analysis with (micro) economic analysis. The result is a discipline which is growing in importance as a tool for enterprise analysis. Statistics and social psychology are less integrated into managerial economics than accounting and economics, but the tendency is to expand the amalgamation. Decision making under conditions of uncertainty is slowly being introduced into entrepreneurial calculations. In production, costing and output considerations, managerial economics has also been well received, possibly because it gives an engineering sense or illusion of exactitude to problems for which exactness cannot be discovered.

Economics by itself, and also managerial economics, often provide vague answers which have only a conceptual persuasiveness. Exact quantification in time, dollars or quantities have not been an outstanding successful accomplishment of economics. Like management science, managerial economics relies on statistics and often industrial engineering to provide an analysis which is essentially numerical and so permits quantitative answers which again have the illusion of accuracy. This is not intended as an adverse criticism. A number which purports to be uniquely accurate, and which does fall somewhere within some defined range of probable answers is better than a range of answers whose numerical geography is unknown.

Unfortunately, the elemental disciplines and their derivatives—e.g., marketing, management and finance—or managerial economics and management science have not dealt well with changes (from whatever source) in the setting of the problems being analyzed. Technological change occurring (sometimes only slightly) in the future, or social change related to technology or to other forces, has not successfully been introduced into the disciplines we have been discussing. Yet to confine analysis and decision theory to situations or models which are essentially static is an onerous limit. Our world, in the gross or in the detail of an institution, has possibilities of change, of dynamism, which cannot be denied in any serious long-range decision.

Toward Contingency Management

The foregoing implies that analysis of a traditional formal sort is not enough. The disciplines, by themselves, are so analytically restrictive as to lead the responsible actors to make decisions which may be quite wrong or ineffective. The foregoing also suggests that insight, experience, guess, and preconception are all indeed in planning—and that they supplement the conventional tools of analysis. Answers to the question "What does the management wish enterprise to be?" will be changed by the brute realities of time and opportunity as well as by the probabilities of the future. Contingencies are always in the wings waiting to come on stage at unexpected moments. The future is always dark seen through a glass.

Contingencies, which is to say unexpected change, and hence new opportunity and risk, may occur in several levels:

- *The Market Level.* Consumers may change their habits or patterns of purchase very quickly. The acceptance by men, after World War II, of synthetic fiber in their clothing, and their acceptance of slacks and sport coats instead of more conventional lounge or business suits, came as a surprise to many firms in the conventional men's clothing industry. The shift of consumers away from butter to oleomargarine was rapid after restrictive legislation was repealed and after the fear of serum cholesterol became widespread.
- *The Competitive Level.* The competitors may begin to act in an unconventional manner and so may require initiative or defensive action by the enterprise. The system of "rebates from the manufacturer" in the American automobile industry, begun by one firm, spread not only to other U.S. firms, in and out of the automobile trade, but to some foreign firms doing business in the U.S.
- *The Environment Level.* The ideologies of the societies in which an institution operates have obvious potential effects on planning and operations. Different ideologies in a work force with respect to productivity, loyalty to employer or to the job specifications require a different course of action by the enterprise.

Contingencies may also appear in the market. No one, or very few persons, as late as 1968, planned to avert or avoid the inflation of the 1970s. Nor was the strange marriage of inflation and unemployment of the 70s expected in the early 1960s. The oil embargo and OPEC price increases have been used as an excuse in explaining all sorts of enterprise and market dislocations. Yet in hindsight, the OPEC actions are not so strange that they might not have been anticipated. But very few expected the persistence, power and harsh policies of the oil producers.

The litany of contingencies faced in the last decade is long and sad. That number would be raised almost beyond measure if the unexpected happenings to particular enterprises were included. The failure is not only risky, it is also uncertain. It might seem that a series of short term successes will assure long run success. This is not necessarily a valid view. The effective handling of contingencies might divert the enterprise from a path, which in the long run has greater rewards than the sum of the short-run contingency successes. To stop every leak in every pipe with chewing gum may be less effective than putting in a new and costly water system or selling the house.

Political uncertainty may not be so important as social uncertainties. For example, the business cycle has been studied for years. Various theories attempt general explanation, but each cycle seems to have characteristics which are unique to it, as well as having characteristics which are common to other cycles. Political activity, however, is usually more reactive to acknowledge and perceived social problems. The alternatives are debated in the press, in Congress, and on T.V. Alternatives of action are thereby fairly well laid out before one is undertaken. This gives enterprise the opportunity to plan and adjust.

Can Risk Be Controlled?

It is common for business and, generally speaking, social and political analysts, to distinguish between the long run and the short run. In its simplest (nontechnical) sense the long run is a time period which extends for a year to as many as 10 or 15 years into the future. The short run on the other hand is assumed to be concerned with current activities. For many purposes the time consideration is useful.

But the investment horizons of several industries may be appreciably different. A firm operating in a market in which technology changes rapidly (e.g., electronics) may feel that an investment in machinery and equipment which cannot be recaptured in one to three years would be a risky, long-term, venture. On the other hand steel technology tends to develop slowly, so investments in steel making are not quickly outmoded. Even when new technologies appeared, as in the years directly after World War II, the U.S. Steel Industry adopted these techniques only slowly. The shrinking nature of the industry pushed the investment horizon back. Government too tends to have a limited horizon. Long range projects, e.g., Social Security or farm policy, are not planned for the long term but rather require constant shoring up.

The short run, insofar as it consists of meeting current problems, does appear to have more homogeneity than the long run. Current problems must be met by borrowing or from the reserve cash, regardless of the current state of inventory, cash or sales. But the certainty of the wage bill being due is 100% and the results of not meeting that obligation are clear. On the other hand some activities which require current outlays are postponable or avoidable. A most perplexing example is repair and maintenance. To one who has been around public and private universities for many years, it is painfully apparent that often short-run requirements are pushed into the future to the disadvantage of long-run interests. Failure to meet depreciation, maintenance and repair costs reduces the value and the life of long-run real investment. That many enterprises other than universities suffered through the 1970s into the 1980s under this handicap is a frequent complaint of management.

We can then urge that (soft pedaling the long and short runs) Strategic Planning can divide the future for any action into segments, by reference to risk and uncertainty. Low risks or unavoidable commitments are akin to the short run, regardless of the time frame. By low risks we mean the opportunity benefits of other behavior (including no action) seem somewhat less than the benefits of the behavior in question. Akin to the long run is the situation in which alternative actions, including no action, have possible and probable benefits which approach or appear to exceed the value of benefits of a given course of action. This is to say opportunity costs (that is, costs of opportunities foregone) may approach, equal or exceed the benefits expected from the given course of action.

Since uncertainty is a large factor in times of inflation, social unrest, and aimless public policy, the willingness to make long time commitments is lower than in the future if fairly certain. (At the end of 1980 banks paid more for 6 month time deposits than for 2½ year deposits.) If Strategic Planning approaches market analysis with a concern for risk, uncertainty and productivity, the certainty of market outlook is more important than calendar time. The need for the flexibility and liquidity of financial investments may cause the postponement of investment in physical plant. If we add to these uncertainty elements the current ideologies which set high store by social and enterprise mobility, upward and laterally, for young executives, and high store by the protection of high managerial incomes, the tendency toward short run concerns in enterprise is strengthened at the expense of long run considerations. These considerations seem to match the circumstance of the present era. If such observations have validity, strategic planners should be able to expose, and possibly convert, some uncertainty to risk. This means as well that the goals of the fortunate industries would then be placed on a more reasonable base than otherwise.

What Management Internal Structure Is Best?

These remarks have little bearing on management's internal structure and operation. The inwardly directed aspects of management are, in our opinion, different from the plans and goals of enterprise. The former are more weighted by administrative matters than the latter, which are more oriented to what should be undertaken rather than how the tasks shall be done. Of course if a new direction is given to enterprise, internal reorganization might be indicated. Should we centralize or decentralize? What is a "business" unit?

A big problem of Strategic Planning is to minimize risk, and convert uncertainty to risk, so that enterprise is in position to take advantage of the present and a future better than if it is only seen through a dark glass.

Given uncertainties due to the inflation, off again on again depression, high capital costs, plus required investment in environmental repair and maintenance (e.g., antipollutive devices which implies investment not directly related to production), and ordinary depreciation costs, enterprise often finds itself in a quandary as to the future. Research and development as futurity elements, has been neglected. However, much of the handwringing over this is not justified in our opinion. First of all, in spite of the decline or slow growth of productivity, gross industrial production has increased as more of the population is employed. This may well be a phenomenon which cannot be extended for long, because plant and the labor force will ultimately be unequal to the task compensating for declining productivity due to whatever cause. The cause is, primarily we believe, a lower rate of capital accumulation and a tired technology. R&D has been slighted, probably because of uncertainty. But science and scientific research are quite independent of industrial R&D. So long as there are universities, graduate schools and Ph.D. candidates there will be workplaces for science. Even as the industrial market oriented toward R&D is starved for funds, the scientific inventory continues to grow.

When, as, and if the depression and inflation are under some control, thereby lessening uncertainty, R&D will again expand. At that time the scientific choices and the new sophistication available to technology will be great, due to the period of scientific accumulation. Industry might even advance as rapidly as it did after World War II. The scientific resource will have become relatively large, and so technology might avoid some of the false starts and adaptations that a more constant rate of technological growth typically exhibits.

The Change Resistors Must Be Dealt With

Institutions require planning. A family, an insurance company, a fire department always have a history and a future. The present is ephemeral, quickly becoming history. So an institution is always hurtling into the unknown. As the future becomes the present, managers of institutions reassess the past, always hoping to be able, thereby, to guess the shape of things to come. Then the institution can adapt to the forming reality or change it.

George Odiorne[2] speaks of the Change Resistors, and quite properly faults them for their failure to adjust to the reality of change or to try to use it. They want the good past to persist, not really recognizing that the good old past is their rosy reassessment of the past to make it seem more pleasant than the present realities and future uncertainties. Odiorne has a valid argument, but one which cannot be generalized in asserting that we or institutions live only in the future. Life is lived in the past, present and future, simultaneously.

As Talcott Parsons[3] taught us, institutions, which is to say people acting in some persistent, organized and concerted way, are constrained in their behavior by the customary, therefore historical, modes of behavior. A family, insurance company, or fire department does not face each day or each new problem by casting behavior into its most efficient form to face the day or to solve the day's problem. The habits, personal and social, which were developed over time, largely control behavior. The minor inefficiencies of habitual behavior are more efficient than a new learning exercise for each novelty. Imagine trying to learn a new knot for every package to be tied or shoe to be laced! Persistence of behavior pattern is essential.

But novelty and the unknown are constant threats to the efficiency of an institution. So planning, providing new goals and/or means, is essential to the persistence of the institution. The institution persists by changing the Change Resistors. Those who cannot and therefore do not want to change, are doomed. Tenure, seniority, and other bulwarks of tradition may become tools of bitter reaction and instruments of failure. Business, hospitals, universities, probably all institutions after a time, may become, in part at least, museums which house, feed, and support Change Resistors. They convert social lag into a virtue and thwart colleagues who have imagination, creativity and drive, despite their years and familiarity with the past. Change Resistors, however, do also provide a brake on change, a brake which sometimes may preserve some significant values of the institution.

It is the Change Resistors who make strategic planning difficult, because such people are by definition without discrimination and wrong headed in what they want to preserve. They are not conservative so much as they are reassessors of history, especially their own place in the history of the institution. They often hope to somehow

---

[2]*The Change Resistors*—Spectrum Books 1981.

[3]Parsons and Smelser—*Economics and Society*, Free Press 1965.

stop change and hold back the future. The serious personnel limitations on Strategic Planning are not only ones inherent and implicit in
attempts to wrestle with the future as history. Some resistance to
change serves the purpose of maintaining the social configuration of
an institution.

At the other end of the spectrum are those for whom any or most
changes seem desirable. Such thoughtless people are as dangerous to
institutional life as change resistors.

THE ETHICS OF LEADERSHIP

Different from Change Resistors, the mindless proponents of change,
and the morally delinquent, are those who will be in commanding
posts, and who will determine the nature of the enterprise given the
new goals and means. The type of leadership, the organizational structure, the enterprise as a system, have to be defined. Strategic Planning,
then, has an important personnel aspect. The planners, who in the first
instance are analysts, have the task of formulating, for further discussion, alternative models of the future setting of the enterprise. The possible adaptations of the enterprise are exposed by the model, whose
implications are the chain of logically derived events from alternative
simulations. The evaluations of the hypothesized chains of events in
terms of social values is essentially an exercise in ethics. To the extent
that the enterprise adopts "ethical" lines of conduct, that it directs
itself toward a chain of events which have implications or externalities
which provide benefits beyond the conventional, then the enterprise,
through Strategic Planning, is planning ethically.

Law and regulations are the formal protection of the society and its
members against entities which, by their actions, produce ill will. But it is
not very likely that an institution or administration, knowing the authority and power of law, would or could consciously undertake a course of
action which is harmful for the sake of harm. In general, for example, a
great anti-pollution ideology has not yet found dedicated enemies in business, as an institution. No business is in favor of pollution for all and by
all. What business agitates for is time, knowledge of what to do, and the
consideration of costs and returns of anti-pollution efforts. That some business firms and other enterprises play the role of Change Resistors is obviously true. This is a function of the internal personnel composition of
leadership. The fault is not implicit in business or government as institutions, but rather in the *ideological attitudes of particular individuals* who
are in positions of power. It is simplistic to see business or government as a
monolithic enemy of a (monolithic) "people." It is the self-consciousness of
Strategic Planning which may be a force to reduce the nonsensical resistance to change to tolerable, smaller, limits.

The very power of large-scale business and government may permit each to affect its settings. This might make the future more agreeable than it otherwise would be, but power is a two-edged sword. The power of business might become a market force which actually reduces the need for the full exercise of administrative power by government. For if social problems were to be eliminated or reduced before they arose, or at least mitigated for the future, the details of regulation would be fewer than otherwise. Rules and laws could then be directed toward general behavior. Specific behavior would be subject to the particular needs and capacities of enterprise, and arise from the need and analysis of enterprise. This is not to negate government policy and administration as The Rulemaker.

So much harmony would be suspect. It is to suggest that general rules organizing markets are probably better than specific ones which regulate particular behavior. But general rules also permit a role for the exercise of authority. The paradox is inevitable.

The criteria of success of an economy can be measured in output, prices, income distribution, and similar current economic data. Considerations of freedom of entry for new business, technical innovation, economic growth and similar criteria, too, are important and mensural. Both kinds of criteria, those which measure and evaluate the present and those which evaluate the future, are essential in a dynamic society. Strategic Planning is a technique which ideally is a tool of big enterprise and of regulatory agents which are flexible. Strategic Planning may turn out to be a notable social invention.

THE LABOR QUESTION AND STRATEGIC PLANNING

Any analysis of the future, for an enterprise or economy, includes of course the labor factor. Some ideas about the future with respect to labor are fairly well known. For example the population, by age and sex, is known for the next couple of generations for the people already born. Immigration and emigration, participation rates, changes in the demographic structure and the natures of other social structure due to war or catastrophe are, however, not known. Ranges (profitability distributions) which have the promise of being valid can, in general, be estimated.

The effectiveness of education and training is probably less well known than the demographic information because of the turmoil of U.S. public (and private) education, and because of the training and education needs.

What is less well known than any of the foregoing, probably, is the state of social values and ideologies of 5–10–20–50 years hence. By ideology we mean (social) values in action. The world is not very stable ideologically. Public moods, social and personal values have shifted and changed markedly in the past few decades. The general ideology of working people during the 1930s and early 40s may have been critical and even hostile to management. But the trade union and political movements captured the minds and values of many of the working class (and other classes), and so developed a group or class ideology which included institutional mechanisms of law and of the market (trade unionism). This reliance on rule and law caused radical individual values or radical social (revolutionary) values to subside or become irrelevant. The period from 1938 until long after World War II was one of economic growth, union strength, business prosperity (generally speaking) and social and political harmony, as compared to the troubled 1960s and 1970s. The Great Depression and World War II were more periods of reform than radical change. World War II and the Korean War were not generally associated with internal social upheaval. National preservation against ideologies suffused the American scene.

It was the Vietnam War period which was concomitant with the rise of what may be considered aberrant individualism, the search for different "life styles," changes in the canons of art and behavior, etc. The great ideological changes occurred then. Many forces and factors converged to generate the social maelstrom or perhaps social convulsion. Enterprise was affected, but business, in the main, seems to have come through the erupting times fairly well. *After* the scene quieted (in the early 1970s) did business find itself moving without its traditional guidelines and expectations. The system seemed to falter (as in the thirties), and ideology seems to have been an important force for change. The oil embargo of OPEC, inflation, unemployment, declining capital accumulation, and an anti-regulation ideology, low productivity, foreign nations' developing highly competitive export industries, the relative growth of the service industries, the growing rate of women in the labor force, seemed to almost swamp American industry. The value systems of business and people are in transition, and no one knows quite to what.

Yet it is pretty clear that the movement toward automation will continue. The older concept of automation is concerned with the use of equipment to do "heavy work" or light work of a singularly repetitive sort. The new notion, robotization, is automation enhanced to do more complex jobs. The computer and computer technology are coming into their own in industry. Obviously novel social arrangements, training and education will be required as robotization becomes more widely applied. How will the trade unions react, how will laboring people react, what will the new movement do to the organization of enterprise?

From 1935 to the 1960s trade unions were a stabilizing factor. Dissident personal and political views of market and labor leaders, alternative social solutions and interests were submerged in the development of the union movement and its regulation. Left and right wing unionism were restrained by the power of the mainstream movement. Management had the leisure, indeed the need, to deal with a labor institution, not with a myriad of smaller, individual problems. In living through the period, Management complained. In retrospect both capital and labor gained in absolute economic position because the whole economy expanded. The rate of labor's income growth surely exceeded that of capital, but prosperity was endemic or at least quite widespread. At present, however, the ideologic novelty and input of unionism seems minimal. The future is less clear than the interpretation of the past, as is always the case.

Industrial and market labor needs of the future probably will stress *(a)* the professionally and technologically trained personnel, and *(b)* the semi-skilled. The former, if history is a guide, tends to develop loyalties to skill and trade. Engineers, toolmakers, and other kinds of skilled and professional people also tend to have great geographic and industrial mobility. How will enterprise hold them? Already we see that the need for administrators and managers has constructed an enormous Master of Business Administration (M.B.A.) program in the U.S.; already we see young M.B.A.s moving from job to job, ever upward, ever toward more power, responsibility and income. The settling down procedure has not begun. Will the 1980s continue to foster geographic and social mobility for the more highly skilled and professional classes? This is a question which has a great bearing on Strategic Planning exercises.

The second class, the semi-skilled, probably will require rather less job training and skill than the 1960 or 1970 factory and office workers. But might not the need for social and interpersonal skills be greater? And will the new "individualism," possibly an outgrowth of the rebellious 1960s, lead to labor turnover and long periods of individual withdrawal from the labor market? With a new breed of "cosmopolitans," i.e., people loyal to skill and profession and a new breed of "locals" (people with relatively minor skills), how will management deal with the work force?

The ideologies of management and labor, as well as of investors and government regulators, are all likely to undergo changes in the next 20–30 years. How will enterprise strategically plan for these changes? Strategic Planning in the labor field is clearly a vital issue. Government policy toward education and training is implicit in the problems of change.

INFORMATION AND STRATEGIC PLANNING

Predating the information revolution we are living through, business, government, science, the arts, clubs, families, all institutions in short, persistently accumulated information. Births and deaths were marked in family bibles and on charts filed in some local government office long before the data were inscribed on tapes or cards for instant referral by a monster computer. Records and other information of a general sort such as imports and exports, employment, sales, and so on, have been sedulously put together by government, banks and business because such data are useful in understanding some future or past situation, as well as because such information is deemed useful in decision making at some private or public level. But the recall of such information has not been efficient. The memory of people as individuals is sharper than the memory of institutional leaders. A change in leadership is not necessarily accompanied by a transfer of information.

The information revolution, a revolution which makes memory and information retrievable, came about because of the electronic capacity to maintain even greater quantities of data, call them forth quickly, and manipulate and analyze them with speed and complexity. The complexity of the world needs the data, and the data help make the world more complex. Sometimes the analysis is beyond the capacity of the data to support the complexity employed. The science of statistics is, generally speaking, beyond the sophistication of most executives. Not that modern administrative capacity is a loss, or confused. On the contrary. The information flow, the ability to analyze data correctly and effectively may be the saving grace in a situation in which the world is likely to find itself with a growing population, with raw material and natural resource scarcities, with rising expectations, and with political and social uncertainties and discontinuities. These will place ever heavier burdens on the planning and productive mechanism of the world and its constituent societies and institutions. Information and analysis gain in value as the difficulty of the problems increase. The inviting parts of the world have largely been preempted and settled and the more obvious resources tapped; but the demands on the world, both per capita and total, are far from satisfied. Even leisure is a demand trap, for while people may weigh work against leisure, leisure itself turns out to be costly. The wants of leisure are no less significant than the wants, private or social, of society.

A major thrust of information and analysis then should be to reduce the cost burdens of the productive, the "supply side," aspects of the economy. If the costs of information gathering, analyzing and storing are not less than the economic benefits produced, then the great dilemma of the world is not addressed. That issue is how to produce more and at lower cost per unit.

The great abuse of potential information capacity, in our view, is to restrict its use, or at least, concentrate its use on problems which if solved or reduced provide a lesser valued resultant than if applied to other uses. This at once raises the question of *value to whom?* Banks and government probably use the information resource to a greater extent than other undertakings. The full scale of their activities would probably be curtailed without the modern resource. Imagine running Social Security without a vast information network. Imagine keeping track of all the domestic and foreign money transactions without computers. The tasks could be performed, but at greater cost in money outlay and time. There also are procedures which require skill and machines to keep inventories or bill orders which are cheaper than if these tasks were done by hand. But the machines performing the task may, in effect, be underutilized. Their capacities may outstrip the requirements of the task. If imagination and creativity were let loose, might not the information resource be more economically and widely used, by both the social (public) and private calculus? We suggest there is the need for both simpler and more complex machines.

The control of costly energy, the better physical and procedural planning of activities, novel inventions and production practices, more effective menu planning for institutionalized populations and even families, in brief the more effective (private and social) allocation of scarce resources, seems to be a more reasonable use of information control than what the enterprise complex presently enjoys. The more effective use of information processing will probably occur in time, not by merely shifting the information resource from its present uses, but by increasing the size and complexity of the resource, and so shifting about the pattern of use. What are now rare or novel uses will become commonplace. Already programmed regulators (computers) have been made a part of the driving mechanism of new automobiles. Already computers do exhaustive simulations for the consideration of new drugs, new industrial designs and so on.

We suggest that for many operations there is a size limit. The obvious limit is if the cost of additional information is greater than the value of the additional output (sales or knowledge). Also, and more important, however, is that the future probably cannot be fully known by simulation exercises. But simulation plus judgement probably provides a better grasp of the future than judgment alone or judgment buttressed by analysis which is less sophisticated than it might be. Strategic Planning is simulation plus judgment.

CONCLUSION

Strategic Planning is a growing necessity as the world of affairs grows larger and more complex. Strategic Planning is possible because of the information revolution and the growing sophistication of social analysis. But two pristine elements are ever present, made even more significant by the very size of the Strategic Planning tasks. They are judgment and responsibility.

The essence of Strategic Planning is that it is based on analysis and judgment. Therefore Strategic Planning entails the need for responsibility restraint. Responsibility ultimately entails the idea of the compromise of ideological values, as well as the respect for such values. Restraint is indicated not only because individuals and their welfare may be involved, but of even greater importance is the involvement of the body politic in the decisions of enterprise. The setting of enterprise is the society itself.

In essence strategic planning means managing change, learning to adjust, getting the feelers of the organization out into society more effectively, having goals and making choices according to those goals, and learning how to turn uncertainty to risk where it can be insured against.

A yawning gap in most strategic planning is a real grasp of the impact of such planning of the human element and labor. Apart from some quite trivial exercises in "human resources" management, most planners have not dealt very intelligently with the issues of unions, popular opinion, and the ideological changes which follow.

Lastly, despite the astonishing gains in electronics and hardware, with complex software not far behind, most planners have not done very well at devising a conceptual grasp of information theory and how to use the power that lies within their grasp.

Tough Questions for Developing Strategies

George S. Day

Corporate management is concerned with the paucity of creative new ideas and evidence that crippling implementation problems are being overlooked. They wonder why many businesses are continually caught off-balance by unanticipated market and competitive actions. This leads naturally to doubts that the effort put into strategic planning is being returned by superior performance. Experience has also taught senior managers to be deeply suspicious of the rosy forecasts of revenue and profit performance that come from the business units. As one CEO complained, "I'm tired of looking at hockey stick forecasts. . . . The focus of most business managers is on the first year of the plan, because this is the basis for their budget and performance appraisals. The rest of the planning period is simply wishful thinking designed to persuade us to give them the budgets they want. . . . It's frustrating because we don't have the detailed information to challenge them."

Meanwhile, many operating managers seem uncertain about what corporate management is seeking. As one division general manager admitted, "We hadn't done our homework on some key questions, and were badly cut up when the executive committee reviewed our strategy. . . . But frankly, I don't know what they are looking for, and since the questions we get seem to change every year I'm not sure they know either."

The real cost of an arid and unfocused strategy dialogue between corporate and operating management is felt when the strategy fails to deliver the promised outcomes. Postmortems of these failures conducted by several multidivisional companies have found that most problems are eventually traced to unrealistic assumptions, distorted resource allocations or a lack of management commitment. Other studies of problems with planning systems have also been pointing to these as endemic problems. These insights have been very helpful in improving the strategic dialogue

Source: George S. Day, "Tough Questions for Developing Strategies," *The Journal of Business Strategy* 6, no. 3 (1986), pp. 60–68.

within planning teams and between operating and corporate management, and reducing the prevalence of these types of failure. At the heart of all efforts at improvement is the development of robust and mutually acceptable criteria for testing and refining business strategies.

WISHFUL THINKING

The bane of managers and planners is the "hockey stick" forecast, also known as the rolling-J-curve forecast. The following comparison of three sets of long-range earnings forecasts against actual business performance is a familiar illustration of this type of wishful thinking (Exhibit 1). Despite the growing discrepancy between actual and forecast earnings in 1979 and 1980, the management of this business was still holding to optimistic assumptions about share stability and strengthening margins. Their only concession to reality was an admission that the turnaround would be more difficult than first anticipated.

What accounts for this pattern of wishful thinking? Does it simply reflect a natural desire of those making the projections to do better in the future? While this impulse colors all forecasts, the real reasons are more deeply rooted in the way managers cope with ambiguity.[1] Three sources of bias have been identified:

- *Anchoring.* Decisionmakers tend to "anchor" on a particular outcome they believe will occur. This outcome dominates their thinking about the option and suppresses consideration of uncertainties. As a result, downside risks are understated.
- *Selective Perception.* There are several biasing elements here: People tend to structure problems in light of their past experience (marketing people will interpret a general management problem as a marketing problem), the anticipation of what one expects to see will influence what one actually sees, and as a consequence conflicting evidence will be disregarded.
- *Illusion of Control.* Planning activities may give decisionmakers the illusion they can master and control their environment. At the same time, decisionmakers have a tendency to attribute success to their own efforts and failures to external events and "bad luck."

These three problems are compounded when top management has unrealistic expectations and requires operating management to make commitments that may not be possible. Texas Instruments (TI) is

---

[1]See Amos Tversky and D. Kahneman, "Judgment Under Uncertainty Heuristics and Biases," *Science*, 1974, pp. 1124–1131; and Robin M. Hogarth and Spyros Makridakis, "Forecasting and Planning: An Evaluation," *Management Science*, Feb. 1981, pp. 115–138.

EXHIBIT 1   Earnings History and Forecast

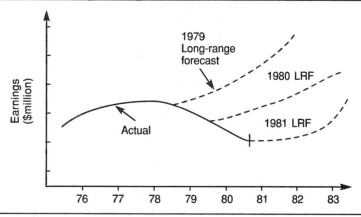

reputedly a company where senior management created a number of long term problems by forcing operating managers to accept nearly impossible goals.[2] Meetings to review operations and plans were designed to generate a "we'll make it happen" attitude. The result was that after senior management got the commitment they wanted, operating management then had to figure out how to make it happen. In the view of one consultant who worked with TI, "The planning sessions generate false hope, not business plans."

As in all facets of planning, the key is hard-nosed reality, and willingness to support challenging objectives with adequate resources. This has worked well for TI in some areas, such as its terrain-following radar system for the F-18 jet fighter and its seismographic system for oil exploration that shows underground formations in three dimensions. These were ambitious programs based on capabilities that TI managers were able to assemble from within their organization. Adroit reassignment of people ensured that these programs would succeed. But the pressure of ambitious objectives also can force operating management to attempt programs beyond their capabilities, as when TI lost ground in the home computer market by trying to write most of its own software.

MYOPIC ANALYSIS

Evaluations of strategies are likely to be dominated by facts and opinions that are easy to retrieve. Often this is evidence of the past success of a strategy. Because this hard data is given more weight

---

[2]P.B. Ultal, "Texas Instruments Regroups," *Fortune*, Aug. 9, 1982, pp. 40–45.

than soft assessments of future threats, management may be unrealistically complacent. This is an especially dangerous posture within industries such as life insurance or telecommunications, which are in the midst of a major restructuring. Larger companies tend to underestimate the ability of new competitors to get needed resources, gain market acceptance, and penetrate previously stable markets. They may also rely for too long on actions—such as shoring up regulatory barriers—that have worked in the past without facing up to the inevitability of change.

Myopia can cut both ways, however, and lead managers to give too much weight to their immediate problems. This is an understandable posture for managers in capital goods industries who have been preoccupied until recently with the problems of managing plant utilization rates of 60 percent or below. Yet the strategies of cost containment developed under these conditions often are not very robust because they cannot easily be adapted to new conditions. While strategies should be changed when the underlying assumptions are no longer valid, frequent changes are both expensive and disorienting. Here is where corporate management has a major role in forcing business units to consider the questions of the long-run adaptability of their strategy.

The myopia and biases that afflict managers' judgments have especially serious consequences for financial evaluations of investments in strategies and projects. For example, while much effort is devoted to projecting market growth, simplifying assumptions are often made that prices will move and shares will behave as they have in the past. But subsequent price levels may be depressed, either by too much added capacity or by low-cost capacity additions that displace high cost facilities. The problem is even encountered in straightforward discounted cash flow analyses of the gains from cost-reducing investments. Such analyses often overlook the effects of competitors making parallel investments to reduce their labor, material, or processing costs. If prices reflect the changing cost structure of a competitive industry, the actual earnings may be lower than expected. This helps explain why the profitability of most business units falls far short of the corporate hurdle rates for investment.

DISTORTED RESOURCE ALLOCATIONS

Corporate allocations of resources for maximum impact are often thwarted by the "gamesmanship" of operating managers manipulating the planning process to serve their own ends. The resulting distortions are magnified when the measures of prospective performance used to compare strategies are themselves misleading. The result is a bias toward short-run payoffs from investment in mature businesses. In one company, this is called the Golden Rule of Planning: "Those that have the gold set the rules."

Gamesmanship

"Our planning process has a life of its own that often has little to do with competitive realities or market opportunities," complained one division general manager recently. "Business unit managers pad their plans and resource requirements because they know corporate will cut everyone back. Corporate knows we do this so they try and outguess us and adjust their approvals of budgets and programs accordingly. So they're at least condoning the game." As each business unit maneuvers to get more than its fair share of the resources, important differences in strategic prospects get blurred.

This problem is a serious concern in many companies. A recent study[3] of planning problems in six regional commercial banks found that two of the three most critical behavioral problems were that managers primarily bargained for resources rather than identifying new resources, and "padded" their plans to avoid close measurement. What was more revealing, however, was that these problems appeared to be a response by the managers to uncertainty about the expectations of corporate management. "When in doubt, leave lots of room for maneuvering," is a credo in many companies.

Misleading Signals

Sales growth and earnings remain the most popular benchmarks for evaluating strategies. As they are readily available from the financial accounting systems they are also influential measures of performance. Mounting criticism of these measures has properly emphasized the ease with which they can be manipulated and their inability to reflect differences in risk exposure or the timing of the earnings flows.[4] A more fundamental problem is that they may deflect the strategic dialogue within a company from the important questions. A promise of high rates of profit is not credible unless it is based on solid evidence of anticipated scarcity or competitive advantage.

---

[3]Marjorie A. Lyles and R. T. Lenz, "Managing the Planning Process: A Field Study of the Human Side of Planning," *Strategic Management Journal*, 1982, pp. 105–18.

[4]Alfred Rappaport, "Selecting Strategies That Create Shareholder Value," *Harvard Business Review*, May–June 1984, pp. 139–49.

LACK OF COHESION AND COMMITMENT

Strategy failures often boil down to the whole being less than the sum of the parts. Too often we have seen individually competent departments working at cross-purposes with one another, and behaving as though their success were coming at the expense of some other department. How else can one account for the manufacturing department that resisted investments in quality assurance programs, and seriously jeopardized a major product line, because they didn't bear the costs and consequences of warranty repairs?

A lack of cohesion is often evident in strategies that have evolved over time and are held together by shaky alliances among functional departments. These are vulnerable to changes in the environment that demand major adjustments, for the mechanisms to make those changes are not in place. However, the consequences of a lack of cohesion—and resulting absence of commitment to integrated action—are greatest when the business embarks on a new strategy. If the new direction is based on a network of reluctant compromises, the temptation to revert to the old strategy will be great. Many insurance companies are finding it difficult to disengage themselves from costly agency networks despite compeling reasons to find more economical ways to go to market. At the heart of the problem is often found a group of managers who are not convinced of the need for change, or whose authority might be compromised by the new approaches.

New strategies are like new ideas. Without a determined and credible champion—who has a vision that galvanizes the management team and the energy to overcome the resistance that change provokes—the odds of a strategy failure are great.

ASKING THE TOUGH QUESTIONS

What could be done to avoid the predictable reasons for strategy failure identified during the postmortems? The answer lies in the observation that a contributing factor in all failures was the absence of useful debate and dialogue at critical points in the formulation of the strategy. The right questions had clearly not been asked at the right time, and indeed it was not even clear there was agreement on what questions should be asked. This leads to the development of a series of evaluation criteria, with the participation of corporate and operating managers. These criteria are cast in the form of seven "tough" questions that are understood and accepted as appropriate ground rules by all participants in the strategic dialogue.

1. Suitability: Is There a Sustainable Advantage?

The essence of strategy formulation is the matching of competencies with threats and opportunities. An important first question is therefore whether a strategy makes sense in light of anticipated changes in the environment. Until the early 1980s, "systems houses" dominated the market for turnkey computer systems.[5] These firms prospered by offering a total solution to a customer's problems by providing both applications software and computer hardware. The market growth of packaged systems of 40 percent per year unfortunately attracted the attention of hardware manufacturers. Faced with rapidly declining hardware prices, these new competitors were beginning to emphasize software. Thus any strategy option for a systems house had to recognize the impact of much larger, better-funded, and highly visible hardware makers and computer service companies.

But strategy is also about the pursuit of competitive advantage. Unless a strategy offers some basis for future advantage, or adaptation to the forces eroding the current competitive position, then it does not stand the test. By mid-1980, it was apparent that systems houses that continued to emphasize general business applications such as accounting and payroll were most vulnerable because it was relatively easy for new entrants to acquire expertise in these applications. By contrast, systems houses specializing in technically complex markets—chromatography systems, for example—with the capability to provide a range of products, including remote data processing and systems consulting, had a protected advantage and attractive growth prospects.

Here are four key steps to follow when subjecting each alternative strategy to the suitability test:

- *Step 1. Review the potential threats and opportunities to the business.* The major sources of these threats or opportunities include: changes in the environment, and especially changes in customer and distribution requirements, the actions of present and prospective competitors, and changes in the availability of critical skills and resources.
- *Step 2. Assess each option in light of the capabilities of the business.* How well can the business ward off or avoid threats, exploit opportunities, or enhance current advantages or provide new sources of advantage? At this stage it is worth asking whether the strategy can work under a broad range of foreseeable environment conditions. Some strategies are only effective when inflation is high, or low, for

---

[5]"New Rivals in Turnkey Systems," *Business Week*, June 23, 1980.

example. Other strategies don't travel well to new geographic markets. A robust strategy that can be readily adapted to a variety of conditions is generally preferred.

- *Step 3. Anticipate the likely competitive responses to each option.*   Can competitors match, offset, or "leap frog" any advantages conferred by this option? Role playing by management teams, taking the perspective of different competitors, can be valuable in assessing competitive responses. To complete this step, ask how the business would cope with the anticipated competitive actions.
- *Step 4. Modify or eliminate unsuitable options.*   If the strategy option does not meet these suitability tests, it should either be modified or dropped from further consideration.

2. Validity: Are the Assumptions Realistic?

Choices among alternative strategies are among the least structured of all decisions that any manager must make. The manager has little hard data on which to rely. He must choose based on judgments, forecasts, and assumptions.

At the heart of these choices lie assumptions.[6] All those with a stake in choosing and implementing the strategy must share those assumptions. Otherwise the strategy will be formulated through compromise and implemented without understanding or conviction.

The difficulty lies in distinguishing sound assumptions from faulty ones. One must be on the lookout for assumptions that are accepted as conventional wisdom, but have either never been thoughtfully examined or cannot be justified in light of past events or probable trends. Whenever a major departure from past performance is anticipated, it is important to test whether there is adequate basis for the forecast. Exhibit 2 shows how this was done in the case of a proposed strategy for an industrial components business that forecast an increase of $51 million in sales and $7 million in net income between 1983 and 1987.

The first step in the validity test is to isolate each of the assumptions about the reasons for the forecast changes; for example, sales and profits are expected to benefit from a combination of price increases close to the rate of inflation, real market growth of 7 percent per year in the forecast period, and substantial share gains in both market segments. The next step is to evaluate the evidence used to support each assumption. Here the basis for the assumptions about share gains and real market growth appears especially tenuous. How can any share gains be

---

[6]Richard O. Mason and Ian I. Mitroff, *Challenging Strategic Planning Assumptions: Theory, Cases and Techniques* (1981).

EXHIBIT 2 Testing Key Strategic Assumptions

Sources of Change	1983-1987 ($ in millions)		*Key Assumptions/Actions*	*Validity*
	Sales	*Net Income*		
Price increase	$23	$12	• 5.5% per year (inflation rate forecast = 6%)	• 7.6% increase in 1981 • 5.3% increase in 1982 • 80% industry capacity and Japanese threat • Simultaneous growing share
Share improvement	17	4	• 31–34% in industrial segment • 20–27% in commercial segment	• .6% per year increase in 1979–1982 but with minimal price increase • Industrial segment is a high-price sensitivity market • New products in the commercial segment are catch-up
Real market growth	10	2	• 7% per year	• 2% per year, 1980–1982 • 20% from unproven new market x
Cost Productivity increase	1	1	• 3% per year	• 70% of annual productivity increase (3% per year, 1978–1982) was a single technical process breakthrough
Compensation increase	____	(12)	• 24% increase in head count	• 1983 head count same as 1980 with 10% less volume
Total change	$51	$ 7		

realistically justified when the new products in the commercial segment do not appear to offer a competitive advantage, and the business is trying to hold prices in the industrial segment close to inflation while countering potential Japanese competition? On this evidence, one has little confidence the proposed strategy could deliver the promised results. New evidence has to be provided and the forecasts adjusted to fit market realities and reflect trade-offs between conflicting performance objectives.

Quality of Information.   All assumptions rely on information which itself may be inaccurate, misleading, or simply out of date. Thus it is important to constantly ask how the data were collected, by whom, and for what purpose. These questions apply equally to internal information (such as costs or salesmen's calling frequency) and environmental data (on growth, market size, and price levels). Information on changes in competitor's capabilities and customer requirements should be scrutinized with special care. The consequences of not doing so were graphically described by the president of the Becton-Dickinson Consumer Products Group in 1980 as he reflected on their experience with strategic planning:

> Four years ago I went through a planning session with the Diabetic Care SBU, which makes, among other products, the syringes diabetics use to give themselves insulin. We had an excellent profiling session, and the strategy we developed seemed like a perfect one.
>   During the next year we suffered a serious loss of market share.
>   What happened was that a competitor introduced a syringe with a finer-gauged needle. We had known the competitor's plans and had tested the finer gauge on a machine that showed no appreciable reduction in drag from the thinner needle. But we didn't test it with the consumers, who have to stick these needles in themselves five or six times a day. They could feel the difference without even asking our machine, so they switched brands. Our problem was that even though we understood our competitors very well, we didn't have a good enough understanding of the market's unfulfilled needs. The planning session had given us a clear picture of the industry and the market, but only a static one. We weren't looking ahead.[7]

3. Feasibility: Do We Have the Skills, Resources and Commitments?

The feasibility test poses two questions for each strategy option:

1. Does the business possess the necessary skills and resources? If not, is there enough time to acquire or develop them before the strategic window closes?
2. Do the key operating managers understand the underlying premises and elements of the option, and are they likely to be committed to implementing the option?

Assessing Skill and Resource Constraints.   Financial resources (capital funds or cash flow requirements) and physical resources are the first constraints against which the strategy option is tested. If these limitations are so constraining that undertaking a strategy would actually jeopardize the competitive position, then the strategy has to be modified to overcome or live within the constraint or perhaps be

---

[7]*Becton-Dickinson Corp.* (D) Case, University of Virginia, 1982.

rejected. Imaginative solutions may be necessary, such as innovative financing methods using sale and leaseback arrangements or tying plant mortgages to long-term contracts.

The next constraints to be tested are access to markets, technology, and servicing capabilities. Do we have adequate sales force coverage? Is the sales force adaptable to the selling job demanded by the strategic option? Is the advertising effort and effectiveness likely to be sufficient? What about the cost, efficiency, and coverage of the present distribution system—including order handling, warehousing and delivery? Are relationships with jobbers, distributors and/or retailers sufficiently secure to adapt to the proposed new strategy? Similarly, do we have sufficient knowledge and experience with the next generation of appropriate product and process technology? Negative or uncertain answers should trigger a search for modifications to overcome problems, or perhaps will lead to eventual rejection of the option.

The most rigid constraints stem from the less quantifiable limitations of individuals and organizations. The basic question is whether the organization has even shown it could muster the degree of coordinative and integrative skills necessary to carry out the change in strategy. Any strategy option that depends on accomplishing tasks outside the realm of reasonably attainable skills is probably unacceptable.

Measuring the Capacity for Commitment. A broad-based commitment to successful implementation requires these two conditions:

- The premises and elements of the strategy must be readily communicable. If they are not understood, then not only will the strategy option likely be flawed, but its capacity to motivate support will be seriously compromised. A good strategy is one that can be easily understood by all functions, so they are not working at cross-purposes. For this reason a good strategy is one that can be adequately explained in two or three pages.
- The strategy should challenge and motivate key personnel. Not only must the option have a champion who gives it enthusiastic and credible support, but it must also gain acceptance by all key operating personnel.

If managers either have serious reservations about a strategy, are not excited by its objectives and methods, or strongly support another option, the strategy must be judged infeasible.

4. Consistency: Does the Strategy Hang Together?

A strategy is internally consistent if all its elements "hang together"; that is, there is minimal conflict among these elements. Planners need to be concerned about two levels of consistency. The first level is the fit of specific functional strategies with the basis for competitive advantage and the investment strategy that make up the strategic thrust. The second level of fit is concerned with the couplings among the functional strategies. Without an acceptable degree of fit at either level, effective coordination cannot be achieved. The obvious price is management energy needlessly devoted to organizational conflict and functional "finger pointing" to shift blame. A less obvious price is the diffused and uncertain impression of the business in the market.

The "consistency test" is seldom pivotal in that few strategies are rejected outright for inconsistency. But it can be useful in improving and refining the strategy to ensure that all elements are pointing in the same direction. This test may also indicate that the degree of change necessary to bring the elements into line is simply not feasible within the limitation of the available resources. Functional managers can only cope with a few changes simultaneously while trying to maintain continuing operations. Thus it may not be possible to upgrade old product lines, enter new markets, modernize the costing system, and build a new manufacturing plant all at once.

5. Vulnerability: What Are the Risks and Contingencies?

Each alternative strategy and the associated projects have a distinct risk profile. The overall level of risk reflects the vulnerability of key results if important assumptions are wrong or critical tasks are not accomplished. For example, an aggressive build strategy that increases investment intensity will increase the break-even point. This alternative is riskier because it makes the firm more vulnerable to shortfalls in sales forecasts than a "manage for current earnings" option.

The Vulnerability/Opportunity Grid.   As virtually any trend and internal capability is a potential risk factor, it is essential to isolate those few that would cause the most damage and deal with them explicitly. The vulnerability grid in Exhibit 3 is useful for this purpose. The *strategic importance* of the risk factors is a combination of (1) a sensitivity analysis of the potential consequences of extreme but plausible values—either positive or negative—of each factor on an overall performance, and (2) the likelihood that these extreme values could occur during the planning period. The appropriate response to important risk factors will depend on an assessment of the *degree of control* the business has over the factor. For example, those that are strategically important, and also subject to company control, need to be understood very well, made the focus of major strategic action steps, and controlled tightly.

EXHIBIT 3   Vulnerability/Opportunity Grid for a Mining Company

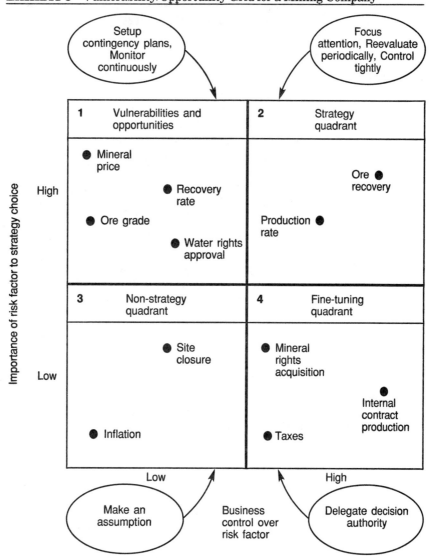

The specific risk factors illustrated in Exhibit 3 come from an assessment by a mining company of a major development proposal. The risky nature of the proposal is highlighted by the large number of strategically important risk factors, such as mineral prices, that are not controlled by the business. These become the focus of contingency plans, and must be continuously monitored. For less important risk factors it is sufficient to simply make an assumption or delegate authority to deal with the issue.

6. Adaptability: Can We Retain Our Flexibility?

In an uncertain environment it is important to ask whether, and at what cost, the strategy could be reversed in the future. The purpose of the questioning is to direct strategic thinking toward finding the best ways to make major investment commitments so that, if a major contingency occurs, it will not be necessary to write off the entire investment. Therefore, one must evaluate how each strategy offers possibilities for flexibility in design, multiple uses, or risk hedging—perhaps at a higher initial capital cost.

The question of adaptability applies as much to decisions about delaying changes in strategic direction as to decisions about undertaking major investment programs. The implications of a delay are difficult to assess, especially when they are buried in the implicit assumption of discounted cash flow analysis that investments are reversible.

In capital budgeting decisions, it is typically assumed that if an investment is postponed, it can always be made later with no penalty other than that implied by the company's discount rate. In fact, to regain this lost ground the business may have to spend a good deal more than if it had made the investment when first proposed. If the strategic window has closed, there may be no opportunity to adapt to the new situation, and all flexibility will have been lost.

7. Financial Desirability: How Much Economic Value Is Created?

The ultimate test of the final candidate options is the attractiveness of their forecast performance relative to the probable risk. At a minimum, an acceptable strategy must satisfy growth and profit objectives negotiated with corporate management. However, these are fallible measures and susceptible to manipulation. They may also myopically emphasize a short-run orientation.

Clearer signals may come from evaluating the merits of a strategy option in light of its capacity to enhance the economic value of the business or to improve competitive position. A forecast of substantial creation of economic value—or of high rates of profitability—cannot be taken as automatic indicators of the acceptability of a strategy option.

Both these measures must be based on persuasive evidence of competitive advantage. Thus, further tests of the outcome require forecasts of the likelihood the option will gain or sustain an advantage.

TOWARD A PRODUCTIVE STRATEGY DIALOGUE

Effective business strategies are formed in a crucible of debate and dialogue between and within many levels of management. The challenge is to encourage realism in the dialogue—so critical decisions are not distorted by wishful thinking and myopic analysis—while not suppressing creativity and risk-taking. If the dialogue is limited to an annual confrontation in which new ideas are challenged by corporate management, then few business unit managers will be inclined to venture beyond safe extensions of their present strategies.

What is needed is a continuing dialogue based on a shared understanding of strategic issues and mutually accepted and understood criteria for evaluating strategy options or strategies in progress. These criteria work best when they are embedded in the organization as "tough questions" that cannot be evaded. These tough questions also clearly communicate that an effective strategy does the following:

- Exploits environmental trends and creates an enduring advantage.
- Is based on realistic assumptions and accurate information.
- Can be achieved with available resources.
- Is internally consistent.
- Is acceptable to the operating managers who will be responsible for implementation.
- Is flexible enough to respond to unexpected developments.
- Will create economic value within acceptable risk limits.

Strategies that do not meet these criteria are unlikely to succeed. No champion will be willing to step forward and galvanize the operating managers into action, and no CEO will award it total support. Such strategies are especially vulnerable to the actions of competitors with a strong commitment to their own well-reasoned strategy.

The Strategy Audit

Milton Lauenstein

- Beatrice Foods announces a $280 million write-off and plans to divest about fifty businesses acquired in a diversification program.
- As a move toward vertical integration, DuPont goes deeply into debt to acquire Conoco. It turns out that DuPont could have bought its raw materials more favorably on the open market.
- Over fifty years ago, GM demonstrated that a strategy of offering a broad line of cars to appeal to the customers was superior to Henry Ford's rigid standardization approach. Since then, Ford and Chrysler have continued to compete on a head-to-head basis with their larger competitor, with poor results.
- Gulf & Western absorbs a $470 million charge to earnings when it decides to sell operations accounting for over $1 billion in sales.

Nearly every day, the press carries news of such "strategic" moves which have gone sour. Why is it that so many corporations make what in hindsight are so clearly serious errors? How is it that chief executive officers, who are paid hundreds of thousands annually, could make such proposals? Why aren't these mistakes caught by the board?

Actually, the way corporate top managements work makes it natural for these blunders to occur. Most chief executives have been selected primarily on the basis of their ability to execute rather than to formulate strategy. Moreover, the pressures and incentives of their positions provide powerful motivations to concentrate on addressing immediate, short-run problems. Their orientation is toward getting things done on time and within budget. It should not be surprising that few CEO's interests or skills qualify them as expert strategists.

As research by Professor Mace and others has clearly shown, the board of directors does not usually attempt to second-guess operating management, even on strategic issues; it is understood that those responsible for implementing it should formulate strategy. Moreover, the operating relationship between the board and the CEO usually

Source: Milton Lauenstein, "The Strategy Audit," *The Journal of Business Strategy* **4**, no. 3 (1984), pp. 87–91.

makes it difficult for directors to have a meaningful input into strategic decisions. The CEO often avoids discussions of overall strategy, the result of which could easily be to restrict his freedom of action. Proposals for capital investments, acquisitions, divestitures, and other long-range matters typically are made on their own merits, with only perfunctory consideration of their strategic implications. Thus the judgment of outside directors is seldom used effectively in the very areas in which it could be of greatest value to the firm.

Strategic errors such as those cited above can be enormously costly and can even threaten the survival of the enterprise. Responsible directors have a duty to participate in decisions of such great consequence. CEOs should welcome such participation, which can be of real help to them.

One potentially useful approach to this problem is an annual audit of corporate strategy. Such a strategy audit should not take the form of a backward-looking critique of what has been done. Rather, it should be designed to take full advantage of the experience, knowledge, and judgment of the directors in determining the best strategy for guiding the corporation in the future.

Managers and directors alike should recognize that there are many factors that can contribute to faulty strategy. The very word "strategy" has been so over-used and misused that few people have any clear idea of what it is and what it should do for an enterprise. Almost any approach to business has been called "strategic." Writers and consultants in large numbers recommend a great variety of simplistic schemes under the rubric of strategy. It is small wonder that so many so-called strategies do more harm than good. The examples mentioned at the outset of this article are typical of how misguided strategies can lead to problems.

A number of factors tend to pull executives away from adopting sound strategies. Some of these factors are grounded in the business situation itself. Others are simplistic and counterproductive schemes promoted by so-called experts. An important function of the strategy audit is to assist management and the board to recognize and avoid these pitfalls and dangerous nostrums.

WHAT THE PITFALLS ARE

There are a number of pitfalls to which companies fall prey, including:

- *Habit.* Older companies in mature industries often continue to invest in fixed assets for years after the business has ceased to offer adequate returns. For example, until it bought Marathon Oil in 1981, U.S. Steel was investing over $1 billion per year in operations which over the previous two decades had returned only about 6 percent on equity.

- *Follow-the-leader.*   There is a natural tendency to emulate success. In many fields, most of the competitors pattern their operations after the industry leader. The behavior of Ford and Chrysler in aping GM is an example. Trying to compete head-to-head with stronger rivals is strategic folly.
- *Incremental thinking.*   In the short run, incremental volume appears to be very profitable. Companies often yield to the temptation to reach outside their areas of competence to get added sales, only to incur unexpected costs which more than offset any additional margin. Sears Roebuck had similar problems when it strayed from offering basic value and tried to sell items such as mink coats and oil paintings.
- *"Graduating."*   Successful smaller companies sometimes fail to realize that the basis of their performance is specialization in specific market niches. When they extend their operations to compete in the industry's mainstream, they often lose their advantage and get into trouble. This has happened repeatedly in the airline industry, when successful regional feeder airlines have "graduated" to compete with major trunk lines. A most recent example is Frontier Air Lines, which was a profitable feeder line based in Denver. Now that it is competing with United and other carriers on the routes to the coast, Frontier is losing money.
- *"Paper entrepreneurialism."*   This phenomenon as described by Harvard Professor Robert Reich, involves manipulating the *symbols* of wealth as contrasted with real industrial activity. For example, adding to per-share earnings by using high P/E stock to acquire other companies is a seductive strategic alternative. However, many who have pursued it have found it led to serious problems in the longer term.

THE DANGEROUS CURE-ALLS

Dangerous cure-alls to guard against include the following:

- *Diversification.*   Probably the most common single theme of corporate strategists is diversification. The usual stated objective is to avoid the cyclicity and vulnerability of single-industry companies. Perhaps a more important motivation is a desire for growth or the excitement of acquisition. However, diversification involves serious risks. Entering a new field is uncertain at best and always complicates the task of management. It is not at all clear that diversification contributes to reducing risk or improving performance. What is quite clear is that many companies have gotten into serious trouble by entering new fields in which they had no experience or management competence.
- *Market share.*   The notion that market share is the key to profitability has gained wide currency in recent years. As a result, companies

have indulged in various forms of destructive price-cutting and premature investment in capacity, often with disastrous results. Despite numerous articles pointing out how many smaller companies are outperforming industry leaders, many firms cling to the notion that market share is the key to success.

- *Standard success patterns.* Masses of statistical data on a wide variety of businesses have been analyzed to find correlations between financial performance and various business characteristics. The implication is that by moving toward generally successful patterns, a business may be able to improve its results. This thinking suffers from basic flaws. What succeeds in most industries may be counterproductive in a specific case. Moreover, correlations do not differentiate between cause and effect. The fact that profitable companies may give much to charity does not justify the conclusion that philanthropy generates earnings.

- *Portfolio management.* Another popular approach to strategy is to attempt to structure a portfolio of businesses with balanced cash flows. A "cash cow" may acquire a dynamic growth company needing continuing cash infusions or vice versa. What is unclear is how this represents a significant value. Many successful companies operate for years with continuing net cash inflows or outflows. Any advantage in balancing cash flows may be more than offset by the difficulty of managing businesses that are so dissimilar. Exxon's failure with high technology companies is a typical result of a strategy of portfolio management.

These simplistic approaches are not inappropriate in all cases. The point is that each involves costs and risks and may prove to be counterproductive in a specific situation. No approach is a cure-all. Each company needs a strategy formulated carefully for its particular circumstances.

The fact that a company goes through an annual five-year planning exercise is no assurance that it has an effective strategy. Companies such as International Harvester and A.M. International were bragging in their annual reports about their strategic planning systems shortly before they met disaster. Had the directors conducted a careful audit of the strategies these procedures produced, they might have been able to avert some of the problems.

WHAT TO LOOK FOR IN A STRATEGY

Basically, a strategy should represent a reasonable basis for expecting to achieve attractive financial results. This normally requires gaining a competitive edge. Thus a sound business strategy should provide a reasonable expectation of developing and maintaining competitive advantages.

When several firms are addressing the same business segment, it is not possible for more than one of them to have a reasonable basis for expecting to excel. In such a situation, the "strategies" being followed by most of them are unsound. Continuing to compete against the company best equipped to serve a specific market segment yields poor results.

Fortunately, markets are diverse. Different customers have different needs. The capabilities that are appropriate for serving one group of customers are inappropriate for serving another. Brooks Brothers and a second-hand clothing store cannot compete effectively with each other—their markets are too different. The highly automated plant of the "low-cost producer" is rarely suitable for making short-run specials. The local convenience store serves a different need from that of the nearby supermarket and can thrive despite charging higher prices for the same products.

A sound business strategy must:

- Define the specific business segments to be served. This definition can be in terms of geography, kinds of products and services to be offered, types of customers, distribution channels, pricing policies, or any other factor that affects the business.
- Identify the particular capabilities that are required to serve the defined business segments most effectively. They could be manufacturing cost, advertising, ready availability, user friendliness, after-sales service, or any of a myriad of others. In a typical situation, one or two such factors are critical.
- Outline a realistic program for developing and maintaining superiority in the key capabilities for serving the selected market segments.

Because of the diversity of customers and their needs, finding a winning strategy is not so difficult, even in an industry dominated by one or more giants. It is nearly always possible to identify groups of customers that could better be served by a different approach.

For example, Crown Cork & Seal Co. was able to outperform its larger competitors in the can industry for decades by concentrating on hard-to-contain products and by offering superior customer service. Heileman has made outstanding progress in the beer industry by using local brands to cater to local tastes in competition with larger brewers with national brands. Digital Equipment, Apple, and Wang have been enormously successful in the computer industry by concentrating their capabilities in specific market segments rather than trying to compete with IBM in mainframes.

The preceding paragraphs deal primarily with what to look for in a strategy of an individual business unit. In auditing overall corporate strategy, directors must also be sensitive to broader corporate issues. These include objectives, finance, scope of operations, and organization.

Corporate objectives extend far beyond economics. Personal values of top management, obligations to employees, and responsibilities to community, government, and society as a whole all influence corporate behavior. Even in the economic area, objectives may vary with respect to risk tolerance and the relative importance of sales growth, absolute earnings, earnings per share, return on capital, and other performance measures.

Financial strategy can have a telling effect on corporate success. The trade-off between reducing financing costs through leveraging and maintaining financial flexibility and the ability to withstand adversity can be crucial. Other issues, such as cash management, control of current assets, capital allocation, and dividend policy often have a powerful influence on corporate performance.

The operations of most corporations extend beyond providing a single product or service to a homogeneous market. Extending the scope of operations represents opportunity not only for growth, but more importantly for developing competitive advantages through combining resources. On the other hand, diversification incurs serious risks and management costs which have plagued many firms. Finding an appropriate balance in determining the scope of operations of any corporation is a key strategic issue.

Organization is closely related to the scope of operations. When several business units are based on the same technology, for example, it may be possible to gain a significant technical advantage over competitors by combining R&D efforts in a single technical center. On the other hand, some business units are likely to succeed only if they have more flexibility and autonomy. Centralizing service functions, such as control, personnel, and engineering can have a positive or negative effect on the competitive positions of individual units, depending on the nature of the businesses and how they are organized.

For a strategy to be fully effective, it must integrate all of the activities of the firm to build the competitive position it has chosen for itself. The manufacturing, marketing, and development functions must be consistent with each other and with the overall objective. So must financial policy, scope of operations, and organization. Top management must place high priority on its long-term program for further development of the key capabilities required to serve the market segments it has targeted for leadership.

Few corporations succeed in developing strategies that are sound, internally consistent, and understood by those responsible for implementing them. A regular systematic strategy audit can reveal inconsistencies and weaknesses and thus provide a stimulus for corrective action. The alternative of waiting until the results are apparent can be extremely painful or even fatal.

AUDITING THE STRATEGY

Auditing corporate strategy requires nothing more than subjecting it to a number of tests of its validity, consistency, and probable effectiveness. A list of questions, such as that presented below, is useful to make the exercise more efficient and thorough.

The board of directors is responsible for corporate performance and for seeing to it that the firm has an effective strategy. The board or one of its committees can either perform the audit itself or review it in much the same fashion as it reviews the annual financial audit. It can assign responsibility for performing the audit to operating management or arrange for a joint effort. While outside counsel can often be helpful, the benefits of participation in this type of exercise are so great that having it performed by outsiders alone may be shortsighted.

The following list of questions is illustrative of the areas a strategy audit might encompass. Not all of these questions will apply to every situation. In some cases, questions not included here may be important. Each company should satisfy itself that the questions relevant to its particular situation have been answered.

Is the company adequately informed about its markets? What further information would be worth the cost of getting? How should it be obtained?

How well informed is the company about its competitors? How well is it able to forecast what competitors will do under various circumstances? Is there a sound basis for such competitive appraisals? Is the company underestimating or overestimating its competitors?

Has management adequately explored various ways of segmenting its market? To what extent is it addressing market segments in which the company's strengths provide meaningful advantages?

Are the products and services the company proposes to sell ones that it can provide more effectively than competitors? What is the basis for such a belief?

Do the various activities proposed in the strategy provide synergistic advantages? Are they compatible?

Does the proposed strategy adequately address questions of corporate objectives, financial policy, scope of operations, organization, and integration?

What specific resources (personnel, skills, information, facilities, technology, finances, relationships) will be needed to execute the strategy? Does the company already possess these resources? Has management established programs for building these resources and overall competence which will provide telling competitive advantages over the long run?

To what extent does the strategy define a unique and appropriate economic role for the company? How different is it from the competitors' strategy?

Has the issue of growth rate been raised? Are there good reasons to believe that investment in growth will pay off? Does the company's track record support such a conclusion?

Does the proposed dividend policy reflect the company's growth policy, based on a demonstrated ability or inability to reinvest cash flow advantageously? Or is it just a "safe" compromise, conforming to what others usually do?

Is management capable of implementing the strategy effectively? What leads to this conclusion?

How and to what extent is the strategy to be communicated to the organization? Is it to be distributed in written form? If competitors are aware of the company's strategy, will that help or hurt?

What provision is to be made for employing the strategy as a guide to operating decisions? To what extent is it to be used by the board? How?

How is it to be kept up-to-date? Are there to be regular reviews? How often and by whom?

Has a set of long-range projections of operations following the strategy been prepared? Have the possible results of following alternative strategies been prepared?

Does the strategy focus on the few really important key issues? Is it too detailed? Does it address genuine business questions (as opposed to "motherhood" statements)?

In its strategic thinking, has management avoided the lure of simplistic approaches such as:

- Growth for growth's sake?
- Diversification for diversification's sake?
- Aping the industry leader?
- Broadening the scope in order to secure "incremental" earnings?
- Assuming it can execute better than competitors without objective evidence that such is the case?

Are there other issues, trends, or potential events that should have been taken into account?

CONCLUSION

Strategic errors by American corporations are common. Misallocation of resources is widespread. Such mistakes can be enormously costly to a company and are a serious drain on the overall economy.

Operating management is usually not in a good position to establish corporate strategy alone. Lack of objectivity, pressures for current performance, and inexperience in strategic planning tend to make executives vulnerable to simplistic approaches that are not effective substitutes for a sound strategy.

A board of directors representing broad business experience can make a valuable contribution to a corporation by conducting a regular audit of corporate strategy. By addressing itself systematically to basic questions about the firm's strategic approach, it can uncover potentially dangerous shortcomings and can initiate action for improvement.

Failure to accept responsibility for seeing to it that the firm is following a sound strategy is a serious breach of a director's responsibility. As directors increase their contributions to the quality of corporate strategy, the performance of individual companies and of the economy as a whole can be expected to improve.

Reading 6

Principles of Strategic Planning Applied to International Corporations

Ellen C. Fingerhut and Daryl G. Hatano

I. INTRODUCTION

> *From the provinces of Cathay itself, as well as from the other provinces of the empire, whatever there is of value is carried thither, to supply the demands of those multitudes who are induced to establish residence in the vicinity of the court. The quantity of merchandise sold there exceeds also the traffic of any other place; for no fewer than a thousand carriages and pack horses, loaded with raw silk, make their daily entry; and gold tissues and silks of various kinds are manufactured to an immense extent.*

The Travels of Marco Polo, *1298 AD[1]*

For centuries before Marco Polo's journey, for the centuries spanning his time and ours, and surely for centuries to come, business searches beyond its national boundaries for new opportunities. Unlike its historic counterparts, business today gets advice from professional planners who apply theoretical strategic planning models. Much of the literature on these models, however, ignores the unique problems of firms engaging in international business.

We will examine strategic planning models in an international arena by analyzing the conceptual difficulties the models encounter when applied to international firms and by noting issues multinational corporations (MNCs) need to include in their plans. A common method for performing strategic planning is to first examine the firm's external situation for opportunities and threats, second perform an internal analysis to determine the firm's strengths and weaknesses, and finally

Source: Ellen C. Fingerhut and Daryl G. Hatano, "Principles of Strategic Planning Applied to International Corporations," *Managerial Planning* 32, no. 2 (September/October 1983), pp. 4–10, 12–14.

develop strategies to capitalize on the strengths, pursue the opportunities, and thwart the threats.[2] We will follow this approach of external analysis, internal analysis, and strategy as we explore the problems of strategic planning in the global marketplace.

II. EXTERNAL ANALYSIS

The goal of the external analysis is to find a firm's opportunities and threats in its environment. We have organized the external analysis in three levels: the competitors, the market/industry, and the macro-environment, presented in order of increased remoteness to the firm.

The Competitors

Several aspects of a strategic planner's competitive analysis are unique to an international firm. First is the problem of competing with foreign firms in general, and second are the distinct problems of competing with entities sponsored or subsidized by the foreign governments. The impacts for these two novelties of the international firm will be discussed in turn.

In analyzing foreign competitors, an important consideration is the size of their home market. Firms usually produce first locally and expand overseas later because of the various competitive advantages they have in their home market, including familiarity with the distribution system, laws, local tastes, and markets; consumer loyalty to home produced products; a closer nexus with headquarters; and economic cost advantages. However, firms with larger home markets acquire cumulative volume faster and thus slide down the experience curve quicker than firms with smaller home markets. IBM's larger home market, combined with an earlier entry, explains why the French computer industry, which enjoyed neither advantage, needed joint ventures with American firms to remain competitive. It has been suggested that a firm can counter foreign competitors by penetrating their home markets before they enter the U.S. market, thus draining the foreign firms' cash flow and slowing their experience curve advance before they have gained the resources to penetrate the American market. For instance, IBM's 25% share of the Japanese mainframe computer market has drained Fujitsu and Hitachi in this way, denying them the resources to invade IBM's U.S. market.[3]

A survey of competitors and possible competitors must include an examination of the newly developed or recently industrialized countries of Brazil, Mexico, Taiwan, Hong Kong, Singapore, and South Korea. Peter Drucker defines this group of countries as able to "do any one thing it decides to do—but it cannot yet do many things at the same time."[4] They have enough capital resources to finance some of their own expansion and large semi-skilled labor forces. Drucker warns that from among these countries an economic power may arise much as Japan has risen in the past few decades.[5] These countries will increasingly threaten the developed world in traditional industries such as steel, fibers, and autos. As the emerging or industrializing nations of Latin América and Africa also become more active competitors, the choice of governments and firms in the developed world will be to resist, by adopting or seeking protectionist policies, or adjust to the evolving new order. (It is interesting to note in this context that the French planning agency in 1978 concluded that "France has more to gain by being actively engaged, as importer and exporter, in Third World industrialization than by trying to protect itself against it.")[6] The function of industrial policies and their impact on American firms will now be the focus of our attention.

A major issue for the MNC in its competitor analysis is the importance of foreign government industrial policies. Industrial policy is defined as actions taken by a government to encourage and develop the competitiveness of the domestic economy, and includes setting targets for specific industries or companies for growth, policies to control foreign presence, and macroeconomic policies. The first category will be discussed in this section, and the remaining two under the environment section below.

Lawrence Franko more narrowly defines European industrial policy as a set of "public policy measures consciously aimed at promoting or maintaining particular kinds of industries by upgrading their efficiency or altering their ownership structure."[7] In implementing their industrial policies, governments can set the goals or targets for local firms, provide R&D funds and other subsidies, erect protectionist barriers to entry and, in many other ways, dictate these firms' global competitive position.[8] The choice of tools varies significantly worldwide and is often much more extensive than in the U.S. They include establishing national champions, supporting prestige industries, taking over companies, and subsidizing local firms.

National champion strategy, writes Erhard Friedberg, aims to "develop and if necessary create a few important companies able to hold their own on world markets."[9] In the 1970s, the French government promoted its champions in the international arena, offering generous subsidies, low interest loans and technical assistance. These policies had varied results. The computer services industry, today the world's second largest, benefited greatly from these programs. However, France's mainframe computer company has continued to perform dismally despite over 20 years of government assistance and many foreign firms have gained a strong foothold in the French mainframe market.

In Japan, the contact and coordination between business and government has been so close and effective that "some experts doubt whether a clear distinction can be made between government and business."[10] Some have referred to this relationship as "Japan, Inc.," referring to the Japanese Government, particularly MITI (Ministry for International Trade and Industry) as corporate headquarters, and each enterprise as a branch or division of the corporation.[11] MITI's policies in establishing economic and industrial development priorities or targets, bear a close resemblance to French indicative planning. However, rather than targeting one "national champion," Japan channels resources into several champions within a given industry. In fact, "there has been a national consensus since the Meiji Restoration as to which industries are important to Japan."[12] Intervention to achieve desired targets takes many forms. "The government acts as catalyst and gadfly, guide and arbitrator, banker and patron, to assure the desired pattern of industrial development."[13]

Programs aimed at developing national champions to aggressively compete worldwide should be distinguished from bailout programs such as Britain's steel industry and America's Chrysler. A bailout's major purpose is to maintain employment in labor intensive and politically powerful industries. Both national champions and bailouts present higher exit barriers for a firm's competitors, but must be analyzed differently since they clearly have distinct and opposite goals.

Governments promote some industries, such as national airlines, solely for national prestige. If sustained by government subsidies, in spite of considerable financial losses, exit barriers are increased, making it difficult for a new entrant (or existing comperitors) to sustain comparable losses.

A common industrial policy tool is to nationalize, wholly or partially, a firm or industry. Government owned competitors present a new set of threats and opportunities for the MNC. For example, the recent French nationalization plans call for restructuring and vertical integration of several industries, eliminating weaknesses in the flow from raw material to finished product.[14] This kind of policy may cut off vital supply sources for foreign competitors, raising entry barriers. When coupled with massive R&D support and an aggressive government procurement policy, these competitors may well threaten existing market-share relationships, especially as non-economic objectives by government become more important.

On the other hand, considerable destabilization and/or reorganization of an industry may well provide new opportunities for a foreign competitor able to take advantage of uncertain times either by becoming a new entrant or by expanding its market share of an existing business. Such opportunities would be especially attractive in sectors where experience curves are steep—and timing crucial.

Often industrial policy, particularly in Europe and Japan, includes extensive government subsidies for R&D, promotion of exports, or restructuring of targeted industries or firms. In the semiconductor industry, for example, the Japanese government spends over $600 million a year, the French $140 million, the West German $150, and the American only $55.[15] By reducing their short-term costs of capital and labor, foreign firms may gain competitive advantages over their U.S. counterparts. (An analysis of U.S. industrial policy is included under "Internal Analysis" below.)

Governments can influence the competitive nature of their domestic industries in a number of other ways. They can provide ready, and sometimes mandatory, markets for certain products, and implement procurement policies to favor domestic industries, thus creating an entry barrier to foreign firms. Governments can also offer tax benefits and other incentives to develop certain sectors in the economy, provide loan guarantees and risk insurance, and finally, promote mergers or cooperation among enterprises to achieve economies of scale. To the extent that these measures offer the national firms a competitive advantage in economies of scale, access to raw materials or markets, decreased risk, or learning curve advantages, they become more threatening competitors.

The Market/Industry

A second stage in the external analysis is to examine the firm's market or industry. This section will first look at the customer, second, list traditional economic cost factors given in classical international trade theory, and finally, examine market segmentation and product life cycle problems.

Foreign governments exercise considerable influence over a firm's potential customers, either directly through procurement policies, or indirectly, through its influence over national firms. To the extent that a company is cut off from foreign governments (and firms within their sphere) their set of potential customers is limited. On the other hand, a U.S. firm can gain access to a ready and willing set of customers through a coalition with a "national champion." The merger of Honeywell-Bull with the French champion, CII (Compagnie Internationale d'Informatique) guaranteed to Honeywell customers willing to buy their products and eliminated in major part the costs and risks of bidding for new contracts. The American firm also enjoyed extensive subsidies from the French government to buoy up the new entity.

Michael Porter's recent book, *Competitive Strategy*, nicely summarizes the traditional economic cost factors used to explain international trade. Among the factors favoring global operations are: a country's comparative advantage in labor, raw material, or other resource costs; production, marketing, logistical, purchasing, and R&D economies of scale achieved by serving a global market; sliding down the experience curve at a quicker rate as a result of greater cumulative volume; and an enhanced reputation or image from an overseas presence. Among the factors impeding global operations are: high transportation and storage costs; difficulties in serving diverse needs in a variety of local markets; distribution problems where established channels favor local sales forces; and higher lag times for repairs, servicing, or deliveries—especially in short fashion cycles, rapidly changing technology, or costly "down time" situations.[16] In some markets, foreign firms can turn their nationality to their advantage. Levi Strauss markets its jeans in Japan with Caucasian models and stresses the prestigious "Made in USA" label. Sumitomo Bank of California and Bank of Tokyo owned California First Bank stress the Japanese trait of politeness in their American markets.

Several market segmentation issues in the international context are exaggerated cases of issues facing firms with operations only in the U.S. First is the question of geographic segmentation. It is common for MNCs to have country specific segments because of the legal differences between countries. While firms operating in the U.S. must consider different state laws, the problem is more complex for MNCs facing a greater variety of legal jurisdictions and the need to maintain relationships with numerous host governments. (The importance of these differences will be discussed in "The Environment" section below.)

While country-specific segments represent the most atomistic unit of analysis, the large number of countries makes it desirable to aggregate nations into larger groups. Geographic proximity is the most common method of grouping because (1) distant regions are more likely to be discrete markets due to the increased transportation costs, and (2) the desire to keep division managers in closer contact with their subordinates leads many organizations to divide into divisions by continents. While geographic proximity is a popular and useful market segmentation method, MNCs have other methods of grouping their country-specific segments. Grouping countries by their level of economic development is a particularly useful segmentation scheme since income levels are a key factor in consumer demand for a product. This also allows firms to overlap product life cycles by entering developing areas after the product has reached maturity in developed areas. Due to experience effects on costs, the product's price is lower when it is later introduced to less affluent countries.

Cultural or language based segments may be a more rational segmentation scheme for other firms, such as a publishing company. Even a cross-cultural industry like computers may find a language-segment scheme useful as word-processing equipment expansions shift the customer base from multi-linguistic scientists to secretaries typing in their native language. In such a segmentation scheme, Spain should be grouped with Latin American countries in a "Spanish" market segment rather than in a "European" segment. Because of the problems peculiar to negotiating with the communist states, they too may be grouped into a separate market segment. Other examples of segmentation schemes might be a birth control company grouping countries by dominant religions, a transportation company grouping by population densities, or an air conditioning grouping by climates.[17]

The Environment

Since forces outside the industry can have significant effects on the players inside the industry, strategic planners must pay attention not only to the firm's competitors and market, but also to the environment in which all operate. Economic, social, political, and technical changes are often mentioned as key environmental elements.[18] Planners in international firms must be especially diligent in assessing the environment because it varies widely between countries, and it poses threats and opportunities of the largest magnitudes. The vicissitudes of foreign affairs is an obvious environmental risk facing MNCs as RCA found when Carter's cancellation of U.S. participation in the 1980 Olympics cost the NBC network $36 million in lost television contracts. Two other environmental problems will be discussed below: macroeconomic issues and host government interventions.

The growth of an integrated world economy cannot be ignored in an environment analysis. Since the early 1970s when the dollar was allowed to float, world currencies have fluctuated greatly, inflation and recessions have become increasingly linked to the health of the international economy, and the capital market has moved towards a frictionless plane which ignores national boundaries.[19] Planners have the aid of computer based macroeconomic models, but must augment the output with gut feelings before drawing conclusions.

The management of foreign exchange risk poses a great challenge to financial planners and can be viewed from an accounting or economic perspective. An accounting approach is concerned with the problems of translating the results of foreign operations from local to home currencies for consolidation in the parent's balance sheets and income statements. Under *FASB 56,* translation exposure is the difference between exposed assets and liabilities, calculated by using the current exchange rate in the country in which a firm primarily generates and expends cash. Accounting exposure also includes transaction exposure, for example, trade and note payables and receivables which require remittance in a foreign currency. The economist's approach examines the effect of currency devaluation or revaluation on the present value of a firm's future cash flows.

Firms can manage foreign exchange exposure in a variety of ways. The most popular techniques include forward contracts, borrowing at the spot rate and investing, and leading and lagging payments. A firm can also invoice sales in domestic currency, try to create offsetting transactions, pair transactions with a different currency, and ultimately, either do nothing to hedge against risk, or choose not to trade. Forecasting exchange rates can be done by using a monetary approach, purchasing power parity, or projecting balance of payments. However, each approach yields varying forecasts and many firms choose to construct leading economic indicators based on historical data to manage their international funds flow, rather than rely on forecasting models.

A major force shaping the economy is the population's demographic transitions. Here predictions are easier to make since the mothers of the next generation are already alive today. Computer models have projected the world's population to reach 10 billion by the year 2000.[20] The developed world is projected to grow at a 0.6% annual rate and the less developed regions at a 2.1% annual rate. Mexico's annual growth rate of 3.1% means it will double in size in the next 25 years. These figures point not only to growing markets, but also to new labor source possibilities as Part III will discuss. The social pressures arising from this population explosion provide much of the impetus for wealth redistribution underlying government actions discussed immediately below.

Threats and opportunities can arise from government changes in pollution standards, safety regulations, products liability law, tax law, or numerous other government activities. An exhaustive treatment of host government relations is beyond the scope of this paper, but three areas especially important for international strategic planning will be discussed. These are protectionism, nationalizations, and technology transfers.

Economic protectionism includes not only explicit government actions such as tariffs or import quotas, but also ostensibly neutral actions having a protectionist effect. Safety and pollution regulations, for example, would have protectionist effects if foreign firms were geared to producing for the lower standards of their home markets.[21] Since 1948, the General Agreement on Tariffs and Trade (GATT) provided a forum to negotiate reductions in protectionism. GATT's future has become uncertain, and it has been argued that without a "hegemonic power," a position the U.S. held after WWII, there is no country with the dominance to force others to follow a trade liberalization policy. This theory contends that as the U.S. loses its hegemonic position and power is shared by the U.S., Japan, and Europe, efforts like GATT will become increasingly impotent, and protectionism will rise.[22]

Host governments often work to increase ownership and control over companies doing business in their country. The state can expropriate the firm's assets or nationalize the company. If the firm's assets are confiscated without adequate compensation, obviously the firm suffers heavy financial losses. Firms can mitigate this risk by borrowing from local banks to fund local operations; insuring with the Overseas Private Investment Corporation, a U.S. government agency; and incorporating various parts of the organization in safer countries. Some countries, such as Mexico and the Philippines, are requiring local participation when foreigners do business in their countries, and are mandating gradual equity transfers to assure local majority control in a few decades. Nationalizations can also hurt a company dependent on the foreign subsidiary as a source of supplies, such as Gulf Oil's change from a crude-rich to a crude-short company when its Kuwait oil fields were taken over by the Kuwaiti government. However American public opinion incorrectly viewed the French nationalizations as an invasion of private sector rights and an expropriation of private property. Shareholders have been adequately compensated and some firms have benefited from the new government policies. In the plans to nationalize CII-HB, Honeywell was able to reduce its interests in a troubled partnership and received a $28 million bonus for its shares.

Gaining technology from multinationals is an important objective of many host governments. Developing countries often require technology transfers to local businesses as a condition for a MNC's entry.[23] However even in the developed countries, technology transfer considerations influence governmental policy, as in the French government's encouragement of the CII-Honeywell-Bull joint venture. Japan's MITI has used its persuasive authority to allocate technology imports among Japanese corporations, ensuring that they did not compete and bid up the technology's price to Japan.[24]

III. INTERNAL ANALYSIS

After performing an external analysis, strategic planners proceed to an internal analysis of the firm's capabilities. This corporate introspection seeks to identify "distinctive competences,"[25] or the company's strengths and weaknesses relative to competitors. Much of the analysis focuses on the firm's financial health, management expertise, facilities, brand acceptance, or other resources varying in importance depending on the firm's unique situation. Three problems of the internal analysis of international firms are the application of product portfolio matrices, the issue surrounding a firm's optimal size, and the U.S. government's response to foreign industrial policies.

Portfolio Planning

There has been an increase in the use of portfolio planning as a strategic planning technique, and today some 45% of the *Fortune* 500 industrials use portfolio planning to some extent.[26] In both the BCG matrix and the GE-Business Attractiveness matrix the key step is defining the strategic business unit (SBU) to be analyzed. While firms operating solely in the U.S. have the problems of deciding if there are several regional markets or a single national market, this problem is exacerbated when the choice is between separate national markets, regional markets, or a single global market.

In determining SBUs, two key factors are: (1) the separation of markets which "are essentially different in terms of competitors, strategies, growth rates and share achieved,"[27] and (2) the company's organizational constraints from past organizational structure decisions.[28] Many of the issues discussed in "The Market/Industry" section, especially in terms of segmentation, can be applied to the first factor. Cultural preferences, legal requirements, and economic development stages are examples of differences that may require a firm's SBU to be smaller than the global market. Whether the SBUs will be defined down to an individual country level will be determined by a balancing of the need to recognize these differences with the desire to keep the SBUs down to a number that retains the matrix's value of visual clarity. Most companies with experience in portfolio planning have averaged 30 SBUs.[29] A firm's organizational structure influences the definition of SBUs since the firm allocates resources along organizational lines. SBUs often aggregate existing operating units, but rarely cut across organizational lines, so an organization with several geographic divisions may aggregate Oceania, Asia, and Africa into a single SBU, but is unlikely to put Japan with an European SBU even though Japan may have more in common with European markets. Since SBUs are for strategic planning purposes, often organizational changes are made to match structure with the SBUs. Drastic changes, however, may take several planning cycles before the ideal SBU matches the firm's structure.

An additional factor to consider in defining an SBU for the BCG Product Portfolio matrix is to ensure that the relative market share is related to the cost relationships that underlie the BCG cash flow assumptions. Consequently, the SBU definition must be tied to "the shared experience or economies of scale arising from shared production or marketing activities."[30] To the extent a separate learning curve can be drawn relating a firm's cumulative knowledge of foreign cultures or laws, it can be argued that a firm's foreign operations should be separate SBUs. This is especially true if the learning curve for learning about the foreign environment is steeper than the other experience curves of the product. Thus a MNC expanding into China may have one SBU for all its products in China, and separate SBUs for each of its products in the rest of the world.

Size Considerations

Firms have long grappled with the problem of finding an ideal size. Part of the answer depends on the strategy choices, an issue discussed below. Organizational behavior issues will be reserved for the "Organizational Design" section. This section will focus on production sharing, learning curves, and visibility considerations.

Peter Drucker has noted the developing world's problem of surplus labor and the developed countries' shortage of people willing to do traditional work, especially in traditional manufacturing. He has concluded that the result will be increased "production sharing," where a single product may be designed, produced, and assembled in different countries.[31] A portent of what is in store is consumer electronics, designed in Japan with semiconductor chips from Silicon Valley and steel housing from Singapore, assembled in Indonesia, labeled "Made in Japan" in a Yokohama free port, and sold worldwide by the Japanese. General Motor's "world car" is a second example of production sharing. Clearly in industries where production sharing applies, firms with global operations will have a distinctive advantage over smaller rivals.

As was mentioned in "The Market/Industry" section above, a MNC can slide down the experience curve faster because it can attain greater cumulative volumes than its domestic rivals. What is often ignored in experience curve discussions is that the experience effect is not automatic, but rather management must diligently work to lower costs. Given that the firm has a certain market share, a production question is whether to produce the product with several smaller factories or a single larger plant. This question is usually addressed in economies of scale terms, but experience curve considerations can also come into play. Defenders of a single plant contend that there is a greater transfer of learning when workers are located at a single location. Others, however, have noted a healthy rivalry developing between plants, and suggest that this competitive drive leads to steeper learning curves at both plants. If creativity is the key variable, industries which rely on innovation, such as computer design, may warrant separate plants. The point is size in terms of number of plants is a factor in making the experience curve theory a reality.

Larger firms generally have greater visibility than smaller firms. Drucker argues that large firms are too conspicuous politically, and hence will have political problems adjusting quickly to market changes. As an example he cites Ford's Fiesta model, a production-sharing product faced with import restrictions by politically powerful American labor interests. In contrast, Drucker notes Melville's success with the production-sharing manufacture of shoes. Despite being the largest shoe retailer, Melville markets under a number of brands, such as Thom-McAn, and hence does not attract the attention of political impediments.[32] The large firm's visibility can also hurt when actions in one part of the globe provoke a boycott of all the firm's products. The well publicized consumer boycott of Nestlé for its sale of infant formula in the Third World is an obvious example.

U.S. Government Policies

Legal constraints are normally not part of an internal analysis since all competitors are similarly constrained and none receive a distinctive competence. In the international arena, however, the variety of laws from one nation to the next means that companies are not similarly affected. There is an endless list of corporation, tax, labor, and other laws that translate to strategic strengths or weaknesses for American firms. Enumeration of them is beyond the scope of this paper; however, the Foreign Corrupt Practices Act which outlaws bribery by American companies doing business overseas is especially notable. The Act, passed in 1977 after the disclosure of Lockheed bribes to Japanese public officials brought an outcry to Congress for reform, is often cited as putting American business at a disadvantage in competing in areas where the indigenous culture accepts bribery as the norm. Also of note are the antitrust statutes that are often cited as impediments to efficient production, hampering American competitiveness against less burdened foreign firms, especially the Japanese.[33] The Sherman Act applies not only to business done in the U.S., but also activities in foreign countries affecting U.S. markets.[34] In the "Industrial Policy" section, we explained the importance of assessing foreign government industrial policies, including subsidizing "national champions," protecting local firms through a variety of tariff and non-tariff barriers, or blocking entry of foreign firms into the local market. Here we analyze the effects of U.S. industrial policy on American firms; to the extent that the U.S. government chooses, or chooses not, to enact a similar set of policies has a direct bearing on the international competitiveness of U.S. firms.

Robert B. Reich's recent article in the *Harvard Business Review* argues that the U.S. relies mostly on macroeconomic policies concerning short-term allocative efficiency and aggregate supply and demand. Through its military procurement and R&D programs, currently, the federal government funds a third of all U.S. industrial R&D and employs (directly or indirectly) 35% of the nation's scientists and engineers.[35]

The NASA space program virtually transformed the computer, semiconductor and aerospace industries by granting subsidies of over $20 billion and assuming many of the long-term R&D risks. Jonathan Kaufman's extensive study of NASA's experience concludes NASA and the military allowed computer and semiconductor makers to improve quality, drive down costs and gain valuable technical know-how—all the time guaranteeing them increasing sales.[36] (Ironically, the French national champion strategy was modeled on the perception that American firms, particularly IBM, were successful due to American government support.)[37]

IV. ALTERNATIVE STRATEGIES

After performing the external analysis for opportunities and threats and carefully considering the firm's strengths and weaknesses, the strategic planner is ready to develop the firm's alternative strategies to utilize its distinctive competences in pursuing opportunities and avoiding threats. The best alternative is then selected as the firm's strategic plan. In this final stage as well, there are areas where MNCs face problems their domestic rivals do not. This part has three sections: generic strategies, mission statements, and organizational structure.

Generic Strategies

In order to successfully outperform a firm's competitors, Porter outlines three generic strategies. "Overall cost leadership," requires the pursuit of significant cost reductions drawing from the experience curve concept, the construction of efficient scale facilities and tight cost and overhead control. "Differentation," involves creating a product or service that is perceived industry wide as being unique, either in design or brand image, technology, features, customer service, or dealer network. Finally, "focus," builds around serving a specific target very well, either a buyer group, segment of a product line or geographic market. These generic strategies can be integrated into an international strategy by choosing to compete globally or to find defensible niches in one or a few national markets.[38] According to Porter, the firm has available four alternatives. First, a broad line global strategy aims at competing worldwide in the full product line of the industry, using the advantages of a global operation. Implementing this strategy requires substantial resources and a long time horizon. Second, "global focus" involves targeting a particular segment of the industry where the impediments to global competition are low and the firm's position can be easily defended from global competitors. "National Focus," as its name implies, focuses on serving the particular needs of a national market in order to out compete global firms. A fourth alternative, "protected niche," builds a strategy to deal effectively in national markets where a number of governmental restrictions restrict entry by tariffs, quotas, requiring a high proportion of local content, etc. Combinations of these strategies are also possible.

Mission Statement/Objectives

A fundamental strategic question is "what is the firm's mission?"[39] An issue a MNC faces in defining its business is deciding whether the corporation will be a true supra-national corporation or if it will be an American corporation with foreign operations. This issue of allegiance may not arise in the initial stage of expansion, but will become increasingly important as foreign operations form a significant part of the firm's total business.

ITT's history demonstrates the epitome of a corporation with no allegiance to any one country. During World War II, ITT chairman Colonel Behn had extensive ties with Nazi Germany, while ITT's Swiss and Spanish subsidiaries continued to supply the Axis powers, even after the Pearl Harbor attack. ITT biographer Anthony Sampson concluded, "Thus while ITT Focke Wulf planes were bombing Allied ships, and ITT lines were passing information to German submarines, ITT direction finders were saving other ships from torpedos . . . Whether Behn was ultimately more helpful to the Allies may never be known . . . the only power he consistently served was the supra-national power of ITT."[40] The company's bribes to the Nixon administration to settle its Hartford Insurance antitrust suit and its use of the CIA to overthrow President Allende in Chile are more recent, well-documented examples of ITT's self-image as a corporation with no national allegiances.[41]

Less spectacular, and also less pejorative examples of supra-national corporations exist. The top contenders for the CEO position at Coca-Cola were Cuban-born Roberto C. Goizueta and Jan R. Wilson, a South American born Canadian citizen. The president of Coca-Cola's U.S. subsidiary is an Argentinean and Coca-Cola's chief financial officer is an Egyptian native.[42] The fact that this Atlanta based firm does not limit itself to American nationals in its selection of top officers demonstrates the firm's self-image as a supra-national corporation. One consequence of a supra-national mission statement could be promotions on the basis of merit over nationality.

A firm's characterization as a supra-national or an American-overseas in its mission statement has several impacts on the firm's strategic plan. If the firm is a supra-national, ROI/risk expectations alone determine where the firm will invest. A firm with an allegiance to the U.S., however, would feel more of a commitment to the U.S. economy and hence might invest in the U.S. even though the ROI/risk expectations were better overseas. Defense manufacturers might consider the extent to which they want their growth plans shaped by American foreign policy considerations. A final example of the allegiance issue's effect on a firm's plans would be how it would allocate its product among customer countries if supply shortages required rationing. The large petroleum companies are an obvious example of firms facing this type of problem.

Transnational Coalitions

In order to gain access to technologies or existing markets, or reap the cost and size benefits by expanding internationally, a company may find it advantageous to form alliances or coalitions with foreign firms. Its strategic choices will inevitably lead it to favor certain kinds of links with foreign affiliates over others. In this section we will first outline the broad types of coalitions, and second discuss how a firm's external and internal analysis, as well as its strategy, dictate its choice of strategic linkages.

Raymond Vernon delineates four "pure" types of linkages, presented in ascending degree of parental control: licensing or technical assistance agreements; foreign-local joint ventures (between a foreign parent and local interests); foreigners' joint ventures (a number of parents, all foreign to the area in which they operate); and wholly owned subsidiaries or branches.[43]

Insights gained from the external and internal analysis constrain a firm's choice of possible alliances. External factors, such as foreign government control, may limit the degree of ownership possible. In Japan, where local ownership is an important national objective, licensing agreements are preferred to ownership, similarly, joint ventures to wholly owned subsidiaries. A host government may impose other restrictions through tax laws, dividend repatriation, required debt/equity ratio or labor policy.

Internal factors play an even more important role in the choice of linkages. For many firms, experience in a foreign country plays a key role in the evolution of coalitions. A firm's preliminary forays will include technical and marketing agreements or the estabishment of sales offices. As the firm gains a successful base of operations it will set up joint ventures and then evolve to wholly owned subsidiaries. The degree of desired control is also crucial. "Complete ownership of local subsidiaries gives the multinational enterprise greatest flexibility in such areas as organization, inter-company pricing, and dividend policy."[44]

In addition to experience and control considerations, the type of link the firm will seek follows directly from its choice of strategy. Firms such as IBM which concentrate on a narrow product line, will tend to prefer wholly owned subsidiaries. Firms with a broad product line and more of a global focus will favor financing agreements or joint ventures. A firm following a strategy of differentiation with a strong trade name will have a lesser need for tight production and marketing control and would therefore find joint ventures more acceptable.

Management styles differ widely among countries and are often a source of failure for many transnational coalitions. In Europe, managers have traditionally focused on production and technical superiority over marketing, are more centralized and bureaucratic, and emphasize medium and long term economic performance.[45] In contrast, American managers focus on short term performance, organize in profit centers to serve specific markets, and are more committed to formal strategic planning and incentive compensation systems. Advancement in U.S. firms is based on achievement rather than formal status and rank, common in Europe. Labor-management relations also contrast vividly: Germany's co-determination law offers workers substantially more recognition and influence in corporate decision making than is found in the U.S. Labor representatives sit on boards (with the power to hire and fire senior executives) and on works councils which negotiate and monitor labor agreements.[46] The difference between American and Japanese management styles has been extensively commented upon in recent years.[47] Japanese "consensus" decision making can strain relations with American partners who are uncomfortable with the diffusion of authority. Many transnational merger failures result from these differences in management styles and disparate corporate goals.

Organizational Design

The choice of a particular strategy also determines organizational design. "Organization in this sense includes both the structure inside the parent enterprise that is intended to guide and control the multinational network and the structure of the network itself which develops through the choice of foreign links."[48] The design of the network traditionally involves a hierarchical ordering of three subgroups: functions (production, finance, marketing, control, personnel, research and development); products or product groups (grouped according to a key product or market characteristic); and countries or areas.

Which organizational structure an international firm adopts depends on its "maturity" and its strategies. At an early stage, firms set up separate international divisions to handle exports. As products reach a stage of rapid growth in overseas demand, marketing and production functions will be spun off. Vernon comments that, "Typically, however, the production and marketing specialists in the international division find themselves obliged more and more to consult with their counterparts in the varicus home product divisions."[49] At an advanced stage they are replaced by product divisions having worldwide responsibility for production and marketing. The choice of a particular strategy also determines structure. For example, IBM's differentiation strategy organizes each of their worldwide operations on a highly integrated basis and then links the separate production and marketing facilities of the region into fairly tight interdependent patterns.[50]

V. CONCLUSION

Strategic planning has proven to be a valuable tool in the successful firm's repertoire. The models being used, however, have certain conceptual difficulties and applications problems when used by firms engaged in international business. We have tried to fill in this gap by suggesting approaches to the theoretical problems and by pointing out issues international firms must address in their plans. Firms traveling on the path of international business face more risks than their domestic counterparts, but also may reap greater rewards. Properly done, strategic planning offers these firms a map to guide them on their journey through the perilous paths of international business. Much as Marco Polo's trip to China forges new and exciting paths for Western traders to follow, strategic planning offers firms new and exciting approaches to business in the international arena.

NOTES

1. *The Travels of Marco Polo,* 1298 (New York: The Orion Press, 1956), pp. 52–155.
2. Phillip Kotler, *Principles of Marketing* (Englewood Cliffs, New Jersey: Prentice Hall, 1980), pp. 66–85. See also William Gluck, *Business Policy and Strategic Management.* 3rd ed. (New York: McGraw-Hill, 1980) and Kenneth R. Andrews, *The Concept of Corporate Strategy* (Homewood, Illinois: Richard D. Irwin, Inc. 1980)
3. Craig M. Watson, "CounterCompetition Abroad to Protect Home Makets," *Harvard Business Review,* 60, No. 1 (January-February 1982), p. 41.
4. Peter F Drucker, *Managing in Turbulent Times* (New York: Harper and Row, 1980), p. 171.
5. Ibid., p. 174.

6. Albert Bressand, "The New European Economies," *Daedalus,* 108, No. 1 (Winter 1979), 60.

7. Lawrence Franko, "European Industrial Policy: Past, Present and Future," The Conference Board in Europe (February 1980), 2.

8. Michael E. Porter, *Competitive Strategy* (New York: The Free Press, 1980), p. 291.

9. John Zysman, *Political Strategies for Industrial Order* (Berkeley, California: University of California Press, 1977), p. 62.

10. Charles-Albert Michalet, "France," *Big Business and the State,* Ed. Raymond Vernon, (Cambridge, Mass.: Harvard University Press, 1974) pp. 105–125.

11. Eugene J. Kaplan, *Japan: The Government-Business Relationship* (U.S. Department of Commerce, February 1972), p. 12.

12. Ibid., p. 19.

13. Ibid., p. 20.

14. Terry Dodsworth, "France to Test its Grand Design for Electronics," *Financial Times,* January 15, 1982.

15. Robert B. Reich, "Why the U.S. Needs an Industrial Policy," *Harvard Business Review,* 60, No. 1 (January-February 1982), p. 20.

16. Porter, pp. 278–285.

17. For groupings using various variables, see S. Prakash Sethi and Richard H. Holton, "Country Typologies for the Multinational Corporation: A New Basic Approach," *California Management Review* (Spring 1973).

18. Derek F. Abell and John S. Hammond, *Strategic Market Planning, Problems and Analytic Approaches* (Englewood Cliffs, New Jersey: Prentice-Hall, Inc., 1979), pp. 54–55.

19. Drucker, pp. 154–181.

20. Gerald O. Barney, Study Director, *The Global 2000 Report to the President: Entering the Twenty-First Century,* 1. (Washington, D.C.: Government Printing Office, 1980), p. 9.

21. See Mordechai Elihau Kreinen, *International Economics, a Policy Approach.* 3rd ed. (New York: Harcourt, Brace, Jovanovich, 1979), pp. 333–335 for other examples.

22. Susan Strange, "The Management of Surplus Capacity," *International Organization* (Summer 1979), p. 303.

23. Raymond Vernon and Louis T. Wells, Jr., *The Economic Environment of International Business.* 3rd ed. (Englewood Cliffs, New Jersey: Prentice Hall, Inc., 1981), pp. 140–143.

24. Norman Macrae, "Must Japan Slow?" *The Economist,* February 23, 1980, p. 27.

25. Abell and Hammond, p. 62.

26. Philippe Haspeslagh, "Portfolio Planning: Uses and Limits," *Havard Business Review,* 60, No. 1 (January-February 1982), p. 59.

27. Abell and Hammond, p. 186.

28. Haspeslagh, p. 65.

29. Ibid.

30. Abell and Hammond, p. 186.

31. Drucker, pp. 95–103.

32. Ibid., pp. 102–106.

33. Lester Thurow, *The Zero Sum Society* (New York: Basic Books, 1980), pp. 145–153.
34. *Timkin Roller Bearing Co. v. United States,* 341 U.S. 593, (1951). See also Lawrence A. Sullivan, *Handbook of the Law of Antitrust* (St. Paul, Minn.: West Publishing Co., 1977), pp. 714–717.
35. Reich, p. 75.
36. Jonathan Kaufman, "How NASA Helped Industry," *Wall Street Journal,* August 28, 1981, p. 20.
37. Raymond Vernon, "Enterprise and Government in Western Europe," *in Big Business and the State*, Ed. Raymond Vernon, (Cambridge Mass.: Harvard University Press, 1974).
38. Porter, p. 294.
39. Abell and Hammond, pp. 389–407.
40. Anthony Sampson, *The Soverign State of ITT* (New York: Stein and Day, 1973), pp. 40, 43.
41. Ibid., pp. 149–215, 259–288.
42. Milton Moskowitz, et al., *Everybody's Business 1982 Update* (San Francisco, California: Harper & Row, 1981), pp. 19–21.
43. Vernon and Wells, p. 24.
44. Stefan H. Robock and Kenneth Simmonds, *International Business and Multinational Enterprises* (Homewood, Illinois: Richard D. Irwin, Inc., 1973), p. 224.
45. "Europe's New Managers," *Business Week,* (May 24, 1982), p. 116.
46. Robert Ball, "The Hard Hats in Europe's Boardrooms," *Fortune,* (June 1976), p. 180.
47. See for example: William G. Ouchi, *Theory Z: How American Business can Meet the Japanese Challenge,* (Reading, Mass.: Addison Wesley, 1981); Vogel, Ezra F., *Japan as Number One,* (Cambridge Mass.: Harvard University Press, 1979); Root, Franklin R., *Foreign Market Entry Strategies,* (NY, NY: AMACOM, 1982).
48. Vernon and Wells, p. 32.
49. Ibid., p. 3. See also Prahalad, C.K., "Strategic Choices in Diversified MNC's," *Harvard Business Review* (July-August 1976), pp. 67–78.
50. Ibid.

Corporate Mission Statements: The Bottom Line

John A. Pearce II and Fred David

Developing a mission statement is an important first step in the strategic planning process, according to both practitioners and research scholars.[1] Several recent books on strategic management include entire chapters on mission statements, which attest to their perceived importance in the strategy formulation process. Nevertheless, the components of mission statements are among the least empirically examined issues in strategic management. No reported empirical studies describe the composition of business mission statements, only a few conceptual articles suggest desirable component characteristics, and no reported attempts have been made to link mission statements to corporate performance.

This neglect is surprising since several studies have concluded that firms that engage in strategic planning outperform firms that do not.[2] Thus, the research reported in this paper focused on the nature and role of mission statements in organizational processes; its goal was to improve our understanding of the link between strategic planning and firm performance.

THE MISSION STATEMENT

Function

An effective mission statement defines the fundamental, unique purpose that sets a business apart from other firms of its type and identifies the scope of the business's operations in product and market terms.[3] It is an enduring statement of purpose that reveals an organization's product or service, markets, customers, and philosophy. When pre-

Source: John A. Pearce II and Fred David, "Corporate Mission Statements: The Bottom Line," *Academy of Management EXECUTIVE* 1, no. 2 (1987), pp. 109–15.

pared as a formal organizational document, a mission statement may be presented under a maze of labels, including "creed statement," "statement of purpose," "statement of philosophy," or a statement "defining our business." Yet regardless of the label, a mission statement provides the foundation for priorities, strategies, plans, and work assignments. It is the starting point for the design of managerial jobs and structures. It specifies the fundamental reason why an organization exists.

A mission statement should create an organization identity larger than the limits placed on the firm by any individual. An effective statement helps to satisfy people's needs to produce something worthwhile, to gain recognition, to help others, to beat opponents, and to earn respect. Thus, it is a general declaration of attitude and outlook. Free from details, a mission statement has breadth of scope; it provides for the generation and consideration of a range of alternative objectives and strategies because it does not unduly stifle management creativity.

Components

A mission statement may be the most visible and public part of a strategic plan. As such, it is comprehensive in its coverage of broad organizational concerns. Although no empirical research has been published to guide corporate mission statement development, the limited evidence available suggests eight key components of mission statements:

1. The specification of target customers and markets.
2. The identification of principal products/services.
3. The specification of geographic domain.
4. The identification of core technologies.
5. The expression of commitment to survival, growth, and profitability.
6. The specification of key elements in the company philosophy.
7. The identification of the company self-concept.
8. The identification of the firm's desired public image.

A STUDY OF MISSION STATEMENTS

Based on previous theoretical and conceptual work focusing on the composition of mission statements, the present empirical investigation was undertaken to assess the relationship between mission statements with the eight components listed above and corporate financial performance. The present study specifically addressed the following hypothesis: The mission statements of high performing *Fortune* 500 companies will exhibit more of the desired components than will those of low performing *Fortune* 500 firms.

Our rationale for this hypothesis was prior theoretical and conceptual writing suggesting that eight components characterize an effective mission statement. Prior research also suggested that firms that engage in strategic planning outperform firms that do little or no planning. We reasoned that because a mission statement is increasingly perceived as an indication of a high-quality strategic planning effort, firms that have developed a comprehensive mission statement should outperform those with a weak or no mission statement. Such a finding would not, of course, indicate causation, because many diverse factors affect organizational performance. However, a comprehensive mission statement, we reasoned, should provide a basis for making better strategic decisions which, in turn, should contribute to improved organizational performance.

SURVEY RESULTS

Response Raters

Completed surveys were returned by 218 of the *Fortune* 500 companies mailed the research instrument. Of the respondents, 61 (28%) supplied mission statements that were analyzed for this report. As indicated in Exhibit 1, of the remaining respondents, 40.4% replied that their organization did not have a mission statement; 5% replied that their mission statement was confidential; and 26.6% sent material, such as an annual report, from which a statement of mission could not be confidently extracted.

Nature and Prevalence of Components

One of the most valuable insights the survey results provide is a realistic portrayal of the components of corporate mission statements. For managers who are asked to participate in constructing or modifying a firm's mission, such information is helpful for comparative purposes. In this section, we will review the survey results for popularity of each of the eight components identified above. We will also present examples of each component excerpted from the corporate mission statements we evaluated.

1. Target Customers and Markets. Did the mission statements specify the firm's intended major customer or market targets? Many did—48%. We were somewhat surprised that more firms were not willing to commit openly to customers and markets. Those we questioned

EXHIBIT 1　The Survey Responses	
Number of mailings	500
No response	282 (56.4%)
Responses	218 (43.6%)
Responses replying:	
That the organization had no mission statement	88 (40.4%)
That the organization had a confidential mission statement	11 (5%)
With material that we could not use	58 (26.6%)
With usable mission statements	61 (28%)

provided three reasons for this intentional omission: First, specifying certain groups might unintentionally signal "no interest" to others; second, merger and acquisition activity might violate any predetermined definition of customers or markets; and third, the various markets of many diverse business units effectively dictated a worldwide corporate market focus, and limiting that focus in any way could be confusing to some readers acquainted with smaller markets for individual product lines.

From the mission statements of Johnson & Johnson and CENEX came these clear commitments to specific customer groups:

> We believe our first responsibility is to the doctors, nurses, and patients, to mothers and all others who use our products and services. (Johnson & Johnson)
>
> . . . to anticipate and meet market needs of farmers, ranchers and rural communities within North America. (CENEX)

2. Principal Products or Services.　Did the mission statements convey the firm's commitment to major products or services? Yes—a solid majority (67%) were unequivocal in specifying their major products or services.

Consider, for example, the following excerpts from the mission statements of AMAX and Standard Oil Company of Indiana, respectively:

> AMAX's principal products are molybdenum, coal, iron ore, copper, lead, zinc, petroleum and natural gas, potash, phosphates, nickel, tungsten, silver, gold, and magnesium.
>
> Standard Oil Company (Indiana) is in business to find and produce crude oil, natural gas and natural gas liquids; to manufacture high quality

products useful to society from these raw materials; and to distribute and market those products and to provide dependable related services to the consuming public at reasonable prices.

3. Geographic Domain.   Did the mission statements specify the firm's intended geographic domain for marketing? Only 41% did. Those who talked to us about the omission said it seemed unnecessary to state the "obvious" global nature of their marketing efforts. "This is undoubtedly an important issue to smaller firms" was the frequent comment of the *Fortune* 500 spokespersons.

Exemplary statements that included this component were the following by Corning Glass and Blockway:

> We are dedicated to the total success of Corning Glass Works as a worldwide competitor. (Corning Glass Works)
> Our emphasis is on North American markets, although global opportunities will be explored. (Blockway)

4. Core Technologies.   Did the mission statements describe the firm's core technologies? Overwhelmingly, they did not. By the far the least frequently included component in the 61 mission statements we evaluated was the "core technology" component, which was specified by only 20% of the firms. The principal reasons company spokespersons gave to our follow-up questioning about the omission were (1) the impossibility of succinctly describing the many technologies on which their multiple products depended, and (2) the inappropriateness of trying to describe the core technologies of their service-based business units. Once again, this component was judged to be far more relevant to smaller, more narrowly focused businesses.

Two of the corporations providing noteworthy exceptions were Control Data and NASHUA, which clearly specified their core technologies:

> Control Data is in the business of applying micro-electronics and computer technology in two general areas: computer-related hardware; and computing-enhancing services, which include computation, information, education and finance. (Control Data)
> The common technology in these areas relates to discrete particle coatings. (NASHUA)

5. Concern for Survival, Growth, and Profitability.   Did the mission statements specify the firm's plans regarding survival, growth, and target levels of profitability? Overwhelmingly, they did. The most popular component in the mission statements was an organizational commitment to survival, profitability, and growth. Of the 61 firms, 55

(90%) included statements at least as explicit as the following excerpts from Hoover Universal and McGraw-Hill:

> In this respect, the company will conduct its operations prudently, and will provide the profits and growth which will assure Hoover's ultimate success. (Hoover Universal)
>
> To serve the worldwide need for knowledge at a fair profit by gathering, evaluating, producing, and distributing valuable information in a way that benefits our customers, employees, authors, investors, and our society. (McGraw-Hill)

6. Company Philosophy. Did the mission statements disclose the firm's basic beliefs, values, aspirations, and philosophical priorities? Yes—more than three-fourths (79%) of the respondents did include clear indicators of the firm's strategic, operating, and human resources philosophies. Several did so by attaching elaborate statements of philosophy to more product/market-oriented statements.

The following brief excerpts from two statements provide a sense of how philosophies were embedded in the mission statements:

> We believe human development to be the worthiest of the goals of civilization and independence to be the superior condition for nurturing growth in the capabilities of people. (Sun Company)
>
> It's all part of the Mary Kay philosophy—a philosophy based on the golden rule. A spirit of sharing and caring where people give cheerfully of their time, knowledge, and experience. (Mary Kay Cosmetics)

7. Company Self-concept. Did the mission statements express the company's view of itself? Did they provide an explanation of the firm's competitive strengths? The answer to these questions is "yes" for 77% of the respondents. As part of their corporate self-concept, Hoover Universal and Crown Zellerbach stated the following:

> Hoover Universal is a diversified, multi-industry corporation with strong manufacturing capabilities, entrepreneurial policies, and individual business unit autonomy.
>
> Crown Zellerbach is committed to leapfrogging competition within 1,000 days by unleashing the constructive and creative abilities and energies of each of its employees.

8. Desired Public Image. Did the mission statements express the firm's desired public image? They clearly did in 87% of the cases, which makes this the second most included component in 61 formal statements. Among the ways in which desired public images were expressed were the following statements from Dow Chemical, Sun Company, and Pfizer:

To share the world's obligation for the protection of the environment. (Dow Chemical)

Also, we must be responsive to the broader concerns of the public including especially the general desire for improvement in the quality of life, equal opportunity for all, and the constructive use of natural resources. (Sun Company)

. . . to contribute to the economic strength of society and function as a good corporate citizen on a local, state, and national basis in all countries in which we do business. (Pfizer)

Mission Statements and Financial Performance

In summary, the analysis of the 61 mission statements revealed some common characteristics. Specifically, the 90% and 87% values (55 and 53 of 61 firms, respectively) indicate that nearly all of the corporate statements included the "concern for survival" and "desired public image" components. In contrast, the 19% and 41% values (12 and 15 of 61 firms, respectively) suggest that sample corporate statements tended to omit discussions of "core technology" and "geographic domain." As shown in Exhibit 2, significantly more of the mission statements of the highest performing *Fortune* 500 firms exhibited three of the eight components than did the statements of the lowest performing firms. Further, mean scores of the highest performers were greater than those of the lowest performers for six of eight components. These findings were all supportive of the research hypothesis. Thus the inclusion of the desired mission statement components was positively associated with a firm's financial performance.

Of course, many variables affect organizational performance, so the present findings do not suggest that the inclusion of desired components in a firm's mission statement will directly improve organizational performance. Quite to the contrary, a firm may have a comprehensive mission statement and still experience declining sales and profits for any number of reasons. Thus, it would be inappropriate, based on this study alone, to label the desired components as "essential" characteristics of mission statements. Rather, further research is needed to determine particular industries, conditions, and situations when specific components are most desirable.

However, the current findings are important for two major reasons. First, they lend empirical support to the notion that higher performing firms have comparatively more comprehensive mission statements. Specifically, for the organizations included in the study, higher performing firms more often exhibited the components suggested as important in the literature. Second, the findings suggest

EXHIBIT 2 A Comparison of Mission Statements of *Fortune* 500 Companies

Component	High Performers' Mean Score[a]	Low Performers' Mean Score[a]	Statistical Difference Between Mean Scores?[b]
Philosophy	.8947	.6000	Yes
Self-concept	.8947	.5333	Yes
Public image	1.0000[c]	.7333	Yes
Customer/market	.4737	.6000	No
Product/service	.5789	.8667	No
Geographic domain	.4211	.3333	No
Technology	.1579	.0667	No
Concern for survival	.9474	.8667	No

a. High performers were firms in the top quartile of a profit margin distribution of all responding *Fortune* 500 companies. Low performers were the lower quartile firms.
b. A "Yes" indicates a *t*-value significant at less than .05.
c. A mean value of 1.00 indicates that all 61 mission statements included the evaluative criterion.

that corporate philosophy, self-concept, and public image are especially important components to include in an organizational mission statement.

DISCUSSION

Developing a Mission Statement

An intended practical and immediate contribution of the present research was to provide some benchmarks against which future studies could gauge the nature and direction of mission statement development. Because such large sample baseline data are otherwise unpublished, the information gathered in this research effort may provide a useful standard of comparison for managers responsible for coordinating the development of mission statements.

This research disclosed that 40% of the 218 responding *Fortune* 500 companies did not have a written mission statement. If mission statements are so important to the strategic development process, why is this so? The respondents may have provided an unsolicited answer, in that 10% of all corporate CEOs specifically requested guidance from the researchers in helping them develop effective mission statements. It may well be that a lack of knowledge about desirable components hampers or even prevents mission statement development.

This initial attempt at empirical research in the area of mission statement composition provides some encouraging evidence of the accuracy of previous conceptual writings and case studies. All eight of the components described as desirable in the normative literature were found to exist in the mission statements; in fact, they appeared with an average frequency of 66%. This finding is important because evaluators of mission statements—such as industry analysts, stockbrokers, and directors of investment funds—may express as much concern for components that are excluded as for those that are included. With the general and macronature of mission statements, perhaps it is at least as important for a firm to demonstrate concern for a particular content issue as it is to express a particular preference for outcomes.

It may in fact be that the findings of this study understate the importance of a carefully and comprehensively developed mission statement. It seems reasonable to theorize that organizations that differ dramatically in such areas as profit motive, stakeholders, and geographic marketplaces would also differ in the components included in their mission statement. In fact, had the corporations responding to the study been more homogeneous, or had business units rather than corporations been contacted, the observed differences might have been greater both in number and in magnitude. For optimal effectiveness, mission statements may need to be as distinctive as the relatively unique competitive situations in which organizations conduct their strategic planning.

Questions Remain

Not only is additional research needed to assess the degree to which the findings of this initial empirical effort can be generalized, but several critical questions about mission statements merit special attention. Three of the more intriguing questions are the following:

1. *What is the nature of the link between mission statements and organizational performance?* An important likely finding is that comprehensive mission statement development sets the stage for comprehensive planning efforts. Since such efforts have been associated with improvements in organizational performance, mission statements may be found to act as outlines for top managers to use to direct and focus their own planning and that of their subordinates.

2. *In what ways should the composition and intent of useful corporate and business-unit mission statements differ?* Corporate missions must often reflect the diverse concerns of several distinct strategic business units, even though corporate and business-unit missions may differ in their contributions to performance. Corporate missions may be best used to establish organizational values and strategic planning priorities, while business missions may be best when they suggest more specific directions that business strategies should incorporate.

3. *How closely associated are publicly pronounced mission statements and "in-house" strategic planning documents?* Our discussions with strategic planners revealed that public statements of corporate mission are designed to be of little value to other firms as a basis for competitive planning. Thus, they are unlikely to spell out specific plans for strategic action. It is perhaps more likely that public statements provide only competitively harmless overviews of competitively potent strategic intentions. In such cases, the mission's strategic substance, which serves as the framework for competitive action, may be communicated among key managers on a classified basis.

CONCLUSION

Practitioners and researchers alike believe there is value in mission development and in the written statements that result. Perhaps it is asking too much to prove that they guarantee direct financial consequences. However, it is not unreasonable to demand empirical evidence of the presumed integral role of mission statements in linking strategic planning with corporate performance. The research we have described puts the first piece of that evidence in place.

Research Methodology

The Research Sample.   A letter requesting a copy of the organization's mission statement was mailed to the chief executive officer of each of the *Fortune* 500 corporations. Responses were received from 218 of the 500 companies, producing a 44% response rate. Of the respondents, 61 companies supplied a mission statement that could be evaluated.

Content Analysis.   To evaluate the 61 corporate mission statements, content analysis, a qualitative research technique for analyzing message contents, was used. Specifically, content analysis involves selecting a written message to be studied, developing categories for measurement, measuring frequency of appearance of the categories by using coding rules, applying an appropriate statistical test to the data collected, and then drawing conclusions. The mission statements were evaluated to determine whether they exhibited the eight components identified from the literature review. Three independent raters evaluated each of the 61 usable statements to determine the degree to which they contained the eight desired components. Prior to conducting their evaluations, the raters read and discussed mission statement articles; they also rated and discussed their ratings of several example mission statements.

When a rater determined that a mission statement contained a specific component, a value of "1" was assigned to the statement. When a particular mission statement did not "clearly" exhibit the component, a "0" was assigned. Inter-rater reliability coefficients revealed no significant differences ($< .01$) among the three independent raters on their evaluations of the corporate statements' total scores.

Statistical Analyses.   Pearson intercorrelations of the eight mission statement components disclosed that only one of the 28 computations ("concern for survival" with "public image") was statistically significant, and only one of the coefficients was above .2701. Thus, the evaluated mission statement components were considered distinct variables. In addition, the low intercorrelations lend some empirical support for the heretofore theoretical notion that mission statements may be examined in terms of their components.

Parametric *t*-test analyses were performed to test the hypothesis that mission statements of high performing companies would exhibit more of the components than those of low performing firms. The selected indicator of performance was the profit margin of each of the sample *Fortune* 500 companies. The distribution was first divided into quartiles; then mission statements of the top quartile firms were compared with those of lower quartile firms. The results are discussed in association with Exhibit 2.

NOTES

1. Among recent authors who have stressed the critical role of mission statements as the starting point in strategic management are W. A. Staples and K. U. Black in their article, "Defining Your Business Mission: A Strategic Perspective," *Journal of Business Strategies,* 1984, 1, 33–39; V. J. McGinnis in "The Mission Statement: A Key Step in Strategic Planning," *Business,* November–December 1981, 39–43; and D. S. Cochran, F. R. David, and C. K. Gibson in "A Framework for Developing an Effective Mission Statement," *Journal of Business Strategies,* 1985, 4–17.

2. For the reader interested in a better understanding of the nature of the empirically evidenced positive relationships between strategic planning and firm performance, three articles should be of particular interest: (1) G. G. Dess and P. S. Davis's "Porter's (1980) Generic Strategies as Determinants of Strategic Group Membership and Organizational Performance," *Academy of Management Journal,* 1984, 3, 467–488; (2) J. W. Fredrickson and T. R. Mitchell's "Strategic Decision Processes: Comprehensiveness and Performance in an Industry with an Unstable Environment," *Academy of*

Management Journal, 1984, 2, 399–423; and (3) R. B. Robinson, Jr. and J. A. Pearce II's "The Impact of Formalized Strategic Planning on Financial Performance in Small Organizations," *Strategic Management Journal,* 1983, 3, 197–207.

3. Probably the most often referenced work on mission statements, the one on which strategic management texts heavily rely, and the one that provided much of the impetus for the present study, is an article by J. A. Pearce II, "The Company Mission as a Strategic Goal," *Sloan Management Review,* Spring 1982, 15–24.

Objectives and Alternatives in the Context of Systems Analysis and MBO

Gil R. Mosard

INTRODUCTION

Setting objectives and developing alternatives are essential steps in the systems analysis framework for problem solving. For example, Mosard (1982) proposed the following systems analysis framework of seven steps based on the earlier work in systems engineering by A.D. Hall (1969):

1. Defining the problem.
2. Setting objectives (and developing evaluation criteria).
3. Developing alternatives.
4. Modeling alternatives.
5. Evaluating alternatives.
6. Selecting an alternative.
7. Planning for implementation.

The focus of this paper will be on steps 2 and 3 of this framework. Fundamental tasks will be proposed with respect to setting objectives and developing alternatives. These tasks presuppose that step 1 of the systems analysis framework—defining the problem—has been accomplished in a comprehensive manner (Mosard, 1983).

The significance of the tasks will be discussed in both the context of the system analysis framework and in the context of the management by objectives (MBO) approach to planning. Managerial techniques to accomplish the fundamental tasks will be described and demonstrated.

Source: Gil R. Mosard, "Objectives and Alternatives in the Context of Systems Analysis and MBO," *Engineering Management International* 3, (1984), pp. 15–28.

SETTING OBJECTIVES: FUNDAMENTAL TASKS

The following set of fundamental tasks is designed to accomplish the second step in the systems analysis process:

a. Identify major needs or goals, objectives, and sub-objectives.
b. Develop a hierarchical structure of the identified needs or goals, objectives, and sub-objectives.
c. Identify degree of interaction between objectives, constraints, alterables, and persons/groups involved.
d. Identify major premises and assumptions.
e. Identify or develop objective measures.
f. Develop preliminary evaluation criteria.

Each of the above tasks will be briefly discussed and illustrated.

The identification of major needs or goals, objectives, and sub-objectives is a complex process whereby broad needs or goals are explicitly developed and then broken down into more specific objectives and sub-objectives.

The generation of a list of goals, objectives, and sub-objectives by a manager/analyst can be stimulated and focused by a comprehensive problem-definition analysis which identifies specific problems, sub-problems, and causal problem factors.

If the objective setting effort is not in response to specific problems, but is rather a formal planning process like MBO, then objectives can be generated by soliciting responses from individuals in the various levels of the organization.

In either case, systems analysis or MBO, there is difficulty in clearly stating needs or goals, objectives, and sub-objectives. Accordingly, Warfield (1973) emphasizes the importance of using a precise syntax in stating objectives, namely the following:

(infinitive verb) (object) (qualifying phrase)

An example would be: to develop a transportation plan for the North Central Texas region.

The use of the recommended syntax does not guarantee that a stated objective will be clear and significant. Other guidelines include:

1. Use an active, rather than passive, verb.
2. Use adjectives with the object in the objective statement for full clarification.
3. Provide additional descriptive information about the objective (such as a target completion date along with cost or resource constraints) with the qualifying phrase.

If the objectives are carefully stated, then it may be possible to construct an objectives tree—a hierarchical structure of objectives—connected by lines and arrows (as shown in Figure 1). The logic of the objectives tree is that lower level sub-objectives contribute to the attainment of the middle level objectives which contribute to the upper level needs or goals (Warfield, 1973).

The development of an objectives tree is very difficult in complex organizations for several reasons:

1. Sheer volume of objectives and sub-objectives: it may be appropriate to partition, or divide, a large scale objectives tree into several smaller trees in order to effectively handle a large volume of objectives.
2. Conflicting objectives: an "or" box can be used to show conflicting objectives.
3. Complex interrelationships among objectives: additional lines with arrows in both directions can be used as necessary along with lines that describe "feedback" characteristics of some objectives.
4. Hidden or secret objectives: some individuals may be very reluctant to reveal their true objectives.

The actual construction of an objectives tree is an iterative, trial-and-error process. Revised versions of an objectives tree can be less time consuming if each need, objective, and sub-objective is written on a separate slip of paper. Each succeeding version of the hierarchical structure is then relatively easy to develop by rearranging and/or adding slips.

MBO and the Objectives Tree

It should be emphasized that an objectives tree can be a useful technique in the management by objectives (MBO) approach to planning. MBO requires identification of major goals, objectives, and sub-objectives, but some MBO efforts stop short of developing a hierarchical structure. Unfortunately, identifying a complex set of objectives can be of little management value without the ability to link the objectives together in a logical manner and display the linkages.

There are several distinct ways that the objectives can be displayed: (1) The objectives tree can be partitioned to show groups of routine objectives, problem-solving objectives, and innovative objectives—which are the three major categories of objectives as suggested by Odiorne (Murdick, 1977). (2) Objectives can also be related directly to organizational structure and sub-systems (Baylin, 1980), or (8) related to the functional aspects of an organization or system (Tripp and Wahi, 1980).

FIGURE 1 Objectives Tree

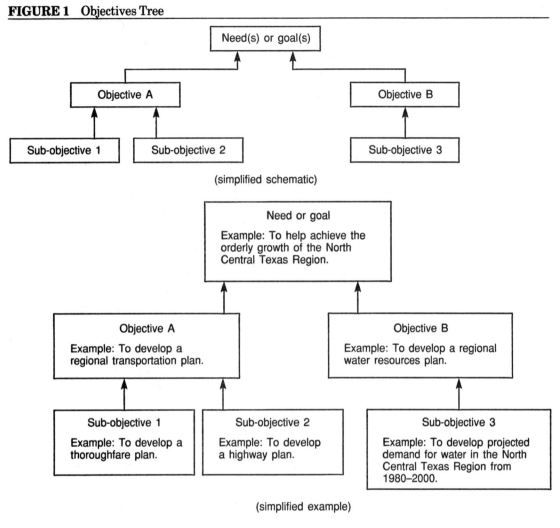

(simplified schematic)

(simplified example)

Interpretive notes:
1. An arrow from one box to another indicates that pursuit of the lower level objective or sub-objective contributes to the accomplishment of the higher level need, objective, or sub-objective.
2. When two or more arrows lead to a box, there is an implied "and" relationship. For example, sub-objective 1 and 2 contribute to the accomplishment of Objective A.

In light of the flexibility of the objectives tree in displaying objectives, the objectives tree has been recognized as a fundamental MBO analytical product (Weihrich, 1977). It is crucial, though, that the manager/analyst chooses the focus of the objectives tree in a deliberate manner to achieve the desired analytical and communication purposes.

Problem Elements

After identifying needs, objectives, and sub-objectives, and developing a hierarchical structure, a more detailed level of analysis may be warranted. Hill and Warfield (1972) recommend identifying the degree of interaction between the following problem elements:

1. Needs—basic goals in the problem-solving effort (example: to help achieve the orderly growth of the North Central Texas Region).
2. Constraints—barriers to the achievement of needs, objectives, and activities (examples: insufficient funding; lack of federal, state, and local cooperation).
3. Alterables—things that can be changed to help achieve needs, objectives, and activities (example: work programs; funding; staffing).
4. Persons/groups involved—anyone who is involved in or affected by the problem-solving effort including the "problem-solvers" and the stakeholders (example: citizens, local planning organizations, federal and state agencies).
5. Objectives—specific sub-goals designed to help achieve needs (example: to develop a regional transportation plan by a specified date).
6. Objective measures—a standard by which to judge the successful attainment/completion of objectives (example: completion of a regional transportation planning document that has the approval of persons/groups involved by a specified date).
7. Activities—specific tasks designed to help achieve objectives (example: collect city housing construction data from 150 cities in the North Central Texas Region by a specified date).
8. Activity measures—a standard by which to judge the successful attainment/completion of activities (example: completed file of city housing construction data from 150 cities by a specified date).

Initially, the attention to problem elements is focused on the needs and objectives already identified and the corresponding constraints, alterables, and persons/groups involved. A list of items for each problem element can be generated in an iterative fashion. A "problem element interaction table" can be developed as shown in Table 1.

This information can be portrayed and stored more precisely by using an analytical tool called a cross-interaction matrix. Hill and Warfield (1972) developed this tool to show the degree of relationship between each pair of problem element lists. Figure 2 shows an example of a cross-interaction matrix for needs and persons/groups involved.

The attention to problem elements can serve a "feedback" function to help improve the preciseness and thoroughness of the objectives tree. For example, a list of alterables should include the "objects" in objective statements. Likewise, the list of constraints and persons/groups

FIGURE 2   Simplified Example of Cross-interaction Matrix (needs versus persons/groups involved)

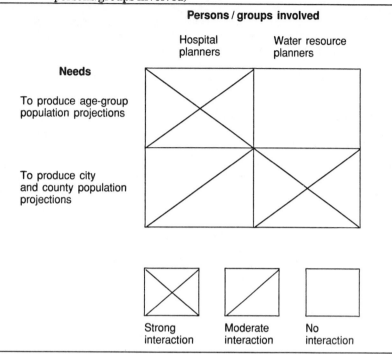

should provide some of the "qualifying phrases" in the objective statements. If the lists of problem elements include items that are not represented on the objectives tree, then the objectives tree is probably incomplete.

In some large scale problem analyses, it might be appropriate to develop an array of interaction matrices to help accomplish the first three major steps of the systems analysis process: (1) Interaction matrices for the first four problem elements represent an initial information-gathering effort in the problem definition step. (2) In step two, after the scope and depth of the problem have been determined, specific objectives and objective measures can be identified. Interaction matrices can then be generated using objectives, objective measures, constraints (more specific), alterables (more specific), and persons/groups. (3) Furthermore, this array of interaction matrices can be extended in step three to consider specific activities and activity measures that are intended to help accomplish the objectives along with very specific constraints, alterables, and persons/groups.

TABLE 1   Problem Element Interaction Table

Needs/Objectives	Constraints	Alterables	Persons/Groups
Need 1: To help achieve the orderly growth of the North Central Texas Region	Political competition among cities Federal, state and local funding	Kind of cooperative programs pursued	Regional planners City officials State officials Federal officials
Objective 1: To develop a regional transportation plan	State funding Federal funding	Priority project list Highway plan Thoroughfare plan	State transportation agency City officials Regional planners
Objective 2:			
.	.	.	.
.	.	.	.
.	.	.	.
.	.	.	.
.	.	.	.
.	.	.	.
.	.	.	.
.	.	.	.

The utility of a large array of interaction matrices is, of course, dependent on the scale of the problem-solving effort. Warfield developed this "unified program planning" approach as a large-scale systems planning technique, but judicious use of this technique can also lend analytical efficiency and communication clarity to some moderate-size problem-solving efforts (Hill and Warfield, 1972; Warfield, 1976; Sage, 1977; Sage (ed.), 1977; Baldwin (ed.), 1975).

After the scope of the problem-solving effort has been identified by carefully setting objectives and sub-objectives, major premises and assumptions associated with the objectives should be explicitly stated. Probabilistic statements, objective or subjective, can be developed to take into account the possible impact of future economic, political, technological, and management conditions that might affect the proposed problem-solving effort.

Specific objective measures, or targets, can then be set for each objective with reference to the explicitly stated premises or assumptions.

A list of objective measures for each objective can be generated if the objectives have been precisely stated. The objective measures can be used by management to monitor the progress of a project after the systems analysis. Although objective measures can be easily specified for some objectives, the objective measures for upper level needs or goals on an objectives tree are sometimes very difficult to specify and many times unnecessary. At the lower levels of the objectives tree, the objective measures may be stated as qualifying phrases in the statement of the objectives themselves.

In a systems analysis, after setting objectives and objective measures, preliminary decision criteria can then be developed. Decision criteria are specific bases of evaluation that will be used to compare alternative sets of activities for accomplishing an objective or goal. Decision criteria usually include the various risk, cost, and benefit characteristics of alternatives for decision-making purposes.

In practice, some decision criteria may emerge in the course of developing alternatives. The major decision criteria categories, though, are usually evident after setting objectives.

There is no general agreement in the systems analysis literature on the use of the terms "measure" and "criteria." In this paper, an objective measure refers to a management control standard that is used to determine progress toward a specific objective after the systems analysis is over and the alternative is actually being implemented. The decision criteria are evaluation standards used in the systems analysis to compare alternative sets of activities prior to selecting and implementing an alternative.

DEVELOPING ALTERNATIVES: FUNDAMENTAL TASKS

The following set of tasks is designed to accomplish the third step in the systems analysis process:

a. Specify alternative sets of activities for attaining objectives and sub-objectives.
b. Identify or develop activity measures.
c. Portray the alternative sets of activities on the objectives tree.

After setting the objectives, the alternative ways of achieving the objectives must be developed and eventually evaluated. These alternative ways can be specified explicitly as sets of activities or tasks. In other words, a working definition of alternative is: a set of activities designed to accomplish an objective.

Quade (1975) recommends that a wide range of alternatives be developed by identifying major classes of alternatives and then developing distinct alternatives within each class. If this process is allowed to be truly creative, then there is a greater possibility of developing noteworthy "hybrid" alternatives for evaluation.

After a suitable range of alternatives is fully developed by explicitly designing a set of activities for each alternative, then activity measures can be developed for each activity in order to specify each alternative set of activities more completely and precisely for management planning and control purposes.

FIGURE 3   Objectives/Activities Tree (a simplified schematic)

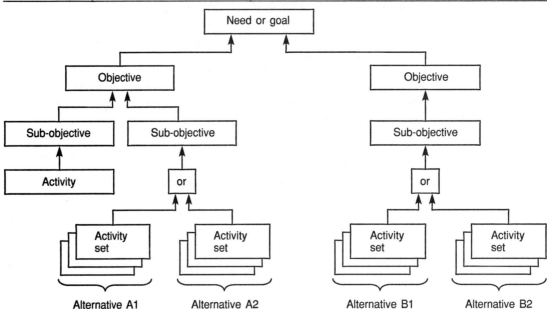

Interpretive notes:
1. An arrow from one box to another indicates that pursuit of the lower level item contributes to the accomplishment of the higher level item.
2. When two or more arrows lead to a box, there is an implied "and" relationship. "Or" relationships are explicitly shown using "or" boxes.

In complex systems analysis problems, there may be several alternatives for each of several different objectives. Accordingly, there may be multiple evaluations to perform. Therefore, in order to organize the analysis effort, it may be very helpful to extend the hierarchical structure of objectives—the objectives tree—to portray alternative sets of activities. A simplified schematic diagram showing the use of an objectives tree to portray alternative sets of activities for a multiple evaluation is shown in Figure 3. The diagram is simplified to clearly show major hierarchical levels. A more realistic objectives/activities tree might show complex interrelationships, and perhaps feedback loops, among objectives and sets of activities. Figure 4 shows a simplified example of an objectives/activities tree for choosing an alternative to accomplish a sub-objective.

In the following case study discussion, emphasis will be placed on selecting the best way to design a regional planning research department that is capable of developing methodologies and regional planning research products, like population estimates and projections, for functional planning efforts.

FIGURE 4 Objectives/Activities Tree (a simplified example). (See interpretive notes in Figure 3.)

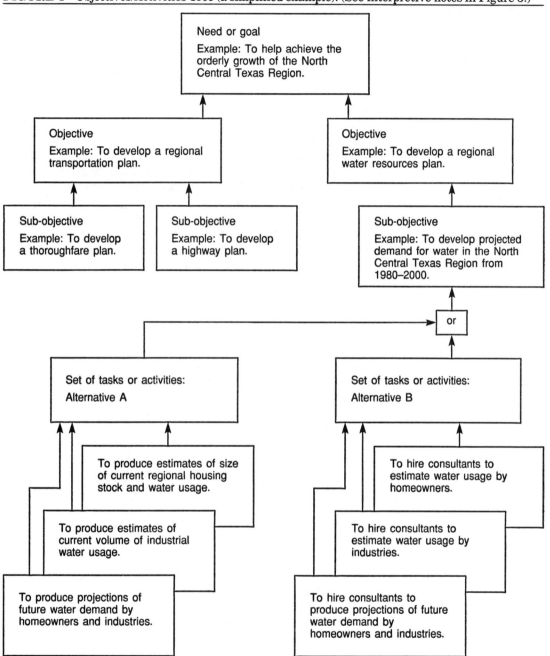

CASE STUDY: DESIGN OF A REGIONAL PLANNING RESEARCH DEPARTMENT

Scenario

You are involved in establishing a research department in a regional planning agency. The department will have planning support responsibilities in transportation, energy, land use, air quality, housing, human resources, water resources, health, criminal justice, and solid waste. You want to design a research environment that will efficiently accomplish the planning support activities and utilize the latest techniques of urban analysis. Current plans in each of the functional planning areas mentioned above are based on significantly varying population growth projections for the Dallas-Fort Worth area, as shown in Figure. 5. You want all projections based on common estimates that are produced in a reliable, timely manner. Eventually you want to help a body of decision-makers determine a preferred regional growth policy that is based on the integrated planning activities of all of the functional planning areas.

Defining the Problem

A first step, usually overlooked, in a large scale systems analysis problem is to explicitly define the sub-problems. An efficient way for all persons involved to gain an understanding of the sub-problems is to develop a problem factor tree. Problems are briefly and carefully stated and then arranged to form a logical structure based on causal interrelationships.

FIGURE 5   Conflicting Population Projections for the Dallas-Fort Worth SMSA (Standard Metropolitan Statistical Area)

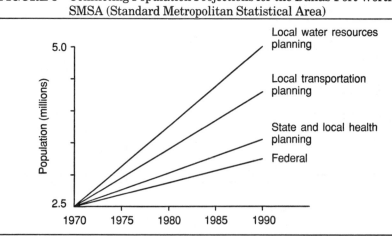

Figure 6 is a simplified problem factor tree for the problem: lack of a regional growth policy. Only major problems, sub-problems, and problem factors are shown. The problem factor tree has purposely been kept to a manageable size for greater communication impact of the most important aspects of the situation.

The development of the problem factor tree is an iterative, trial-and-error process that requires precise wording and consistent logic applied to the interrelationships between problems, sub-problems, and problem factors. The lower level problem factors "contribute to" or help "cause" the sub-problems which in turn "cause" the upper level problems. It is not uncommon to have feedback loops that complicate the causal connections on the tree.

After giving a very broad understanding of the problems by developing a problem factor tree, the problem can be defined in greater detail, as shown in Table 2, by listing problem elements such as needs, alterables, constraints, and persons/groups involved. These problem element lists could be displayed alternatively as a problem element interaction table or a series of cross-interaction matrices, as described previously in this paper. It is often more efficient, though, to begin the second step of the analysis—setting objectives and developing evaluation criteria—without undue delay. Systems analysis should be an iterative process that strikes a balance between attention

FIGURE 6   Problem Factor Tree (simplified)

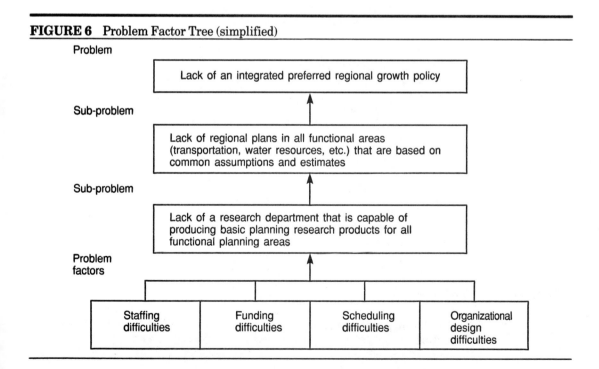

TABLE 2   Problem Element Interaction Table

Needs:
1. To provide agency with common planning data for all functional areas of planning.
2. To develop credible population estimates and projections.
3. To develop and maintain the agency's analytical tools.
4. To provide policy-related research to the policy makers.
5. To provide major research support to transportation and water resources planning.

Constraints:
1. To staff the research department with existing agency employees.
2. To acquire no more than 3 employees from another department.
3. To fund the department with existing grants.
4. To continue development of the Urban Growth Simulation Model.
5. To utilize the agency's present computer facilities.
6. To utilize existing agency floorspace.

Alterables:
1. Number of employees from other departments.
2. Funding allocations from existing departmental grants.
3. Agency emphasis on in-house Urban Growth Simulation Model.
4. Computer firm sub-contracting.
5. Departmental floorspace.

Persons/Groups Involved (and Disciplines):
1. Executive Board of Agency (policy makers).
2. Directors of agency departments.
3. Other agencies—federal.
4. Other agencies—state.
5. Other agencies—local.
6. Businesses.
7. Universities.
8. Builders, developers.
9. Consulting firms—engineering, market research, planning.
10. Newspapers.

---

to detail and emphasis on major aspects of the whole process. The problem factor tree and the lists of problem elements can help achieve the desired balance.

Setting Objectives and Developing Evaluation Criteria

After analyzing the list of needs, constraints, alterables and persons/groups, it is relatively easy to begin stating objectives and developing evaluation criteria for selecting the best alternative for achieving

TABLE 3   Evaluaion Criteria (preliminary)

Scope and Effectiveness	Risk of Failure	Cost	Benefits
Capable of meeting all needs on a timely basis	Due to technological difficulty and/or lack management control	Short run Long run	Spillover to all clients of regional planning research Analytical reputation of agency

the objectives. Figure 7 shows an objectives tree, as described previously in the paper, at the most general level. The specific objectives and sub-objectives associated with the proposed research department represent another level—a "middle" level of the objectives tree as shown in Figure 8. Objectives trees are developed in a trial-and-error fashion in order to precisely represent the intent or purpose of the problem-solving effort. After the objectives are set, then it is possible to develop evaluation criteria, as shown in Table 3, prior to designing, modelling, evaluating, and selecting alternatives to accomplish the objectives.

Creating Alternatives

After setting objectives and developing evaluation criteria, it is appropriate to begin the third step of systems analysis: creating alternatives. Distinctly different alternative classes should be created along with alternatives that differ slightly within each class. Eventually, a manageable number of alternatives must be selected for evaluation. A broad range of alternatives is usually desirable if the feasibility of the whole range of alternatives is not in question.

Figure 9 shows an example of creating alternatives and portraying them on the lower level of the objectives/activities tree. These three alternative approaches to designing a research department differ considerably with respect to organizational structure and personnel requirements. The operational activities of each alternative therefore differ accordingly, although each alternative could conceivably accomplish the objectives shown in Figures 7 and 8.

SUMMARY

In this paper, a set of tasks has been proposed for accomplishing the following steps of systems analysis:

1. Setting objectives.
2. Developing alternatives.

FIGURE 7   Objectives Tree (general level). (See interpretive notes in Figure 3.)

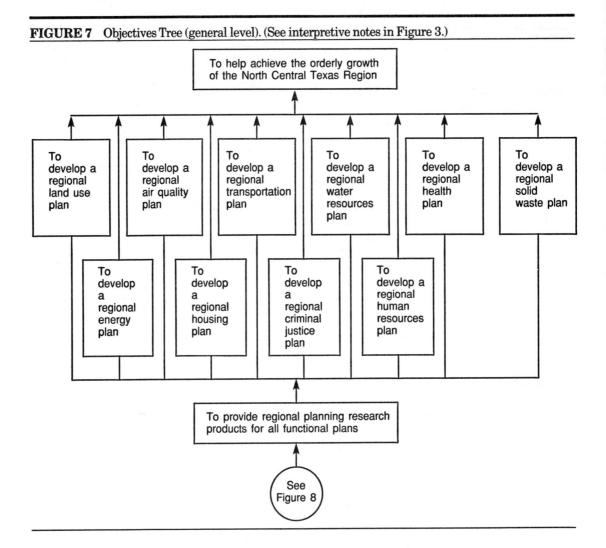

Analytical techniques, including the objectives tree, problem element interaction table, cross interaction matrix, and the objectives/activities tree, have been illustrated.

The proposed tasks and recommended techniques are designed to improve the analysis and communication efforts associated with large scale systems analyses and also management-by-objectives (MBO) planning efforts.

Figure 10 shows the sequence of major tasks and techniques associated with objectives and alternatives in systems analysis.

FIGURE 8 Objectives Tree (middle level). (See interpretive notes in Figure 3.)

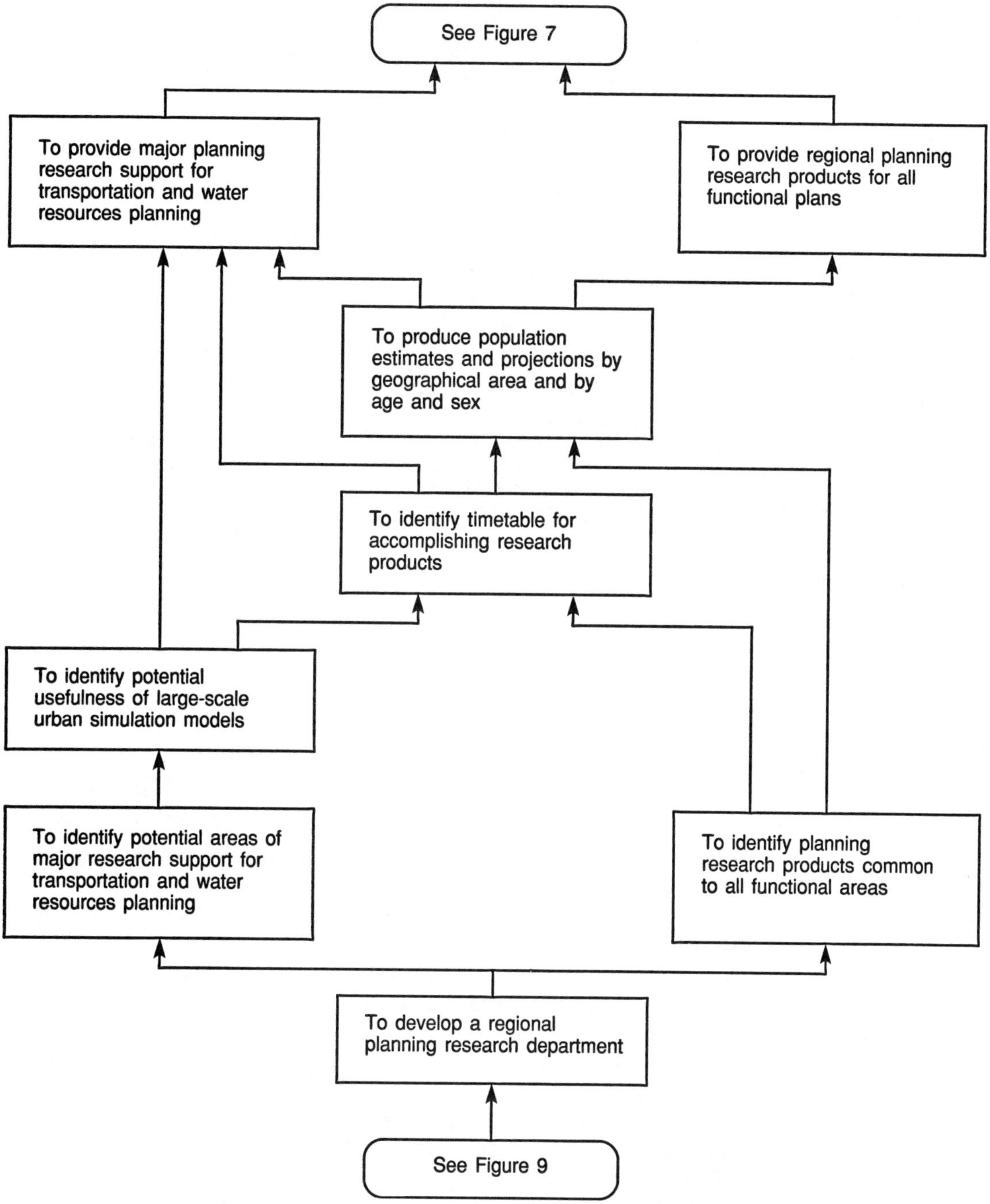

FIGURE 9   Objectives/Activities Tree (lower level). (See interpretive notes in Figure 3.)

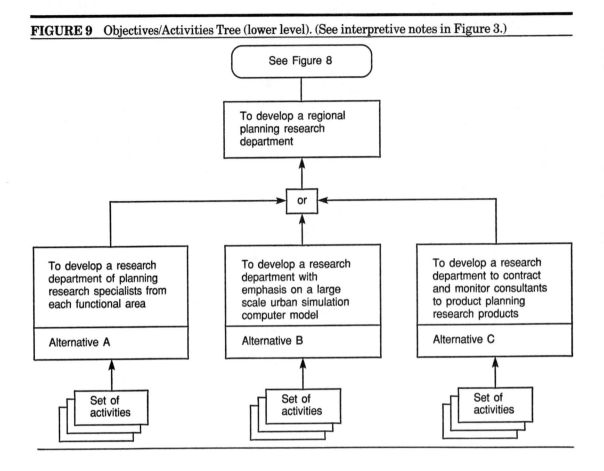

REFERENCES

Baldwin, M.M. (Ed.), 1975. Portraits of Complexity. Battelle Memorial Institute, Columbus, Ohio, 222 pp.

Baylin, E., 1980. Logical systems structure. Journal of Systems Management, August: 37–46.

Hall, A.D., 1969. A three dimensional morphology of systems engineering. IEEE Transactions on Systems Science and Cybernetics, Vol. SSC-5: 156–160.

Hill, J.D. and Warfield, J.N., 1972. Unified program planning. IEEE Transactions on Systems, Man, and Cybernetics, Vol. SMC-2, No. 5: 610–621.

Mosard, G.R., 1982. A generalized framework and methodology for systems analysis. IEEE Trans-actions on Engineering Management, Vol. EM-29, No. 3: 81–87.

Mosard, G.R., 1983. Problem definition: tasks and techniques. Journal of Systems Management, June: 16–21.

FIGURE 10 Summary of Major Tasks and Techniques for Setting Objectives and Developing Alternatives (Single-headed arrows indicate the sequential order of the tasks. Double-headed arrows indicate the iterative nature of the tasks.)

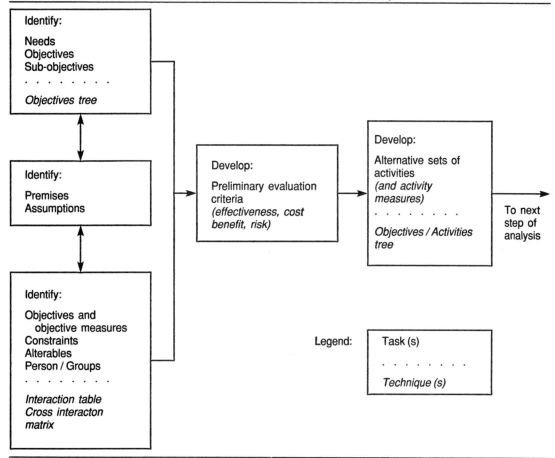

Murdick, R.G., 1977. MIS for MBO. Journal of Systems Management, March: 34–40.

Quade, E.S., 1975. Analysis for Public Decisions. American Elsevier, New York, 380 pp.

Sage, A.P., 1977. Methodology for Large Scale Systems. McGraw-Hill, New York, 445 pp.

Sage, A.P. (Ed.), 1977. Systems Engineering: Methodology and Applications. IEEE Press, New York, 401 pp.

Tripp, L.L. and Wahi, P.N., 1980. How much planning in systems development? Journal of Systems Management, October: 6–15.

Warfield, J.N., 1973. Intent structures. IEEE Transactions on Systems, Man, and Cybernetics, Vol. SMC-3, No. 2: 133–140.

Warfield, J.N., 1976. Societal Systems: Planning Policy, Complexity. Wiley, New York, 490 pp.

Weihrich, H., 1977. Getting action into MBO. Journal of Systems Management, November: 10–13.

PART II

Analysis of the Competitive Environment

A host of external and often largely uncontrollable factors influence a firm's choice of direction and action and, ultimately, its organizational structure and internal processes. These factors, which constitute the firm's competitive or external environment, involve three subcategories. The remote environment is composed of a set of conditions that originate beyond and usually irrespective of any single firm's operating situation; namely, ecological, economic, political, social, and technological factors. The industry environment includes such potent competitive forces as entry barriers, supplier power, buyer power, the availability of substitutes, and the level of competitive rivalry. Finally, the operating environment, which is specific to the firm, includes the company's direct competitors, creditors, customers, labor market, and suppliers.

The seven articles in this second section will help you to better understand the nature of these forces and to better anticipate their impact on strategic decision making and performance. The articles are particularly useful in helping to acquire important planning skills in competitive analysis, environmental scanning, and forecasting. A special dimension of several of these articles is the extent to which the authors both describe and critique the strategic management tools and techniques. Additionally, you will find explanations of the tools and techniques that can be applied to a variety of business settings, nationally and internationally, for small and large businesses.

Abstracts

COMPETITIVE ANALYSIS FROM A STRATEGIC PLANNING PERSPECTIVE

In the presence of market changes, the first step for a strategic planner is to analyze the state of the industry and then the company's position with its competitors. Once this is known, one can establish alternative strategies for long-run profits. As a planner begins this task, he or she is faced with an immediate problem in terms of the data required to perform the analysis. In this article the authors present an organized approach which allows a planner to utilize publicly available data to carry out competitive analysis.

The proposed methodology utilizes strategic planning concepts developed by the Boston Consulting Group (BCG). The focus of analysis for the BCG approach is the large corporation with distinct operating subsidiaries. The primary emphasis of this study is its focus on changes in growth and market share. The process attempts to explain both the structural changes taking place in an industry and the competitive forces involved.

The second half of this article uses the BCG approach to analyze the competitive position of the top six California banks with respect to three types of loan and deposit portfolios. The spread of growth among these banks reflects some possible transition taking place in terms of competition among the banks. The proposed methodology can be utilized for the analysis of any industry where similar public data exists.

DEVELOPING AN EFFECTIVE ENVIRONMENTAL ASSESSMENT FUNCTION

Business environmental assessment is gaining widespread recognition as an integral part of strategic planning. In this article, the author discusses nine steps which must be taken to create an effective environmental scanning effort. He proposes that by following these steps it is possible to develop a tailor-made business environment function for any organization. These nine steps require organizations to:

1. Examine the company's needs and evaluate the extent to which performance is impacted by outside events.
2. Learn about the nature of environmental assessment and its potential benefits.
3. Define goals in light of company philosophy, organizational behavior, and planning sophistication/maturity.
4. Organize the environmental assessment function to meet goals.
5. Develop tactical plans which describe specific short-term actions.
6. Obtain information to identify management needs and establish priorities for these needs.

7. Obtain a variety of analytical tools to forecast the future business environment.
8. Develop communication devices to communicate an analysis of external environment trends and events to management.
9. Use the results of steps 1 through 8 to put an environmental assessment function in place.

The primary use of the environmental assessment effort should be in generating assumptions for the long-range and strategic planning processes. Its effectiveness will depend on if and how the results are used. Environmental scanning should be employed as a control function to monitor this environment for changes which might alter the plan.

INTERNATIONAL COMPETITOR ANALYSIS

Growing competition from foreign firms entering U.S. markets and greater penetration of foreign markets by U.S. firms has made international competitive intelligence a critical skill for more firms than ever before. A systematic approach to international competitor analysis enables decision makers to concentrate their efforts on the most viable overseas market opportunities.

The analysis process is a blend of researching the market, making cross-cultural comparisons, and judging the fit between strategies and situations. The steps to international competitor analysis include: (1) studying the environment of the country or overseas market of interest, (2) analyzing strengths and weaknesses of international competitors with respect to the environment, (3) investigating the goals and strategies of international competitors, (4) assessing the firm's competitive position, and (5) selecting strategies to compete internationally and globally, taking into account possible competitor reactions. International competitor analysis requires unique sets of information. Types and location of data sources differ depending upon the data needed for each step.

In the future, the successful firms will be the ones that broaden their domestic competitor intelligence capabilities. This requires a strong commitment from top management to conduct ongoing international competitor analysis. Such a commitment includes resource allocation, studying international competitors' culture and philosophies, and creating strategic plans based on international intelligence.

A MANAGER'S GUIDE FOR EVALUATING COMPETITIVE ANALYSIS TECHNIQUES

Virtually all business managers recognize the importance of understanding their industry and their competitors. As a result, the use of competitive analysis techniques have become a popular means of helping managers formulate and implement strategy. However, the wide variety of competitive analysis techniques available to managers presents a problem of choosing the most appropriate set for the objectives of an assignment.

This article develops a reference guide of 21 competitive analysis techniques, evaluated along 11 dimensions, in order to assist managers in their selection of an appropriate method for their needs. The key characteristics of each technique are highlighted along with their typical advantages and limitations.

Few competitive analyses can be successfully completed using a single technique; the guide is designed to help managers choose the combination of techniques that will address their particular situation most effectively and efficiently. References are provided that present additional operational details for each technique. While these evaluation dimensions vary in importance across competitive analysis assignments, recognizing them can greatly facilitate choices when groups of managers and analysts are working together.

ENVIRONMENTAL FORECASTING: KEY TO STRATEGIC MANAGEMENT

A crucial responsibility for managers is to ensure their firm's survival by anticipating and adapting to environmental change in ways that provide new opportunities for growth and profitability. Therefore, the impact of change in the firm's external environments must be predicted and understood. The search for opportunities and constraints in the future includes four key aspects of strategic planning.

First, strategic planning must begin with selection and analysis of the key variables in a firm's environment. Many external and often uncontrollable conditions influence a firm's choice of direction, its actions, and, ultimately, its organizational structure and internal processes. Such conditions constitute the external environment of a business and can be categorized as parts of the remote environment or task environment.

Second, the manager must identify appropriate sources of environmental information. The casual gathering of strategic information that is part of the normal course of executive reading, interaction, and meetings is subject to bias and must be balanced with alternative viewpoints.

Third, strategic planning must include the evaluation of forecasting techniques. Ultimately, the choice of a technique depends not on the environmental factor under review, but on such considerations as the nature of the forecast decision, the amount and accuracy of the information available, the accuracy level required, and the resources available.

Finally, the results must be tied into the strategic management process. In formulating strategy, the resulting predictions become part of the assumed environment. Dealing with the uncertainty of the future is a major function of the strategic manager, and the forecasting task requires systematic information gathering coupled with the ability to combine and utilize a variety of forecasting approaches. Sensitivity and openness to new and better approaches and opportunities are essential for good strategic management.

ANALYZING THE COMPETITION

Many top managers recognize that to survive in a competitive environment, it is not enough to analyze the market as a whole. Business owners must understand and anticipate their individual competitors in the marketplace. Because competitor information is difficult to gather, many businesses abandon this important strategy. However, these forms may have good sources of competitor information already available. The key is knowing where to gather relevant information and how to combine separate pieces of data into a coherent profile of each competing operation.

The first step is to develop a list of goals that the program will achieve, including what information is needed. An effective competitor analysis focuses on key factors that drive companies to act and react in the marketplace: assumptions, objectives, strategies, and capabilities. The second step is to discover sources of information. Discovering where to find reliable information about rival firms may seem a formidable task. Fortunately, many managers will find they already have a good starting base when they review the information available in-house. This information should be supplemented with data available from outside sources.

Once a competitor's capabilities are assessed, a summary of findings, including assumptions, objectives, strategies, and capabilities should be developed. Planned activities should be documented in the form of a business plan so that progress toward the original goals of the program can be monitored.

ENVIRONMENTAL SCANNING FOR SMALL AND GROWING FIRMS

Small businesses are beginning to recognize the need for conscious and continuous study of their environment. Timely and accurate knowledge of the relevant environment is a major element in the success or failure of a small and growing business.

Imitation of large firm environmental forecasting techniques by small firms seldom work for three basic reasons. First, small businesses lack the capital and human resources that many techniques require. Second, large firms are usually systems oriented while small businesses tend to be personality oriented. Third, the greatest strength of the small business lies in its flexibility and maneuverability.

Choosing and modifying a firm's environmental scanning techniques can best be done through a structured analysis of small business forecasting needs and priorities. The firm should figure out what the technique provides, evaluate the firm's need for the information the technique provides, analyze the cost/benefit ratio of the technique, and establish an acceptable level of risk.

The basic differences between large and small firms also suggest general guidelines for profitably implementing environmental scanning in small and growing firms. Responsibility for implementing and modifying a technique should lie with the strategic planner, since the ultimate aim is to mold the technique to his personality and needs.

Competitive Analysis from a Strategic Planning Perspective

Syyed T. Mahmood and M. Munir Moon

INTRODUCTION

There are three types of current market trends in banking that highlight the need for strategic planning in banks as never before. The first trend is in the deregulation of financial institutions in general and of banks in particular. The second trend, related to the first, is of reduced margins in traditional banking services caused by high interest rates and operating costs. Finally there are the opportunities and problems posed by new and recent technologies in communications and data processing.

In the presence of these changes, the first step for a strategic planner is to analyze the state of the industry and then the bank's position with its competitors. Once this is known, one can establish alternative strategies for long run profits.

As a planner begins this task, he or she is faced with an immediate problem in terms of the data required to perform the analysis. Suppose a strategic planner wants to determine the profitability of a particular type of loan. He or she decides to begin by considering the bank's market share and its growth relative to other banks for that type of loan. After considering this information, the next logical question is related to the profitability of the loan for other competing banks. This information will generally not be available since it is regarded as proprietary. If it were available we could then consider issues like ROI and other criteria to judge the efficacy of proceeding with (1) increasing market share, (2) pulling out of the market, and/or (3) aggressively reducing operating costs.

Source: Syyet T. Mahmood and M. Munir Mood, "Competitive Analysis from a Strategic Planning Perspective," *Managerial Planning* 33, no. 1 (July/August 1984), pp. 37–42, 63.

FIGURE 1   BCG Approach

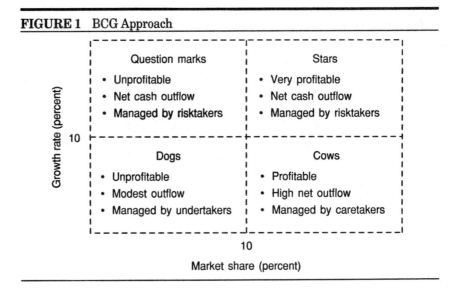

In this article an organized approach is presented which allows a planner to utilize the publicly available data to carry out the first task of strategic planning, including competitive analysis. Since the methodology utilizes strategic planning concepts originally developed by the Boston Consulting Group (BCG), Part 1 summarizes the essential features of the BCG approach.

In Part 2 this approach is utilized to analyze the competitive position of the top six California banks with respect to three types of loan and deposit portfolios. Part 3 considers the implications to be drawn from a strategic perspective.

1. A SUMMARY OF THE BCG APPROACH TO STRATEGIC PLANNING

The focus of analysis for the BCG approach is the large corporation with distinct operating subsidiaries. By considering a few aggregate variables such as rates of growth and market share, a simple portfolio approach is utilized to determine resource allocation among them to maximize long run profits. The initial choices are further refined by considering other decision criteria such as ROI, technological change, etc. These ideas are summarized in Figure 1.

Usually the growth rate of the industry separates the high growth from the low growth cells. For a diversified company, its desired growth rate is the dividing line. Thus products above the line have above average market growth and vice versa. In the figure the products on the left have a lower market share relative to the largest competitors. This is somewhat different from usual convention yet the concept is similar. The characteristics of each type of product or subsidiary is written under the title.

The strategic planning implications of this portfolio approach are to divest "dogs" and use cash rich "cows" to develop "stars" or to turn "question marks" to "stars." The actual business of strategizing is of course more complex yet this summary is sufficient for this paper.

2. STRATEGIC PLANNING FOR BANKING

Since the key objective of a bank is to provide services in various forms to consumers, we have replaced the products as defined in BCG approach by services provided by the banks.

For the purpose of analysis, we have selected three categories of loans and deposits in domestic branches of California's top six banks, for the last three years. The top down approach is followed in that the most general categories such as total loans and total deposits are examined first followed by specific categories of loans and deposits. Personal loans, real estate loans, commercial-industrial loans, demand deposits, saving deposits and time deposits represent a significant share of total loans and total deposits of a bank and are used for analysis in this article. The top six banks used for this study are:

Name	Abbrev.	No. of Branches
Bank of America	BOA	1,163
Security Pacific Bank	SPNB	659
Crocker National Bank	CNB	394
First Interstate Bank	FIB	349
Wells Fargo Bank	WFB	426
Union Bank	UB	60

Figure 2 shows the competitive position of the banks over time with respect to total deposits. The diameter of the circle is directly proportional to the volume of the deposits. One can make the following observations:

- Aggregate growth rate for total deposits has been around 2–3% in the last three years.
- Bank of America carries a significant share of the market share while Union Bank has the lowest market share among the six from 1979 to 1981.

FIGURE 2   Total Deposits for California Top 6 Banks (bubble: volume in dollars)

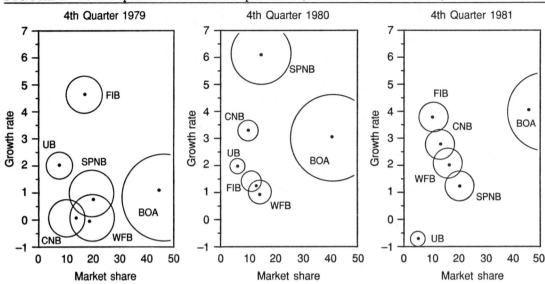

- Competition for deposits among the top six banks is between FIB, CNB, SPNB and WFB with SPNB leading the trend.

Also a few questions arise from these observations. First, what is the relative mix of deposits among the banks? Second, what accounts for the deposit size hierarchy of the banks in which BOA is so dominant and UB so far behind during the last three years? The competition for market share would seem to be among the four middle banks. Third, why is total deposit growth smaller than total loan growth, and what are its implications? Figures 3 through 9 will help us in addressing these issues.

Demand deposits (less NOW accounts), which are a highly desirable business for banks (with the maintenance of certain minimum balances) since banks do not have to pay interest on them, have had either flat or negative growth. The only exception is UB in 1979 which had relatively higher growth. This surge of growth in 1979 was caused by infusion of capital from Standard Chartered Bancorp which acquired it in 1979. The dominant role played by BOA and the relatively insignificant role of Union Bank is associated with the number of branches that they have. BOA and UB have 1163 and 60 branches, respectively, while the number of branches in the other four banks varies from 350 to 650. Since deposits have more of a retail orientation, number of branches do make a difference in terms of volume. It is obvious that this relative decline in the growth of

FIGURE 3   Demand Deposits for California Top 6 Banks (bubble: volume in dollars)

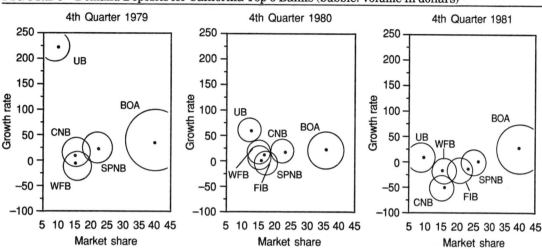

demand deposits is an artifact of deregulation as consumers take advantage of higher interest rates in other financial institutions.

Saving deposits, commonly known as passbook accounts, show a negative growth in 1979 and 1980 and then growing at about 2% in 1981 (see Figure 4). It is difficult to find a logical answer for their growth in 1981 specially when short term interest rates were at their peak of 20–21% while saving accounts paid only 5 1/4%. At best they represent temporary consumer inertia.

Union Bank which had relatively lower growth in saving deposits in 1979 showed a significant improvement in 1980 and 81 after its acquisition in 1979.

Time deposits which have grown from 6–8% during the 1979–81 period seem to have played a dominant role in overall growth of total deposits. Besides BOA and UB, the other four have tried to change their strategies to pursue or gain extra share as reflected in Figure 5 by higher growth of FIB in 1979 and SPNB in 1980. Unfortunately those changes in strategies turned out to be short term as can be seen from 1981 numbers, where all four are clustered together as before.

Now, we turn to an analysis of loans made by the same banks. Figure 6 shows that total loans grew at about 3–4% on the average during the 1979–81 period. BOA is maintaining its dominance over the same period. An interesting observation is the relatively higher growth of total loans for FIB and CNB. Figures 7–9 would provide some insight to this upsurge in growth for these two banks.

Real estate loans (as shown in Figure 7), once a highly desirable part of a bank's loan portfolio, still seem to do well. Real estate loans grew at

FIGURE 4   Saving Deposits for California Top 6 Banks (bubble: volume in dollars)

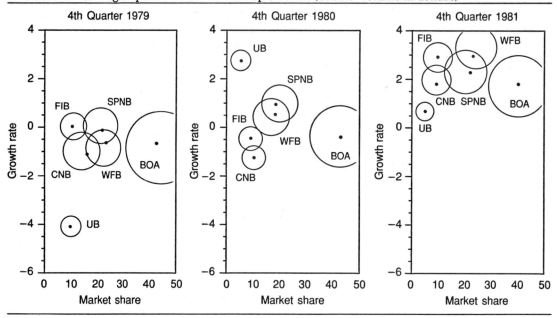

FIGURE 5   Time Deposits for California Top 6 Banks (bubble: volume in dollars)

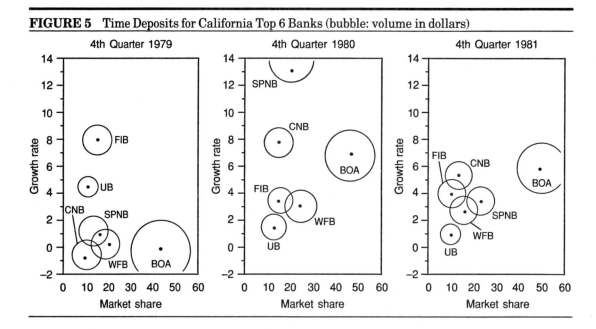

FIGURE 6   Total Loans for California Top 6 Banks (bubble: volume in dollars)

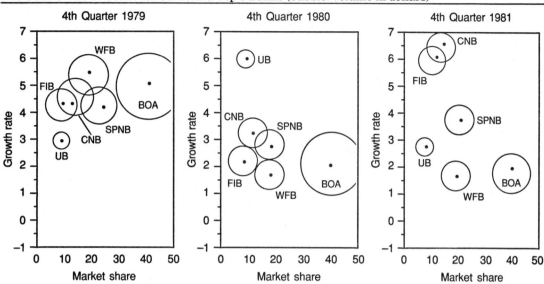

about 4.5% on the average in the last three years, higher than the growth in total loans, which reflects the desirability of these loans on a bank's portfolio. While old fixed low interest mortgage loans have been disasters for all financial institutions, the birth of variable mortgage loans have made them less risky. As the proportion of the old fixed low interest loans in the portfolio declines, real estate loans as a whole become more desirable for banks. Underlying demand for housing in California is still strong due to net immigrations and the higher percentage of the 24–34 age group, the prospective buyers of homes. The key problem in the last three years has been that of affordability which has been circumvented to some extent in 1980–81 by developers subsidizing the buyers in order to liquidate their inventory. Creative financing and various new kinds of mortgage instruments seem to have a positive effect on real estate loans which grew at about 2% even in 1981 when mortgage rates were about 17%. None of the six banks seem to have any new approach or strategy to approach this market and that is why the relative share and growth pattern for all of them has been the same in the last three years.

Personal loans, shown in Figure 8, one of the key services of a retail bank were disastrously affected by higher short term rates. They had a negative growth of about 2% during 79–80. Need for personal loans, which are generally used to finance vacations, and consumer durables would certainly be lower at about 20–25% financing cost. Besides the

FIGURE 7   Real Estate Loans for California Top 6 Banks (bubble: volume in dollars)

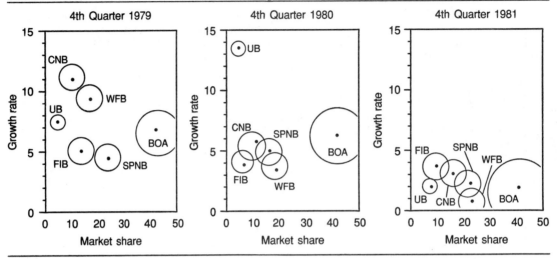

FIGURE 8   Personal Loans for California Top 6 Banks (bubble: volume in dollars)

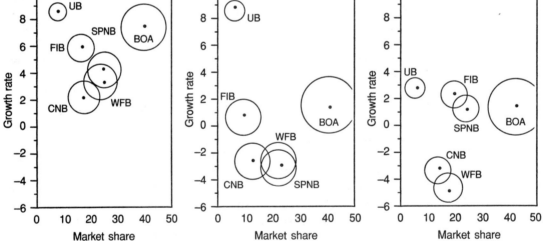

high cost of money, rising unemployment causes uncertainty among employed workers and reduces consumer spending.

Realizing that personal and real estate loans did not grow at the same level as total loans, one can say that commercial and industrial

FIGURE 9 Commercial and Industrial Loans for California Top 6 Banks (bubble: volume in dollars)

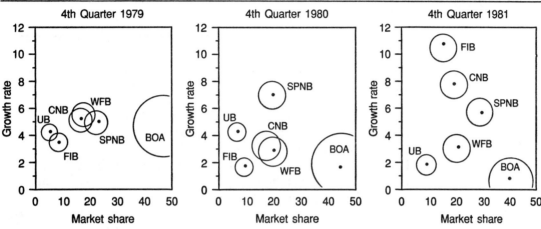

loans played a greater role in the overall growth of total loans. Figure 9 shows that commercial and industrial loans grew at about 6–8% in the last three years. Apparently the shift in demand and supply for loans is very clear. During the beginning of a recession the corporations' revenue declines faster than operating expenses. This causes serious cash flow problems for many companies that they have to resolve through short term borrowings. Also corporations are competing with the government's own borrowing needs to finance deficits (also higher because of reduced revenue) which keeps long term interest rates high. Businesses tend to satisfy their short term financial needs through short term higher interest loans rather than slightly lower but longer term financial obligation. For banks it was desirable to lend money at 2–4% spread above prime. FIB and CNB seem to have shifted their approach towards the commercial and industrial loan market in 1981.

The spread of growth in 1981 among these banks reflects some possible transition taking place in terms of competition among the middle four banks.

3. IMPLICATIONS

Given the data and trends presented earlier what useful implications can we draw for the future of the banking industry in California? It was pointed out at the beginning of the article that the banking industry is in the midst of unprecedented changes due to deregulation, new technology and higher operating costs. The analysis suggests that:

- A bank with a larger network of branches tends to have larger market share.
- The foreign acquisition of CNB and UB does not seem to have had any significant impact on overall competitive position of these banks except for a very short period.
- There has not been much growth in traditional banking services, therefore, competition among the middle four banks is very stiff in order to gain any further market share.
- Loans have grown at relatively higher rates than deposits resulting in negative impact on liquidity. This has resulted in greater emphasis on asset-liability management.
- There has been a shift away from the demand and saving deposits towards money market funds and T-Bill accounts reflecting the greater awareness and sensitivity of consumers to get the most of their money and a move away from the traditional saving instruments.

We have tried to use secondary sources of information and simple graphics utilizing the BCG concept to help us understand the structural changes taking place in the industry and competition among the top California banks from a strategic perspective. As mentioned earlier California was used as a sample state. The methodology can be utilized for other financial institutions or even other industries where similar public data exists. Since our primary emphasis has been on studying changes in growth and market share, we have not concerned ourselves with the impact of these changes on income statements of these banks.

We believe that strategic planning, complex as it is, could be simplified by utilizing simple concepts as we have used in this article. A lot more work needs to be done in this area of competitive analysis and strategic analysis. We hope to generate further discussion on the subject through this analysis. Some of the questions that need further attention are:

1. Would new technology (ATM etc.) result in fewer branches and move away from traditional banking services? The success of BOA's decision to cut its retail branches by one third would help in understanding this effect.
2. With the government's emphasis on deregulation, can aggressive regional banks expect to be acquisition targets of larger or foreign banks as a vehicle for their entry into the California market? A case in point is CNB's and UB's acquisition in 1980 and 1979, respectively.

3. With the emergence of the one stop financial service center concept, will the banks form the seed of such a center or will some other type of financial or retail institutions absorb banking services?
4. The new technologies such as ATMs, electronic fund transfers and global banking are having an important impact on the economies of scale of the banking industry. Will these changes benefit the larger banks? While on the face of it size should be an advantage smaller banks may enjoy greater flexibility in adapting to and initiating changes in the industry.

REFERENCES

• Abel, Derek F. and Hammond, John E. Strategic Market Planning, New Jersey: Prentice Hall, 1979.
• Fox, Harold W. "The Frontiers of Strategic Planning: Intuition or Formal Models?" *Management Review* 1981, 70: 8–14.
• Naylor, Thomas H. "Strategic Planning Models." *Managerial Planning* 1981, 30: 3–11.

Developing an Effective Environmental Assessment Function

ALLEN H. MESCH

Business environmental assessment is gaining wide-spread recognition as an integral part of strategic planning. In this article I will describe the process necessary to develop an environmental assessment function.

There are nine steps which must be taken to create an effective environmental scanning effort:

- Step 1. Examine the company's needs.
- Step 2. Learn about environmental assessment.
- Step 3. Define goals.
- Step 4. Organize to meet goals.
- Step 5. Develop tactical plans.
- Step 6. Obtain information.
- Step 7. Obtain analytical tools.
- Step 8. Develop communication devices.
- Step 9. Use the results.

By following these steps it will be possible to develop a tailor-made business environmental assessment function for your organization.

This article is based on experiences at an operating division of Sun Exploration and Production Company. Following a recent reorganization, the operating division no longer exists as a separate entity. The major tasks of the division were to produce and process natural gas, as well as market natural gas, gas liquids and energy related services.

The Dallas based division contained three organization groups: (1) Operations, (2) Marketing, and (3) Business Development. The Operations Group was responsible for producing natural gas through explor-

Source: Allen H. Mesch, "Developing an Effective Environmental Assessment Function," *Managerial Planning* 32, no. 5 (March/April 1984), pp. 17–22.

atory and development drilling. The Marketing Group sold the gas to natural gas transmission companies. The Business Development function was responsible for new business ventures including gas production from unconventional sources.

STEP 1.   EXAMINE THE COMPANY'S NEEDS

Does your organization need a business environmental assessment function? In order to answer that question you need to evaluate the extent to which your performance is impacted by events beyond your control. Let us consider the following questions:

- Does the external business environment influence your capital allocation and decision-making process?
- Have you had to scrap previous long-range plans because of unexpected changes in the business environment?
- Has there been an unpleasant surprise in the external business environment?
- Is competition growing in your industry?
- Is your business more marketing oriented and are you more concerned about the ultimate consumer?
- Do more and different kinds of external forces seem to be influencing your decisions (politics, social issues, emissions to air and water, government regulations, etc.), and does there seem to be more interplay between them?
- Are you unhappy with past forecasting/planning efforts?

If you have answered yes to any or all of these questions, adding a business environmental assessment function to your organization could be the answer.

STEP 2.   LEARN ABOUT ENVIRONMENTAL ASSESSMENT

Business environmental assessment has evolved out of the needs identified in Step 1. In this step we examine the nature of environmental assessment and its potential benefits.

The business environment is changing more rapidly and less predictably than in the past. This has caused difficulty in predicting that change. As a result, managers have found it increasingly difficult to react to their environment. Some of our problems may be due to past misconceptions about ourselves and the environment. We have viewed our companies as isolated and distinct from the environment. In past strategic planning processes, the environment has been treated as a given from which we have taken a series of assumptions necessary to produce the plan. This isolated perspective has fostered the problems we are now experiencing with the planning and forecasting process.

Business environmental assessment can help us deal with our dynamic business surroundings by formally recognizing environmental influences. Business environmental assessment is a methodology for handling external issues that will have significant impact on the organization. It attempts to identify emerging threats and opportunities which are the results of environmental changes. Effective environmental scanning helps us anticipate problems before they occur rather than react after they happen. It focuses on future events and issues and the necessary current decisions to profit by them.

Environmental assessment covers a wide range of topics and influences. Indeed it is this breath of analysis that makes it unique. Some of the areas of interest include the following:

- Economics.
- Technology.
- Government and politics.
- Social.
- Marketplace and competition.
- Manpower and capital resources.
- World affairs.
- Corporate environment.
- Employees and shareholders.

Based on the above description, an environmental assessment function can make the following contributions:

- Create a proactive planning system which will attempt to anticipate changes rather than react to them.
- Look at a wide range of emerging situations, their interrelationships, and their impact on the company.
- Provide a focal point on which to coordinate and facilitate the environmental scanning effort.
- Heighten management's overall awareness of events in the external environment and thus sensitize them to look for opportunities in these changing surroundings.

These contributions can result in a more aggressive organization that is seeking opportunities in a changing world rather than reacting and coping with events.

STEP 3.   DEFINE GOALS

Environmental assessment goals should be defined in light of company philosophy, organizational behavior, and planning sophistication/ maturity. Environmental scanning is a relatively new function in the

---

FIGURE 1   Questions of Environmental Assessment Factors

---

(1)   If you could have perfect information about five external factors which impact on our operation, what would they be? (For example, crude oil prices, GNP deflator, etc.)

(2)   What five external factors do you see as the major threats to our business?

(3)   What five factors would you like to know about our competitors' future plans?

(4)   If you were asked to define a company strategic direction, what five external factors would you feel would be the most critical in performing this task?

(5)   What five external areas would be the most likely to show changes which would be most favorable to the company's future?

---

young discipline of strategic planning. In introducing such a function to an organization, the following questions should be addressed:

- How does the organization accept new ideas and new processes?
- Is there open communication within the company or will this function have to establish new links?
- Does the company have an established strategic planning process and how is it viewed?
- Does the company environment foster creative thought?

The answers to these questions will indicate if the environmental assessment concept will be accepted into the organization.

One way of testing the organization's acceptance of such a group would be through interviews with senior management from each of the operating and staff functions. These interviews could be used to obtain management's perception of the expected contribution of such a function, which external issues they felt most important, and how they might participate in the external scanning process.

This interview process was conducted at Sun Exploration and Production's operating division. Environmental assessment was depicted as a source of help and guidance rather than another activity to consume management time. The help would be provided by guiding management in interpreting and understanding the business setting in which the company operated and in developing a perspective of possible future events which provide threats and opportunities.

The interviews were preceded by a memo describing the environmental assessment concept and posing a series of questions on the external environment. Responses to the questions were discussed in the interviews. Suggested questions are shown in Figure 1.

These interviews achieved several results. First, they were a formal introduction of the environmental assessment concept to management.

Second, the interviews initiated the environmental scanning process by getting people to think about the critical factors in their environment. Lastly, the results were used to define those variables which management felt were worth watching most carefully.

Based on these interviews a series of three goals can be developed. The first goal should be to become very knowledgeable about the external business environment. This intelligence should be focused, but not limited to, the major management concerns. The next goal is to define threats and opportunities in this environment. The third goal is to incorporate these findings in the management decision making process.

These goals translate into three basic duties which every environmental assessment function must perform.

- Obtaining information about the external environment.
- Assessing, analyzing and evaluating this information.
- Communicating this information to management.

STEP 4. ORGANIZE TO MEET GOALS

In organizing the environmental assessment function a number of different organizational formats can be considered:

- Irregular, periodic or continuous effort.
- Internal vs. external group.
- Full-time vs. part time effort.
- Centralized vs. decentralized.

There are three basic approaches to environmental scanning efforts: irregular, periodic and continuous. Irregular systems are characterized by the reactive nature of planning as well as environmental scanning. This system is created to solve a current crisis. This approach attempts to reduce uncertainty in the current and short-term future. As a result, they tend to be band-aid approaches to problems which rely on past coping techniques.

Periodic systems are more sophisticated and complex. While the focus of these systems is still problem solving, they exhibit greater proactive characteristics. While they are forecasting oriented, the forecasts that they produce are limited in their scope and methodologies. Such systems analyze problems on a periodic basis and do not provide for continuous environmental monitoring.

Continuous systems represent the ideal environmental assessment process. In these systems the focus shifts from problem-solving to opportunity-finding. There is also a realization that planning systems contribute to the growth and survival of the organizations in a proactive way. Because of this realization, these systems draw on a variety of company expertise and environmental scanning becomes a structured activity. These systems attempt to enhance the organization's capability to deal with environmental uncertainty. It is this ideal system that we would propose installing in our organization.

Should an environmental assessment function be an internal group or an external function? This is primarily a consequence of the expenditures the company is willing and able to make in this area. Organizations can have an effective process by selecting either alternative. A small internal group can be developed. This group would coordinate the environmental scanning process, develop information sources, prepare analyses and forecasts, and lead discussions on environmental issues. Alternatively, an outside consultant can be retained to perform these same duties. Outside consultants have the advantages of a broad information base and an unbiased viewpoint. The disadvantage in using consultants is their lack of knowledge of company philosophy and strengths and weaknesses. For the situation discussed here we are assuming that an internal group is created.

Generally, the environmental assessment function is established within the planning organization. Placing the effort here provides for good communication with the strategic planners and allows environmental assessment to take advantage of already existing lines of communication.

At Sun Exploration and Production's operating division, the group was established as a full-time continuous function in the Planning Department. The group contained two professionals and one secretary.

Most organizations perform environmental assessment on a part-time basis. The persons assigned to identify emerging environmental issues are pulled from other groups and have other responsibilities and interests competing for their time. Unfortunately, in many organizations such a part-time task force is not effective. The person's main job takes so much time that the environmental scanning effort becomes diluted. Balancing this drawback is the necessity to include representation from all the company line and staff functions in the environmental scanning process. We chose to address this problem through use of an external environment council.

The purpose of the external environmental council was to develop a consensus viewpoint of the future and to explore opportunities and threats for the division. The council was composed of planning representatives from the line and staff functions. This group met monthly to discuss topics in the external business environment and what effect they might have on operations. In this way the group served as a permanent environmental assessment scanning function.

The monthly meeting consisted of a presentation by the environmental assessment group and/or outside consultants followed by discussion. Follow-up work, based on questions posed during the meeting, was done by the environmental assessment group. By having the follow-up work done by the environmental assessment group, the participants were relieved from a great deal of the work load. They were allowed to make their most effective contributions by guiding and directing the environmental scanning effort through focusing the group's investigations onto new and different external areas.

Another organizational question is the appropriate division of such activities between corporate headquarters staff and divisional management. In general, the closer you can perform environmental scanning to the operations most affected the more attention it will get and the better intelligence you will be able to retrieve. However, there is some work which might best be left to corporate headquarters staff. Specifically, headquarters staff should serve as a focal point for all economic and federal regulatory monitoring efforts. Other issues such as the local regulatory situation, operating costs, machinery and manpower availability should be addressed by the specific divisions which they impact.

At this point it will be necessary to name an individual to lead your environmental scanning effort. This person should be a dedicated career planning professional with at least ten years of experience. Selection of the appropriate candidate should be based on experience, organizational fit, and analytical and communication skills.

STEP 5.   DEVELOP TACTICAL PLANS

In order to meet the goals set in Step 3, it is necessary to develop a set of tactical plans which describe specific short-term actions. For example, at Sun Exploration and Production's operating division, the following short-term actions (grouped by primary duty) were defined:

1. Obtain information about the external environment by developing a series of historical data bases.
2. Assess, analyze, and evaluate this information.
   a. Hire and train necessary staff.
   b. Obtain a natural gas supply/demand model.
   c. Obtain a gas price forecasting program.
   d. Produce long-range forecasts for the strategic planning process.
3. Communicate this information to management.
   a. Develop an environmental assessment newsletter.
   b. Produce special topic reports on critical environmental factors.
   c. Organize and lead an external environmental council.

In the next three sections we will examine these tactical plans in more detail.

STEP 6.   OBTAIN INFORMATION

As no army can run without food, no environmental assessment group can function without data. The primary tasks in obtaining this information are:

- Identify management needs for business environment information and establish priorities for these needs.
- Identify and secure both raw and processed information and data relevant to management needs from both internal and external sources.
- Develop and manage data bases to facilitate rapid access to and analysis of such information.

The identification of management needs of data was aided by the management interviews in Step 3. These needs were defined by a series of discussions with senior managers from each of the operating and staff functions. The interviews indicated management's perceptions of the most critical issues and the supporting statistics which environmental assessment needed to obtain.

The environmental scanning group also needs to be aware of specific data needs required for the company planning process. The information requirements should be coordinated with line and staff planners.

The last information need could be described as the library function. Invariably, other groups in the organization will come to an environmental assessment group to ask for statistics and reports. Unfortunately, in some cases, this becomes the primary function of this group.

After the required data needs are identified, it is necessary to obtain the information to support these needs. There are several sources for this information:

- Information media—newspapers, journals, radio and television, and libraries.
- Data bases—public, private, computer, and/or hardcopy.
- Consultants.
- Internal sources—for company specific information and competitor information.

Most people are familiar with published journals and periodicals. However, computer data bases are now becoming more available. According to *The Wall Street Journal*, computer data bases are being sold by about 240 marketers. Almost 1,600 data banks in about 275 subject areas are now available to the public. Even personal computer users can access information on stock quotes, financial information, newsletters, descriptive indexes of articles, economic forecasts, etc.

The availability of computer data banks allows the environmental assessment function to satisfy the last duty which is to develop and manage data bases to facilitate rapid access to and analysis of information. With the variety of data bases available there is really no need to develop your own. The problem becomes choosing the appropriate bases for your organization. In choosing a computer data base system, the following factors should be considered:

- Cost effectiveness.
- Information compatibility—time series match needs.
- Ease in retrieval.
- Reporting systems available tables, statistical analysis, graphs.
- Overall system support—technical and programming help.

With an information system in place, environmental assessment can then begin work on analyzing and evaluating the data.

STEP 7.   OBTAIN ANALYTICAL TOOLS

The assessment and analysis function requires the environmental scanning group to integrate, interpret and assess environmental information to determine impacts on the company's current business operations and decisions and to project trends and scenarios relevant to future business directions. Essentially, environmental scanning must identify threats and opportunities facing the company based on a forecast of the future business environment.

Environmental assessment needs techniques and analytical tools to forecast this future environment. Subjective and objective methods are generally used to make these forecasts. The least structured of these methods are based on experience and intuitive judgments. Subjective methods make the assumption that the past is a valid guide to the future. Objective methods are designed to reduce the impacts of personal bias. Objective methods use models to describe interactions among many variables in complex systems. These models can be used to test system responses to a number of different stimuli. The choice of techniques available to a particular company, time period, or circumstance is a matter of judgment. However, the use of several techniques is generally recommended. The results from a model should be evaluated against expert experience and judgment.

Planning professionals have rated the potential usefulness and actual usage of various scanning and forecasting methodologies. This survey indicated that scenario writing was the single most important technique.

Our techniques centered around scenario building using objective models. For example, in producing our long-range forecast we developed a series of natural gas pricing scenarios. We then assessed the impact of these prices on supply and demand by using gas supply forecasting and energy demand modeling computer programs.

The environmental assessment group should have a variety of tools and techniques available which can be applied as the situation warrants. The tools should be easy to use and cost effective. Generally, it is more economical to purchase and use existing models and techniques rather than to develop your own. The techniques must be easy to use so that time will not be wasted in initial training and re-learning programs each time they are applied.

Our environmental assessment group used a variety of computer based techniques:

- General statistical packages.
- Simple rapid plotting programs.
- Price forecasting programs.
- Timesharing access to energy and economic models.
- Operating cost forecasting programs.

These programs and models gave us the arsenal necessary to analyze and assess some of the problems we faced.

STEP 8. DEVELOP COMMUNICATION DEVICES

One of the most important duties of the environmental assessment function is to communicate an analysis of external environment trends and events to management. Therefore, to have an effective environmental assessment function there needs to be good communication between the group and its constituents. There are several devices which can be used to achieve this communication. We employed a number of different methods.

The first techique we used was a monthly newsletter to highlight current and future environmental trends. This newsletter contained a concise reporting of the business environment situation with an emphasis on the strategic perspectives. The audience for this newsletter was senior level managers. The newsletter was a one page document which was punched for saving in a three-ring binder. The copy was printed on both sides of the page with three columns on each page. The format included liberal use of graphs and charts.

Another communication device was the environmental assessment special topic report. These analyses were prepared periodically on a variety of topics and included a formal written report followed by a brief oral presentation. These reports were distributed to interested company and corporate managers. The environmental assessment group developed special topic reports on the impact of the electric heat pump on residential natural gas consumption, industrial sector gas consumption, the available supply of Canadian and Mexican Gas exports, and trends in drilling costs.

An external environment council was created with representation from the company planning staffs. This council served as an additional means to present information to management as well as to provide a formal device for dialogue on external environment issues.

There should also be good informal communication between the rest of the planning group and the environmental assessment group. The environmental assessment group should be included in all phases of the strategic planning process so that they can see first hand the effect external forecasts have on company performance projections.

The communication role of environmental assessment should not be treated lightly. Good information and analysis are useless unless put into the right hands at the right time. The success of an environmental assessment organization can be compared to a three-legged stool. The first leg is information, the second is analysis, and the third leg is communication. Without strength in all of the legs the stool soon collapses.

STEP 9.   USE THE RESULTS

After performing Steps 1 through 8 your organization should have an environmental assessment function in place. Its effectiveness will depend on if and how the results are used.

The primary use of the environmental assessment effort should be in generating assumptions for the long-range and strategic planning processes. Environmental scanning should also be employed as a control function to monitor this environment for changes which might alter the plan.

In addition to this primary contribution, with wide-spread use of environmental scanning, your organization should expect to experience the following results:

- Heightened management awareness in the external environment resulting in a broader management perspective.
- Development of early warning systems which anticipate threats or opportunities for the company.
- A practive rather than reactive management posture.
- Improved planning and forecasting efforts.
- Greater ownership in the assumptions used to generate long range and strategic plans.

I hope these steps will serve as useful guidelines in developing your own environmental scanning effort.

REFERENCES

Liam Fahey, William R. King, Vadake K. Narayanan, "Environmental Scanning and Forecasting in Strategic Planning—The State of the Art," *Long Range Planning,* (February 1981, Volume 14, No. 1), pp. 32–39.

John D. Stoffels, "Environmental Scanning for Future Success," *Managerial Planning,* (November-December 1982, Volume 31, Number 3), pp. 4–12.

The Wall Street Journal, May 12, 1983, p. 1.

"A Budding Mass Market for Data Bases," *Business Week,* (January 17, 1983), pp. 128–131.

International Competitor Analysis

Diane J. Garsombke

Irwin Magnetics, a medium-sized office equipment firm located in Ann Arbor, Michigan, was faced with a slumping U.S. market due to increased domestic competition. In trying to find new markets, a key requirement was locating areas where competitors were not already entrenched. After performing a competitor analysis, managers of Irwin identified both a large demand for personal computers and an absence of their U.S. multinational competitors in India. Within two years Irwin became one of that country's top suppliers of microcomputers. This success was triggered by Irwin's ability to gather data on its competitors, determine markets with high demand, and quickly supply appropriate technology to a new-found market opportunity.

- S. D. Warren, a pulp and paper firm located in Westbrook, Maine, discovered that its international rivals from Germany and Japan were gaining a competitive advantage by adopting automation, computerization, and robotization. Warned by this competitor intelligence, the mill manager and vice president developed resource-allocation strategies that would help the firm's major U.S. plant achieve an 80 percent level of computerization. Top management at S. D. Warren became convinced that technological adaptation was the critical success factor for firms in the globally competitive forest products industry.
- When General Mills agreed to produce and market Yoplait, the yogurt product of the French firm Sodima-Yoplait, GM discovered that its international competitors catered to cultural differences in customer's eating habits. The French consider yogurt a dessert to be eaten after lunch or dinner, whereas the American consumer regards yogurt as a meal at lunchtime or a healthful snack. From an analysis of the size of international competitors' packages, the company real-

Source: Diane J. Garsombke, "International Competitor Analysis," *Planning Review* 17, no. 3 (May/June 1989), pp. 42–47.

ized that meal-sized containers of yogurt would be needed for the American market and snack-sized containers for the French market. In the U.S., Yoplait yogurt was packaged individually, but for the French market it had to be put up in packs of four, six, or eight individual containers for family-style desserts.

These three businesses shared two common experiences. One, competition forced them to gather intelligence about their international competitors. Two, by studying the goals of their competitors, and the methods these rivals used to accomplish their goals, the three firms rethought their marketing strategies.

THE CATALYST TO INTERNATIONAL COMPETITOR ANALYSIS

What underlies this growing use of international competitor analysis? A major factor, emphasized almost daily in the media, is the growth of competition, particularly international competition, in the U.S. market. As a responding offensive strategy, many U.S. firms are choosing to attack international competitors in their home markets. American executives expect their foreign-based competitors to respond by withdrawing resources or redirecting their emphasis away from the U.S. market in order to defend their "home turf." This would appreciably ease the stress on U.S. markets.

Another factor spurring international competition is increased U.S. government emphasis on exporting and overseas business opportunities. Federal programs and legislation, such as The Export Trading Company Act of 1984, the U.S. Trade Bill with Canada, and the Caribbean Basin Initiative, were developed to encourage the over 2,000 U.S. small businesses to take another look at the international opportunities awaiting them. This internationalizing trend, in turn, fuels the need and desire for information regarding competitors in countries and regions around the globe.

The companies that thrive in global markets will be those that know their international competitors well and create plans to gain competitive advantage from this knowledge.

CHARACTERISTICS OF INTERNATIONAL COMPETITOR ANALYSIS

Increasing numbers of U.S. firms are entering foreign markets that are both unfamiliar and untested. They are competing against new as well as established thriving international firms from both developed and developing countries. To protect themselves, U.S. firms will need to anticipate how the players, the playing field, and the approach and processes in international intelligence gathering differ from the domestic variety.

The International Players

Many U.S. firms are already gathering information about the international firms with whom they battle for the U.S. market. But the *modus operandi* of these competitors may differ from country to country. Ford and General Motors executives, for instance, have learned, via their international competitor analysis, that Honda's method of selling cars in Japan is more personalized than the approach they use in America. In Japan, salespeople visit their customers' homes with car style/color catalogs and drive the selected car to the buyer's doorsteps to close the deal.

Adapting the Systematic Approach

A systematic approach to international competitor analysis enables decision makers to concentrate their efforts on the most viable overseas market opportunities.

For example, in the availability of information resources, the investigator will have to rely on new sources such as foreign embassies/consulates; special collection libraries in the U.S. (like Harvard's Yenching Library's collection on China); international computerized data bases (such as D & B-International: Dun's Market Identifiers, Moody's Corporate News-International, and the BBC's External News Service); foreign periodical services (like German News Company and Overseas Courier Service); and the resource centers of the Department of Commerce's district/state offices.

Competitor analysis usually involves research using both secondary and primary information sources. There is normally a time lag involved with all published secondary sources (the time it takes to gather and publish information) as compared to primary sources (executives can speak directly to the sales force—and customers, suppliers, and other industry experts are usually only a phone call away). In addition to an even longer time lag for foreign published sources (due to distance and time for translation), it is often more difficult to call upon primary sources for international competitor analysis.

Primary research through interviews with customers, suppliers, and security analysts should be carefully and continually compiled. Be aware that informal "cold" calls on foreigners are often unacceptable in business cultures that value formality or social ties such as in the Middle East, South America, and Asia. This means that information must be gathered through official introduction or by friends, contacts, and carefully developed networks in the country of interest.

Source Credibility

Especially in developing and lesser developed countries, the credibility and reliability of secondary sources should be suspect. Census data can be tampered with by government officials for propaganda purposes or it may be restricted. A U.S. CEO reports that in South Korea, for instance, even official figures can be conflicting depending on the source (there are discrepancies in data from the Bank of Korea, the Trade Ministry, and the Commerce Ministry). A U.S. textbook representative suggests that in Singapore the government inflates the student enrollment figures in order to get higher World Bank assistance. Also, even in developed countries where information may be gathered systematically, it can be categorized differently than in the U.S., making comparisons of facts and figures across countries misleading. International economic advisors to countries like Taiwan are quick to point out that their calculations of the foreign trade deficit, for example, do not match those of their U.S. counterparts.

Unlevel Playing Field

U.S. firms will have to investigate both business and sociocultural factors to truly understand the strategies of their foreign competitors. These include:

- Strong country nationalism.
- Market pioneer advantage.
- Protectionist trade measures, both tariff and nontariff.
- Special treatment by the government in the form of subsidies, contracts, and resources.

FIVE STEPS TO INTERNATIONAL COMPETITOR ANALYSIS

International competitor analysis deductively links the macro and micro environments. A manager selects the scope of the market and analyzes a particular market niche in one country or a global perspective of the marketplace. The analysis process is a blend of researching the market, making cross-cultural comparisons, and judging the fit between strategies and situations.

The steps to international competitor analysis include:

- Studying the environment of the country or overseas market of interest.
- Analyzing strengths and weaknesses of international competitors with respect to the environment.
- Investigating the goals and strategies of international competitors.
- Assessing the firm's competitive position.
- Selecting strategies to compete internationally and globally, taking into account possible competitor reactions.

These five process steps of international competitor analysis require unique sets of information. Types and location of data sources differ depending upon the data needed for each step.

Step 1.   Study the Environment of the Country or Overseas Market of Interest

To get a picture of an industry in a foreign country or market, a company needs to study the external environment. Top priority must be given to defining the market/competitor issues. Is there a big enough market in this country or region to provide an opportunity? How intense is the competition (the number of foreign competitors, their fierceness, do they go in for extreme price cutting or cutthroat tactics)? A second priority should be delineating the sociocultural issues. Are there changes in the fabric of society that will present unique opportunities for U.S. firms? For example, in developing countries, young peoples' desires for high-tech Western products are growing.

Eliminate Ethnocentrism.   In international competitor analysis one of the crucial premises is that "to really understand a competitor, the decision maker must put on the competitor's shoes." Thus, a successful competitor analysis of a South Korean firm, for example, begins with a holistic understanding of the South Korean business environment. If American CEOs fail to see the world as their South Korean counterparts see it, there is a great risk that they will be unable to predict future moves accurately.

U.S. executives should search for any distinct advantages that international firms may have because of laws, trade barriers, regulations, technology, local economic conditions, and preferential governmental policies. For example, careful study of the royal Saudi family uncovered the special relationships of each family member to the government, allowing Citgo to penetrate the Saudi Arabian market and overcome the stranglehold its international competitor, Aramco, had developed by monitoring the Middle East for decades.

Another illustration in the electronics industry shows the value of a thorough investigation into the laws of a country. Brazilian law regarding local manufacture and local sourcing of raw materials strongly favors Brazilian electronics firms. This protectionism has effectively limited the sales of U.S. computer firms for the last five years. Recently, however, IBM found a loophole. Technically, the Brazilian law only pertains to new, not used, equipment. As a result, IBM initiated an upgrade buy-back arrangement with existing U.S. customers and is gaining a foothold in the South American market by selling used computer hardware to Brazilian customers.

Sometimes changes in government policies are brought about because of a change in political parties or a shift in the economic situation. In his environmental scanning, the French subsidiary manager of a Chicago-based multinational, Evans Machinery, read a *Business Europe* article in which the author concluded that "pressure from the government and the French business community to 'buy French' had increased dramatically." To corroborate this piece of information, the manager consulted a key executive at Renault, who confirmed that policy makers were convinced the government now felt that French firms needed protection. This means the French subsidiary executive must develop new strategies to cope with the political and economic pressures that are changing his firm's environment.

General environmental information of this type can be found in secondary sources such as *Citibank World Outlook,* and the Department of Commerce's *Overseas Business Reports, Global Market Surveys,* and *Country Market Sectoral Surveys.* Embassy trade officials from the country of interest and District Officers from the Department of Commerce in Washington, D.C., are primary resources for market-specific data. Country- or region-specific information can be found in special collection libraries (like the African and Middle Eastern Division of the Library of Congress, Washington, D.C.; the American Academy of Asian Studies Library in San Francisco; and the Latin American Data Bank Library at the University of Florida in Gainesville.

Step 2.   Analyze Strengths and Weaknesses of Competitors with Respect to the Environment

Look at each of the functional aspects of international competitors in light of the local environments. Summarize the strengths and weaknesses of each rival firm. In marketing, for example, do any environmental characteristics create greater capabilities or vulnerabilities for your firm? Some questions to ask are:

- Does the firm have a strong brand image in the local market? Are local consumers highly nationalistic?
- Are there any unique features or packaging? In particular, are these specs geared toward the values or characteristics of local consumers (for example, the baking dishes and kitchen utensils sold by Japanese firms are much smaller so they will fit the typically small oven sizes and tinier hands of Asian housewives).
- Does your firm excel in delivery to buyers? This could be an important competitive advantage in a nation with a variegated and complicated distribution system.
- Is location critical? Retail space may be at a premium in some cities.
- Are there vulnerabilities in the price-quality relationship?
- How effective are the themes and messages used in the promotional effort? Are they targeted toward a particular international, regional, or country market?

In finance, it is important to assess the profitability, efficiency and soundness of each international firm in relation to the industry posture. In human resources, a key question might be: Does the corporate culture promote or detract from competitiveness?

For a manufacturing business, the processes of researching how competitors produce products in an efficient and effective manner are important. Service firms will need to evaluate how well international rivals are providing what they promise. Are product/services meeting the desires of customers? How innovative is the firm in product/service development? Does the company take advantage of economies of scale on a local, regional, or worldwide basis?

To illustrate the relative capabilities of different international firms, the world market for kraftlinerboard (a product that is used primarily for the packaging of industrial or fruit products on a worldwide basis) is a good example. U.S. companies on the whole have superior cost position because of abundant forest resources, lower relative labor costs, and energy availability. Their Scandinavian and Japanese rivals have developed higher value-added paper products such as printing and writing papers to offset their cost disadvantage.

Brazilian firms in the industry are currently developing their softwood forests and conserving foreign currency for needed infrastructure improvements. They will most certainly become major competitors in the next decade. To remain cost leaders in the world market, U.S. firms need to maintain their relatively lower costs of raw materials, labor, and energy. But they must also monitor currency fluctuations and economic developments in Latin America and Asia, which could threaten their future competitiveness.

Some well-established sources of information on individual international competitors resemble familiar U.S. publications. Britain's Extel is similar to Moody's Investors manuals; in Europe, "Informations Internationales" is comparable to Value Line; two companies in Japan, Nilekei and Toyo Keizai, produce summaries of annual and quarterly reports, much like Standard and Poor's; foreign brokerage houses in New York, such as Nikko Securities, compile analytical reports on companies from their home country.

A few examples of the available international business and trade journals include: *World Construction,* the Asian and European editions of *The Wall Street Journal, Ekonomska Politika* (a weekly business magazine of Yugoslavian companies), *Canadian Business* (like *Fortune,* it ranks the leading 500 Canadian firms) and *International Business Week.*

Actual product comparisons require more direct approaches. Such comparisons can be found by carefully reading product brochures, watching competitor advertisements, talking with other firms' salespeople/customers, or by conducting reverse engineering—taking the competitor's product apart. General Motors routinely buys the products of rival firms and analyzes them to see if the models have any unique advantages. Some say that the first personal computer designed in the U.S.S.R. was a result of reverse engineering performed on Apple Computer Inc.'s Apple II model.

Step 3. Investigate the Goals and Strategies of International Competitors

Identifying the goals of an international competitor provides information on the direction and intensity of the competition.

Quantitative and Qualitative Goals. More quantitative goals such as profitability, growth, leverage, and market share can be found in financial reports, stock exchange reports, prospectuses, or annual reports.

Qualitative goals refer to image, customer loyalty, stockholder stability, and employee satisfaction. Information on these areas can also be found in annual reports and articles written about firms being researched. For example, when the CEO of a Hungarian medical equipment multinational firm explained in a press release that his goal was to make a profit in Africa in 10 to 15 years, reporters were stunned— why such a modest goal? He explained that the company anticipated that it would take a decade or longer to get established in the African markets. Such long-term goals signal the staying power and tenacity of international competitors.

CEO Watching. This is often a useful way to assess an overseas competitor firm's goals. In firms with a strong corporate culture, the philosophy, values, and style of the top executives form the organizational value system and shape the future direction of the firm. Are the CEOs aggressive or conservative; risk oriented or risk averse; authoritarian or people oriented; lazy or tireless? This information can provide subtle clues that lead to accurate guesses on where an international firm is heading.

In addition, the goals of the firm set the stage for future actions and strategies. For example, if the international competitor chooses aggressive goals, the strategies could be more daring, such as joint ventures with host national firms or strong emphasis on new product/service development which are region-, country-, or culture-specific rather than more status quo types of strategies, such as exporting without any product modifications or more passive modes of entry.

Sometimes strategies and goals are revealed explicitly by top managers. For example, when Akeo Morita, chairman of the Sony Corporation, announced Sony's intention to enter the business machine market against IBM and Xerox, he revealed the corporate goal by predicting that eventually business machine sales would exceed a third of Sony's total sales volume.

Step 4.   Assess Firm's Competitive Position Vis-à-Vis International Competitors

Michael Porter, a strong proponent of competitor analysis, emphasizes following up on five areas of analysis:

- Present and future capabilities in the core functional areas.
- Future resource capacity for growth.
- Existing resource capacity for quick response to a competitive move.
- Flexibility and adaptability to changes in the industry or external environment.
- Ability to sustain a fight.

This framework is useful in the global arena as well. What's more important is how a firm compares with its competitors in the targeted country or overseas market. In other words, does the firm have stronger functional capabilities, greater future growth capacity, a quicker response to competitive moves, more flexibility, or a more sustainable advantage than its rivals? A competitive position matrix for each international market of interest (or different countries, regional groupings, or global customer segmentation) can be very useful in visualizing a firm's international stance. For example, Exhibit 1 analyzes a U.S. specialty seafood firm's competitive profile in the country market of Malaysia.

Here's where the firm sizes itself up against the facts gathered about the competition. It answers the key question: "What is the firm's com-

EXHIBIT 1 A U.S. Firm Compared with Its International Competitors in Malaysian Market

Comparison Criteria	A (U.S. MNC)	B (Korean MNC)	C (Local Malaysian Firm)	D (Japanese MNC)	E (Local Malaysian Firm)
Marketing capability	0	0	0	0	−
Manufacturing capability	0	+	0	0	0
R&D capability	0	0	0	−	0
HRM capability	0	0	0	0	0
Financial capability	+	−	0	0	−
Future growth of resources	+	0	−	0	−
Quickness	−	0	+	−	0
Flexibility/adaptability	0	+	+	0	0
Sustainability	+	0	0	0	−

Key: + = *firm is better relative to competition.*
  0 = *firm is same as competition.*
  − = *firm is poorer relative to competition.*

petitive position in the international market?" In this case, the U.S. CEO notes that the firm's access to resources gives it a sustainable advantage; however, size and bureaucracy weigh against the company's ability to respond quickly to market opportunities in Malaysia's seafood industry when compared to South Korean, Japanese, and Malaysian competitors. The next step is to focus on the implications of this strength and weakness analysis for future strategies.

Step 5. Select Strategies to Compete Internationally and Globally Taking into Account Possible Competitor Reactions

The final step is to translate these relative comparisons into action. What are the implications of the analysis for international strategy formulation?

This analysis should both highlight company needs (resources, training, product development, and market research) and pinpoint which markets maximize opportunities. Firms may find they can avoid costly battles or collision courses with resource-rich competitors by selecting "safe" market niches. By studying a market's history, firms can develop strategies that will avoid others' mistakes, or that will take advantage of opportunities others have missed.

For example, Chrysler's international competitor analysis showed the company had a weak competitive position—particularly against the Japanese. Chrysler's deteriorating position was caused by high labor and parts costs in the U.S., low trade barriers for Japanese firms in the U.S. (lifting of Voluntary Restraint Agreement by the Reagan Administration), and high tariff barriers for Chrysler in Japan. To overcome these weaknesses, the company shifted to a more global-oriented strategy, which included sourcing of parts in Malaysia and Mexico as well as a joint venture with Mitsubishi Motors to make a low-priced, largely plastic modular component car by 1989. International competitor analysis enabled Chrysler to strengthen its position against rival Japanese firms, and it considerably opened up the Asian market.

Sometimes a firm is faced with international competitors who have been in a country market for many years and have made considerable investment in adapting their strategies to fit the local environment. In this situation, new entrants may be more successful with innovative responses and niche strategies.

This was Canon's choice when it analyzed competitors' actions in the Japanese copier market. All the existing international competitors had made major modifications to their machines to handle oversized Japanese paper (larger than the typical legal-sized paper in other countries). Upon further research, Canon determined that design changes would create a major price disadvantage because of the resource outlay required. Therefore, instead of trying to copycat rivals, Canon came up with a creative solution: a model that offers an added feature—exact copies of Japanese business cards. The changes were easily made, and the company capitalized on an opportunity that international rivals had overlooked—the common Japanese business practice of exchanging business cards.

CRITICAL ISSUES FOR THE FUTURE

At present, there is no centralized sourcebook or clearinghouse for categorizing the wide variety of information on international firms. The worldwide yellow pages service being compiled by International Business Clearinghouse, Western Union, and ITT will be an excellent sourcebook but limited in the type of information given, such as location, telephone, telex, and product or service offered by specific international businesses.

There is a need for a real commitment on the part of U.S. businesses to gather and share international competitor information. It will undoubtedly involve considerable time, effort, money, and specialized resources (telecommunications and translators) to gain an in-depth knowledge of international competitors.

Also, with the growing need for up-to-date and accurate information on international competitors in the U.S., there will be a greater demand for computerized global data bases. (See "Using On-Line Information for Strategic Advantage" by James McGrane in the November/December 1987 issue of *Planning Review* for the case study in which Mead conducted international competitor analysis using the global NEXIS data base, DIALOG, and ECLIPSE computerized services.) Commercial service firms like Business International are broadening their publication offerings with more extensive and current reviews of industries within certain countries and regions.

In the future, the successful firms will be the ones that broaden their domestic competitor intelligence capabilities. This requires a strong commitment from top management to conduct ongoing international competitor analysis. Such a commitment includes resource allocation, studying international competitors' culture and philosophies, and creating strategic plans based on international intelligence.

FURTHER READING

Aggarwal, Raj, "The Strategic Challenge of the Evolving Global Economy," *Business Horizons,* (July–August, 1987).

Callahan, Joseph M., "Chrysler's New Market-Driven Global Strategy," *Automotive Industries,* (June, 1985).

Chandran, Rajan; Hernandez, Sigfriedo; and Stanton, John L., "The Marketing Research Problems in Latin America," *Journal of the Market Research Society,* 2, 24, (1983).

Eells, Richard and Nehemkis, Peter, *Corporate Intelligence and Espionage: A Blueprint for Executive Decision Making.* New York: Macmillan Publishing Company, 1984.

Engel, Alan K., "Number One in Competitor Intelligence," *Across the Board,* 24 (December, 1987).

Fuld, Leonard M., "How to Gather Foreign Intelligence Without Leaving Home," *Marketing News,* (January 4, 1988).

Fuld, Leonard M., *Monitoring the Competition: Finding Out What's Really Going On Over There.* New York: John Wiley & Sons, 1988.

Hayes, Robert H., *Restoring Our Competitive Edge: Competing Through Manufacturing.* New York: John Wiley & Sons, 1984.

Hershey, Robert, "Commercial Intelligence on a Shoe String," *Harvard Business Review,* (September–October, 1980).

Levitt, Theodore, "The Globalization of Markets," *Harvard Business Review,* (May–June, 1982).

Mascarenhas, Briance, "International Strategies of Non-Dominant Firms," *Journal of International Business Studies*, 17 (Spring, 1988).

McNally, George, "Global Marketing: It's Not Just Possible—It's Imperative," *Business Marketing,* (April, 1986).

Montgomery, D. B., and Weinberg, C. E., "Towards Strategic Intelligence Systems, *Journal of Marketing,* (Fall, 1979).

Pezeshkpur, Changiz, "Systematic Approach to Finding Export Opportunities," *Harvard Business Review,* (September–October, 1979).

A Manager's Guide for Evaluating Competitive Analysis Techniques

John E. Prescott and John H. Grant

Virtually all managers acknowledge the importance of understanding their industries and their competitors. As a result, interest has grown rapidly in the use of various competitive analysis techniques to help formulate and implement strategy. However, managers who want to conduct competitive analyses are faced with perplexing choices among a wide variety of techniques with different strengths and weaknesses, an abundance of internal and external data sources, an array of computer software packages, and constraints in terms of time, money, information, and personnel. Many managers are asking, "Where do I start?"

The efficient selection of appropriate techniques for a particular situation depends on a three-phase process of awareness and choice. First, what relevant techniques are available and how do they relate to one another? Second, what is the focus and scope of the competitive arena of interest? Third, what constraints on time and other resources limit the extent of analyses that can be undertaken? Our extensive review of the literature and of applications in several industries can help managers and analysts complete these three phases effectively.

UTILIZATION PROFILES

In order to assist managers to select and apply competitive analysis techniques, we developed a reference guide consisting in part of profiles describing various competitive analysis techniques (Table 1). These

Source: John E. Prescott and John H. Grant, "A Manager's Guide for Evaluating Competitive Analysis Techniques," *Interfaces* 18, no. 3 (May–June 1988), pp 10–22. Used with permission.

profiles can assist managers in several ways. We chose a broad array of techniques to illustrate the increasing variety of analytical options available. The key characteristics of each technique have been highlighted along with their typical advantages and limitations. This should help managers to identify the techniques best suited to their situations. Few competitive analyses can be successfully completed using a single technique; the guide can help managers to choose the combination of techniques that will address the issue most effectively and efficiently. We provide references that present additional operational details for each technique.

COMPETITIVE ANALYSIS TECHNIQUES

The utilization profiles array a diverse set of 21 techniques and evaluate them along 11 important dimensions. The techniques described below are sequenced beginning with broad industry-level techniques and moving to narrower functional area techniques. However, most of the techniques are applicable at either the corporate or the business-unit level. Detailed descriptions of the techniques can be found in Hax and Majluf [1984], Grant and King [1982], Porter [1980], and Prescott [1987].

- *Political and country risk analysis* assesses the types (asset, operational, profitability, personnel) and extent of risks from operating in foreign countries.
- *Industry scenarios* develop detailed, internally consistent descriptions of what various future structures of the industry may be like.
- *The economists' model of industry attractiveness* analyzes the five basic forces (bargaining power of suppliers and customers, threat of substitute products, threat of entry, and industry rivalry) driving industry competition.
- *BCG industry matrix* identifies the attractiveness of an industry based on the number of potential sources for achieving a competitive advantage and the size of the advantage that a leading business can achieve.
- *Industry segmentation* identifies discrete pockets of competition within an industry. The bases of segment identification are often product variety, buyer characteristics, channels of distribution, and geography.
- *PIMS* is an on-going data base of the Strategic Planning Institute which collects data describing business units' operating activities, their industries and competitors, their products and customers. The purpose is to assist planning efforts of the participating businesses.
- *A technological assessment* develops an understanding of the technological relationships and changes occurring in an industry.

- *Multipoint competition analysis* explores the implications of a situation in which diversified firms compete against each other in several markets.
- *Critical success factor analysis* identifies the few areas in which a business must do adequately in order to be successful.
- A *strategic group analysis* identifies groups of businesses which follow similar strategies, have similar administrative systems, tend to be affected by and respond to competitive moves and external events in similar ways.
- A *value chain analysis and field maps* identify the costs, operating characteristics, and interrelationships of a business's primary activities (that is, inbound logistics, operations, outbound logistics, marketing and sales, service) and supporting activities (that is, firm infrastructure, human resources management, technological development, procurement).
- *Experience curves* show that the costs of producing a product (service) decrease in a regular manner as the experience of producing it increases. The decrease in costs occurs over the total life of a product.
- *Stakeholder analysis and assumption surfacing and testing* identify and examine any individual or group goals that affect or are affected by the realization of the businesses' goals.
- *Market signaling* is any action by a competitor that provides a direct or indirect indication of its intentions, motives, goals, or internal situation.
- *Portfolio analysis* locates a corporation's businesses along dimensions of industry attractiveness and competitive position to help managers to make resource allocation decisions and to evaluate future cash flows and profitability potential.
- *Strengths and weaknesses analysis* identifies advantages and deficiencies in resources, skills, and capabilities for a business relative to its competitors.
- *Synergy analysis* examines tangible (raw material, production, distribution) and intangible (management know-how, reputation) benefits of shared activities among business units.
- *Financial statement analysis* assesses both the short-term health and long-term financial resources of a firm.
- *Value-based planning* evaluates strategies and strategic moves in light of their probable stock market effects and financing implications. (It does not refer to managerial values in our usage.)
- *Management profiles* examine the goals, backgrounds, and personalities of the individuals making strategic decisions in a competing firm or institution.
- *Reverse engineering* is purchasing and dismantling a competitor's product to identify how it was designed and constructed so that costs and quality can be estimated.

TABLE 1   Utilization Profiles of Competitive Analysis Techniques

Note: Twenty-one techniques are evaluated along 11 important dimensions. To use the table, locate the technique and evaluative dimension of interest. In the row and column intersection (cell), our assessment of a technique's characteristics as they apply to the dimension will be summarized. The

Dimensions	Resource Needs				Data Needs		
	Time			Managerial			
Techniques	Development	Execution	Costs	Skills	Sources	Availability	Timeliness
Political and country risk analysis	Long	Long	High	Conceptual Analytical Diagnostic	Literature search Informants Personal interviews	From analysis	Historical Current
Industry scenarios	Long	Long	High	Conceptual Analytical Diagnostic	Focus Groups Literature search Personal interviews	Customized	Future
Economists' model of industry attractive- ness	Moderate	Long	Medium	Technical Conceptual Diagnostic	Case study Personal interviews Literature search	Off-the-shelf but basically derived from analysis	Current
BCG industry matrix	Short	Moderate	Medium	Technical Conceptual Diagnostic	Literature search Personal interviews	From analysis	Current
Industry segmenta- tion	Moderate	Moderate	Medium	Conceptual Diagnostic Analytical	Case study Personal inverviews Literature search	From analysis	Current
PIMS	Moderate	Short	Medium	Technical Analytical	Data bases	Off-the-shelf	Current
Technological assessment	Long	Long	High	Technical Conceptual Analytical	Direct observation Participant observation Data bases Documents	From analysis Sometimes Customized	Future
Multipoint competition	Short	Moderate	Low to Medi- um	Conceptual Diagnostic	Literature search Personal interviews	From analysis	Current
Critical success factors	Short	Moderate	Medium	Conceptual Diagnostic Analytical	Literature search Case study	From analysis	Current
Strategic group analysis	Moderate	Short	Low	Conceputal Diagnostic	Literature search Personal interviews Case study	From analysis	Current

TABLE 1 *(continued)*

techniques are arranged in descending order from a broad industry level to a narrower functional level. Multiple entries for the managerial skills and sources and evaluative dimensions are in descending order of importance and priority, respectively.

Accuracy Constraints	Updating Requirements		Advantages	Limitations	References
	Frequency	Difficulty			
Availability	Periodic	Reanalyze	Understand other cultures or political positions and potential problem areas	Often evaluated using own norms Language problems Data often difficult to evaluate and can change rapidly if power positions change	Desta, 1985 Hofer and Haller, 1980
Assumption of sources	Ad hoc	Reconceptualize	Sensitize management to the need to adapt to industry evolution	Based upon assumptions subject to change Costs	Wack, 1985a, b Porter, 1985
Managerial skills	Ad hoc	Reconceptualize	Structured approach to examining industries Identifies competitors Basis for other in-depth analysis	Basic assumption that economic structure of industry is root of competition Drawing of industry boundaries	Porter, 1980
Managerial skills	Ad hoc	Reanalysis	Primarily a diagnostic tool for identifying profitable industry segments	Needs to be used in conjunction with other techniques such as industry analysis and CSFs	Pekar, 1982
Conceptual skills	Ad hoc	Reanalysis	Identifies pockets of opportunity Identifies pockets of future profits or areas under attack	Choosing segmentation dimensions Piecemeal approach to competition	Bonoma and Shapiro, 1983 Porter, 1985
Representativeness of businesses in data base	Periodic	Repetitive	Flexibility of use Variety of operations	Lack of organizational variables	Wagner, 1984 Schoeffler, Buzzell and Heaney, 1974 Ramanujam and Venkatraman, 1984
Financial support	Continuous	Reconceptualize	Keep abreast of key technological drivers	Expensive, continuous, difficult process	Petrov, 1982 Hayes and Wheelwright, 1979a, b
Sources	Ad hoc	Reanalysis	Identifies areas where a competitor may retaliate (vice-versa)	Typically ignores motives, skills, etc. of competitor	Karnani and Wernerfelt, 1985
Managerial skills	Periodic	Reanalysis	Fast, inexpensive method for focusing efforts	Often is superficial	Rockart, 1979 Leidecker and Bruno, 1984
Managerial skills	Periodic	Reanalyze	Fast, cheap, easy way to understand key competitors	Superficial; ignores firms outside industry	McGee and Thomas, 1986 Porter, 1980

TABLE 1 *(continued)*

Dimensions / Techniques	Resource Needs				Data Needs		
	Time			*Managerial Skills*	*Sources*	*Availability*	*Timeliness*
	Development	*Execution*	*Costs*				
Value-chain analysis and field maps	Short	Long	High	Technical Diagnostic	Case study Personal interviews Literature search	Customized	Current
Experience curves	Short	Moderate	Medium	Technical Diagnostic	Documents Personal interviews Direct observation	From analysis	Current
Stakeholder analysis and assumption surfacing and testing	Short	Moderate to High	Medium	Conceptual Diagnostic Analytical	Personal interviews Focus groups Literature search	Customized	Past Current
Marketing signaling	Moderate to Long	Continuous	Low	Conceptual Diagnostic Analytical	Documents Personal interviews Direct observation	From analysis	Future
Portfolio analysis	Moderate	Short	Low	Technical	Literature search Case study Personal interviews	From analysis	Current
Strength and weaknesses analysis	Short	Long	High	Interpersonal Technical Diagnostic	Personal interview Direct observation Case study	Customized	Current
Synergy analysis	Moderate	Long	High	Technical Diagnostic Conceptual	Documents Case study Personal interviews	Customized	Current
Financial statement analysis	Short	Short	Low	Technical Analytical	Documents Historical records Data bases	Off-the-shelf From analysis	Historical
Value-based planning	Long	Moderate to Long	Medium	Technical	Historical records Data bases	From analysis	Historical
Management profiles	Short	Short	Low	Interpersonal Technical	Personal interviews Informants Documents	From analysis	Current
Reverse engineering	Short	Varies	Varies	Technical	Product purchasing	Off-the-shelf	Current

TABLE 1 *(concluded)*

| Accuracy Constraints | Updating Requirements | | Advantages | Limitations | References |
	Frequency	Difficulty			
Sources	Ad hoc	Reanalyze	Best techniques for understanding operating details of a competitor or one's self	Data often difficult to obtain Slow, expensive	Kaiser, 1984 Porter, 1985
Sources	Ad hoc	Repetitive	Provides an understanding of cost and thus pricing dynamics Gives a picture of whether to compete on basis of costs	Based upon history which may not carry through to future	Hall and Howell, 1985 Hax and Majluf, 1984
Managerial skills	Periodic	Reanalyze	Introspection Attempts to get at underlying causes of behavior	Subject to misinterpretation	Freeman, 1984 Rowe, Mason, and Dickel, 1985
Managerial skills	Continuous	Reconceptualize	Early warning indicator	Misinterpretation Get off on the wrong direction	Porter, 1980
Sources	Periodic	Reanalyze	Visual summary Requires managers to think systematically about industry and competitive position Heuristic method of decision making	Superficial Assumes cash flow/profit drives decision	Hax and Majluf, 1984 Grant and King, 1982
Sources	Ad hoc	Reanalyze	Provides in-depth understanding of entire business capabilities Provides feedback for remedial action	Costly; long; cooperation of personnel essential Hierarchical position of manager influences perception	Stevenson, 1985, 1976
Sources	Ad hoc	Reanalyze	Shows cost or differentiation advantage as a result of sharing—staying power, exit decisions, response times	Data difficulties Time consuming	Porter, 1985
Sources	Periodic	Repetitive	Fast, easy, cheap handle on financial picture	Data problems Usually limited to public corporations	Hax and Majluf, 1984 Hofer and Schendel, 1978
Sources	Periodic	Repetitive	Simplicity—ability to compare alternatives and competitors	Basic assumption that maximizing stock price is primary goal. Difficult to implement for individual business units of multidivision company (private firm)	Reimann, 1986 Kaiser, 1984 Fruhan, 1979
Recency of sources	Continuous	Repetitive	Development of management profiles and manpower (succession) charts Managers do not always act in a rational manner	Past is good predictor of future	Ball, 1987
Managerial skills	Ad hoc	Reanalyze	Best way to understand a competitor's product characteristics and costs	Can be time consuming May not be CSF	–

DIMENSION DESCRIPTIONS

For each of the 11 dimensions developed to evaluate the techniques, we selected criteria to enhance its meaningfulness. The criteria reflect our experience and understanding of what considerations are important for evaluating a particular technique. While firms often use external consultants for some aspects of competitive analysis, we assume that internal personnel will be conducting all phases of the analyses.

Time.   The time required to implement a technique can be separated into development (Dev.) and execution (Ex.) phases. The developmental phase involves specifying objectives and determining any initial constraints that will be imposed on the project. The execution phase involves the collection of data, analysis, and dissemination of the findings to the appropriate individuals.

Financial Resources.   The financial resources required to conduct any analysis with a given technique can be categorized as low (under $10,000), medium ($10,000 to $50,000) or high (over $50,000).

Managerial Skills.   To complete an assignment a manager may need a number of specific skills; these may be classed in five groups: technical, interpersonal, conceptual, diagnostic, and analytic. Technical skills are those necessary to accomplish specialized activities. Interpersonal skills involve the ability to communicate with, understand, and motivate both individuals and groups. Conceptual skills are the abilities of a manager to think in the abstract and understand cause-and-effect relationships. Diagnostic skills allow a manager to study the symptoms of a problem and determine the underlying causes. Analytical skills involve the ability to identify the key variables in a situation, understand their interrelationships, and decide which should receive the most attention.

Sources.   Sources are persons, products, written materials, anything from which information is obtained. Sources are of two primary types, "learning-curve" and "target" [Washington Researchers, 1983]. Learning-curve sources are those that provide general rather than specific knowledge; they are used when time is not critical and to prepare for a target source. For example, industry studies and books are typical learning-curve sources. Target sources, on the other hand, contain specific information and provide the greatest volume of pertinent information in the shortest period of time. Trade associations, company and competitor personnel are typical target sources. They are often one-shot sources that cannot be used repetitively.

The sites from which one obtains information can be classified as either "field" or "library." By combining the sources and sites of information, we developed a typology of data collection techniques. Figure 1 contains 15 data collection techniques that can be used for competitive analysis assignments [Miller, 1983]. For each we have recommended the most appropriate sources. If a particular technique presents problems in availability or application, then nearby techniques in the figure should be considered. For example, if product purchasing is desired but is too expensive or unavailable, then direct observation or a literature search should be used.

Availability.   While data can be obtained for almost any project for a price, the ease with which one can secure data can be classified. Three categories we have found useful are "off-the-shelf," "derived from analysis," and "customized." Off-the-shelf refers to data in the form the manager needs. If the essential raw data are available but require some analyses to put them in the desired form, then we classify the availability as "derived from analysis." When the information for a study must be developed, we call it "customized."

Timeliness.   Data, analysis, and implications that deal primarily with the past are historical; those that address the present and future, we call current and future.

Accuracy Constraints.   The value of a particular technique is limited by the quality of the resources and validity of the data used. Using the above dimensions, we identified the key constraint that would potentially hinder the usefulness of the given technique. This dimension is analogous to a warning label for the user.

Updating Requirements.   Competitive analyses are seldom one-time phenomena. In order to understand the updating requirements for each technique, two useful dimensions are "frequency" and "difficulty." The frequency dimension can be divided into ad hoc (when the need arises), periodic (according to an established schedule), and continuous.

The difficulty dimension addresses the extent and nature of skills that may be required during an update. If the same analysis can be performed again with no modifications, then we have labeled it repetitive. If modifications must be made because the format or content of the information has changed, we describe it as re-analysis. If the assumptions of the analysis need to be challenged or changed, then the updating requires a reconceptualization.

Advantages and Limitations.   The final two dimensions summarize the major advantages and limitations of the technique. While these

FIGURE 1   Sources of Data

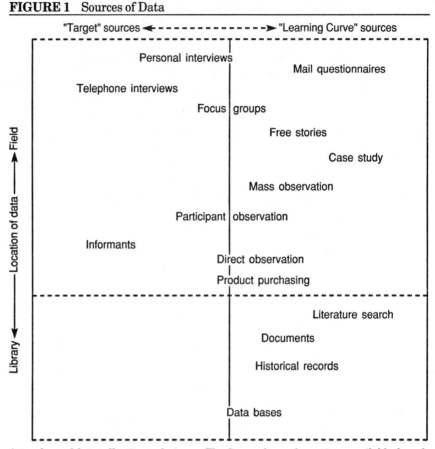

A typology of data collection techniques. The figure shows the options available for collecting data given the desired source and location. A source of data can either provide specific target information or general learning-curve information. The location of the data can reside in a field setting or in a library.

assessments are implicit once the preceding criteria have been applied to a specific analytical assignment, they are intended to underscore special considerations. Examples of advantages could be insight into cultural constraints or an industry's evolution; whereas limitations could be communications difficulties or conflicting assumptions, either of which may lead to misunderstandings.

References.   The publications chosen are from a much broader list of strategic management references. We based our choice on their availability, managerial orientation, and relative recency. Most contain bibliographies that further extend the resources.

While these evaluation dimensions vary in importance across competitive analysis assignments, recognizing them can greatly facilitate choices when groups of managers and analysts are working together.

SELECTING AND USING THE TECHNIQUES

The transition from a description of techniques to their selection for application is best conveyed by an actual example.

The competitive environment of an electric utility company has recently been undergoing significant changes. A great many industrial customers, the utility's "bread-and-butter," have been closing or reducing operations. Other industrial and commercial customers have been threatening partial backward integration into cogeneration systems. Residential customers have been voicing concerns before the public utility board because they pay some of the highest rates in the country. Because of potentially low returns and increasingly high risks, the investment community seems less willing to finance the large capital expenditures necessary in this industry. The utility's geographic service area, vigorously engaged in attracting new businesses, is looking for high technology and service businesses, which typically consume modest amounts of electricity.

To further complicate its competitive problems, a variety of governmental bodies are openly discussing the benefits of deregulation. Since electricity can be distributed cheaply over wide geographical areas, the need to restrict the boundaries of each utility is being questioned. Deregulation, some argue, would benefit consumers by allowing them to choose among a wider set of competitors.

The managers in the company are faced with an internal situation of severe financial constraints, top management's desire to take immediate corrective action, and a lack of skills in formal strategic planning. The newly hired planners charged with addressing the above issues need a method for organizing their competitive analysis efforts. They must choose techniques for understanding their industry and competitors.

SELECTING TECHNIQUES

Many competitive analysis assignments begin when top executives become dissatisfied with their firm's prevailing emphasis and understanding of the competitive environment. This was the case in the electrical utility company described above. Management initiated a series of meetings which focused on the strategic planning efforts at the firm. One of the outcomes was an assignment to conduct an analysis of the

TABLE 2   A Competitive Analysis at an Electical Utility Company

| | Techniques | |
Needs	Chosen	Rejected/Deferred
To understand the dynamics of the industry	Economists' model of industry attractiveness Strategic group analysis Critical success factors	Industry scenarios Industry segmentation Stakeholder analysis
To identify its strategic position relative to its key competitors	Financial analysis Management profiles Strengths and weaknesses analysis	Value-based planning Value-chain analysis

industry and competitors. The planners, facing the constraints of a limited budget, perceived urgency, and after a series of meetings, an inexperienced support staff decided to focus on two fundamental issues: first, to understand the contemporary dynamics of the broadly defined electrical utility industry; second, to address the strategic position of the firm relative to its key existing and potential competitors. The managers needed to identify those competitive analysis techniques that would best answer their questions within their existing constraints. The outcome is shown in Table 2.

Table 2 also illustrates several important aspects of the process of initiating a competitive analysis assignment. Even the most basic assignments, like those described in the table, present the manager with a variety of choices. The firm in this case concentrated its efforts on basic analyses that would lay the foundation for later in-depth studies. As a result, several possible alternatives were rejected because they were too costly, time-consuming, complicated, or not relevant to the circumstances at that time. For example, industry scenarios were deferred for two interrelated reasons. The team needed to understand the industry better before it could address more sophisticated issues. Second, developing industry scenarios would have been too costly and time-consuming. Techniques, such as political and country risk analysis, multi-point competition, synergy analysis, and market signaling were viewed as not relevant to the immediate issues. The competitive analysis team examined each of the 21 techniques and chose those which best suited the assignment and the constraints imposed on the project.

The team applied three interrelated techniques in order to better understand the industry. First, the economists' model of industry attractiveness provided a comprehensive picture of the industry. It revealed that competition should be viewed from both a regional and a national perspective. Further, deregulation (a concern of top management) was not likely to occur for another three-to-five years, and then the transmission systems of electrical utilities would be the first area to be deregulated. Finally, while the bargaining power of electrical utilities is not strong, their profitability was expected to increase over the next five years due in part to a construction cycle coming to an end.

Second, using the industry analysis as a foundation, strategic group analysis identified those key competitors important in identifying the firm's relative position. Strategic groups were developed on a national level using publicly available operating and financial data for a set of about 70 firms. On a regional level, a group of eight electrical and gas utility firms were selected, which were either in the firm's transmission grid or which competed in their geographical territory.

Third, critical success factors were identified at two levels. During the industry analysis, CSFs were identified for the industry as a whole. Then CSFs were identified for the strategic groups. The layering or combining of techniques within an analysis allows managers to address multiple aspects of a question.

Having narrowed the field of competitors to a manageable number through the strategic group analysis, the team turned to the second issue. It sought to build profiles of the competitors to depict the relative positions of the firms. The choices were to conduct a financial analysis of the firms, to examine their management teams' profiles and to analyze their strengths and weaknesses. These methods were chosen because the data were easily available, the time for the analysis was relatively short, and the result would be a set of reports that other managers in the firm could use easily. This last point was very important. Since most managers were not really convinced that it was necessary to consider the competition, the competitive analysis team felt it extremely important to choose those techniques that were understood by virtually all managers. When the managers saw the usefulness of these analyses, the team would then move to other analyses that were less familiar but which could provide additional intelligence. Most of the techniques rejected or deferred (Table 2) fit in this category.

From this example, it is clear that even seemingly simple competitive analysis assignments pose important issues and questions. In this case, questions concerning the relative position of the firm could not be tackled until the managers understood the industry as a competitive arena. This new perspective on the environment required customer feedback, technical appraisals, and regulatory understanding.

The assignment in this case took approximately three months to complete, with approximately one-third of the time being spent on the developmental aspects of the study.

Conclusions   Growing competitiveness in many markets and along many combinations of dimensions is increasing the complexity of competitive analysis problems facing managers. Our descriptions of techniques, evaluation dimensions, and information types should provide managers with helpful guidance in making competitive analyses.

REFERENCES

Ball, Richard, 1987, "Assessing your competitor's people and organization," *Long Range Planning,* Vol. 20, No. 2, pp. 32–41.

Bonoma, Thomas V. and Shapiro, Bensen P., 1983, *Segmenting the Industrial Market,* Lexington Books, Lexington, Massachusetts.

Desta, Asayehgn, 1985, "Assessing political risk in less developed countries," *Journal of Business Strategy,* Vol. 5, No. 4, pp. 40–53.

Freeman, R. Edward, 1984, Strategic Management: *A Stakeholder Approach,* Pitman Publishing Company, Boston, Massachusetts.

Fruhan, William E., Jr., 1979, *Financial Strategy: Studies in the Creation, Transfer and Destruction of Shareholder Value,* Richard D. Irwin, Homewood, Illinois.

Grant, John H. and King, William R., 1982, *The Logic of Strategic Planning,* Little, Brown and Company, Boston, Massachusetts.

Hall, Graham and Howell, Sydney 1985, "The experience curve from the economist's perspective," *Strategic Management Journal,* Vol. 6, No. 2, pp. 197–212.

Hayes, Robert H. and Wheelwright, Steven C., 1979a, "The dynamics of process-product life cycles," *Harvard Business Review,* Vol. 57, No. 2 (March–April), pp. 127–136.

Hayes, Robert H. and Wheelwright, Steven C., 1979b, "Link manufacturing process and product life cycles," *Harvard Business Review,* Vol. 57, No. 1 (January–February), pp. 133–140.

Hax, Arnoldo C. and Majluf, Nicolas S., 1984, *Strategic Management: An Integrative Perspective,* Prentice-Hall, Englewood Cliffs, New Jersey.

Hofer, Charles W. and Haller, Terry, 1980, "Globescan: A way to better international risk assessment," *Journal of Business Strategy,* Vol. 1, No. 2, pp. 41–55.

Hofer, Charles W. and Schendel, Dan, 1978, *Strategy Formulation: Analytical concepts,* West Publishing Company, New York.

Kaiser, Michael M., 1984, *Understanding the Competition: A Practical Guide to Competitive Analysis,* Michael M. Kaiser Associates, Inc., Washington, DC.

Karnani, Anell and Wernerfelt, Birger, 1985, "Multiple point competition," *Strategic Management Journal,* Vol. 6, No. 1, pp. 87–96.

Leidecker, Joel K. and Bruno, Albert V., 1984, "Identifying and using critical success factors," *Long Range Planning,* Vol. 17, No. 1 (February), pp. 23–32.

McGee, John and Thomas, Howard, 1986, "Strategic groups: Theory, research and taxonomy," *Strategic Management Journal,* Vol. 7, No. 2, pp. 141–160.

Miller, Delbert C., 1983, *Handbook of Research Design and Social Measurement,* Longman, New York.

Pekar, Peter P., 1982, "The strategic environmental matrix: A concept on trial," *Planning Review,* Vol. 10, No. 5, pp. 28–30.

Petrov, Boris, 1982, "The advent of the technology portfolio," *The Journal of Business Strategy,* Vol. 3, No. 2, pp. 70–75.

Porter, Michael E., 1980, *Competitive Strategy,* The Free Press, New York.

Porter, Michael E., 1985, *Competitive Advantage: Creating and Sustaining Superior Performance,* The Free Press, New York.

Prescott, John E., 1987, "A process for applying analytic models in competitive analysis," in *Strategic Planning and Management Handbook,* eds. David I. Cleland and William R. King, Van Nostrand Reinhold Company, Stroudsburg, Pennsylvania, pp. 222–251.

Ramanujam, Vasudevan and Venkatraman, N., 1984, "An inventory and critique of strategy research using the PIMS data base," *Academy of Management Review,* Vol. 9, No. 1, pp. 138–151.

Reimann, B. C., 1986, "Strategy valuation in portfolio planning: Combining Q and VROI ratios," *Planning Review,* Vol. 14, No. 1, pp. 18–23, 42–45.

Rockart, John F., 1979, "Chief executives define their own data needs," *Harvard Business Review,* Vol. 5, No. 2 (March-April), pp. 81–92.

Rowe, Alan J.; Mason, Richard O.; and Dickel, Karl E., 1985, *Strategic Management and Business Policy,* second edition, Addison-Wesley Publishing Company, Reading, Massachusetts.

Schoeffler, Sidney; Buzzell, Robert D.; and Heany, Donald F., 1974, "Impact of strategic planning on profit performance," *Harvard Business Review,* Vol. 52, No. 2, pp. 137–145.

Stevenson, Howard H., 1976, "Defining corporate strengths and weaknesses," *Sloan Management Review,* Vol. 17, No. 3 (Spring), pp. 51–68.

Stevenson, Howard H., 1985, "Resource assessment: Identifying corporate strengths and weaknesses," in *Handbook of Business Strategy,* ed. William D. Guth, Warren, Gorham and Lamont, Boston, Massachusetts, Chapter 5, pp. 1–30.

Wack, Pierre, 1985a, "Scenarios: Shooting the rapids," *Harvard Business Review,* Vol. 63, No. 6, pp. 139–150.

Wack, Pierre, 1985b, "Scenarios: Uncharted waters ahead," *Harvard Business Review,* Vol. 63, No. 5, pp. 73–89.

Wagner, Harvey M., 1984, "Profit wonders, investment blunders," *Harvard Business Review,* Vol. 62, No. 5, pp. 121–135.

Washington Researchers, 1983, *Company Information: A Model Investigation,* Washington Researchers Ltd., Washington DC.

Environmental Forecasting: Key to Strategic Management

John A. Pearce II and Richard B. Robinson, Jr.

Even large firms in established and stable industries will be actively involved in transitions in the 1980s. For example, by 1985 Sears will have opened new financial centers in 250 retail stores. Forecasting the business environment for the second half of the 1980s has led some firms, such as Sears, to expand.

Other corporations have forecast a need for massive retrenchment. One such firm is the Weyerhauser Company, which laid off 2,000 employees in 1982 in order to streamline its cost of doing business. Still other companies have cut back in one area of operations in order to underwrite growth in another. This year General Electric has decided to close 10 plants and reduce its work force by 1,600 employees while simultaneously making a commitment to spend $250 million by 1986 to upgrade its facilities.

Although change in the 1970s was rapid, most observers agree that greater changes and greater challenges for strategic managers are the reality of the 1980s. The crucial responsibility for managers is to ensure their firm's survival by anticipating and adapting to environmental change in ways that provide new opportunities for growth and profitability. Therefore, the impact of change in the firm's external environments must be predicted and understood.

The search for opportunities and constraints in the future includes the following aspects of strategic planning:

1. Selecting the key variables in the environment critical to the firm.
2. Selecting the major sources of environmental information.
3. Evaluating forecasting approaches or techniques.
4. Integrating the results of forecasts into the strategic management process.

Source: John A. Pearce II and Richard B. Robinson, Jr., "Environmental Forecasting: Key to Strategic Management," *Business* (Georgia State University Business Press), 33, no. 2 (July–September 1983), pp. 3–12.

SELECTING KEY ENVIRONMENTAL VARIABLES

Strategic planning must begin with selection and analysis of the key variables in a firm's environment. Many external and often uncontrollable conditions influence a firm's choice of direction, its actions, and, ultimately, its organizational structure and internal processes. Such conditions constitute the external environment of a business and can be categorized as part of the *remote environment* or part of the *task environment*.

The remote environment is composed of political, economic, social, and technological forces that originate beyond and usually irrespective of a firm's operating situation. The remote environment therefore presents opportunities, threats, and constraints, and a company rarely possesses the strength to exert any meaningful reciprocal influence on them.

The task environment, which is also called the competitive or operating environment, encompasses many of the challenges a firm faces when attempting to attract or acquire needed resources or to market goods and services in a profitable manner. Among the most prominent task-environment factors are a firm's competitive position, its customer profile, its reputation among suppliers and creditors, and an accessible labor market. The task environment differs from the remote environment in that a company typically has a much greater degree of control over the former. Thus individual businesses can be much more flexible in their strategic planning when they consider the task environment than they can when they are studying only the remote environment.

Several management experts have argued that the most important factors are the changes in population structure and dynamics. These changes, in turn, produce turbulence in the remote and task environments.

Historically, population shifts have tended to occur every 40 to 50 years and, therefore, have had little relevance to business decisions. However, during the second half of the twentieth century, population changes have become radical, erratic, contradictory, and therefore of great importance.

If forecasting was as simple as predicting population trends, strategic managers would need only to examine census data to predict future markets. For example, all of the adults who will be producing and buying goods in 1995 are alive today. But economic interpretations are actually very complex; many variables are involved and the entire environment must be considered. Migration rates; mobility trends; birth, marriage, and death rates; and racial, ethnic, and religious structures confound population statistics. Too, the political aspects of resource development in this interdependent world further confuse the problems—as evidenced by the actions of oil countries such as Saudi

Arabia, Iraq, Libya, and Kuwait. Changes in political situations, technology, or culture further complicate forecasting.

In the United States, the turbulence is no less severe. Changing products, services, and competitors; uncertain government priorities; rapid social change; and major technological innovations all add to the complexity of planning for the future. In order to grow, to be profitable, and, at times, even to survive in this turbulent world, a firm's strategic managers must have the sensitivity, the commitment, and the skill to recognize and predict the variables that will most profoundly affect the company's future.

Who Selects the Key Variables?

Although planning executives or committees may be responsible for obtaining forecasts, the responsibility for environmental forecasting lies with top management. For example, the Sun Company, a large oil firm, assigns the responsibility for the long-range future of the corporation to the chairman and vice-chairman of the board of directors. One of the key duties of the vice-chairman is "environmental assessment." In this context, "environment" refers not to the air, water, and land but rather to the very general environment of economics, technology, politics, and society in which the Sun Company operates today and will have to operate in the future.

The environmental assessment group consists of the chief economist, a specialist in technological assessment, and a public issues consultant; the group reports to the vice-president of environmental assessment. The chief economist evaluates and forecasts the state of the economy; the technological assessment specialist covers technology and science; and the public issues consultant concentrates on politics and society.[1]

However, headquarters' capability and proficiency for analyzing political, economic, and social variables around the world may be limited. Therefore, "on the spot" personnel, outside consultants, or company task forces may be assigned to assist in forecasting.

Selecting Specific Variables

Each firm must develop a list of variables that will have specific make-or-break consequences. Some variables may have been crucial in the past, and others may become important in the future. The list can be kept manageable by limiting specific variables in the following ways:

- Include all variables with high impact despite low probability of occurrence (for example, trucking deregulation) as well as variables

with high probabilities regardless of impact (for example, a minimal price increase by a major supplier). Delete variables with low impact and low probabilities.
- Disregard major disasters such as nuclear war.
- Consolidate variables when possible, if smaller variables are linked to larger ones. (For example, a bank loan is based more on the dependability of a company's cash flow than on its component sources.)
- Watch for variables with multiple impacts so that their importance is not underestimated.[2]

Limits on money, time, and skill in forecasting often prevent a firm from predicting many variables in the environment. The task of predicting even a dozen variables is substantial. Frequently firms try to select a set of key variables by analyzing the environmental factors in the industry that are most likely to force sharp growth or decline in the marketplace. As an example, housing starts are significant for the furniture, appliance, and textiles industries; housing, in turn, is greatly affected by high interest rates.

SELECTING INFORMATION SOURCES

Before forecasting can begin in a formal way, the manager must identify appropriate sources of environmental information. The casual gathering of strategic information that is part of the normal course of executive reading, interaction, and meetings is subject to bias and must be balanced with alternative viewpoints. Although *The Wall Street Journal, Business Week, Business, Fortune, the Harvard Business Review, Forbes* and other trade, popular, and scholarly journals are important sources of forecasting information, more formal, deliberate, and structured searches for information are desirable for strategic forecasting.

A list of published sources that may be used in forecasting can be found on pages 194 to 197. These sources provide information on specific forecasting needs. If a firm can afford the time and expense, primary data should also be gathered by special research in such areas as market factors, technological changes, and competitive and supplier strategies.

EVALUATING FORECASTING TECHNIQUES

In today's ever-changing world, strategic managers depend on a wide range of forecasting techniques. This section will evaluate several of the more typical techniques and will suggest the types of forecasting for which they are most commonly used. (See Exhibit 1.)

EXHIBIT 1   Popular Approaches to Forecasting

Technique[1]	Short Description[2]	Cost	Popularity[3]	Complexity	Association with Life Cycle Stage[4]
QUANTITATIVE					
Casual					
Econometric models	Simultaneous systems of multiple regression equations	High	High	High	Steady state
Single and multiple regression	Variations in dependent variables are explained by variations in the independent one(s)	High/ Medium	High	Medium	Steady state
Time series					
Trend extrapolation	Linear, exponential, S-curve, or other types of projections	Medium	High	Medium	Steady state
	Forecasts are obtained by smoothing averaging, past actual values in a linear or exponential manner	Medium	High	Medium	Steady state
QUALITATIVE OR JUDGMENTAL					
Salesforce estimate[5]	A bottom-up approach aggregating salespersons' forecasts	Low	High	Low	All stages
Juries of executive opinion	Marketing, production, and finance executives jointly prepare forecasts	Low	High	Low	Product development
Anticipatory surveys; market research	Learning about intentions of potential customers or planes of businesses	Medium	Medium	Medium	Market testing and early introduction
Scenario	Forecasters imagine the impacts of anticipated conditions	Low	Medium	Low	All stages
Delphi	Experts are guided toward a consensus	Low	Medium	Medium	Product development
Brainstorming	Idea generation in a noncritical group situation	Low	Medium	Medium	Product development

1. Only techniques discussed in this article are listed.
2. Adapted in part from S. C. Wheelwright and S. Makridakis, *Forecasting Methods for Management,* 3rd ed. (New York: Wiley, 1980), 34–35.
3. Adapted in part from S. C. Wheelwright and D. C. Clark, "Corporate Forecasting: Promise and Reality," *Harvard Business Review* (November–December 1976).
4. Adapted in part from J. C. Chambers, J. K. Mullick, and, D. D. Smith, "How to Choose the Right Forecasting Technique," *Harvard Business Review* (July–August 1971). The associations shown are "most common," but most techniques can be used at most stages.
5. For details see N. C. Mohn and L. C. Sartorius, "Sales Forecasting: A Manager's Primer," *Business* (May–June 1981 and July–August 1981).

Debate exists over the accuracy of quantitative versus qualitative approaches, with most research supporting quantitative models. However, the difference in predictions between the two types of approaches is often minimal. Additionally, subjective or judgmental approaches may often be the only practical methods to forecast trends in the political, legal, social, and technological areas of concern—in the remote external environment. The same is true for several of the factors in the task environment, especially for customer and competitive considerations.

Ultimately, the choice of a technique depends not on the environmental factor under review, but on such considerations as the nature of the forecast decision, the amount and accuracy of the information available, the accuracy level required, the time available to make the forecast, the importance of the forecast to the firm, the cost of the forecast, and the competence and interpersonal relationships of the managers and forecasters involved.[3] Frequently, assessment of these factors leads to the selection of a combination of quantitative and qualitative techniques, thereby strengthening the accuracy of the ultimate forecast.

Economic Forecasts

At one time, only forecasts of economic variables were made to facilitate strategic management. Economic forecasts were primarily concerned with remote economic factors such as general economic conditions, disposable personal income, the consumer price index, wage rates, and productivity. Derived from government and private sources, these economic forecasts serve as the framework for industry and company forecasts. Industry and company forecasts deal with task-environment concerns such as sales, market share, and other economic trends pertinent to the firm.

With the advent of sophisticated computers, the government and some wealthy companies contracted with private consulting firms to develop *econometric models*. Econometric models utilize complex simultaneous regression equations to relate occurrences in the economy to areas of corporate activity. They are especially useful when good information is available on causal relationships and when large changes are anticipated. During the relatively stable decade of the 1960s and on into the 1970s econometrics became one of the nation's fastest growth industries. However, since early in 1979 the big three econometric firms—Data Resources (McGraw-Hill), Chase Econometrics (Chase Manhattan Bank), and Wharton Econometric Forecasting Associates (Ziff-Davis Publishing Co.)—have fallen on hard times. The explosion of oil prices, inflation, and the growing interdependence of the world economy have created problems beyond the inherent limits of the econometric models. Despite their enormous technological resources, these models still depend on the judgment of the model builders. Recently, that judgment has not been dependable.[4] Three more widely used and less expensive approaches to forecasting are *time series models, judgmental models,* and *causal models.*

Time series models attempt to identify a pattern in a combination of trend, seasonal, and cyclical factors based on historical data. This technique also assumes that the past is a prologue to the future. Time series techniques, including exponential smoothing, decomposition, and trend extrapolation, are relatively simple, well-known, inexpensive, and accurate.

Of the time series models, *trend analysis* is most frequently used. This model assumes that the future will be a continuation of the past in some long-range trend. If sufficient historical data, such as annual sales, are readily available, a trend analysis can be done quickly and inexpensively.

In the trend analysis depicted in Exhibit 2, concern should focus on long-term trends, such as Trend C, which represents 10 years of fluctuating sales. Trend A, where three excellent years were used in the trend analysis, is too optimistic. Similarly, the four bad years depicted in Trend B represent a much too pessimistic outlook.

EXHIBIT 2   Interpretations in Trend Analysis

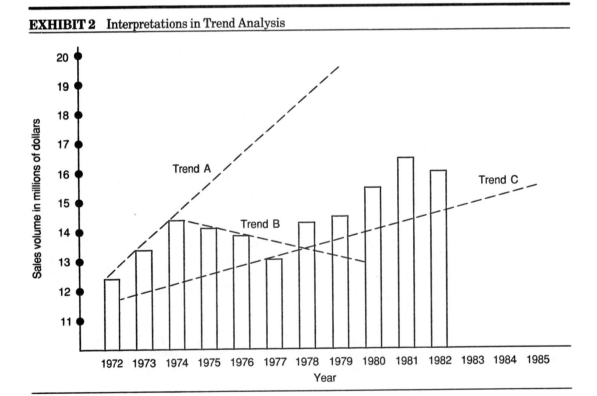

The major limitation of trend analysis is the assumption that all relevant conditions will remain relatively constant in the future. Sudden changes in the conditions upset the trend prediction.

Judgmental models are useful when historical data are not available or when they are hard to use. Examples of judgmental or qualitative approaches are *salesforce estimates, juries of executive opinion,* and *customer surveys.* Salesforce estimates consolidate salespersons' opinions of customers' intentions and opinions regarding specific products. These can be relevant, if customers respond honestly and remain consistent in their intentions. Juries of executive opinions combine estimates of executives from marketing, production, finance, and purchasing and then average their views. No elaborate math or statistics are required. Customer surveys may be conducted by personal interviews or telephone questionnaires and require well-stated, easily understood questions that are asked of a random sample of the relevant population. Surveys can provide valuable in-depth information. However, they are often difficult to construct and time-consuming to administer. Many market research firms use such surveys to anticipate market response.

Causal models are useful if specific relationships between variables are known. For example, knowledge of personal income and growth of certain population segments are usually good predictors for certain basic consumer products. Thus, if a change in one economic variable signals a future change in a major business variable, such as sales demand for a given type of product, a causal model can be developed. Econometric models and single- and multiple-regression techniques are the most popular of the causal approaches.

Social Forecasts

Sole reliance on economic indicators for strategic forecasting neglects many important social trends that can have a profound impact upon the nation and its organizations.[5] Some firms have recognized this importance and have forecast social issues as part of their environmental scanning in order to identify social trends and underlying attitudes.[6] Social forecasting is a very complex undertaking. Recent efforts have analyzed such major social areas as: population, housing, Social Security and welfare, health and nutrition, education and training, income, and wealth and expenditures.

A variety of approaches is used in social forecasting, including time series analysis and the three judgmental techniques described earlier. However, a fourth approach called *scenario development* is probably the most popular of all techniques for social forecasting. Scenarios are imagined stories about the future that integrate objective and subjective parts of other forecasts. They are designed to help managers anticipate changes for the firm. Because scenarios can be presented in an

Sources for Task Environment Forecasts

Competition and Supplier Considerations

Target group index

U.S. industrial outlook

Robert Morris annual statement studies

Troy, Leo, *Almanac of Business and Industrial Financial Ratios*

Enterprise Statistics (U.S. Bureau of the Census)

Securities and Exchange Commission (10-K Reports)

Annual reports of specific companies

Fortune 500 Directory, The Wall Street Journal, Barrons, Forbes, Dun's Review

Investment services and directories: Moody's, Dun & Bradstreet, Standard & Poor's, Starch Marketing, Funk & Scott Index Trade association publications

Industry surveys

Market research surveys

County Business Patterns

County and City Data Book

Industry contacts, professional meetings, salespeople

NFIB Quarterly Economic Report for Small Business

Customer Profile

Statistical Abstract of the U. S., first source of statistics

Statistical Sources by Paul Wasserman (a subject guide to data—both domestic and international)

American Statistics Index (Congressional Information Service Guide to statistical publications of U.S. Government—monthly)

Office of the U.S. Department of Commerce: Bureau of Census reports on population, housing, and industries

U. S. Census of Manufacturers (statistics by industry, area, and products)

Survey of Current Business (analysis of business trends, especially February and July issues)

Market research studies *(A Basic Bibliography on Market Review,* compiled by Robert Ferber, et al., American Marketing Association)

Current Sources of Marketing Information: A Bibliography of Primary Marketing Data by Gunther & Goldstein, American Marketing Association

Sources for Task Environment Forecasts *(concluded)*

Guide to Consumer Markets, Conference Board (provides statistical information with demographic, social, and economic data—annual)

Survey of Buying Power

Predicasts (abstracts of publishing forecasts of all industries, detailed products, and end-use data)

Predicasts Basebook (historical data from 1960 to present covering subjects ranging from population and gross national product to specific products and services)

Market Guide (individual market surveys of over 1,500 U.S. and Canadian cities; data includes population, location, trade area, banks, principal industries, colleges and universities, department and chain stores, newspapers, retail outlets, and sales)

County and City Data Book (includes bank deposits, birth and death rates, business firms, education, employment, income of families, manufacturers, population, savings, wholesale and rental trade)

Yearbook of International Trade Statistics (UN)

Yearbook of National Accounts Statistics (UN)

Statistical Yearbook (UN— covers population, national income, agricultural and industrial production, energy, external trade, and transport)

Statistic of (Continents): Sources for Market Research (includes separate books on *Africa, America, Europe)*

Key Natural Resources

Minerals Yearbook, Geological Survey (Bureau of Mines, Department of Interior)

Agricultural Abstract (U.S. Department of Agriculture)

Statistics of electric utilities and gas pipeline companies, Federal Power Commission

Publications of various institutions (American Petroleum Institute, U.S. Atomic Energy Commission, Coal Mining Institute of America, American Steel Institute, Brookings Institution)

Sources for Remote Environment Forecasts

Economic Considerations

Predicasts (most complete and up-to-date review of forecasts)

National Bureau of Economic Research

Handbook of Basic Economic Statistics

Statistical Abstract of the U.S. (also includes industrial, social, and political statistics)

Publications of the U.S. Department of Commerce:

Office of Business Economics (example: *Survey of Business)*

Bureau of Economic Analysis (example: *Business Conditions Digest)*

Bureau of Census (example: *Survey of Manufacturers,* and various reports of population, housing, and industries)

Business and Defense Service Administration (example: *U.S. Industrial Outlook)*

Securities and Exchange Commission (various quarterly reports on plant and equipment, financial reports, working capital of corporations)

The Conference Board

Survey of Buying Power

Marketing Economic Guide

Industrial Arts Index

The Chamber of Commerce

American Manufacturers Association

Federal Reserve Bulletin

Economic Indicators, annual report

Kiplinger Newsletter

Worldcasts

Master key index for business international publications

U.S. Department of Commerce

Overseas business reports

Bureau of Census—*Guide to Foreign Trade Statistics*

Business Periodicals Index

Social Considerations

Public opinion polls

Surveys such as *Social Indicators and Social Reporting,* the Annals of the American Academy of Political and Social Sciences

Abstracts services and indexes for sociological, psychological, and political journal articles

Sources for Remote Environment Forecasts *(concluded)*

Indexes for *The Wall Street Journal, New York Times,* and other newspapers

Bureau of Census reports on population, housing, manufacturers, selected services, construction, retail trade, wholesale trade, and enterprise statistics

Various reports from groups such as the Brookings Institution and the Ford Foundation

World Bank Atlas (population growth and gross national product data)

World Bank *(World Development Report)*

Political Considerations

Public Affairs Information Services Bulletin

CIS Index (Congressional Information Index)

Business periodicals

Funk & Scott (regulations by product break-down)

Weekly compilation of presidential documents

Monthly Catalog of Government Publications

Federal Register (daily announcements of pending regulations)

Code of Federal Regulations (final listing of regulations)

Business International Master Key Index (regulations, and tariffs)

Information services (Bureau of National Affairs, Commerce Clearing House, Prentice-Hall)

Technological Considerations

Applied Science and Technology Index

Statistical Abstract of the U.S.

Scientific and Technical Information Service

University reports, congressional reports

Department of Defense and military purchasing publishers

Trade journals and industrial reports

Industry contacts, professional meetings

Computer-assisted information searches

National Science Foundation, *Annual Report*

Research and Development Directory, patent records

Sources: Adapted from C. R. Goeldner and Laura M. Kirks, "Business Facts: Where to Find Them," *MSU Business Topics* (Summer 1976): 23–76; François E. deCarbonnel and Roy G. Donance, "Information Source for Planning Decisions," *California Management Review* (Summer 1973): 42–53; and A. B. Nutt; R. C. Lenz, Jr.; H. W. Landford, and M. J. Cleary, "Data Sources for Trend Extrapolation in Technological Forecasting," *Long Range Planning* (February 1972): 72–76.

easily understood form, they have gained popularity in social-forecast situations. Scenarios can be developed by the following process:

1. Prepare the background by assessing the overall social environment under investigation (such as social legislation).
2. Select critical indicators and search for future events that may impact the key trends (growing distrust of business).
3. Analyze reasons for past behavior for each trend (perceived disregard for air and water quality).
4. Forecast each indicator in at least three scenarios, showing the least favorable environment, the likely environment, and the most favorable environment.
5. Write the scenario from the viewpoint of someone standing in the future and describe conditions at the time and how they developed.
6. Condense the scenario length for each trend to a few paragraphs.

Scenarios prepare strategic managers for alternative possibilities if certain trends continue, thus enabling them to develop contingency plans.

Political Forecasts

Some strategic planners want political forecasts treated with the same seriousness and consideration given to economic forecasts. They believe that shifts toward or away from a broad range of political conditions can have profound effects on business success. Examples of such political influences are the size of government budgets, tariffs, tax rates, defense spending, the growth of regulatory bodies, and the extent of business leaders' participation in government planning.

Political forecasts of foreign countries are also important. Political risks increase the threat to businesses that are in any way dependent on international subsidiaries or suppliers for customers or critical resources. The increasing world interdependence makes it imperative for firms of all sizes to consider political implications on their strategies.

Because billions of U.S. dollars were lost in the 1970s as the result of revolutions, nationalizations, and other forms of political instability, a number of multinational firms and consultants have developed a variety of global forecast approaches. Among the better known are:

- Haner's Business Environmental Risk Index (monitors 15 economic and political variables in 42 countries).
- Frost & Sullivan's World Political Risks Forecasts (predicts the likelihood of various catastrophes befalling an individual company).

- Probe International's custom reports for specific companies (examines broad social trends).
- Arthur D. Little's (ADL) developmental forecasts (examine a country's progress from the Stone Age to the computer age).[7]

Of all the approaches, ADL's forecasting techniques may be the most ambitious and sophisticated. With computer assistance, they follow the progress of each country by looking at five criteria: social development, technological advancement, abundance of natural resources, level of domestic tranquility, and type of political system. When a country's development in any one of these areas gets too far ahead of the other, tension builds and violence often follows. Using this system, political turbulence was forecast in Iran as early as 1972. These development forecasts by ADL also foresee that uneven development will likely produce similar turmoil in 20 other countries such as Peru, Chile, Malaysia, and the Philippines. The assumption behind the ADL forecast is that the world is highly predictable, if one asks the right questions. Unfortunately, too many executives fail to use the same logic in analyzing political affairs that they use in other strategic areas. Political analysis should be routinely incorporated into economic analyses. Ford, General Motors, Pepsi, Singer, DuPont, and United Technologies are among the many companies that follow ADL's advice.

Technological Forecasts

Such rapid and revolutionary technological changes as lasers, nuclear energy, satellites and other communication devices, desalinization of water, electric cars, and miracle drugs have prompted many firms to invest in technological forecasts. Advance knowledge of the probable development of the technological improvements helps strategic managers prepare their firms to benefit from change. To make technological forecasts, all of the previously described techniques, except econometrics, can be used. However, the uncertainty of information about a technological change favors scenarios, plus two additional forecasting approaches—*brainstorming* and the *Delphi technique*.

Brainstorming is a technique used to help a group generate new ideas and forecasts. Analysis and criticism of individual contributions are postponed so that creative thinking is not stifled or restricted. Because of the absence of interruptions, group members are encouraged to offer original ideas and to build on the innovative thoughts of other group members. At a later time the most promising of the ideas are thoroughly evaluated.

The Delphi technique uses a systematic procedure to obtain a consensus from a group of experts. The procedure includes a detailed survey of the expert opinion, usually through a mail survey; a reading of the anonymous exchanged answers by the experts; and one or more revisions of answers to the same problems until convergence occurs.

The Delphi technique, although expensive and time-consuming, can also be successfully used for social and political forecasting.

INTEGRATING FORECAST RESULTS

Once the techniques are selected and the forecasts made, the results must be tied into the strategic management process. For example, the economic forecast must be related to the analyses of the industry, the suppliers, the competition, and key resources. Exhibit 3 presents a format for displaying the interrelationships between forecasted remote environmental variables and task or operating environmental variables. In formulating strategy the resulting predictions become a part of the assumed environment.

Strategic decision makers must understand the assumptions that serve as the basis of the environmental forecasts. An example of this critical need is illustrated by the experience of Itel, a computer leasing firm. In 1978, largely because IBM was unable to make delivery of its newest systems, Itel was able to lease 200 of its plug-in computers made by Advanced Systems and by Hitachi. As a consequence, Itel made a bullish sales forecast for 1979 that it would place 430 of its systems—despite the rumor that IBM would launch a new line of aggressively priced systems in the first quarter of that year. Even Itel's competitors felt that customers would hold off their purchasing decisions until IBM made the announcement. However, Itel signed long-term purchase contracts with its suppliers and increased its marketing staff by 80%. This forecasting mistake and the failure to examine sales forecasts in relationship to competitors and suppliers were nearly disastrous. Itel slipped close to bankruptcy within less than one year.

Forecasting external events enables a firm to identify the probable requirements for success in the future, to formulate or reformulate its basic mission, and to design strategies to achieve goals and objectives. If the forecast identifies any performance gaps or inconsistencies between the firm's desired position and its present position, strategic managers can respond with strategic plans and actions. Forecasts can also be used as the basis of contingency planning by facilitating the design of alternatives that reflect a range of confidence about the predictability of the future. For example, a firm might wish to construct a set of scenarios under conditions that it views as "optimistic," "most likely," and "pessimistic."

Dealing with the uncertainty of the future is a major function of the strategic manager, and the forecasting task requires systematic infor-

EXHIBIT 3 Impact Matrix for Task and Remote Environments Showing Example Impacts

| | TASK FACTORS | | | |
	Key Customer Trends	*Key Competitor Trends*	*Key Supplier Trends*	*Key Labor Market Trends*
REMOTE FACTORS *Economic*	Trends in inflation and unemployment rates		Annual domestic oil demand and worldwide sulfur demand through 1983	
Social	Increasing numbers of single-family homes			Increasing education level of U.S. population
Political	Increasing numbers of punitive damage awards in product liability cases		Possibility of Arab oil boycotts	
Technological		Increasing use of superchips and computer based instrumentation for synthesizing genes	Use of cobalt-60 gamma ray to extend shelflife of perishables	

mation gathering coupled with the ability to combine and utilize a variety of forecasting approaches. It also demands a high level of insight to integrate risks and opportunities in formulating strategy. Intentional or unintentional delays, or lack of understanding of certain issues, may prevent an organization from using the insights gained from its assessment of the impact of broader environmental trends. Therefore, sensitivity and openness to new and better approaches and opportunities are essential for good strategic management.

NOTES

1. Eric Weiss, "Future Public Opinion of Business," *Management Review* (March 1978): 9.
2. Robert E. Linneman and John D. Kennell, "Shirt-Sleeve Approach to Long-Range Plans," *Harvard Business Review* (March–April 1977): 145.

3. Steven C. Wheelwright and Darral G. Clarke. "Corporate Forecasting: Promise and Reality," *Harvard Business Review* (November–December 1976): 42.
4. "Where the Big Econometric Model Goes Wrong," *Business Week,* 30 March 1981, 70–73.
5. Fremont Kast, "Scanning the Future Environment: Social Indications," *California Management Review* (Fall 1980): 22–32.
6. Liam Fahey and William R. King, "Environmental Scanning for Corporate Planning," *Business Horizons* (August 1977): 27.
7. Niles Howard, "Doing Business in Unstable Countries," *Dun's Review* (March 1980): 49–55.

Analyzing the Competition

James E. Svatko

The highly competitive nature of today's business environment demands that companies not only identify primary rivals in the marketplace, but also understand competitors' strengths, weakness, and overall business strategies. Business owners are beginning to recognize this need, reports a study by The Conference Board; more and more companies are systematically tracking their competitors. Many firms are intensifying current competitive intelligence efforts, and a sizable majority of surveyed executives say competitive intelligence in their companies will expand even further in coming years.

Competitive intelligence is vital to corporate survival for a number of reasons. Most important, the practice of predicting competitor movements in the market helps shape corporate strategy. With an effective corporate competitive intelligence program, top managers can work toward achieving five critical objectives: (1) avoiding surprises, (2) identifying threats and opportunities, (3) gaining competitive advantages by decreasing reaction time, (4) improving planning, and (5) understanding their own companies better.

Considering this new trend, firms that hold analyzing the competition low on the list of marketing priorities are operating at a great disadvantage. Some managers may assume that because the company competes on a daily basis with its rivals that it is already familiar with competitor strategies and tactics. Others may believe that it is impossible to analyze the competition on a systematic basis. However, the company that relies solely on intuition and informal bits of information to monitor its competitors is leaving itself open to attack.

Any firm can establish a competitor analysis system that provides management with essential information about the wide range of

Source: James E. Svatko, "Analyzing the Competition," *Small Business Reports* 14, no. 1 (January 1989), pp. 21–28.

strategies that rivals are likely to pursue. The key is knowing where to gather relevant information and how to combine separate pieces of data into a coherent profile of each competing operation.

What Information Is Needed

The first step is to develop a list of goals that the program will achieve, including what information is needed. Identify the departments in the company that will use the information, and consult with department heads as to what specific data is desired. Information sought by the program should then be classified into useful categories. An effective competitor analysis focuses on four key factors that drive companies to act and react in the marketplace. These include competitor assumptions, objectives, strategies, and capabilities.

ASSUMPTIONS

Every company operates according to assumptions about its own position in the marketplace. While these assumptions may or may not be true, they form the basis for the firm's marketing strategy. For example, a firm that believes its product has captured a certain degree of brand loyalty may be slow to react to a competitor's price cut. As a result of its false assumption, the company stands to lose a substantial portion of market share.

Firms also formulate basic assumptions about competitors and the industry environment. Again, these may or may not be correct. Assumptions are, essentially, "weak points" that can be exploited. A competitor analysis program should identify as many of these weak points as possible. The company gains a powerful advantage by identifying a rival firm's assumptions because these beliefs are usually adhered to rigidly. Consequently, when a competitor's assumptions are challenged, the competitor typically has no contingency plans with which to counter.

With regard to each competitor identify the following:

- Beliefs that a firm holds about its position in the market.
- Capabilities and objectives that the rival firm attributes to other competitors, and whether these are valid.
- Historical identification with any particular product or products selling approach, distribution arrangement, or operational policy.
- Beliefs about industry trends and market demand, and to what degree these are optimistic or pessimistic.

- Rigid corporate policy that dictates the way the company conducts business or reacts in a crisis.

OBJECTIVES

When a company knows the objectives a rival firm has set for itself, it can better predict how a competitor will react to market forces. This information can prove invaluable in enabling a company to fine-tune its own marketing plans.

Objectives may be difficult to identify. One approach is to examine the way the firm handles basic business responsibilities. Then, management must "guess" what objectives could be motivating the actions taken. To create such profiles, answer the following questions:

- What accounting system does the competitor use?
- How are inventories evaluated?
- Is there a correlation between growth in revenues and market share?
- Do activities of the firm indicate aversion to risk?
- How does the organizational structure of the competitor affect its decision-making capacity?
- Does any particular department receive a greater share of the budget?
- What are the professional and educational backgrounds of top management within the rival firm? Is the competitor hiring employees with any specific type of skills?
- What are the backgrounds of members of the board of directors? Does the firm use outsiders to review company operations or policy?
- Has the rival company committed itself to any new contracts, joint ventures, or licensing agreements?
- Is the competitor facing any legal, environmental, or social pressures?

STRATEGY

The third step in analyzing competitive behavior involves developing statements about the competition's marketing strategies. This may be the most straightforward aspect of the competitor analysis, as variables are public knowledge and therefore easily monitored.

Pricing. Are the competitor's prices higher or lower than the industry norm? What are the terms of sale? Is pricing controlled regionally or at a central headquarters?

Sales.   Does the competitor hire in-house staff to handle sales or use independent agents? Are sales groups organized by product line, by accounts, or by region?

Distribution.   What distribution channels does the rival firm use? Does it offer exclusive arrangements to certain distributors?

Product Line.   Do production/marketing efforts concentrate on a specific product line or does the firm produce/market a variety of products?

Advertising Promotion.   Does the firm appear to spend more or less than other competitors on advertising and public relations? Who is the target audience? Which form of media is used the most?

Service.   Does the competitor offer service contracts? Is diservice tied to product sales? What is the company's service reputation among its customers?

Management can use this information to identify a firm's strategic priorities. For example, strong commitment to preserving market share is signaled by the following activities:

- Price-cutting to undersell competitors.
- Launching new products to improve market position.
- Raiding key accounts of rival firms.
- Defending copyright, patent, or trademark infringements vigorously in court.
- Acquiring new firms to improve product line.
- Building new factories.
- Upgrading product packaging regularly.
- Aggressive spending on research and development.

Management should always attempt to determine: (1) whether competitors are gaining or losing share in target markets, (2) whether competitors' current positions can be expected to improve or deteriorate if strategies do not change, and (3) what adjustments will probably be made to improve market position.

CAPABILITY

The assumptions, objectives, and strategies affect the timing, intensity, and direction of a competitor's marketing efforts. The firm's capabilities determine its ability to take on new projects and to defend itself in the marketplace.

To evaluate capabilities, examine product quality, market penetration, sales volume, internal organization, and innovation. Compare strengths and weaknesses in these areas to complete the competitor profile. Consider, for example, a competitor that has a strong sales operation but a weak R&D department. From a strategic standpoint, this company's selling strengths may be offset by another firm's ability to capture market share through new-product development.

Sources of Information

Discovering where to find reliable information about rival firms may seem a formidable task. Fortunately, many managers will find they already have a good starting base when they review the information available in-house. In fact, fostering the interest and enthusiasm of company staff is an invaluable first step in the development of an effective competitor analysis program. Explain the goals of the competitor analysis program, detailing the type of information that will enable the company to meet these goals. Employees should understand that their contribution is crucial to the program's success. Emphasize that the task of intelligence gathering is actually an extension of their present duties, rather than an additional responsibility.

In addition, carefully explain the difference between relevant and unimportant information. Employees need specific guidelines about the subject matters the company hopes to study. For example, indicate whether desired information relates to the competitor's product line, sales force, or current advertising campaign, and emphasize which particular aspects are most important.

The firm should consider providing incentives to its employees in order to keep intelligence efforts on target. Compensation can take the form of a graduated schedule of bonuses, where employees are rewarded a nominal cash award for the amount and quality of information submitted. However, incentives need not be limited to monetary awards. Companywide recognition and personal commendations to those who have contributed significant information—particularly when such information leads to an important strategic benefit—can prove just as effective.

DEPARTMENTS AS SOURCES

Employees should be made aware that they are part of a team effort. In one form or another, each department in the company possesses useful information about the competition. Information contributed by one department will combine with that from other departments to create an overall picture. The following are examples of how a firm's own departments can be used to monitor the competition.

Sales Force. The sales force is probably the most immediate and ready source of competitor information in any organization. Consider requiring sales staff to complete monthly reports about competitor activity they observe during their selling efforts.

Purchasing. The purchasing department works daily with many of the same suppliers that service the competition. Therefore, purchasing may have direct access to information about competitors through conversations with vendors.

Distribution. Like purchasing, the distribution department works or has contact with firms that may also serve competitors. Thus, distribution staff may be able to learn about the distribution networks used by competing firms.

Personnel. Have the human resource department periodically review help-wanted advertisements for same-industry positions. By monitoring these ads, the company can judge the stability of a competitor's staff, and draw general conclusions about the effectiveness of its management.

Research and Development. R&D departments typically keep files on competitors' products, design specifications, and patent information. In addition, researchers are usually in contact with universities or other research institutes that monitor important innovations taking place within the industry. A firm with an R&D department will almost always have access to valuable competitor information. If the company does not have a formal research and development operation, consider appointing a team to generate contacts that can assist in gathering this type of information.

SOURCES OUTSIDE THE COMPANY

Information obtained through employee efforts should be supplemented with data available from outside sources. Usually, these sources require research on the part of company staff, but they can yield critical insights into competitor activities.

Trade Information. Perhaps the most reliable and accessible outside source is the trade show. Monitor the calendars of events in trade publications. Advance trade show information often lists new products slated for exhibition as well as the names of the exhibitors. Exhibitor booths typically overflow with printed material explaining product specifications and service arrangements.

Further, directories distributed at trade shows and conferences should be retained. When a number of these documents have been collected, they can be studied for patterns in competitor participation and product emphasis.

Note that trade journals, magazines, and newsletters can become vital to the competitor analysis system. These publications should be reviewed for leads regarding industry trends and news about other companies.

News Clippings.   Small local publications, as well as major city newspapers, are viable sources for monitoring business activities. The key, however, is to design a system that effectively screens these numerous sources. If in-house staff do not have the time or expertise to gather news clippings, contact a public relations or advertising agency for assistance. These firms usually provide news-clipping service or can refer clients to a news-clip vendor.

News-clipping services will search for specific information as defined by the company. Material can be requested according to general categories (i.e., all the direct marketing activities for a particular type of product) or by targeting one company for study. News-clip vendors usually charge a small fee for each clipping.

Government Filings.   Federal and state public filings are another information source that should not be neglected. The most frequently used federal source of information on publicly held competitors is the Securities and Exchange Commission. Public filings include financial statements as well as information concerning the issuance of new stock or a new acquisition. Further, corporate environmental filings often reveal information on processes and materials used in production.

Advertisements.   Competitors' advertising approaches are, in most cases, tied to the overall marketing strategy. By analyzing the message in print ads and other media, management may gain valuable insights. For assistance, there are firms similar to news-clipping vendors that will provide, for a fee, tearsheets of advertisements from magazines and newspapers.

Companies can also use direct mail as means of tracking competitors' promotional materials. When different employees are put on various mailing lists, a steady influx of competitor marketing information becomes available to the company.

Plan of Action

Once the above data has been gathered, the competitor analysis program requires a detailed plan of action describing how the information will be used. Many companies document planned activities in the form of a business plan so that progress toward the original goals of the program can be monitored. This written document typically includes a mission statement, timetable, and budget.

Mission Statement.   The mission statement sets forth the objectives of the competitor analysis program. It should be a brief paragraph defining what information is being sought and how it will be used. A typical mission statement might read as follows:

> Compile, evaluate, and communicate information about competitors' market activities, advertising strategies, technological capabilities, and future products. The information will be used to keep marketing, sales, and production departments apprised of the competition so that their decision-making capabilities are enhanced.

This statement can also serve as an announcement of the competitor analysis program to the entire company. When used for this purpose, it should be posted where all employees can see it.

Timetable.   A timetable for implementing the activities of the program should be established according to the information needs of the various departments involved. For instance, the sales manager may need information about a competitor's pricing schedule before attending a major trade show.

Budget.   The competitor analysis program should be treated as a profit-centered rather than cost-centered project. This means that financial gains generated from information produced by competitor analysis should be credited to the competitor analysis program.

Conclusion

Once a competitor's capabilities are assessed, a summary of findings, including assumptions, objectives, strategies, and capabilities should be developed. Attempt to answer these questions: What are the most probable strategic changes that the competitor will make? How strong will the move be? Which other rivals will be most vulnerable? Such analysis enables the company to gauge the potential impact of any actions that might be initiated by the competitor.

There are three key elements to the development of a successful competitor analysis program: commitment, continuity, and contribution. The firm must first make a commitment to the time and resources necessary to maintaining the program. There must be a continuous monitoring of the program once it is implemented. Finally, the ultimate success of the competitor analysis effort requires the contribution of all employees within the firm.

BIBLIOGRAPHY

Fuld, Leonard M., Monitoring The Competition: *Find Out What's Really Going On Over There,* John Wiley & Sons (New York), 1988.

Gilad, Benjamin and Tamar Gilad, *The Business Intelligence System: A New Tool For Competitive Advantage,* American Management Association (New York), 1988.

Johnson, William, with Jack Maguire, *Who's Stealing Your Business?: How To Identify And Prevent Business Espionage,* American Management Association (New York), 1988.

Porter, Michael E., *Comparative Strategy: Techniques For Analyzing Industries And Competitors,* The Free Press (New York), 1980.

Environmental Scanning for Small and Growing Firms

John A. Pearce II, Bruce L. Chapman and Fred R. David

INTRODUCTION

The successful business in a complex and competitive world tends to be one that systematically plans for the future. In response to environmental changes, there has been a significant rise in formal strategic planning systems and in the development of environmental scanning to support those systems.

Environmental scanning is an organized way of looking at the world outside the company so that planners can anticipate new opportunities and impending dangers soon enough to deal with them effectively. Strategic planning is the rudder that keeps a business on course; environmental scanning is the radar that informs the pilot of conditions which are likely to be encountered. Scanning techniques range from the regular monthly reading of a business journal to the continuous operation of an information analysis department employing a large staff of researchers and analysts. The information sources for environmental scanning data are similarly broad in range and quality, as described in Figure 1.

Small businesses are beginning to recognize the need for conscious and continuous study of their environment. Today's small business managers often find their futures dependent on events that they might not have noticed ten or twenty years ago. The rise or fall of the dollar in European money markets, or the actions of a foreign power half-a-world distant are examples.

Timely and accurate knowledge of the relevant environment is a major element in the success or failure of the small and growing business. Indeed, many of the most important reasons for small business

Source: John A. Pearce II, Bruce L. Chapman, and Fred R. David, "Environmental Scanning for Small and Growing Firms," *Journal of Small Business Management* 20, no. 3 (July 1982), pp. 27-34.

FIGURE 1 Information Sources of Environmental Scanning Data

Internal Sources	*Sample Techniques*	*Comments*
Production and marketing information	Question salesmen and technical representatives, examine sales records. Record unfilled customer requests.	In general, these techniques organize information you already possess. They are a cheap, easy, first step toward an organized information network.
Internal analysis	Project sales. Compute: —Market boundaries —Marketing effectiveness —Production capacity —Resource capacity —Asset intensity —Common financial ratios.	A basic tool in environmental scanning, information analysis ranges from quick, simple calculations to elaborate computer models. Availability of inexpensive, powerful micro-computers puts fairly sophisticated analysis techniques well within the reach of the small businessman. Be sure that you know the limitations of the results, however, or you could be badly misled into faulty generalizations.
Management's experience	Brain-storming. Position papers. Delphi techniques.	The experience of a company's management is still one of the most valuable sources of strategic information. These techniques are specifically intended to make the most of that resource.

External Sources	*Examples*	*Comments*
Publications: • **General business** • **Trade journals** • **Government publications** • **Required government reports**	*Business Week, Wall Street Transcript. Restaurant News, New Equipment Digest. Official Gazette* of the U.S. Patent & Trademark Office. Environmental impact statements, required federal and state financial reports.	Publications are the cornerstone of any environmental scanning system. They are a cheap, reliable source of information about the world at large as well as a specific industry. Try to strike a balance between general business publications and trade journals. Investigate lesser-known journals and newsletters; they can be a goldmine of information not yet known to most of your competitors.
Consultants: • **Government** • **Non-profit** • **Paid consultants**	Industry analysts in the Commerce Department. Universities, non-profit foundations. Marketing consultants, engineering consultants.	Consultants need not cost a lot of money (though many do). Most government agencies, universities, and non-profit foundations have experts, analysts, and consultants who will answer questions about a specific industry for little or no money; the National Referral Center of the Library of Congress is a good way to find these consultants. Specific questions about your company usually require a paid consultant, but the cost of consultation can be eased by careful shopping.

FIGURE 1   *(concluded)*

External Sources	Examples	Comments
Miscellaneous sources	Tear down competitors' products. Play customers to the competition. Buy shares of competitors' stock. Attend convention and trade shows. Talk directly to your customers.	Many of these techniques skirt the fuzzy line between environmental scanning and industrial espionage: deceiving salesmen by playing customer makes many people uncomfortable, others see it as a harmless smokescreen. Like any ethical question, the final answer must come from the person using the technique.

failures, such as deficient planning, over-investment, unrealistic pricing, low sales, and inadequate cost control, can be traced to small business managers' inattention to the world beyond the office door.

SPECIAL SMALL BUSINESS CONCERNS

Because of the decisive head start of corporate strategists, small business managers may be tempted to copy corporate scanning techniques. But copying the strict form of a technique—instead of its function—is usually inefficient, often ineffective, and potentially disastrous. Imitation of large firm environmental forecasting techniques by small firms seldom works, for three basic reasons.

First, small businesses lack the capital and human resources that many techniques require. Small businesses usually begin with limited capital and have difficulty raising more, so there is seldom cash available to invest in elaborate strategic programs. Also, small firms often lack expertise outside their special area of competence, so that complex and expensive techniques, or those that require specialized knowledge or skills, are unlikely to succeed. Finally, since small businesses seldom have enough people to handle even normal business demands, the adoption of forecasting techniques, especially those that require the time of the CEO, will either overburden the business or will be compromised.

Second, large firms are usually systems oriented, while small businesses tend to be personality oriented. A necessary part of the evolution of a large corporation is its lessening of dependence on individuals. The small firm, on the other hand, is typically headed by one or a few key people. These key people are responsible for the important decisions at every level of the company, from the most routine daily operations to the broadest business strategy; thus their personalities become a controlling characteristic of the firm. An environmental scanning technique must be acceptable to these people, or its output is unlikely to be well received. To be truly valuable, it must fully utilize those key personalities' strengths, and minimize their weaknesses.

Third, the greatest strength of the small business lies in its flexibility and maneuverability. Small businesses are usually labor-intensive, thereby reducing the need to acquire or divert large amounts of capital equipment to enter a venture. Decision chains are shorter, so less time is lost between perceiving a new opportunity and capitalizing on it. In addition, the clear, immediate command of the CEO over a relatively small group of employees often generates a synergistic "team effort"; a unity of purpose that allows the company to accommodate changes normally impossible for larger businesses. A scanning technique must be selected and modified to support and enhance these strengths, or the small company is bound to lose to the overwhelming economies of scale of the large corporation.

ANALYSIS OF SCANNING NEEDS

Choosing and modifying a firm's environmental scanning techniques can best be done through a structured analysis of small business forecasting needs and priorities The following four recommendations can form the basis of such an analysis:

First, figure out what the technique provides. Consider not only the type of data provided by the technique (e.g., industry average ROE) but also the precision, accuracy, timeliness, reliability, completeness, and scope of each type of data.

Analyze the technique completely and accurately; such analysis lays a firm foundation for future decisions about the technique's usefulness. It is often helpful to evaluate each technique, using a standard "method analysis worksheet." These worksheets should later be placed in a permanent file of environmental scanning methods, even if the technique is not going to be used right away. A business's information needs change as the business changes, and this file will be a valuable resource in the future.

Second, evaluate the firm's need for the information the technique provides.

Make a list of the company's information needs that includes the relative importance of each piece of information to the company as well as the level of precision, accuracy, and timeliness that each must have. Compare the list of information needed with the list of information a particular technique can provide, marking those items that match, exceed, or fall short of the business' current needs.

Examine the deficient pieces of information to see if the technique can be modified to raise the data's quality. Look at "over-rich" data to see if money can be saved by relaxing the quality of the data to a lower, but acceptable, level. Finally, carefully consider the pieces of data that the technique provides but that are not on your list of needs—the business may be overlooking a valuable indicator. If a new piece of information seems worthwhile, add it to your list of needs and try using it for a while if possible. Even if a given piece of information is unusable, ask yourself if similar pieces of information might be helpful. Keep the list of information needs in the scanning methods file for future use, but do not scratch "needed" information even after you find a way to obtain it—a scanning method that you encounter in the future may turn out to be cheaper or more efficient.

Third, analyze the cost/benefit ratio of the technique. Consider all costs associated with the scanning technique, including the cost of the strategic planner's time. Be sure to explore every avenue for cutting costs; try to get the most you can for your money. Compare costs with an estimate of the benefits you expect to receive. Aim for a rough estimate, one that you could work up in a few minutes using only paper and pencil. If the technique looks promising, then it merits a more detailed look. The final evaluation of the technique depends on your informed judgment. This is just a way of giving that judgment something to work on.

Fourth, establish an acceptable level of risk. Large corporations often make their money the same way gambling casinos do: by banking on the odds. A casino daily bets huge amounts of money on events that it cannot predict, such as the roll of a die or the order of randomized cards—and it often loses sizable amounts of money on these bets. It prospers in the knowledge that, over the long run, it will keep about 2 percent of the money that flows through its games. In the same way, an oil company will sink millions of dollars into nine dry wells, banking on the statistical prediction that the tenth well will pay for itself and the nine dry holes that went before, with plenty of profit to spare. Unfortunately, the small company cannot play the odds; one major miscalculation may bankrupt the company. The small firm cannot bet high stakes on a 20:1 payoff that is 10 percent certain unless it has no other choice; instead, it must opt for the 10 percent payoff that is 92 percent sure, and its environmental scanning techniques must reflect this requirement.

IMPLEMENTATION GUIDELINES

The basic differences between large and small firms suggest four general guidelines for profitably implementing environmental scanning in small and growing firms.

First, minimize the cost—not only dollar cost, but manpower cost. A surprising number of environmental scanning techniques use information sources that cost little or no money; federal, state, and local government agencies, for example, produce useful information as a byproduct of their normal functioning. Other sources include private and public nonprofit and educational organizations. However, while the information is free for the asking, one may need to invest large amounts of time in locating and analyzing it, and that time may be diverted from critical and demanding day-to-day operations. Luckily, a small business can reduce or eliminate these costs in several ways.

Start by trading precision for cost. The techniques used by a large corporation often provide information that is more exact (and more expensive) than the small business really needs.[1] After all, to a large business, an error of a few percentage points in an estimate can often translate to a loss of many hundreds of thousands of dollars. But at the dollar volume that a small business generates, the same percentage difference might translate to only a few thousands of dollars, and it does not make sense to spend ten times that amount to insure against the potential loss. For example, the small business can accept estimates in round numbers, e.g., $125,000 vs. $123,976. This has the added advantage of reminding one that any predictions of future earnings or expenses are indeed estimates, and should be viewed with reservation.

Try to reduce the amount of data examined. Normally only one or two key factors are of prime interest to the firm,[2] and these factors should be monitored closely and continuously. Business managers should also keep close watch on factors that require a long lead time before an effective response can be made, as well as on those that have only a moderately strong effect on the firm but are likely to change.[3] Other environmental factors can be monitored with much less sensitivity and frequency. This approach does introduce the possibility of significant changes going unnoticed, but it retains the critically important awareness that there might be something "out there" that could strongly affect the company's future. It is this awareness that writers cite as the single most important benefit of initiating a formal environmental scanning system.

Second, streamline the method. One of the great strengths of the small business is its ability to keep employees in touch with what the company is doing and why it is doing it. Even if a sophisticated

---

[1] Jacob Naor, "How to Make Strategic Planning Work for Small Businesses," *SAM Advanced Management Journal*, Winter 1980, p. 37.

[2] Theodore Cohn and Roy A. Lindberg, *Hou Management Is Different in Small Companies* (American Management Association, Inc., 1972), p. 24.

[3] Harold E. Klein and William H. Newman, "How to Integrate New Environmental Forces into Strategic Planning," *Management Review*, July 1980, p. 48.

scanning technique were more efficient than a straightforward approach, the small firm rarely has an employee with the specialized training and knowledge required to implement and monitor it. Thus, the way to preserve this essential strength of the small business is to use a technique in its most straightforward, understandable form.

Third, enhance the effectiveness of scanning by selecting techniques that fit the personalities of the people using them. A technique that requires long hours in a library searching, sorting, and analyzing pages of statistics is almost sure to die of neglect at the hands of the active, outgoing head of a marketing organization, but it might be just the thing for the CEO of an innovative engineering company. By the same token, an extroverted strategic planner could glean mountains of gold from his counterparts at an industry convention, while a more reserved person would leave with only jetlag.

The typical large corporation does not tailor techniques to individuals simply because they cannot expect to have the same people implementing the technique for very long. Corporate environmental scanning often requires a sizable group of people to implement, and over time, members of this group may be promoted or leave the firm for one reason or another. Compensating for turnover would keep the planning staff in turmoil and virtually eliminate their effectiveness.

In the small company, however, environmental scanning techniques will not be used by a large staff, but by one or a few people at the highest operational levels. These people may have been with the firm since its beginning and can be expected to keep their strategic planning responsibilities for a good deal longer. Forcing these executives to learn unnatural or uncomfortable ways of doing things is an intolerable waste of time and talents. Encouraging users to conscientiously adapt given methods to fit their personalities, compensate for their weaknesses, and enhance their strengths will ensure that the technique is used more often, more easily, and more efficiently.

Fourth, never let the technique hobble the firm's flexibility and maneuverability. One strength common to small firms is the ability to exploit business opportunities outside their present scope of operations. In several major industries, important innovations have been made by small firms working in unfamiliar fields.[4] Using an environmental scanning technique that screens and focuses the strategic planner's information too narrowly would nullify this advantage.

Small firms tend to stick too closely to formal plans, and to think too highly of methods used by big business. In the less structured world of the small business, sound judgment sometimes dictates a course of

---

[4]Colin Smith and Lyn Wilson, "The Intelligence of Change," *Management Today*, May 1980, p. 36.

action directly counter to formal plans. The small business manager should never disengage his or her judgment, but should strive to make it an integral part of the strategic process by using information from the various scanning techniques to sharpen and refine it.

Finally, use the technique for a while, and then modify it as required. Pencil and paper analysis cannot tell you everything about a technique; sooner or later you have to make a trial run in the real world. This transfer from theory to practice should take place much sooner in a small business than in a large corporation. The small business does not have either the skilled analysts or the large start-up costs of a large corporation, so a small business usually gets more information for less money by using the technique as soon as analysis shows that it may be worthwhile.

Responsibility for implementing and modifying a technique should lie with the strategic planner, since the ultimate aim is to mold the technique to his personality and needs. A reasonable amount of attention toward refining the technique in the first year of use should markedly enhance its future utility.

Once a year or so, closely examine all of the scanning techniques in use, new and old, to identify those that are valuable and eliminate those that are dead weight. A small business cannot afford waste in the strategy-making process anymore than it can in any of its business operations.

CONCLUSION

Development of a small business environmental scanning process can be enhanced by borrowing the hard-won knowledge of the large corporations. However, corporate scanning techniques cannot be used blindly or haphazardly, but must be carefully adapted with a full understanding of the differences between large and small businesses. Only then can the small and growing business be sure that it is building a strong, efficient base for its overall strategic planning system.

PART III

Alternative Company Strategies

By the term *strategy,* managers are referring to their large-scale, future-oriented plans for interacting with their competitive environments to optimize the achievement of organization objectives. Thus, the number of different strategies is almost as large as the number of different organizations that develop them. However, the differences are often so small and the similarities so many and so great, that it is possible to talk about the competitive settings in which each of several broadly defined types of strategies are most likely to produce desired results.

The first of the eight articles in this section provides an overview of the types of master or grand strategies that are available to a firm. The author describes 12 types of strategies that can be used to focus the profitability, growth, and survival needs of a firm and suggests the conditions under which each strategy is likely to provide specific benefits. Subsequent articles provide a detailed analysis of the specific advantages, disadvantages, and applications of individual options including strategies of concentrated growth, vertical integration, joint venture, divestiture, and turnaround.

The final article in this section focuses on the selection and modification of basic types of strategies for use by service sector businesses. In this award winning manuscript, the authors argue that the traditional view of strategies, as developed by and for manufacturing firms, must be modified to satisfy the special needs of service firms. The article includes guidelines that practicing managers can use to guide them in the development of their own strategic plans.

Abstracts

SELECTING AMONG ALTERNATIVE GRAND STRATEGIES

Despite variations in the implementation of the strategic management approach, there is widespread agreement among designers of planning systems on the critical role of grand strategies to provide direction for strategic actions. Two problems have limited practicing managers' use of grand strategies to indicate how the firm's long-range objectives will be achieved. First, the range of alternative grand strategies available to the decision makers is often not fully understood. Second, strategic decision makers who generate lists of promising grand strategies are often without a logical and systematic approach to the selection of a preferable alternative.

The purpose of this article is twofold: to list, describe, and discuss 12 grand strategy options which should be considered by strategic planners, and to present an approach for the selection of an optimal grand strategy from among available alternatives.

The selection of a promising grand strategy is best guided by the use of matrix analysis. The basic idea underlying the matrix is that two variables are of central concern in the selection process: the purpose of the grand strategy and the choice of an internal or external emphasis for growth and profitability. Using this approach, decision makers are better able to identify alternatives with the highest probabilities of success for achieving the firm's long-term objectives.

CONCENTRATED GROWTH STRATEGIES

Despite the popularity and success of concentrated growth strategies, managers have been left without guidelines to help them in determining when their firm should go about maximizing the advantages of the strategy. This article directs attention to challenges confronted by managers who undertake a concentrated growth strategy through reliance on internal development. The study also identifies several conditions in the firm's environment that are particularly conducive to the concentrated growth strategy.

Systematic analysis of new product successes and failures underscores the risk of deviating from company strengths. Staying with what the firm does best and avoiding areas of undeveloped skills are the bases for their endorsement of concentrated growth.

The greatest influences on the market success of firms that implement a concentrated growth strategy are the ability to assess market needs, knowledge of buyer behavior, customer price sensitivity, and effectiveness of promotion.

Under stable conditions, a concentrated growth strategy poses the lowest risk among grand strategies to a firm's economic stability. However, in a changing environment, a firm committed to concentrated growth faces high risks. It is also vulnerable to high opportunity costs by remaining in a specific product market when other options are ignored that could employ the firm's resources more profitably. Nevertheless, the limited additional resources necessary to implement concentrated growth, coupled with the relatively low level of risk involved, make this strategy desirable for a firm with limited funds.

QUICK CHANGE STRATEGIES FOR VERTICAL INTEGRATION

Finding an appropriate vertical integration strategy is often a matter of common sense, but the optimum solutions are overlooked when managers do not understand potential business unit synergies and other benefits of vertical integration. This dilemma is compounded by a manager's desire to maintain strategic flexibility. Given the nature of competition, it is clear that many firms have either the wrong kind of vertical integration or much more than they need. Their internal arrangements and management systems get in the way of their business units' realizing the most from vertical synergies.

The vertical integration framework is a set of contingencies that suggest an orientation, or desirable ends, not inviolate rules. To bring vertical integration strategy in line with competitive realities, the authors encourage top management to recognize that vertical integration strategies are not static, to know company strengths, to recognize implicit subsidizations, to keep to hospitable industries, to create a new player, to use international alliances, to scrutinize vertical transfer policies, to test all assumptions, and to be wary of short-term pressures.

The key to effective use of vertical synergies is keeping alert to industry changes that affect the firm's opportunities. Managers must also beware of investing far upstream or downstream to acquire capabilities beyond the firm's core strengths. Finally, the costs of cross-subsidization must be justified by the benefits. The key determinants of whether or not a firm should skip a particular stage in its integrated chain of activities are the task's centrality to its corporate mission, the synergies it provides, and the quality of goods or services provided by outsiders.

JOINT VENTURES IN THE FACE OF GLOBAL COMPETITION

As a result of high costs associated with poor timing, loss of control, increased competition, and technology swapping, joint ventures are often unstable. Yet, recent evidence suggests that joint ventures can be more useful in global competition than managers of U.S. multinational corporations have historically thought. This article represents a framework that helps managers decide when to use a joint venture to do business abroad. Assuming that managers are free to choose the ownership structure for a foreign venture, the decision should depend on their strategies for managing the firm's capabilities and geographic scope. The role of the venture in these strategies influences the costs and benefits of joint as compared with whole ownership.

The proposed framework recommends a joint venture when a firm needs to expand its capabilities to compete successfully, but not when it will merely exploit an existing advantage. A joint venture is also not recommended when there are potential conflicts of interest between the partners. Opposing forces are likely to drive the choice of ownership structure for foreign subsidiaries in global industries. The tension between the need to expand globally and the need to control the network is likely to be felt in industry after industry well into the future.

CORPORATE DIVESTITURE: "PRUNING FOR HIGHER PROFITS"

Corporate divestiture of business segments has become an accepted alternative growth strategy to diversification. As the economic environment becomes more competitive, the ability of management to actively direct and control the multibusiness becomes more important than ever before.

In a diversified business, resource allocation becomes an important consideration. The redirection of resources, whether material assets or management talent, to growing parts of the business requires attention and review. If management finds itself spending a disproportionate amount of its time and energy on one part of the corporate entity, that segment may be a candidate for divestiture.

The development of a divestiture strategy is formalized when a situation arises that cannot be solved by continuing to operate the particular business unit. These divestiture candidates are units with no hope of recovery in the present parent corporation. A corporation may develop a divestment and implementation strategy to deal with this emotional subject. The conception of a divestment strategy often begins with a listing of the reasons for possible divestiture. Management must consider the physical interrelationships of facilities, the interdependence of other corporate activities, and the costs of dissociating a business segment. To be effective, a divestment strategy requires an implementation program that is sensitive to all of these issues.

DIVESTITURE: ANTIDOTE TO MERGER MANIA

Corporate divestitures provide an antidote for merger mania. They not only support a psychological equilibrium; they also help firms maintain a desired level of resources, sales, earnings, and stock prices. They illustrate today's practice of asset management, a strategy that concentrates on efficiency and effectiveness. This article examines strategies for divesting subunits and other assets. It then discusses corporate restructuring and gives an example of the strategy.

In reviewing its assets and their profit contributions, a corporation is likely to find some that are not sufficiently profitable. Management also may find that some assets do not fit with those used in its primary activities. Prompt abandonment of poor performers and misfits avoids drains on other resources and keeps employee morale high.

A corporation typically uses one of three methods of divesting a component unit: outright sale, spin-off, or liquidation. Often divestiture has both an immediate, titanic effect on a firm's assets and a longer-run downward influence on earnings, thus significantly affecting its overall strategies. Methods of divesting business units are covered and accounting concepts and divestiture techniques are presented. Finally, some of the tax considerations in divesting are outlined.

FROM WARNING TO CRISIS: A TURNAROUND PRIMER

Long before a business fails, warning signals start flashing. But managers do not always notice the danger signs and even occasionally ignore them. However, with the proper tools and guidance, managers can train themselves to recognize the bad signs, whether they are activated from within the organization or from the outside. Once managers learn the signals, they also can differentiate between the various stages of organizational decline. This article presents a turnaround primer that identifies warning signals, categorizes decline phases, and provides a framework to help managers reverse the direction of an organization that may well be on its way to complete failure.

A turnaround can take several forms. It can be strategic if the business needs to be redefined because of changing markets and products. An operational turnaround involves changing a business's operations, which could include cost cutting, revenue generating, and asset reduction. The financial turnaround restructures the financial operations of a business. The object is to utilize the financial strength of the business as an asset. Each type of turnaround may focus on a particular strategy. These include: revenue generating, product/markets refocusing, cost cutting, and asset reduction. Using the current strategy is part of the art of successfully turning around a company.

CUSTOMIZED STRATEGIES FOR SERVICE SECTOR BUSINESSES

There has been a long-standing perception that the planning problems that service sector firms face differ meaningfully from those of manufacturing companies. Yet, the exact nature of these differences is often elusive. A careful comparison of service with manufacturing firms suggests the possibility for developing a basis for analysis that can be used in the identification and proper evaluation of competitive options particular to service industries.

This article presents a framework for helping consultants recognize and evaluate the planning implications of the factors that distinguish service industries. It is designed to facilitate the analysis of the attractiveness of a service firm's strategic options, given its operational resource and its customer interface characteristics.

It is a basic premise of this article that the profit earned by a service firm will depend directly on the mix of strategies chosen by the firm, and by how well it implements its choices. Major strategic options available to service firms include emphasis on: focus, firm image, chain identification, franchising, service quality, cost position, ancillary services, low price, and financial leverage.

The need to understand the specific character of a business gives rise to the need for a classification scheme for service firms that addresses both their internal and external characteristics. Six such classifications are identified. It is also important to understand how use of each of the nine competitive options may be favorable or unfavorable to firms in each of the six firm classifications. The authors recommend that managers become familiar with the relationships between competitive options and the categories and variables used in each of the classifications.

The model developed in this paper has broad applicability for managers of service firms in their decision making on competitive options. It is a guide to productive idea generation and it provides a powerful, fundamental way to think about service firm opportunities and constraints.

Selecting among Alternative Grand Strategies

John A. Pearce II

Despite variations in the implementation of the strategic management approach, there is widespread agreement among designers of planning systems on the critical role of grand strategies.[1] Intended to provide direction for strategic actions, grand strategies are seen as the basis of coordinated and sustained efforts directed toward the achievement of a business's long-term objectives.

As theoretically and conceptually attractive as the idea of grand strategies has proven to be, two problems have limited practicing managers' use of the approach. First, the range of alternative grand strategies available to the decision makers is often not fully understood. The tendency of strategic managers to build incrementally from the status quo often presents unnecessary limitations on their search to improve corporate performance. Other executives have simply never considered the variety of options available as attractive grand strategies. Second, strategic decision makers who generate lists of promising grand strategies are often without a logical and systematic approach to the selection of a preferable alternative. Few planning experts have attempted to proffer viable evaluative criteria and selection tools.[2]

The purpose of this article is twofold: to list, describe, and discuss twelve grand strategy options which should be considered by strategic planners and to present an approach for the selection of an optimal grand strategy from among available alternatives.

GRAND STRATEGIES

Grand strategies indicate how the firm's long-range objectives will be achieved. A grand strategy can be defined as a comprehensive general approach which guides the major actions designed to accomplish long-term objectives of a business.

There are twelve principal grand strategy options, any one of which could serve to provide the basis for achieving major long-term objectives. However, when a company is involved in multiple businesses, multiple grand strategies are usually required. Each of these options is described in this section with examples to indicate some of their relative strengths and weaknesses.

Concentration

By far the most frequently selected grand strategy is concentration on the current business. The firm directs its resources to the profitable growth of a single product, in a single market, or with a single technology. Some of America's largest and most successful companies have traditionally adopted the concentration approach. Examples include W. K. Kellogg and Gerber Foods, which are known for their product, Holiday Inn, which concentrates on geographic expansion, and Lincoln Electric, which bases its growth on technological advances.

The reasons for selecting a concentration grand strategy are easy to understand. Concentration is often preferred to the others because it is typically lowest in risk and in additional resources required. It is also based on the known competencies of the firm. On the negative side, for most companies a concentration strategy tends to result in slow growth, a more narrow range of investment options, and few opportunities for surges of profitability. Further, because of their narrow base of competition, concentrated firms are susceptible to performance variations resulting from industry trends.

A grand strategy of concentration allows for a considerable range of action. Broadly speaking, the business can attempt to capture a larger market share by increasing present customers' rate of usage, by attracting competitors' customers, or by interesting nonusers to buy the product. In turn, each of these actions suggest a more specific set of alternatives. Some of these options are listed in the top section of Table 1.

Market and Product Development

When strategic managers forecast that the combination of their current products with their current markets will not provide a basis from which they can achieve their company mission, they have two

TABLE 1   Specific Options under Three Grand Strategies

Grand Strategy: Concentration
(increasing use of present projects in present markets)

Specific Options:
- Increase present customers' rate of usage,
  increase unit of purchase size,
  increase rate of product obsolescence,
  advertise other uses,
  give price incentives for increased use.
- Attract competitors' customers,
  establish sharper brand differentiation,
  increase promotional effort,
  initiate price cuts.
- Attract nonusers to buy product,
  induce trial use through sampling and price inducements,
  price up or down,
  advertise new uses.

Grand Strategy: Market Development
(selling present products in new markets)

Specific Options:
- Open additional geographical markets,
  regional expansion,
  national expansion,
  international expansion.
- Attract other market segments,
  develop product versions to appeal to other segments,
  enter other channels of distribution,
  advertise in other media.

Grand Strategy: Product Development
(developing new products for present markets)

Specific Options:
- Develop new product features,
  adapt (to other ideas, developments),
  modify (color, motion, sound, odor, form, shape),
  magnify (make stronger, longer, thicker, of extra value),
  minify (make smaller, shorter, lighter),
  substitute (ingredients, process, power),
  rearrange (patterns, layout, sequence, components),
  reverse (inside out),
  combine (units, purposes, appeals, ideas).
- Develop quality variations.
- Develop additional models and sizes (product proliferation).

Source: Adapted by the author from: H. Igor Ansoff, "Strategies for Diversification," *Harvard Business Review* (September-October 1957); David J. Luck and Arthur E. Prell, *Market Strategy* (New York: Appleton-Century-Crofts, 1968), pp. 174–83; Alex F. Osborn, *Applied Imagination*, 3rd rev. ed. (New York: Charles Scribner's Sons, 1963), pp. 286–87; Arthur A. Thompson and A. J. Strickland, *Strategy Formulation and Implementation* (Dallas, Texas: Business Publications, 1980, p. 104: Philip Kotler, *Marketing Management* (Englewood Cliffs, N.J.: Prentice Hall, 1972), p. 237.

options which are moderate in cost and risk—market and product development.

Market development commonly ranks second only to concentration as the least costly and least risky of the twelve single grand strategy options. It consists of marketing present products, often with only cosmetic modifications, to customers in related market areas by adding different channels of distribution or by changing the content of its advertising or its promotional media. Several specific approaches are listed in the middle section of Table 1.

Product development involves substantial modification to existing products or the creation of new but related items which can be marketed to current customers through established channels. The adoption of the product development strategy is often made either to prolong the life cycle of current products or to take advantage of favorable reputation and brand name. The idea is to attract satisfied customers to try new products as a result of their positive experience with the company's initial product offering. The bottom third section of Table 1 lists some of the many options available to businesses which undertake product development.

Innovation

It is increasingly risky in many industries not to innovate. Consumer as well as industrial markets have come to expect evolutionary, if not revolutionary, changes in the products which are offered. As a result, some businesses find it profitable to base their grand strategy on innovation. They seek to reap the initially high profits associated with customers' acceptance of a new or greatly improved product. Then, rather than face stiffening competition as the basis of profitability shifts from innovation to production or marketing competence, they move on to search for other original or novel ideas. The underlying philosophy of innovation is to create a new product life cycle, thereby making similar existing products obsolete.

While most growth-oriented firms appreciate the need to be occasionally innovative, a few companies use it as their fundamental way of relating to their markets. An outstanding example is Polaroid, which heavily promotes each of its new cameras until competitors are able to match their technological innovation. At that time, Polaroid is normally prepared to introduce a dramatically new or improved product. For example, in short succession consumers were introduced to the Swinger, the SX-70, the One-Step, and the Sonar One-Step.

Few companies succeed using an innovation strategy. The reason stems from the extremely high research, development, and premarketing costs incurred in converting a promising idea into a profitable product.

Horizontal and Vertical Integration

When the long-term strategy of a firm is based on growth through the acquisition of one or more businesses operating at the same stage of the production/marketing chain, its grand strategy is called horizontal integration. Such acquisitions result in the elimination of competitors from the marketplace. For example, Warner-Lambert Pharmaceutical Company's acquisition of Parke Davis in 1970 reduced competition in the ethic drugs field for Chilcott Laboratories, a company which Warner-Lambert had previously acquired, and constituted a horizontal integration. The combinations of two textile producers, two shirt manufacturers, or two clothing store chains would be classified as horizontal integrations.

When the grand strategy of a firm involves the acquisition of businesses which either supply the firm with input, such as raw materials, or serve as customers for the firm's outputs, such as warehousers for finished products, it is engaged in vertical integration. If a shirt manufacturer acquires a textile producer—by purchasing its common stock, buying its assets, or through an exchange of ownership interests—the strategy is a vertical integration. In this case it is a "backward" vertical integration, since the acquisition is of a business operating at an earlier stage of the production/marketing chain. If the shirt manufacturer had merged with a clothing store, it would have been an example of "forward" vertical integration, since it involved the acquisition of a business nearer to the ultimate consumer at the final stage of the chain.

The principal attractions of horizontal integration are readily apparent. The acquiring firm is able to greatly expand its operations, thereby achieving greater market share, improving economies of scale, and increasing efficiency of capital usage. Additionally, these benefits are achieved with only a moderate level of increased risk to the firm, since the success of the expansion is principally dependent upon proven abilities of the company.

The reasons behind the choice of vertical integration are more varied and sometimes less obvious. The main reason for backward integration is the desire to increase the dependability of the supply of raw materials or production inputs. The concern is particularly great when the number of suppliers is few and the number of competitors is many. In this situation, the vertically integrating firm can better control its costs and thereby improve the profit margin of the expanded production/marketing system. Forward integration is a preferred grand strategy for firms when the advantages of stable production are particularly high. A business can increase the predictability of the demand for its output through forward integration, that is, through ownership of the next stage of its production/marketing chain.

There are also some increased risks associated with both types of integration grand strategies. For horizontally integrated firms, the risks stem from the increased commitment of the company to a single business. For vertically integrated firms, the risks result from expansion of the company into areas which require strategic managers of the original business to broaden their competence and assume additional responsibilities.

Joint Venture

Occasionally, two or more capable companies lack a necessary component for success in a particular competitive environment. For example, no single petroleum firm controlled sufficient resources to enable it to construct the Alaskan pipeline, nor was any firm capable of processing and marketing the volume of oil which would flow through the pipeline if it could be constructed. The solution was a set of joint ventures. As shown in Table 2, these cooperative arrangements could provide both the necessary resources to build the pipeline and the processing and marketing capacity to profitably handle the oil flow.

The particular form of joint venture discussed above is called joint ownership.[3] In recent years it has become increasingly appealing for domestic firms to join with foreign businesses through the use of joint ownership. For example, Bethlehem Steel acquired an interest in a Brazilian mining venture as a means of securing a raw material source. The stimulus for this joint ownership was a preference in grand strategy, but such is not always the case. Certain countries virtually mandate that foreign companies entering their markets do so on a joint-ownership basis. India and Mexico are good examples. The rationale of these foreign countries is that such joint ventures minimize the threats of foreign domination and enhance the skills, employment, growth, and profits of local businesses.

Concentric and Conglomerate Diversifications

Grand strategies involving diversification represent distinct departures from a firm's base of operations. They typically involve the acquisition or internal generation (spin-off) of a separate business which offers synergistic possibilities because of the counterbalancing possibilities of the two businesses' strengths and weaknesses. For example, Head Ski initially sought diversifications into summer sporting goods and clothing in order to offset the seasonality of its snow skiing equipment business. However, diversifications are occasionally under-

TABLE 2 Typical Joint Ventures in the Oil Pipeline Industry

Pipeline Company (assets, in millions)	Co-owners	Percent Held by Each
Colonial Pipeline ($480.2)	Amoco	14.3%
	Atlantic Richfield	1.6
	Cities Service	14.0
	Continental	7.5
	Phillips	7.1
	Texaco	14.3
	Gulf	16.8
	Sohio	9.0
	Mobil	11.5
	Union Oil	4.0
Olympic Pipeline ($30.7)	Shell	43.5
	Mobil	29.5
	Texaco	27.0
West Texas Gulf Pipeline ($19.8)	Gulf	57.7
	Cities Service	11.4
	Sun	12.6
	Union Oil	9.0
	Sohio	9.2
Texas-New Mexico Pipeline ($30.5)	Texaco	45.0
	Atlantic Richfield	35.0
	Cities Service	10.0
	Getty	10.0

Source: Testimony of Walter Adams in *Horizontal Integration of the Energy Industry,* Hearings before the Subcommittee on Energy of the Joint Economic Committee, 94th Congress, 1st session (1975), p. 112.

taken as unrelated investments because of their otherwise minimal resource demands and high profit potential.

Regardless of the approach that is taken to diversification—concentric or conglomerate—the motivations of the acquiring firms stem from the same basic set of needs. As summarized by Glueck these motives include:

- To increase the firm's stock value (often in the past, mergers have led to increases in the stock price or price-earnings ratio).
- To increase the growth rate of the firm faster than present internal growth strategy.
- To make a good investment to purchase a unit which makes a better use of funds than plowing the same funds into internal growth.
- To improve the stability of a firm's earnings and sales (by acquiring firms whose earnings and sales complement the firm's peaks and valleys).

- To balance or fill out the product line.
- To diversify the product line when the life cycle of current products has peaked.
- To acquire a needed resource quickly (such as high-quality technology or highly innovative management).
- For tax reasons (to purchase a firm with prior tax losses which will offset current or future earnings).
- To increase efficiency and profitability, especially if there is synergy between the two companies.[4]

When a diversification involves the addition of a business whose activities are related to the firm's current offerings in terms of technology, markets, or products, it is a concentric diversification. With this type of grand strategy the strategic decision makers of the acquiring firm make a conscious effort to select new businesses which possess a high degree of compatibility with their current businesses. The ideal concentric diversification occurs when the combination of company profiles results in increased strengths and opportunities as well as decreased weaknesses and exposure to risk. Thus, the acquiring company searches for new businesses whose products, markets, distribution channels, technologies, and resource requirements are familiar but not identical to its own, synergistic but not wholly interdependent. Examples are plentiful: Eastman Kodak, Procter & Gamble, Johnson & Johnson, United States Steel and dozens of others.

Occasionally, a firm, particularly a very large one, plans to acquire businesses because they represent the most promising investment opportunities available. This type of grand strategy is commonly known as conglomerate diversification. The principal decision criterion of the acquiring firm is the profitability of the venture. There is little concern given to creating product/marketing synergy with existing businesses of the firm, contrary to the approach taken in concentric diversification. However, financial synergy is often sought by conglomerate diversifiers, such as ITT, Textron, American Brands, Litton, U.S. Industries, Fuqua, and I.C. Industries. They may seek a balance in their portfolios between current businesses with cyclical sales and acquired businesses with countercyclical sales, between high cash/low opportunity and low cash/high opportunity businesses, or between debt-free and highly leveraged businesses.

Retrenchment/Turnaround

For any of a large number of reasons, a business can find itself in a period of declining profits. Economic recessions, production inefficiencies, and innovative breakthroughs by competitors are only three examples. In many such cases strategic managers believe that the firm can survive and eventually prosper if a concerted effort is made over the period of a few years to fortify the basic distinctive competencies of the business. This type of grand strategy is known as retrenchment. It is accomplished through one of two ways, employed singly or in combination:

- Cost reduction, accomplished by decreasing the size of the work force by not replacing employees lost through attrition, leasing rather than purchasing equipment, extending the life of machinery, and eliminating elaborate promotional activities.
- Asset reduction, from the sale of land, building, and equipment which are nonessential to the basic activity of the business, and by the elimination of the company airplane and executive cars as perquisites.

If these initial approaches fail to achieve the required reductions, more drastic action may be necessary. It is sometimes essential to lay off employees, drop items from a production line, and even to eliminate low-margin customers.

Since the underlying purpose of a grand strategy of retrenchment is to reverse current negative trend, the method is often referred to as a turnaround strategy. Interestingly, the turnaround most commonly associated with this approach is in management positions. In a study of fifty-eight large firms, researchers Schendel, Patton, and Riggs found that retrenchment for turnaround was almost always associated with changes in top management.[5] Bringing in new managers was believed to introduce needed new perspectives on the firm's situation and to raise employee morale.

Divestiture

A divestiture strategy is the marketing for sale of a business or a major component of a business. When a retrenchment strategy fails to accomplish the desired turnaround, strategic managers often decide to sell the business. However, because the intent is to find a buyer who is willing to pay a premium above the value of fixed assets for a going concern, the term *marketing for sale* is more appropriate. Prospective buyers must be convinced that because of their skills and resources, or the synergy which can be created between their existing businesses and this new addition, they will be able to profit from the acquisition.

The reasons for divestitures vary. Often they arise because of partial mismatches between acquired business and the parent corporation. In time, some of the mismatched parts cannot be integrated into any of the corporation's mainstreams and thus must be spun off. A reason for divesture is the financial needs of the corporation. Sometimes the cash flow or financial stability of the corporation as a whole can be greatly improved if businesses with high market value can be sacrificed. A third, less frequent, reason for divestiture is government antitrust action, which is invoked whenever a corporation is believed to monopolize or unfairly dominate a particular market.

Although examples of grand strategies of divestiture are numerous, the most outstanding example in the last decade is Chrysler Corporation, which in quick succession divested itself of several major businesses in order to protect its mission as a domestic automobile manufacturer. Among major Chrysler sales were its Airtemp airconditioning business to Fedders and its automotive subsidiaries in France, Spain, and England to Peugeot-Citroen. These divestitures yielded Chrysler a total of almost $500 million in cash, notes, and stock and in the relatively short term improved its financial stability. Other corporations which have recently pursued this type of grand strategy include Esmark, which divested Swift and Company, and White Motors, which divested White Farm.

Liquidation

When the grand strategy is that of liquidation, the business is typically sold in parts, only occasionally as a whole, but only for its tangible asset value and not as a going concern. In selecting liquidation, owners and strategic managers of a business are admitting failure and recognize that this action is likely to result in great hardships to themselves and their employees. However, they choose it as a long-term strategy in order to minimize the losses of all stakeholders of the firm. Usually faced with bankruptcy, the liquidating business tries to develop a planned and orderly system which will result in the greatest possible profit and cash conversion as the business slowly relinquishes its market share.

Planned liquidation is worthwhile. For example, the Columbia Corporation, a $130 million diversified firm, liquidated its assets for more cash per share than the market value of its stock.

Combination Grand Strategies

The larger and more diversified a firm is, the more likely it is to require a combination of several grand strategies to reflect the individual needs of its separate businesses. Since a corporation's businesses often compete in different task environments and under significantly different competitive conditions, it is understandable that each single business unit or major division would require a distinctive grand strategy.

TABLE 3   Grand Strategy Selection Matrix

	Areas of Emphasis	
	Internal (redirected resources within the firm)	**External** (acquisition or merger for resource capability)
Overcome Weaknesses	**Quadrant II** Turnaround or retrenchment Divestiture Liquidation	**Quadrant I** Vertical integration Conglomerate diversification
Maximize Strengths	**Quadrant III** Concentration Market development Product development Innovation	**Quadrant IV** Horizontal integration Concentric diversification Joint venture

Purpose of the Grand Strategy

Even a company with a single business typically designs a more complex and multifaceted strategy than any of the independent and isolated approaches just described. For example, a manufacturing business which is divesting its retail outlets may simultaneously plan to sequentially expand its product development activities. Or a corporation may actively seek the concentric diversification of firms which own subsidiaries which can be combined, repackaged, and divested profitably. It was this exact combination strategy which was adopted by the forest products corporation Boise Cascade in the 1960s.

GRAND STRATEGY SELECTION

Selection Matrix

One valuable guide to the selection of a promising grand strategy is the matrix shown in Table 3. The basic idea underlying the matrix is that two variables are of central concern in the selection process: the purpose of the grand strategy and the choice of an internal or external emphasis for growth and profitability.

Although a company profile usually reveals its strengths and weaknesses strategic managers attempt to gain some feel for the basis on which they should develop their grand strategy. In the 1950s and 1960s it was fashionable to advise strategic planners to follow certain rules or prescriptions concerning their choice of strategies. Most experts now agree that strategic selection is much better guided by the unique set of conditions which are seen to exist for the planning period and by the company's strengths and weaknesses. What is valuable to note, however, is that even early approaches to selecting a grand strategy were based on the concern for matching a concern for internal versus external growth with a principal desire either to overcome weaknesses or to maximize strength.

The same two concerns led to the development of the Grand Strategy Selection Matrix in Table 3. A firm in Quadrant I often views itself as overly committed to a particular business which has limited growth opportunities or which involves high risks due to the problems of having all of the company's eggs in one basket. One reasonable solution is vertical integration, which enables the firm to reduce risk by reducing uncertainty either about inputs or about access to customers. Alternatively, a firm may choose conglomerate diversification, which provides a profitable alternative for investment without diluting the attention which management can give to the original business. However, the external orientation for overcoming weaknesses usually results in the most costly grand strategies. The decision to acquire a second business demands both large initial time investments and sizable financial resources. Strategic managers who are considering these approaches must be cautious not to exchange one set of weaknesses for another.

A more conservative approach to overcoming weakness is found in Quadrant II. Firms often chose to redirect resources within the company from one business to another. While this approach does not reduce the company's commitment to its basic mission, it does reward success and enable the further development of proven competitive advantages. The least disruptive of the Quadrant II strategies is retrenchment, which results in the pruning of a current business's activities. In situations where the weaknesses arose from inefficiencies, such retrenchment can actually serve as a turnaround strategy, meaning that the business gains new strength through a streamlining of its operations coupled with an elimination of waste.

However, when the weaknesses of the firm constitute a major obstruction to success in the industry and when the costs of overcoming the weaknesses cannot be afforded or are not justified by a cost-benefit analysis, then the elimination of the business must be considered. Divestiture offers the best possibility for recouping the company's investment, but even liquidation can be an attractive option when the alternatives are an unwarranted drain on organizational resources or bankruptcy.

A commonly repeated business adage argues that a company should "build from strength." The premise is that a company's growth and survival depend on its ability to capture a sufficient market share to enable essential economics of scale. For firms that also believe that their profitability will derive from this approach and which prefer an internal emphasis for maximizing their strengths, four alternative grand strategies hold considerable promise. As shown in Quadrant III, the most frequently adopted approach is concentration on the business—market penetration. The business which selects this strategy is strongly committed to its present products and markets. It will strive to solidify its current position by reinvesting resources in a fortification of its strengths. Two alternative approaches are market and product development. With either of these strategies the business attempts to broaden the basis of its operations. Market development is chosen when strategic managers feel that the existing product offering would be well received by new customer groups. Product development is preferred when existing customers are believed to have interest in products related to the firm's current lines or based on its special technological or other competitive advantages. A final alternative for Quadrant III firms is an innovation strategy. When the business's strengths are in creative product design or unique production technologies it is often strategically attractive to stimulate consumer purchases by accelerating perceived obsolence. This is the principal view underlying the selection of an innovative grand strategy.

When a business seeks to maximize its strengths by aggressively expanding the basis of its operations, external emphasis is usually needed in the selection of its grand strategy. Its preferred options are shown in Quadrant IV. Horizontal integration is attractive because it enables firms to quickly multiply the output capability of the business. The proven skills of the original business's managers are often the critical dimension in converting the new facilities into a profitable contributor to the parent company, thus expanding a fundamental competitive advantage of the firm. Concentric diversification is a good second choice for similar reasons. Because of the relatedness of the original and newly acquired businesses, the distinctive competencies of the firm are likely to facilitate a smooth, synergistic, and profitable expansion of the company's operations. The final option for increasing resource capability through external emphasis is through joint venture. This alternative allows the business to extend its strengths into competitive arenas which for one of various reasons it would be hesitant to attempt single-handedly. However, because of the partner's production, technological, financial, or marketing capabilities, a joint venture can significantly reduce financial investment and increase the probability of success to the point that formidable ventures become attractive growth alternatives.

CONCLUSION

Grand strategies are typically formulated to promote synergy in operations over a period of at least five years. Obviously, their selection merits careful consideration. One way by which the choice process can be improved is through an effort by strategic decision makers to initially consider the comprehensive set of twelve fundamental alternatives discussed early in this article. Allowing for suitable modification and combinations of conceptually pure approaches, these alternatives should provide practical insights to the selection of a firm's most promising grand strategy options.

Additional direction in the selection is provided through the use of the Grand Strategy Matrix. By disciplining themselves to define the basic intent of their grand strategies in terms of purpose and area of emphasis, strategic decision makers are more likely to identify alternatives with the highest probabilities of success for achieving the firm's long-term objectives.

Given the number and strength of competitors in most markets, and the often surprising parity of capabilities which they exhibit, strategic managers need the competitive advantage which an insightfully selected and developed grand strategy can facilitate. The consideration of a comprehensive set of alternatives coupled with selections based on critical success criteria should provide a basis for improvement in the grand strategy choice process.

REFERENCES

1. Among recent models or theories of strategic management are those of J. A. Pearce II, "An Executive Perspective on the Strategic Management Process, *California Management Review,* Vol. XXIX (Fall 1981); G. A. Steiner, *Strategic Planning* (New York: The Free Press, 1979); J. M. Higgins, *Organizational Policy and Strategic Management* (Hinsdale, Ill.: Dryden Press, 1979); H. I. Ansoff, *Strategic Management* (New York: John Wiley & Sons, 1979); R. King and D. I. Cleland, *Strategic Planning and Policy* (New York: Van Nostrand Reinhold, 1978); and G. A. Steiner and J. B. Miner, *Management Policy and Strategy* (New York: Macmillan Publishing, 1977).
2. A noteworthy exception can be found in A. A. Thompson and A. J. Strickland, *Strategy Formulation and Implementation* (Dallas, Texas: Business Publication, 1980).
3. Other forms of Joint ventures include leasing, contract manufacturing, and management contracting.
4. W. F. Glueck, *Business Policy and Strategic Management* (New York: McGraw-Hill, 1980).
5. D. Schendel, G. R. Patton, and J. Riggs, "Corporate Turnaround Strategies: A Study of Profit Decline and Recovery," *Journal of General Management,* Vol. 3 (1976), pp. 3–11.

Concentrated Growth Strategies

John A. Pearce II and James W. Harvey

Many victims of merger mania were once mistakenly convinced that the best way to achieve company objectives was to pursue unrelated diversification in the search for financial opportunity and synergy, only to see corporate performance fall well below expectation. By rejecting that "conventional wisdom," Martin Marietta, Kentucky Fried Chicken, Compaq, Avon, Hyatt Legal Services, and Tenant have demonstrated the advantages of what is increasingly proving to be sound business strategy.

PURSUING A CONCENTRATED GROWTH STRATEGY

These companies are just a few of the majority of American business firms that compete by focusing on a specific product and market combination. Yet, little has been written about—and perhaps as little thought given to—the concentrated growth strategy.

Concentrated growth is the strategy of the firm that directs its resources to the profitable growth of a single product in a single market with a single dominant technology. The main rationale for this approach, sometimes called a market penetration or concentration strategy, is that the firm thoroughly develops and exploits its expertise in a delimited competitive arena.[1]

Despite the popularity and success of concentrated growth strategies, managers have been left without guidelines to help them determine when their firm should employ concentrated growth and how they should go about maximizing the advantages of the strategy. Furthermore, current adopters of the concentrated growth strategy are frequently tempted to expand into unrelated areas without fully

Source: John A. Pearce II and James W. Harvey. "Concentrated Growth Strategies," *Academy of Management EXECUTIVE* 4, no. 1 (February 1990), pp. 61–68.

understanding the consequences. The enticements to stray from this strategy include impatience to grow, pressure to use idle capacity, need to meet short-term goals, and underestimating current opportunities.[2] Fascination with new product development and expansion into new markets should be tempered with the fact that new products fail at an average rate of 40% for consumer goods, 20% for industrial products, and 18% for services.[3]

A further enticement is to accelerate focused growth through horizontal integration. While such a strategy offers the advantage of enabling the firm to retain its basic product and market orientation, it exposes the company to a wide range of financially threatening complications. These potential problems include extended debt involvement; geographic variations in unions, worker contracts, and conditions of employment; added complexity in strategic planning and management coordination; and difficulties owing to multiple suppliers, local competitors, and governmental agencies. So numerous and great are these complications that their discussion is beyond the scope of this article. We restrict our attention to challenges confronted by managers who undertake a concentrated growth strategy through reliance on internal development.

DIVERSITY AND PERFORMANCE

"Stick to the knitting" is the phrase used by Peters and Waterman to describe one of several characteristics of successful corporations.[4] Staying with what the firm does best and avoiding areas of operation of undeveloped skills are the bases for their endorsement of concentrated growth.

Systematic analysis of new product successes and failures further underscores the risk of deviating from company strengths. After examining 195 case histories, Calantone and Cooper identified nine new product introduction scenarios, based on resource compatibility and product superiority.[5] The type of introduction that had the highest level of market success (72%) was described as a synergistic "close-to-home" product. These successful introductions had significant overlap with the firm's existing products, markets, technical expertise, and production proficiency. For example, "The Better Mousetrap with No Marketing" type of new product introduction had a success rate of 36% while the "Me Too" product, with no technical or production synergy averaged only 14%.

This study revealed that the pursuit of growth through expansion into previously unmastered technologies, or new markets, is done so at comparatively great risk. Other evidence adds support to the view that diversification, particularly unrelated diversification, is risky.

An analysis of the 250 largest firms in America's 25 largest industries revealed that firms that have higher measures of concentrated growth show greater financial performance.[6]

Another indictment of unrelated diversification was found in a study of America's best midsize businesses.[7] Among the key findings was that "unrelated diversification is a mortal enemy of winning performance." In contrast, successes often resulted from "edging out." This term refers to strategies based on clear mission statements that are well-understood within the firm, predicated on offerings with value, and serve selected market segments while cautiously moving into related products, related markets, or both. Success with edging out strategies is derived from a commitment to innovation within well-known technology and well-defined market niches.

RATIONALE FOR SUPERIOR PERFORMANCE

Why do concentrated growth strategies lead to enhanced performance? An analysis of product successes and failures across multiple industries suggests several reasons. This study shows that the greatest influences on market success are those characteristic of firms that implement a concentrated growth strategy.[8] These influences include the ability to assess market needs, knowledge of buyer behavior, customer price sensitivity, and effectiveness of promotion. Further underscoring the importance of concentrated growth-based company skills, the study also showed that these core capabilities are more of a determinant of competitive market success than are the environmental forces faced by the firm. High success rates of new products are also tied to avoiding situations that require undeveloped skills, such as serving new customers and markets, acquiring new technology, building new channels, developing new promotional abilities, and facing new competition.[9]

A major misconception about the concentrated growth strategy is that the firm that practices it will settle for little or no growth. This is certainly not true for a firm that correctly utilized the strategy. A firm employing concentrated growth grows by building on its competencies and achieving a competitive edge by concentrating in the product-market segment, it knows best. The firm employing this strategy is aiming for the growth that results from increased productivity, better coverage of its actual product-market segment, and more efficient use of its technology.

The concentrating firm's ability to grow stems mainly from its development of one or more of three important strategic capabilities: marketing abilities, efficiencies of scale and other cost reductions, and product differentiation. Since the firm will try to develop a specific product-market it has two alternatives to no growth: (1) stimulate increased consumption of the product through marketing-related activities achieving efficiencies in production and distribution that allow the firm to cut its costs or to increase the value of the product in the consumer's mind, or (2) to develop special attributes that brands the product as different.

Taken together, these points provide insights into why concentrated growth strategies work. Managers should focus on well-understood markets, competitors, technology, manufacturing processes, promotion, and distribution. This approach significantly improves the likelihood of market success.

CONDITIONS THAT FAVOR CONCENTRATED GROWTH

There are specific conditions in the firm's environment that are particularly conducive to the concentrated growth strategy. The first is when the firm's industry is resistant to major technological advancements. This is usually the case in the late growth and maturity stages of the product life cycle and in product-markets where product demand is stable and industry entry barriers, such as capitalization, are high. Machinery for the paper manufacturing industry, where the basic technology has not changed in more than a century is a good example.

A second especially favorable condition is when the firm's target markets are not product saturated. Markets with competitive gaps leave the firm with alternatives for growth in addition to taking market share away from competitors. The successful introduction of traveler services by Allstate and Amoco demonstrates that even an organization as entrenched and powerful as AAA could not build a defensible presence in all segments of the automobile club market.

A third condition that favors concentrated growth exists when the firm's product-markets are sufficiently distinctive to dissuade competitors in adjacent production markets from trying to invade the firm's segment. John Deere and Co. refrained from its planned growth in the construction machinery business when mighty Caterpillar threatened to enter Deere's mainstay, the farm machinery business, in retaliation. Rather than risk a costly price war on its own turf, Deere scrapped these plans for growth.

A fourth condition favorable to concentrated growth exists when the firm's inputs are reasonably stable in price and quantity and when they are available in the amounts and at the required times. Maryland-based Giant Foods is able to concentrate in the grocery business largely due to its long-term, stable arrangements with suppliers of its private label products. Most of these suppliers are the same makers of national brands that compete against the Giant labels.

With a high market share and aggressive retail distribution Giant controls the national brands' access to the consumer. Consequently, suppliers have considerable incentive to honor verbal agreements, called "bookings," in which they commit themselves to Giant for price, quality, quantity, and timing of shipments for a one year period.

The firm pursuing concentrated growth also benefits from being in a market with minimal seasonal or cyclical swings that would propel the firm to diversify. Night Owl Security, the Washington, D.C. market leader in home security services, commits customers to initial four-year contracts. In a town where affluent consumers tend to be quite transient, the length of this relationship is remarkable. Further reinforcement for Night Owl's concentrated growth strategy comes from the company's success in getting subsequent owners of its customers' homes to extend and renew the security service contract.

The firm can also grow while concentrating when it experiences competitive advantages based on efficient production or distribution channels. These advantages enable the firm to formulate advantageous pricing policies. More efficient production methods and better handling of distribution also allow the firm to achieve greater economies of scale or, in conjunction with marketing, result in a product that is differentiated in the mind of the consumer. Graniteville Company, the large South Carolina textile manufacturer, realized decades of growth and profitability by adopting a "follower" tact as part of its concentrated growth strategy. By producing fabrics only after market demand was well established, and by featuring products that could reflect its expertise in adopting manufacturing innovations and in highly efficient, long production runs, Graniteville prospered through concentrated growth.

Finally, the success of market generalists creates conditions for successful concentrated growth.[10]

When generalists succeed using universal appeals, they avoid making special appeals to different groups of customers. The net result is that markets dominated by generalists leave open many small pockets of markets where specialists can emerge and thrive.

For example, hardware store chains such as Stanbaugh-Thompsons and Hechinger, focus primarily on routine household repair problems and offer solutions that can be easily sold on a self-service, do-it-yourself basis. This approach leaves gaps at both the "semi-professional" and "neophyte" ends of the market—in terms of the purchaser's skill at household repairs and the extent to which available merchandise matches individual homeowner requirements.

PUTTING A NEW "SPIN" ON CONCENTRATED GROWTH

Firms that rely primarily on concentrated growth strategies may wish to modify their courses of action, yet retain their bases of strength. Managerial options represent varying degrees of concentrated growth.

Managers can practice "Pure Concentrated Growth," edge out into related markets (let's call this "Market Extension"), or make minor modifications in products or develop closely related new ones that fit within existing lines ("Product Extension"). A final opportunity for growth is to combine market and product extensions to form a "Hybrid Extension" strategy.

PURE CONCENTRATED GROWTH

The pure concentrated growth strategy involves product improvement, intensifying promotion, expanding channels, and pricing for penetration, as exhibited by Kentucky Fried Chicken. Using the theme "We Do Chicken Right," KFC stresses product specialization, limited menu, expanded distribution, and aggressive advertising, sales promotion, and pricing.

Tenant Corporation, MasterCard and Visa pursued pure concentrated growth through product improvement. Tenant, a manufacturer of mechanized cleaning equipment for industrial markets, recently embarked on a major recommitment to product quality and performance. The results include a 60% share of the domestic market, a 40% share of the international market, and a rebuff to Toyota which had plans for increasing its share of the American market. MasterCard's and Visa's development of "affinity cards," which allows the holder to select an outside organization (usually nonprofit) for a contribution for each transaction, has succeeded in stimulating the use of its credit cards.

MARKET EXTENSION

Market extension allows companies to practice a different form of concentrated growth by identifying new uses for existing products and new demographically, psychographically, or geographically defined markets. Frequently, changes in media selection, promotional appeals, and distribution are used to initiate this approach. Market extension, by finding a new use for a product, was shown by Du Pont's Kevlar, an organic material used by police, security, and military personnel primarily for bullet-proofing. The product is now being used to refit and maintain wooden-hulled boats, since the material is both lighter and stronger than glass fibers and has eleven times the strength of steel.

News in the medical industry provides other examples of new markets for existing products. The National Institutes of Health's report of a study showing that aspirin may lower the incidence of heart attacks in healthy men is expected to boost sales in the $2.2 billion analgesic market. Due to the expansion of this market, it is also predicted that share values of non-aspirin brands, such as industry leaders Tylenol and Advil, will be hurt. Product extensions currently planned include "Bayer Calendar Pak," 28-day packaging to fit the once-a-day prescription for second heart attack prevention.

PRODUCT EXTENSION

The strategy of product extension is based on penetrating existing markets by incorporating product modifications in existing items, or developing new products with a clear connection to the existing line. The telecommunications industry provides an example of product extension based on product modification. To increase its estimated 8–10% share of the $5–6 billion corporate user market, MCI Communication Corp. augmented its product offering by extending its direct-dial service to 146 countries, the same as AT&T, at lower average rates. The recent addition of 79 countries to its network underscores management's belief in this market, estimated to grow 15–20% annually.

Other examples of expansions linked to existing lines include Gerber products' decision to grow through general merchandise marketing to offset the flat baby food industry. Recent introductions include 52 items, ranging from feeding accessories to toys and children's wear.

THE HYBRID EXTENSION

The hybrid extension is the search for new growth opportunities by simultaneously combining market and product modifications. This strategy is used by NAPA, a franchise organization of auto parts aftermarket distributors serving the repair industry and do-it-yourselfers. NAPA has expanded its operations to offer installation of its products. This new service is directed at the market of drivers who want complete services that NAPA has never served, and to those do-it-yourselfers who want to "trade up" to such services.

Using a similar strategy, Dunkin' Donuts now offers a wider variety of breakfast items such as eggs, breakfast meats, and croissants, targeted at the market segment not previously served by its donut and coffee offering, and at existing customers desiring diversity. Additionally, by packaging its coffee in cans for the first time, Dunkin' Donuts is implementing a market extension strategy aimed at new customers who wish to serve its coffee at home or in the office.

RISKS AND REWARDS OF CONCENTRATED GROWTH

Under stable conditions, a concentrated growth strategy poses the lowest risk among grand strategies to a firm's economic stability. However, in a changing environment, a firm committed to concentrated growth faces high risks. The greatest risk is that by concentrating in a single product-market the firm is particularly vulnerable to changes in that segment. Slowed growth in the segment may jeopardize the company because its investment, competitive edge, and technology are deeply entrenched in a specific offering. Sudden changes by the firm are difficult when the product is threatened by near-term obsolescence, a faltering market, new substitutes, or changes in technology or customer needs. For example, the manufacturers of IBM-clones faced such a problem when IBM announced its adoption of the OS/2 operating system for its personal computer line. The change effectively made existing clones "out of date."

By entrenching in a specific industry, the concentrating firm is particularly susceptible to changes in the economic environment of its industry, since the firm does not have a cushion from involvement in other industries. For example, Mack Truck, the second largest truck maker in America, saw an 18 month slump in the truck industry result in a $20 million loss for the company.

Entrenchment in a specific product-market tends to make a concentrating firm more adept than competitors at detecting new trends. However, any failure to properly forecast major changes in the industry can result in extraordinary losses. Numerous makers of inexpensive digital watches declared bankruptcy when they failed to anticipate the competition posed by Swatch, Guess, and other trendy watches that emerged from the fashion industry.

A firm pursuing a concentrated growth strategy is also vulnerable to high opportunity costs by remaining in a specific product-market when other options are ignored that could employ the firm's resources more profitably. Overcommitment to a specific technology and product-market can hinder a firm's ability to enter a new or growing product market that offers more attractive cost-benefit tradeoffs for the firm. Had Apple computers maintained its policy of making equipment that did not interface with IBM equipment, it would have voluntarily ignored the strategic options that instead have proven to be its most profitable.

REWARDS

Examples abound of concentrating firms that report exceptional returns on its strategy. Companies like McDonald's, Goodyear, and Apple Computers have used first-hand knowledge and deep involvement with specific product segments to become powerful competitors in its markets. The strategy is even more often associated with successful smaller firms that have steadily and doggedly improved market position.

The limited additional resources necessary to implement concentrated growth, coupled with the limited risk involved, also make this strategy desirable for a firm with limited funds. For example, through a carefully devised concentrated growth strategy, medium-sized Deere and Company was able to become a major force in the agricultural machinery business even when competing with much bigger firms like Ford Motor Co. While other firms were trying to exit or diversify from the farm machinery business, Deere spent $2 billion in upgrading its machinery, boosting efficiency, and engaging in a program to strengthen its dealership system. This concentrated growth strategy enabled the company to become the leader in the farm machinery business, despite the fact that Ford was 10 times its size.

Firms that remain within a chosen product-market often extract the most from technology and market knowledge and minimize the risks associated with unrelated diversification. The reason for the success of a concentration strategy lies with the firm's superior insights into its technology, product, and customer, as a means of obtaining a sustainable competitive advantage. Superior performance on these aspects of corporate strategy has a significant positive effect on market success.

CONCLUSION

Firms that are tempted to seek revenue streams through commitment to unrelated technology and markets or to lessen their dependence on mature products, must fully understand the risks of such actions. The enticement to develop new products and to expand into new markets must be tempered with the knowledge of high new product failure rates. When assessing strategic options, managers should consider the merits of concentrated growth. While building from a basis of stability and experience, concentrated growth strategies can also provide innovation and expansion at manageable levels of risk.

NOTES

1. For a more detailed and comprehensive description of alternative business strategies, refer to John A. Pearce II, "Selecting Among Alternative Grand Strategies," *California Management Review,* 30(2), Spring, 1982, 23–31.
2. A more complete list of nine reasons for abandoning a concentrated growth strategy is provided by M. Laruenstein and W. Skinner, "Formulating a

Strategy of Superior Resources," *Journal of Business Strategy,* Summer, 1980, 4–10.

3. These results were reported in *New Products Management for the 1980s,* New York: Booz, Allen & Hamilton, 1982.

4. The top selling book in which the term first appeared is T. J. Peters and R. H. Waterman, *In Search of Excellence: Lessons From America's Best Run Companies,* New York: Harper, 1982.

5. For details on this study, see Roger Calantone and Robert G. Cooper, "New Product Scenarios: Prospects for Success," *Journal of Marketing,* 45, Spring, 1981, 48–60.

6. The complete findings of the study are reported in P. Varadarajan, "Product Diversity and Firm Performance: An Empirical Investigation," *Journal of Marketing,* 50, July, 1986, 43–57.

7. A comprehensive and indepth presentation of the study appears as Donald K. Clifford, Jr. and Richard E. Cavanagh, *The Winning Performance: How America's High-Growth Midsize Companies Succeed,* New York: Bantam Books, 1985.

8. The original presentation of the study and its results appeared in Robert G. Cooper, "Identifying Industrial New Product Success: Project NewProd," *Industrial Marketing Management,* 8(2), April, 1979, 124–135.

9. For a complete description and analysis of the study, see Robert G. Cooper, "The Impact of New Product Strategies," *Industrial Marketing Management,* 12(4), October, 1983, 243–256.

10. For a provocative discussion of the corporate strengths of specialists and generalists, see Glenn R. Carroll, "The Specialist Strategy," *California Management Review,* 26(3), Spring, 1984, 126–137.

Quick Change Strategies for Vertical Integration

Kathryn Rudie Harrigan

The decision to make or buy product components or services must constantly be reevaluated as a firm's competitive position changes. But managers often fail to keep fine tuning these important relationships because they don't recognize the dangers of allowing their firm's vertical integration strategy to become obsolete.

- Early nonintegrated personal computer firms such as HeathKit sold their products unassembled. In 1974, electronic hobbyists were purchasing bags of components and building their own personal computers. By 1977, when sales of previously assembled personal computers took off, such forward-integrated firms as Tandy/Radio Shack (TRS), Commodore International, and Texas Instruments (TI) were selling their earliest models through wholly owned retail outlets. IBM established retailing outlets when it introduced its Personal Computer (PC) in 1981, before it became backward integrated and began making its own electronic components.

  Later, as customers learned more about personal computers and their use became more and more widely accepted, heavy involvement in retail access became much less of a critical success factor. TRS and IBM permitted their personal computers to be sold by other retailers, and in fact TRS PCs were manufactured by low-cost offshore producers. TI completely backed away from retailing activities.

  In 1986, now that the demand for personal computers has matured, the paramount concern of successful competitors is the availability of software. Insightful personal computer firms are adjusting to this change by sponsoring software-writing activities through a variety of quasi-integrated business arrangements.

- When crude oil prices fell in the 1980s and demand declined, oil companies adjusted their vertical integration strategy in a number of

Source: Kathryn R. Harrigan, "Quick Change Strategies for Vertical Integration," *Planning Review* 14, no. 5 (September 1986), pp. 32–37.

ways. Sun, Mobil, and others reduced refinery capacity. Some integrated oil firms terminated deliveries to unproductive outlets and closed gasoline stations in low-volume states. Texaco closed over 2,000 stations, and Amoco ceased marketing branded gasoline activities in eleven states. In addition, Amoco and other firms bolstered their marketing campaigns. For example, Amoco offered discounts to retail customers who paid in cash instead of with credit cards, while ARCO eliminated credit card sales altogether.

- A surfit of vertical integration is currently causing problems for the U.S. steel and automobile industries. Many of these firms have been slow to back away from ore mining, cargo shipping, ingot formation, and other vertically related activities in which they no longer have the competitive advantage over outsiders.

Finding an appropriate vertical integration strategy is often a matter of common sense, but the optimum solutions are often overlooked because most managers don't really understand how to realize the business unit synergies and other benefits of vertical integration, or how to avoid the dangers of welding the firm to the wrong kind of make-or-buy relationship.

Their dilemma is then compounded by the desire to maintain strategic flexibility. Vertically integrated businesses are often quite expensive to start up and redeploy. The incremental costs of coordinating fully integrated business units can be so high that SBU managers are reluctant to encourage buyer-seller relationships between their business units. Yet, there can also be significant opportunity costs in having either too little or too much vertical integration.

ADVICE FOR TOP MANAGEMENT

Given the nature of competition in a number of industries, it's clear that many firms have either the wrong kind of vertical integration or much more than they need. Their internal arrangements and management systems get in the way of their business units' realizing the most from vertical synergies. Some business units may still be subsidizing others at huge opportunity costs when the right time to do so has long since passed. Here's how to bring your firm's vertical integration strategy in line with competitive realities:

Recognize that No Vertical Integration Strategy Lasts Forever

Industry conditions change. Bargaining power, like market power, is temporary, and the old logic that might have worked may no longer be valid. Vertical integration strategies must be retuned as competitive circumstances change.

Know Your Strengths

Only produce those components or services that garner premium prices. Spin off noncritical activities and those with the lowest returns through divestitures or fade-out joint ventures. Free up plant space and personnel to concentrate on the activities most crucial to the firm's future.

Recognize Implicit Subsidizations

Question whether corporate policies that encourage vertically related business units to do business with each other—for transfer pricing and intelligence gathering without regard to market realities—are penalizing your business. The benefits of some vertical integration strategies are at best ephemeral once industry conditions change.

Keep to Hospitable Industries

Carefully match the dimensions of vertical integration to the most compatible competitive settings. Once the pioneering era of an industry has passed, take vertical integration risks only where competitors are unlikely to resort to price cutting to remedy excess capacity. Be sure that there are plenty of nonintegrated competitors to keep industry capacity in line with demand.

Create a New Player

Product lives are becoming shorter and shorter in many high-innovation industries. If a firm has harmed its competitive position by filling too many of its needs in-house, thus depriving its business units of knowledge and working relationships with innovative outsiders, now may be the time to create a new supplier or a new channel of distribution through a joint venture or some other form of quasi-integration.

Use International Alliances

Now that improved computing power and communications technology make such systems feasible, it's imperative to deal with global competition by creating an integrated, worldwide logistical system to satisfy demand most efficiently. Acquire partners who can improve your international management system and competitive position.

Scrutinize Vertical Transfer Policies Frequently

The make-or-buy decision must be continuously reassessed to meet competitive realities. Create technological jump-off points for reexamining whether lower costs or superior capabilities are available elsewhere before funding an expansion to do it yourself. Put outsiders to work for your business units.

Keep Testing Your Assumptions

If corporate policies favor vertical integration but business units balk at implementing them, ask why. Inside suppliers and customers often take advantage of their captive audience under the flag of corporate strategy. Find out why vertically related business units prefer using outsiders instead of each other.

Be Wary of Short-Term Pressures

The blinders of short-term performance goals often block managers' overview of the firm's needs for secure customers, a steady diet of technological break throughs, and balanced risks among vertically linked business units. If corporate make-or-buy strategies still seem to be the right way to go after you've given them a thorough shaking out, then adjust your management system to reward business units for being good corporate soldiers. Help them share in top management's vision of the future.

CAUTIONS

The key to effective use of vertical synergies is keeping alert to industry changes that affect the firm's opportunities. Beware of environmental changes that force you to scramble, as Ashland Oil had to do after divesting its exploration and production operations when Federal oil allocation schemes and refinery subsidies were discontinued. Beware also of investing far upstream or downstream to acquire capabilities beyond the firm's core strengths. In an era when businesses are well advised to "stick close to their knitting," managers must be wary of wandering too far afield in search of elusive benefits lest they harm their firm's competitive advantage in the activities that truly matter.

Problems will doubtless arise in implementing these ideas since every organization develops a unique set of relationships among its business units. However, the vertical integration framework is a set of contingencies that suggest an orientation, or desirable ends, not inviolate rules.

What types of vertical integration relationships work best in various competitive environments? What types tend to fail? The key forces to consider are:

- The nature of demand leading to industry growth.
- Competitive behavior.
- Bargaining power between suppliers, distributors, and customers.
- Corporate strategy needs.

NUMBER OF VERTICALLY RELATED STAGES

A move to get involved in several stages of processing is little more than a diversification decision unless a firm's corporate strategy also encourages its business units to:

- Purchase from or sell to each other.
- Share technological and market intelligence.
- Coordinate product traits, specifications, volumes, and other details in some purposeful way.

The decision to subsidize one business unit temporarily at the expense of another makes sense if you're reaching for such industry-wide or cluster-wide strategy benefits as shared resource and experience curve economies, technological leadership, or protection for proprietary information. However, it can be costly to be involved in too many vertical stages of processing. The costs of cross-subsidization must be justified by the benefits, whether they're:

- Higher value-added margins.
- Synergies between processing stages.
- Stronger product differentiation.
- Proprietary knowledge.
- Pioneering new industries.
- Focused competitive advantage.
- Exit barrier reduction, or other desirable outcomes.

Capturing High Value-Added Margins

If intrafirm transfers are made at market prices, the total possible value-added margin—from the entry stage to the stage where its products and services are sold to outsiders—remains more or less the same. The proportion of a firm's total value-added margin captured by a particular business unit in that processing chain can be shifted from one stage to another as transfer pricing mechanisms change.

Successful firms engage in many vertical stages of processing when the value-added margins of adjacent business units are high. The pursuit of high value-added margins leads successful firms to pick and choose carefully among tasks they could perform in-house when they operate at full capacity. And they choose activities that keep their critically skilled people occupied, while they farm out low value-added jobs.

Creating Synergies between Processing Stages

In my study I found that successful firms were involved in the greatest number of vertically related stages where significant synergies could be gained by sharing resources or where other corporate needs could best be served. Unsuccessful firms perform tasks in vertically related processing stages merely to fill excess capacity.

Creating Strong Product Differentiation

Carefully coordinated strategies involving many vertical processing stages may allow a firm to create significant improvements in supplying technologies or distribution practices, provided it has an effective management information system. Superior coordination of services or better control over a product's ingredients and/or components may provide the basis for creating premium-priced, highly differentiated products. These higher prices offset costs arising from coordinating business unit activities. If a firm pursues a strategy of product differentiation, forward integration may be temporarily necessary to control the quality and image of a firm's products and raise customers' switching cost barriers.

However, when a firm's products have successfully created these switching costs, forward integration is less necessary. Instead, the firm should use the bargaining power of these barriers to control outside distributors unless the value added by downstream activities remains unusually high.

Protecting Proprietary Knowledge

Trade secrets and processes for high-quality products are better protected and updated with competitive intelligence faster when a firm masters the complexities of coordinating several vertical processing stages.

- Polaroid stopped purchasing its negative materials from Kodak when its instant photography patent expired. Too much proprietary information was contained in the design of Polaroid's negative to let a competitor continue to produce it.
- Schlumberger, a leading instrument and test equipment firm, acquired its own custom logic semiconductor house, Fairchild Camera & Instrument, to protect its proprietary knowledge of oilwell drilling recording services. That logic was imbedded in the microprocessors of its products.
- Dow Chemical often integrates vertically to prevent other firms from learning too much about its proprietary chemical processes and processing-equipment designs.

Pioneering Strategies

If a vertically integrated firm achieves remarkable successes by virtue of its coordination strategies, its nonintegrated competitors may have to engage in similar strategies. However, as with other sources of competitive advantage, being engaged in many vertical stages may not be sustainable or appropriate for very long. Firms must deliberately adjust the number of stages to changing competitive conditions.

In young industries, where products may be quite different than their substitutes, customers may be confused or reluctant to try something new. This is especially true when complex new products require demonstrations or other substantial explanations and servicing, as did microcomputers in 1978.

In such cases, pioneering firms may have to integrate forward to create an infrastructure where none exists; develop new distribution channels; and explain their products.

- Early in the century, Celanese couldn't prove that its manmade fibers were attractive to consumers because weavers of cotton and wool fabrics were unwilling to run rayon and acetate fibers on their looms. Celanese had to weave its own fabrics from its synthetics, make the fabric into garments, and distribute them for a limited time.
- RCA demonstrated the commercial potential of its television receiver products by engaging first in black and white broadcasting, then in color broadcasting, and most recently in stereo broadcasting. It also produced entertainment programming in order to have something to broadcast.
- When aluminum smelters wanted to produce aluminum cans, they met a wall of resistance from the traditional tin can manufacturers. ALCOA, Kaiser, and other aluminum firms had to forward integrate and develop their own can-making equipment to prove their idea was viable.

- Corning Glass Works promoted the adoption of glass cable for fiber-optic telecommunications networks and other applications through its Siecor venture with Siemens. Corning provided the fiber-optic cable, and Siemens provided the electronic components needed for a turn-key system.
- Genetic-engineering firms such as Cetus, Genentech, and Genex are currently forming joint ventures with partners who have market access.

Piggy-backing on the Pioneer

Vertical integration for missionary purposes doesn't always pay off. A forward-integrated firm must be wary of lighting the way for competitors while bearing the higher fixed costs of pioneering.

When IBM entered the personal computer business, the product had already been legitimized by earlier entrants. IBM profited from their mistakes. It purchased its PC components from the pioneering firms to take advantage of the latest technological improvements and cost reductions. This spared IBM the risk of investing in soon-to-be-obsolete technology.

Focusing on Competitive Advantage

Hiring outsiders to perform intermediate processing steps in volatile industries reduces the likelihood of being stuck with unusable resources. In addition, the same analysis that leads a firm to use outsiders also helps it recognize its own distinctive competences in production and marketing.

Successful firms purchase simple or low-volume components from outsiders when they're constrained by plant capacity. These arrangements allow the skilled personnel to focus on difficult but challenging tasks that build the basis for future competitive advantage.

Reducing Exit and Mobility Barriers

When demand for an industry's products declines, firms must purposefully dismantle vertical integration arrangements that might act as exit barriers.

- When the market for men's tailored suits matured, many forward-integrated firms backed away from retailing operations. Only Hartmarx kept its retail outlets as a barometer for measuring changing consumer tastes.
- As the whiskey market declined, distillers abandoned barrel making, lumber operations, grain elevators, grain brokerage, bottle production, and wholesaling activities.

Similar cautions are appropriate when technology changes very rapidly. Firms can be more successfully engaged in many vertically related processing stages when competition isn't cutthroat and industry structures are stable.

The Dangers of Too Many Stages of Processing

Most firms can't maneuver quickly enough in turbulent settings to enjoy the luxury of engaging in a number of processing stages. Long vertical-processing chains work best where industry structures don't lead to price wars and products or processes change slowly. As Hewlett-Packard discovered when it was confronted with the cost-slashing tactics of Texas Instruments and Casio, too many processing stages can cost you the competitive advantage. The firms that balance many stages the best are technological leaders whose products or components are state of the art.

The key determinants of whether or not a firm should skip a particular stage in its integrated chain of activities are: the task's centrality to its corporate mission; the synergies it provides; and the quality of goods or services provided by outsiders:

- Although many pharmaceutical companies use outside laboratories for clinical testing, research-oriented firms maintain their own clinical and toxicology labs for the developmental stages of drug testing to help in gaining FDA approval The scientists and medical specialists they employ in these clinical and toxicology studies are their most critical strategic resources, especially where errors or inaccurate record keeping by outside clinicians could delay their efforts by months or even years.
- Electronics firms sometimes produce consumer electronic products, as well as microprocessors, photomasks, and silicon wafers, to keep their product and process innovation at the cutting edge. For these firms, such consumer electronic products as digital watches, calculators and personal computers are merely one way to market their components. They regard such tactics as simply another lab test for their more important products.

DEGREE OF INTERNAL PURCHASES AND SALES

Firms that engage in several vertically related processing stages (the diversification decision) must decide not only whether a buyer-seller relationship should exist between business units (the coordination decision), but also how much of a business unit's requirements or outputs to transfer internally.

The appropriate degree of internal transfers depends, in part, on a firm's need to balance production volumes. For example, the volumes purchased from upstream business units cannot exceed the downstream business unit's capacity for processing. The technological scales of assets used in many vertically related processing stages are rarely in balance. An orderly industry needs nonintegrated firms to even out the production imbalances of vertically integrated firms. If few nonintegrated competitors survive, the vertically integrated firms' excess capacity in one stage of processing often takes the form of vicious price wars that rage out of control in an effort to fill their underutilized chains of assets.

Successful firms make good use of such outsiders as subcontractors and distributors, but most unsuccessful firms can't seem to muster the bargaining power needed to treat outsiders as their vassals. The relative bargaining power of a business unit depends on whether:

- Its product designs are highly specific to particular customers.
- Good alternative outlets or suppliers exist.
- The business unit is capable of manufacturing the goods and/or services it buys.
- Suppliers or distributors are dependent on the business unit's patronage.

When balance problems are severe, successful firms employ subcontractors to perform tasks requiring otherwise underutilized assets. Sometimes outside firms perform a specific processing step for all the other firms in an industry, such as bromine chemistry, because it's dangerous or because the step is very specialized but needed infrequently by a single firm.

- Fringe competitors often purchase excess crude oil, extra aged whiskies, bulk pharmaceuticals, piece-work tailoring, electronic subassemblies, or other excess outputs from larger firms. Their presence creates a network of buyers and suppliers that larger firms can rely upon to smooth short-falls in a cyclical market.
- Sources for private branding, plant leasing, and contract manufacturing are often available to allow petrochemical firms to maintain capacity utilization goals while responding to seasonal peaks in demand. In some chemical industries, competitors manufacture for

each other while they take turns shutting down for annual maintenance.

- Firms like Sinclair Research, which has no factory of its own, hire other firms such as Timex to manufacture the products they design and sell.
- Osborne Computer once enjoyed great success by buying other firms' components, sub-assemblies, and software to package into its portable system.
- Several pharmaceutical houses purchase off-patent, bulk drug products made by others to avoid in-house research and manufacturing expenses.

No Internal Transfers

Business unit managers instinctively seek outside suppliers, distributors, and customers because they fear the damaging effects of high degrees of internal transfers. Their resistance to fully integrated buyer-seller relationships with sister business units is healthy. Because business unit managers frequently lack top management's insights, their objections often provide a useful test by reminding corporate strategists of operating difficulties that implementation could create by encouraging high degrees of internal purchases or sales.

Vertical integration was once thought of the same way as being pregnant—one either was or wasn't. Now it's recognized that vertical integration strategies are composed of several strategic dimensions, each of which may be fine tuned to suit changing competitive conditions. While vertical integration strategies need constant reevaluation, this process keeps a company on its competitive toes, and the rewards can be substantial.

FURTHER READING

Buzzell, R. D., "Is Vertical Integration Profitable?" *Harvard Business Review,* January-February, 1983.

Harrigan, K. R., *Strategies for Declining Businesses,* Lexington, MA: Lexington Books, 1980.

Harrigan, K. R. and Porter, M. E., "Endgame Strategies for Declining Industries," *Harvard Business Review,* July-August, 1983.

Porter, M. E., *Competitive Strategy: Techniques for Analyzing Industries and Competitors,* New York: Free Press, 1980.

Porter, M. E., *Competitive Advantage: Creating and Sustaining Superior Performance,* New York: Free Press, 1985.

Joint Ventures in the Face of Global Competition

Benjamin Gomes-Casseres

American firms seem to have discovered a new strategy for competing abroad: joint ventures. Until a decade ago, many U.S. multinational companies (MNCs) shunned joint ventures, arguing that shared ownership led to loss of control and profits. As one General Motors executive put it, "If it was worth doing, it was worth getting all the benefits." In search of ways to bolster their global competitive advantages, these same firms are now finding new merits in joint ventures. (Let us define a joint venture as any affiliate of an MNC where the equity is partly owned by another firm, usually one from the host country. This definition excludes non-equity cooperative ventures, such as licensing.)

General Motors is a case in point. Until the early 1970s, it owned 100 percent of the equity in each of its subsidiaries abroad. By 1975, six of GM's forty foreign subsidiaries were owned jointly with another firm, usually one from the host country. Since then, twelve out of twenty of GM's new foreign subsidiaries have been joint ventures! In the United States itself, the company launched its joint venture with Toyota in 1983, a cornerstone of its strategy to expand its small-car offerings. GM's joint ventures in Korea (with Daewoo) and Japan (with Isuzu and Suzuki) are also important elements in this strategy.

General Motors is not alone in its new-found love for joint ventures. Evidence from industries as diverse as cosmetics and computers suggests that, after insisting on whole ownership abroad in the 1960s, U.S. multinationals began to use joint ventures more extensively in the early 1970s.[1] This trend seems to have accelerated in the early 1980s, to the point where one prominent international consultant claimed that "no company can stay competitive in the world today singlehandedly."[2] Among the U.S. firms forming major joint ventures abroad are

Honeywell (with France's Bull and Japan's NEC), AT&T (with Italy's Olivetti and Holland's Philips), and Whirlpool (also with Philips). In addition, scores of firms have recently entered the Chinese or South Korean markets with joint ventures; these include Johnson & Johnson, Gillette, Heinz, Procter & Gamble, Corning Glass, W.R. Grace, Xerox, General Electric, Rohm & Haas, McCormick, and Allied-Signal.

Business leaders and researchers cite five main reasons for the rising popularity of joint ventures. First, the governments of many countries with attractive domestic markets—including China and South Korea—try to restrict foreign ownership. Second, many U.S. firms have found that host country partners could help them enter new markets quickly by providing management expertise and local connections.[3] Such help is particularly important because of the intensifying competition from European and Japanese carmakers, which is a third reason for U.S. firms' increasing use of joint ventures. These competitors are often willing to settle for joint ventures in host countries where U.S. firms have insisted on whole ownership.[4] Fourth, foreign firms, especially from Europe and Japan, have become more attractive joint venture partners for U.S. multinational corporations as their technological capabilities and market presence have grown. Finally, in many industries global scale is becoming a distinct advantage in R&D and production, leading all but the largest firms to consider joint ventures as a way to achieve such scale and share risks.[5]

JOINT VERSUS WHOLE OWNERSHIP

This evidence suggests that joint ventures can be more useful in global competition than managers of U.S. multinational corporations thought just a decade ago. But does this mean that that old reasoning was wrong? By no means. Joint ventures still entail huge costs when used at the wrong time. The loss of control is real, as are the risks of creating new competitors, damaging the firm's reputation, and eroding its technological edge.

As a result of such costs, joint ventures are often unstable. GM and its South Korean partner Daewoo are blaming each other for the disappointing exports from their formerly promising joint venture. Disagreements between AT&T and its computer partner Olivetti have also made the pages of the business press. And a highly profitable joint venture between the chemical firms Hercules and Montedison was quietly dissolved when the latter bought the former's shares. These are not isolated cases. Empirical studies suggest that anywhere between one-third and two-thirds of joint ventures eventually break up.[6]

But why do so many firms enter into joint ventures that eventually cost them headaches and money? There are two explanations for instability in any joint venture. First, the partners simply made a mistake: they formed a joint venture when it may not have been the thing to do, or they joined up with the wrong partner. Second, their initial decision was right, but conditions changed so that the joint venture was no longer useful.[7] In both cases, the joint venture form itself is not to blame. It is more likely that the process for deciding when to use joint or whole ownership was inadequate.

There is a time and a place for joint ventures in a firm's global strategy. Recognizing that time and place allows a firm's managers to avoid partnerships that end in costly divorces. It also allows them to evaluate from time to time, before serious disagreements arise, whether their joint ventures are still useful. This article presents a framework to help managers decide when a joint venture is appropriate, and when it is not.

Host Government Restrictions

But even when an MNC prefers to own all the equity in a subsidiary, it may not be able to do so. Governments of countries such as India, Mexico, China, and even France try to encourage joint ventures with local firms in a variety of ways. In China, for example, major sectors are reserved for local firms or joint ventures. The French government might use subtler ways to favor local firms and joint ventures, such as national standards and preferential procurement.

Does this mean that the MNC's choice between joint and whole ownership is irrelevant in these cases? No. All governments with restrictive ownership policies have, at one time or another, made exceptions for firms insisting on whole ownership. IBM, for instance, recently negotiated a wholly owned subsidiary in Mexico. Foreign investors in India, too, have found creative ways to respond to the government's demands; sometimes they retained management control of critical activities, while at other times they gained exceptions to the demand for shared equity.[8] In their efforts to attract foreign investors, the governments of South Korea, Venezuela, and even China are also softening their ownership restrictions.

Firms preferring whole ownership in such restrictive countries might thus be able to bargain for an exception. But not every MNC has the bargaining chips necessary to pull this off. My framework also helps managers identify the strengths and weaknesses of their firms in such negotiations.

Evidence from a variety of sources supports the guidelines presented below. I used statistical data collected at Harvard in the 1970s to identify when and why U.S. multinational corporations chose to use joint ventures in the past, and when they did not (see the Appendix).[9] The results of this analysis are consistent with studies based on recent, but more limited, data from researchers at Wharton.[10]

I also interviewed more than forty international executives from five major global companies to understand the dilemmas they faced. I learned that many factors influenced the ownership decision, but that only the few discussed here were critical.

DECIDING WHEN TO USE A JOINT VENTURE

Assuming that managers are free to choose the ownership structure for a foreign venture, the decision should depend on their strategies for managing the firm's capabilities and geographic scope. The role of venture in these strategies influences the *costs and benefits of joint as compared with whole ownership.*[11]

Expanding or Exploiting Capabilities

Whether a joint venture is appropriate depends on the capabilities and goals of the firm. In the GM-Toyota joint venture, each partner contributed in an area in which the other was weak. GM brought its U.S. distribution network to the deal, and Toyota brought its small-car designs and efficient manufacturing methods. Outside the U.S. market, too, GM's need for a low-cost manufacturing base for small cars led to its joint venture with Daewoo in Korea. This venture was to sell 200,000 compact cars in the United States through GM's Pontiac Division. For Daewoo, it was a way to compete against Hyundai in the U.S. market.

The joint venture between AT&T and Olivetti, too, was motivated by complementary capabilities of the two firms. AT&T had little experience doing business abroad, and wanted to sell its minicomputers in Europe. Olivetti, on the other hand, was relatively strong in Europe, but wanted to sell its personal computers in the United States. A similar combination of goals and capabilities brought together Honeywell, Bull, and NEC. The three companies had longstanding supply and licensing relationships, but decided in 1987 to integrate their computer operations further through a freestanding, jointly owned venture. NEC was to supply technology for high-end computers; Honeywell offered an extensive distribution network and customer base in the United States; and Bull was strong in midsize computers and in the French market.

Some Risks of Joint Ventures.   These strategies contrast strikingly with those of other firms I studied. Managers from both Gillette and Johnson & Johnson insist that joint ventures are anything but ideal, at least in their core businesses. Gillette's technological edge in making razor blades makes it unnecessary for them to cooperate with other firms. Furthermore, such cooperation might risk sacrificing the high quality standards for which Gillette blades are known worldwide. Gillette headquarters staff make sure subsidiaries maintain these standards by monitoring their raw material supplies, furnishing process equipment, and regularly spot checking final products. Joint venture partners would have little to add to this process and might dilute the control exercised from headquarters.

A commitment to quality and central control is also what drives Johnson & Johnson to shun joint ventures. J&J's business depends greatly on intangible assets such as trademarks, patents, and reputation. Sharing control of such assets with another firm might risk eroding these competitive advantages. For example, a local partner might cut corners to sell in markets where quality was not valued highly, and so hurt J&J's reputation in other areas. Royalty agreements could provide some protection in these areas, reported one executive, but 100 percent ownership provided the best assurance. This is another case where the MNC has little to gain, and much to lose, from a joint venture.

Even J&J, however, uses joint ventures in some situations. It entered the Japanese pharmaceuticals market with a joint venture, partly because of the presence of strong local competitors who had more experience in pharmaceuticals than did J&J. The company also turned to a joint venture to enter the French consumer products market, after failing with a wholly owned venture. French companies had well-established reputations and distribution networks in this market; J&J found that the only effective way to compete with them was to join them.

Ownership Tradeoffs: Capability.   These cases suggest that *a joint venture is more appropriate when the firm seeks to expand capability into new fields, and less appropriate when it aims to exploit an existing competitive advantage.* In GM's joint ventures in Japan and Korea, AT&T's in European computers, and J&J's in French consumer products, a joint venture was used to expand the firm's capabilities through cooperation with a partner that had the needed know-how and market position. On the other hand, in their core businesses Gillette and J&J (and GM in the 1960s) merely exploited the competitive advantages that they already had. Usually a partnership was unnecessary—and it could dilute the firm's advantages.

The competitive advantages of multinational corporations are typically based on their organizational know-how and skills, or on intangible assets such as patents, trademarks, and reputation. By their very nature, such advantages cannot be readily bought from outsiders, as is the case, for example, with machinery, labor, or raw materials.[12] But

MNCs can acquire such advantages through a joint venture with another firm, which typically involves some transfer of personnel, provision of training and advice, and cooperative marketing and research. Joint ventures are thus more than just convenient financial vehicles for geographical expansion—indeed, they may be costly mistakes where that is their only rationale. Rather, successful joint ventures are arrangements to acquire capabilities and assets that cannot be purchased through arm's-length transactions.

The examples cited above also illustrate the importance of choosing the right joint venture partner. In each case, the U.S. firm chose a partner that could complement its capabilities—one that was strong in precisely those areas in which the U.S. firm was weak. In this sense, the first criterion for choosing a partner is that the firms be different. The potential for joint gains is greater the more *dissimilar* the partners. But it is also important that their goals be compatible, as discussed in the next section.

My statistical analyses supported these conclusions. I found that U.S. MNCs were less likely to form joint ventures in their core business than in fields in which they had less experience. Similarly, those with extensive experience abroad were less likely to form joint ventures than others, and all seemed to prefer whole ownership in countries with which they were relatively familiar. Firms in businesses that depended on intangible assets such as proprietary technical know-how and product image were particularly unlikely to form joint ventures, as these advantages could be eroded by a misbehaving partner. The case data suggests, however, that local firms can sometimes add to an MNC's local market image when they have established brands and distribution networks.

And even in industries where proprietary technical know-how was important, those firms that needed to *acquire* technology to compete effectively often used joint ventures to do so. Thus high-technology firms exhibited two extreme behaviors: either they were dead set against joint ventures or else they found these arrangements critical to success. Until recently IBM took the former position; firms like Honeywell and AT&T now argue the latter. Which side of the debate these high-technology firms are on depends, once again, on whether they are exploiting or expanding their technological capabilities.

Global or Local Scope

The cases discussed above begin to illustrate another factor important to the choice of ownership structure. In insisting on wholly owned subsidiaries, both Johnson & Johnson and Gillette were concerned with the effect of the joint venture on their *global strategies*.

Both maintained global quality standards that upheld their image and reputation worldwide. The risk of a joint venture stemmed from the fact that the partner, often a local firm, was concerned only with *local strategies,* where lower standards might suffice.

This is one specific illustration—probably the most important one—of the old adage that partners in a joint venture need to have compatible goals. That is a second criterion in selecting a partner. In contrast with the condition about complementary capabilities, here the greater the *similarity* between the partners, the lower the likelihood of conflicts. Of course, the geographic scopes of no two firms are alike, especially not those of multinational corporations and local partners. But the goals that each has for the joint venture should be alike, which can often be the case for MNCs following multidomestic, rather than global, strategies.[13]

Ownership Tradeoffs: Scope. The potential for conflict between an MNC's global strategy and a host country partner's more localized concerns appears in many forms. Firms pursuing a global strategy often incur costs in one location to benefit their operations elsewhere.[14] Local profits in such cases are secondary to global profits. But a local partner would, of course, be concerned only with local profitability, and so would try to block policies that represented net costs to the joint venture but net benefits to the MNC. This suggests that *joint ownership with a local firm may not be appropriate for ventures that are to be integrated into the MNC's global strategy.*

IBM followed this rule religiously in the 1960s and 1970s. Originally, IBM had managed its six plants in Europe independently of each other, as each served a local market. In the early 1960s the firm decided to merge them and manage them as parts of an integrated regional system. Products and components were traded among the plants, and all followed similar marketing and product strategies. Since then, explained former CEO Jacques Maisonrouge, "The control issue [has become] critical, because optimization of the whole system was not equal to optimization of the subparts."[15] Partly because joint venture partners would be interested only in optimization of the "subpart" in which they had a share, IBM has traditionally insisted on whole ownership.

The recent disagreements between General Motors and its South Korean partner also point to a conflict of interest based on differences in geographic scope. The joint venture's sales in the United States were running 33 percent below target in mid-1988, and Daewoo lost $40 million on the deal in the first half of that year alone. Daewoo and Korean auto analysts blamed GM for failing to promote the car in the United States and for not placing a high priority on it. On the face of it, GM would seem to have stronger incentives for promoting car sales from its wholly owned divisions than from the joint venture. Similarly, Daewoo wants to expand in its local market, but GM is cold to the idea. As a result, Daewoo has been forced to turn to Japanese suppliers for technology to make a new inexpensive "people's car," a pet project of the president of Korea.[16]

Global Strategies and Expanding Capabilities.   The relationship between the U.S. firm Hercules and Montedison, Italy's chemicals giant, illustrates both aspects of the joint venture decision: management of capabilities and of geographic scope. In 1982, Montedison launched a strategy to "internationalize" the company by using joint ventures. According to one of the company's top planners, joint ventures would be used "where Montedison had good technology and decent business positions, and where it needed to grow, but couldn't do so alone." Two such fields were polypropylene plastics and pharmaceuticals.

Montedison developed a new polypropylene process that slashed electricity costs by 30 percent and steam use by 90 percent. The process also used a lower-grade raw material than other technologies then on the market, and the finished product had a number of advantages. But Montedison's global market position in polypropylene was weak. It held about 17 percent of European capacity, but had failed to enter the U.S. market with a wholly owned subsidiary some years earlier. The costs of learning to operate in an unfamiliar environment and building market share from scratch proved too high for Montedison.

Hercules was the dominant polypropylene producer in the United States. It also had the largest market share worldwide, just slightly ahead of Shell. In addition, Hercules was strong in areas where Montedison was weak: product applications and marketing. On the other hand, Hercules was weak in process technology, having traditionally depended on licenses from Montedison.

This combination was ideal for a joint venture. Montedison could expand its capabilities in down-stream activities and in the U.S. market, while Hercules could do the same in upstream activities. Himont, a new fifty-fifty joint venture between the companies, thus became the world market leader when both parents transferred their polypropylene businesses to it in 1983. Montedison's new technology was installed in all Himont plants, and the joint venture adopted Hercules's successful marketing strategies. In this case, Montedison's global strategy did not seem to conflict with the goals of Hercules, because the latter, too, operated on a global scale.

But such conflicts did appear in another joint venture between these two companies. Before launching Himont, Montedison and Hercules each owned 50 percent of Adria Labs, a pharmaceutical company in the United States that sold a highly successful anticancer drug. To

Montedison, Adria was primarily a sales arm of its pharmaceutical division, which developed and produced the drug. But Hercules wanted Adria to be the core of a new, self-sufficient company capable of manufacturing its own products. The costs of such an effort seemed to conflict with Montedison's plans to integrate Adria into its global strategy, which called for introducing to the U.S. market a number of new drugs developed in Italy. As in the case of IBM's regional integration in Europe, control of this venture seemed critical to Montedison. So, at the same time that Hercules and Montedison formed Himont, they also shifted majority ownership of Adria Labs to Montedison.

My statistical analysis yielded additional evidence of the link between global strategies and ownership. It suggested that vertical integration between a joint venture and its partners could affect the likelihood of conflicts between them. Subsidiaries that sold a substantial share of their output to the MNC or to other subsidiaries in the MNC's system were less likely than others to have joint ownership. Such sales might be part of a global strategy in which each subsidiary produces what it is best at. The transfer prices used in these transactions are likely to be a perennial source of conflict with local joint venture partners. The MNC will want prices that maximize its global profits, which implies shifting profits to wholly owned subsidiaries. The local partner will, of course, want just the opposite.

The effect of vertical integration inside the host country was different. When an MNC's venture depended on raw material inputs from local suppliers, particularly when there were few suppliers, it was likely to have joint ownership. In such situations, MNCs apparently find it advantageous to give the supplier a stake in the venture to assure a constant supply. Transfer prices for the inputs might be a problem here too, but the local supplier has an even greater incentive to insist on high transfer prices if it does not own a share of the venture.

NEGOTIATING WITH HOST GOVERNMENTS

If, based on the analysis above, MNC managers decide that a joint venture is the best structure for a foreign subsidiary, then the host government is likely to agree. Almost without exception, host government policies have aimed to encourage, not discourage, joint ventures. So it is the multinational corporation preferring *whole* ownership that may have to negotiate with restrictive host country governments.[17]

In such ownership negotiations, MNC managers make tradeoffs among a number of issues, including ownership. An analysis as described above should precede these negotiations, because it suggests why the firm needs whole ownership and how important this is. For example, if control really is "critical," as IBM claimed, then the point should probably not be conceded in negotiations. But if the firm only mildly prefers whole ownership, it may well decide to trade this issue off against others.

The ability of the host government to make the MNC change its position on ownership depends on what it can offer the firm in return. The same is true for the firm's ability to gain an exception to the government's rules. This ability of one party to get its way reflects its *bargaining power* in negotiations. Case and statistical studies suggest that the bargaining power of firms and host governments vary according to the circumstances of the investment.[18]

MNC Strength: Contributions to Country Goals

IBM's ownership negotiations with India in 1978 and with Mexico in 1985 suggest when MNCs can expect to "win" at the bargaining table. The governments of both countries had rules restricting foreign ownership of manufacturing subsidiaries. In the first case, the government enforced this rule strictly, and IBM ended up divesting from India rather than ceding 60 percent of its existing operations to local investors. In the second case, IBM gained a rare exception to the Mexican rules, and set up a wholly owned venture to manufacture personal computers. What made the difference?

One difference between the two cases was that Mexico in 1985 was more desperate for foreign investment than India was in 1978. India was pursuing a fairly successful strategy of self-sufficiency and nonalignment that led it to want local control of an indigenous computer industry. Foreign investment was valued only because it brought in skills that contributed to this goal. Clearly, IBM could supply these skills, but so could a number of second-tier U.S. and European companies that were willing to share ownership with Indian firms.[19] IBM, for its part, felt that yielding to India's demand for a joint venture would set precedents that it could not afford, given its previously untarnished record of complete ownership worldwide.

The situation in Mexico was different. The country had just endured its second foreign exchange crisis in a decade and was well on its way to a third. This situation led the Mexican government to soften its restrictions on foreign investment, much as other developing countries had been doing. Mexico, too, wanted computer technology, but in addition it wanted foreign investors for the capital they would bring in, the exports they could generate, and the confidence they might instill in the country's recovery.

IBM's promise to transfer technology to Mexican firms and export a major part of the output from its Mexican operations proved to be just the sweetener the government needed to approve the wholly/foreign-owned investment. During the negotiations, IBM agreed to triple its planned investment to $90 million, export 90 percent of the output, and help the Mexicans set up, run, and fund a semiconductor development center. IBM also agreed to a number of provisions that favored local producers: it promised to buy inputs from local suppliers, develop a local dealer network, and sell its final output in the domestic market at prices that were 15 percent above international levels. (This last provision implicitly protected higher-cost domestic producers.)

The key bargaining chips that IBM wielded in this negotiation were its *technology and degree of commitment to the host market.* In high-technology fields with high barriers to entry, producers from developing countries usually cannot break into world markets without the help of a global firm. And many governments, following Japan's example, are promoting precisely these types of industries. The ownership regulations in a number of countries explicitly make exceptions to projects in high-technology sectors. But even when such exceptions are not mandated by law, MNCs contributing to the host government's goals are in a strong bargaining position in ownership negotiations.

MNCs making major commitments to restrictive host countries are also more likely than others to gain an exception to the ownership rules. My statistical studies suggested that the bargaining power of the MNCs increased with the size of their investment. Aside from the inflow of capital, host country governments also seem to value the substantial managerial skills and domestic linkages that accompany major projects. These factors seem to have been important in the case of IBM in Mexico.

Government Strength: Attractive Markets

Historically, the host governments that have had most success enforcing ownership restrictions were those with *attractive domestic markets.* Numerous U.S. firms were forced to form joint ventures in Japan in the 1960s and 1970s, or to license their technologies, because that was the only way to get access to the booming Japanese market. Today, China is using its large and rapidly growing market to gain concessions from MNCs. Until April of 1986, the Chinese government refused to approve wholly foreign-owned ventures; since then W.R. Grace and others have set up such facilities. But the Chinese have continued to encourage joint ventures through a variety of incentives, and foreign firms are often more than willing to comply. Gillette, for example, did not hesitate to set up a joint venture in China, even though it insisted on whole ownership elsewhere. Johnson & Johnson has already formed two joint ventures there; it owns 50 percent of one venture making pharmaceuticals and tampons, and 60 percent of one making Band-Aid bandages.

India, Mexico, and Brazil also have used the attraction of their domestic markets to force MNCs to form joint ventures with local firms. One reason IBM went out of its way to reach an agreement with Mexico was to gain access to the Mexican market and use it as a base to develop a Latin American business. Smaller countries imposing ownership restrictions, such as those in the Andean Common Market, have had much less success. In these instances, foreign investors sometimes preferred to stay away altogether rather than give in to the government's demands.

Alternative Strategies for Firms.   Even when the country offers an attractive market, however, managers may feel that the risks of joint ownership in some ventures are too high. What are they to do? First, they should consider whether the venture could be modified to reduce these risks. Maybe the subsidiary could be set up to sell exclusively in the domestic market, rather than in world markets, thus reducing the need for control that stems from following a global strategy. Gillette and Johnson & Johnson seem to have done that in China. Where this is not possible, the solution may well be to decline to invest altogether. My statistical analysis indeed showed that ventures in restrictive countries tended to be less tightly integrated than others into the MNCs' networks.

A second option for firms that are forced to concede on the ownership issue is to seek concessions on aspects of control that are less publicly visible. Sometimes restrictive governments hold their ground on the ownership issue, but allow MNCs to have management control of the operations. Gillette, for example, owns only 49 percent of a ballpoint pen business in Mexico, but controls general administration, manufacturing, finance, and product quality through a management contract. General Motors' managers, too, have found that host country governments are usually more willing to make concessions on management control issues than on the basic demand for some local participation.

THE FUTURE OF JOINT VENTURES

Partly for reasons cited above, more and more MNCs have been forming joint ventures abroad in recent years. Are we thus seeing the passing of the traditional form of investing abroad, the wholly owned subsidiary? The answer to this question affects the way global firms will be managed in the 1990s. It depends on trends in the factors that determine the costs and benefits of joint ventures.

The current popularity of joint ventures is not unique. Between 1955 and 1961, the share of joint ventures in the new investments of large American MNCs went from 28 percent to 55 percent. But just as rapidly that share fell to 31 percent in 1969.[20] The 1970s saw another increase in the use of joint ventures abroad, to a new level that seems to have been sustained into the 1980s.

The reasons behind the ebb and flow of joint ventures in the past seem to lie in the changing global strategies of the multinational corporations. The 1950s are sometimes referred to now as a "flag-planting" period; U.S. firms rushed abroad to establish footholds in many countries at the same time. Forming joint ventures with local firms was an ideal way enter new markets quickly. But the trend in the 1960s was toward consolidation and integration of the firms' global networks, as suggested by the IBM Europe example cited above. Conflicts with joint venture partners, who had purely local concerns, became more common in this period. The U.S. firms thus shunned joint ventures in this period, and even bought out many of the partners who had been useful earlier. This pattern may well repeat itself in the future.

Joint Ventures and Globalization

One trend sometimes credited with the popularity of joint ventures in the 1980s is the widening of the competitive arena from national to global markets. Marketers call this the "globalization" of markets; industry analysts point to the increasing need to pursue worldwide economies of scale and scope; and trade statistics reflect the rising competition from a myriad of foreign sources. These trends are probably affecting all industries, even though some, such as telecommunications, are changing more dramatically than others.

Globalization forces led Montedison to launch the polypropylene joint venture with Hercules. Montedison was traditionally an Italian producer, with minor operations in other European countries. But in the early 1980s all the major chemical firms elsewhere became global competitors. Firms like Hoechst, BASF, ICI, and Dow not only exported from their home bases, but also manufactured abroad, raised capital on international markets, and formed supply and other relationships with each other. These companies used their strengths in one country to help them compete in others, and they drew on technological and managerial resources from several countries.

Montedison's joint venture with Hercules was an effort to move in one leap into the league of global chemical producers. As such, it illustrates how *globalization encourages joint ventures when it drives firms to expand their capabilities and access to markets.* Similarly, firms might form joint ventures to do R&D in industries where costs could not be recouped in national markets alone, such as in telecommunications. Or they might join forces to draw on scientific resources in various countries, as is happening in biotechnology.

But there is another side to the globalization of industries. Firms with operations in various countries often find it profitable to manage these in an integrated way, using one plant to supply the other, or following common marketing and manufacturing strategies. Globalization here implies greater central control of worldwide operations; joint ventures are more of a hindrance than a help in this process. Thus, *globalization discourages joint ventures when it drives firms to integrate their worldwide operations.* Given this tendency, it is not surprising that, once Himont established its position as a leader in global polypropylene production, Montedison bought out Hercules's share.

Opposing forces are thus likely to drive the choice of ownership structure for foreign subsidiaries in global industries. The tension between the need to expand globally and the need to control the network is likely to be felt in industry after industry. International managers will thus continue to struggle with this dilemma in the future. That prospect is clearly better than simply following the current joint venture fad, or blindly pursuing the old preference for whole ownership.

A FINAL CHECKLIST

A substantial body of evidence now exists to guide managers struggling with this dilemma. The framework I have presented suggests that six questions are critical. For every proposed business investment abroad, managers should ask these questions.

- **What ownership structure do we prefer, if we are free to choose?** In answering this question managers should consider the next two questions. Even when there are restrictions on foreign ownership, it is important to start with this question, because it prepares the firm for negotiations.
- **Can we exploit an existing competitive advantage, or will we need to expand our capabilities to compete successfully?** The stronger the latter possibility, the more attractive a joint venture will be. Of course, a firm may have an advantage in one area, such as technology, but still need to expand its capabilities in another, such as marketing. A joint venture partner should then be chosen to complement the firm's existing capabilities.
- **Will we be following a globally integrated strategy?** If so, a joint venture with a local partner can lead to costly conflicts of interest. The key is to make sure that the partners agree on the level—global or local—at which profits are to be maximized. Potential problems may arise when the MNC supplies or buys from the joint venture, when quality standards exceed requirements of the local market, and

when exports from the venture compete with those of the MNC's other subsidiaries.

- **If the host government restricts foreign ownership, do we have the bargaining power to win an exception?** Answering this depends on answering the next question. If the firm's bargaining power is limited, it should consider modifying its strategy for the new business so that whole ownership is no longer critical. It is often possible to learn to live with a forced joint venture by limiting the scope of the venture and negotiating management contracts.
- **What will we contribute to the country's goals, and how much will we depend on the host government?** The key here is whether the firm's contributions to the country are valued highly by the government. Firms bringing advanced technology and willing to make major investments are generally in a strong bargaining position. Conversely, the host government's bargaining position will be stronger the more attractive the domestic market is to the MNC.
- **Will answers to these questions change with industry evolution?** The firm's ownership strategies are likely to vary over time, just as they vary across industries and countries. Thus, each proposal should be evaluated on its own merits. Moreover, a decision made today may need to be revised later. Managers sensitive to the global evolution of their businesses will be able to avoid unnecessary surprises and costs in joint ventures.

APPENDIX

The framework presented in this article is based partly on extensive statistical analysis of data from almost 200 large American MNCs collected in the 1970s by Harvard's Multinational Enterprise Project. This database is still the most detailed and comprehensive one available on the activities of U.S. MNCs abroad. The sample used here contained information on ownership structure and other characteristics of 1,877 subsidiaries in a broad cross section of countries and industries. I added country variables from the World Bank and industry variables from the Profit Impact of Marketing Strategies (PIMS) database to the Harvard data. I then used binomial regression methods to develop and test a model describing the conditions under which the MNCs chose joint or whole ownership for the subsidiaries in existence in 1975. I tested the applicability of this cross-sectional model over time with earlier data from the same database. Finally, the results of this analysis were complemented with case data on five large MNCs gathered through field interviews in 1985. The statistical results were consistent with these cases, as well as with statistical data collected by other researchers in the 1980s. Further details on the statistical results are in my "Ownership Structures of Foreign Subsidiaries: Theory and Evidence," forthcoming, and "MNC Ownership Preferences and Host Government Restrictions: An Integrated Approach" (1988).

REFERENCES

1. In 1969, 31 percent of the new foreign manufacturing ventures of large U.S. multinationals were jointly owned with local partners, compared with 41 percent six years later. See B. Gomes-Casseres, "Joint Venture Cycles: The Evolution of Ownership Strategies of U.S. MNEs, 1945–1975" in *Cooperative Strategies in International Business,* ed. F. J. Contractor and P. Lorange (Lexington, MA: Lexington Books, 1988).
2. Kenichi Ohmae quoted in "Are Foreign Partners Good for U.S. Companies?" *Business Week,* 28 May 1984.
3. Extensive anecdotal evidence on the role of joint ventures in providing local connections in China and Japan can be found in S. Goldenberg, *Hands across the Ocean* (Boston: Harvard Business School Press, 1988).
4. Evidence for the automobile, automotive parts, food, computer, and pharmaceutical industries is in L. G. Franko, "New Forms of Investment in Developing Countries by U.S. Companies: A Five Industry Comparison," *Columbia Journal of World Business,* Summer 1987, pp. 39–56.
5. See T. Hout et al., "How Global Companies Win Out," *Harvard Business Review,* September–October 1982, pp. 98–108.
6. In one McKinsey and Coopers & Lybrand study, 70 percent of the joint ventures broke up. See "Corporate Odd Couples," *Business Week,* 21 July 1986, pp. 100–105. In L. G. Franko's pioneering work on the topic, one third of the joint ventures were eventually dissolved. See his *Joint Venture Survival in Multinational Corporations* (New York: Praeger, 1971).
7. Two articles in the Summer 1987 *Columbia Journal of World Business* present unconventional views on joint venture instability. My own "Joint Venture Instability: Is It a Problem?" analyzes the two types of explanations noted in the text. It also suggests that joint ventures can often be transitional forms that are expected to give way to whole ownership after they achieve their purpose. If so, joint venture instability is a sign of success, not failure. Roehl and Truitt argue that partner disagreements are not only inevitable, they are also useful. See T. W. Roehl and J. F. Truitt, "Stormy, Open Marriages Are Better: Evidence from U.S., Japanese, and French Cooperative Ventures in Commercial Aircraft," *Columbia Journal of World Business,* Summer 1987.
8. See D. J. Encarnation and S. Vachani, "Foreign Ownership: When Hosts Change the Rules," *Harvard Business Review,* September–October 1985, pp. 152–160.
9. The data was collected by the Harvard Multinational Enterprise Project, as described in J. P. Curhan et al., *Tracing the Multinationals: A Sourcebook on U.S.-based Enterprises* (Cambridge, MA: Ballinger, 1977).

10. See S. J. Kobrin, "Trends in Ownership of U.S. Manufacturing Subsidiaries in Developing Countries: An Interindustry Analysis" in Contractor and Lorange (1988).

11. For recent theoretical perspectives on the costs and benefits of joint ventures, see my "Ownership Structures of Foreign Subsidiaries: Theory and Evidence," *Journal of Economic Behavior and Organizations,* in press; E. Anderson and H. Gatignon, "Modes of Foreign Entry: A Transaction Cost Analysis and Propositions," *Journal of International Business Studies,* Fall 1986, pp. 1–26; and J. Hennart, "A Transaction Cost Theory of Equity Joint Ventures," *Strategic Management Journal,* July–August 1988, pp. 36–74. Pioneering work on this topic appears in J. M. Stopford and L. T. Wells, Jr., *Managing the Multinational Enterprise: Organization of the Firm and Ownership of the Subsidiaries* (New York: Basic Books, 1972).

12. See D. J. Teece, "The Multinational Enterprise: Market Failure and Market Power Considerations," *Sloan Management Review,* Spring 1981, pp. 3–17.

13. The distinction between global and multidomestic strategies rests on whether the MNC integrates its worldwide operations or pursues separate strategies in each host country. See Hout et al. (1982).

14. See G. Hamel and C. K. Prahalad, "Do You Really Have a Global Strategy?" *Harvard Business Review,* July–August 1985, pp. 139–148.

15. Talk at Harvard Business School, 17 April 1985.

16. See "Is the GM-Daewoo Deal Running on Empty?" *Business Week,* 12 September 1988, p. 55.

17. Of course, in many countries there are other terms to negotiate with host country governments, such as capacity licenses, foreign exchange allocations, tax rates, and so on. This discussion focuses on negotiations about ownership structures.

18. Theoretical discussions and empirical evidence on the role of bargaining power in ownership negotiations are in my "MNC Ownership Preferences and Host Government Restrictions: An Integrated Approach" (Boston: Harvard Business School, working paper, 1988); N. Fagre and L. T. Wells, Jr., "Bargaining Power of Multinationals and Host Governments," *Journal of International Business Studies,* Fall 1982, pp. 9–23; and S. J. Kobrin, "Testing the Bargaining Power Hypothesis in the Manufacturing Sector in Developing Countries," *International Organization* 41 (1987): 609–638.

19. See J. M. Grieco, "Between Dependence and Autonomy: India's Experience with the International Computer Industry," *International Organization* 36 (Summer 1982): 609–632.

20. For a detailed analysis of historical trends in joint venture formation, see my "Joint Venture Cycles" in Contractor and Lorange (1988).

Corporate Divestiture: Pruning for Higher Profits

Richard J. Schmidt

Corporate divestiture of business segments has become an accepted alternative growth strategy to diversification. Components of a corporation are subject to divestiture if they:

- Do not produce an acceptable return on investment.
- Do not generate sufficient cash flow.
- Do not meet corporate strategic uses.

In the words of one author:

> Disinvestment, or getting out of old sunset industries, is just as important a source of growth as getting into new sunrise industries.[1]

There were 642 corporate divestitures during 1983 in the United States. In 284 of these divestitures, an exchange price was disclosed; in 37.5 percent of the sales this price was greater than $25 million, and in 12.6 percent of the sales it was $100 million or higher.[2]

In the present restructuring of the U.S. economy, the major divestitures of the 1980s are of the same magnitude as the acquisition activity of the 1960s and early 1970s. In the 1960s, size and diversity were perceived as strong indicators of corporate vitality. But in the more competitive economic environment of the 1980s, the ability of management to actively direct and control the multibusiness has become more important than ever before.

Source: Reprinted from *Business Horizons*, No. 30, 3, pp. 26–31. Copyright 1987 by the Foundation for the School of Business at Indiana University. Used with permission.

[1]Lester C. Thurow, "The Productivity Problem," in *Macro-Engineering and the Future*, ed. F. P. Davidson and C. L. Meader (Boulder, Colo.: Westview Press, 1982), p. 101.

[2]See "Almanac & Index, 1984," *Mergers and Acquisitions*, January 13, 1984, p. 38.

HISTORICAL PERSPECTIVE

During the 1960s, many industrial firms were acquiring other firms, often in different businesses, to form large conglomerates. In the 1970s a general economic downturn made many companies slow down the acquisition process, and divestiture appeared in its early stages. Dynamic, fast-growth companies were combining with slow-growth, mature companies for a counterbalancing effect.

Many companies found, however, that "if you have too many businesses, you stretch yourself too thin in capital and management."[3] The conglomeration of so many businesses under one corporate umbrella caused concern in the financial community.

SEGMENT REPORTING

In December 1976, under prodding from the Securities and Exchange Commission, the Financial Accounting Standards Board issued Statement on Financial Accounting Standards No. 14, *Financial Reporting for Segments of a Business.*[4] This statement required publicly owned corporations to report assets held and income generated by disaggregated corporate segments of similar products and services.

For the first time, public disclosure was made of many business segments that were obviously unprofitable. The disclosure forced management into explaining to stockholders why certain portions of the corporation were producing low returns on the stockholders' invested capital. For the first time, corporate executives began to develop divestiture strategies to eliminate unsuccessful sections of the business, rather than just spinning off an occasional unprofitable segment.

In the 1980s the chemical process industry joined the growing number of corporations that were shedding unprofitable segments. According to a spokesperson for the management consulting firm of Arthur D. Little Company:

> It's an effort on the part of chemical companies to narrow the scope of corporate interest and activities to those they know best.[5]

---

[3]In the words of John Dansby, vice president for planning at Ashland Oil, as quoted in "Properties for Sale: How Companies Are Deconglomerating," *Chemical Week,* November 7, 1984, p. 32.

[4]Financial Accounting Standards Board, *Financial Reporting for Segments of a Business Enterprise, Statement No. 14* (Stamford, Conn.: FASB, 1976).

[5]"Properties for Sale" (note 2): p. 32.

ALLOCATING AND REDIRECTING RESOURCES

In a diversified business, resource allocation becomes an important consideration. For example, management talent is a scarce commodity, and a corporation is wise to use its management people to its maximum ability in areas they know well. To keep management from being over-extended, priorities must be set and adhered to. If management finds itself spending a disproportionate amount of its time and energy on one part of the corporate entity, that segment may be a candidate for divestiture.

The redirection of resources, whether material assets or management talent, to growing parts of the business requires attention and review. As one author points out, constant attention should be given to identifying resources that "may be of benefit to other strategic business units of the organization in their expanding stages."[6]

Resource review is particularly important when a product is nearing the end of its life cycle (see Figure 1). The dynamics of a product life cycle of conception, birth, growth, maturation, decline, and death can change a company's attitude toward any given activity and may suggest divestiture of the product's operations.

When a portion of a business becomes unprofitable, the corporation can attempt to remedy the situation by various means:

FIGURE 1   The Product Life Cycle and Divestiture Strategy

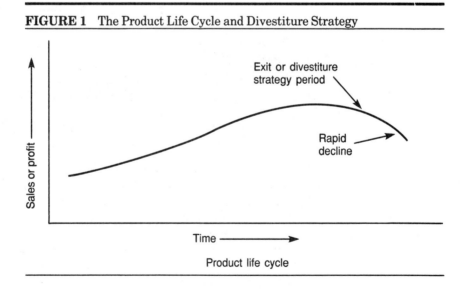

---

[6]K. W. Tourangeau, *Strategy Management* (New York: McGraw-Hill, 1981), p. 127.

1. **Continuing as is.** This is always an alternative.
2. **Reducing costs.** Positive steps can be taken to improve the cost-revenue relationship.
3. **Reviewing prices.** Selling prices may be adjusted to improve the cost-revenue relationship.
4. **Adding products or product lines and introducing new products.** Development of new products may be an acceptable alternative if time permits. Strengthening the existing product market may improve overall profitability.
5. **Exploiting an operation.** A better job of management may be done to strengthen manufacturing, distribution, or sales.
6. **Shutting down the operation.** This exit strategy is a widely explored alternative. Such exit strategies are restricted to pricing, distribution, geographic contraction, and the elimination of a service or product. The company usually exits with a minimum of further investment and a maximum of profit. Overall corporate sales are reduced but cash flows may improve and a positive net income may be realized.
7. **Divestiture.** Disposing of a segment as a going concern.

DEVELOPING A DIVESTITURE STRATEGY

Shutting down an operation or divestiture may not be an acceptable alternative initially. There may be emotional or prestige reasons for continuing a part of a business in spite of circumstances. Among these reasons are:

- The dislike of admitting failure.
- Unpleasantly high losses to be absorbed in one year.
- Employee morale problems.
- The fear that someone else may purchase a divested segment and turn it into a success.[7]

When all attempts at maintaining an operation fail and management recognizes that a strategic business unit is in a problem situation and prospects for a turnaround are bleak, management must realize that getting out of an industry in an expedient fashion, even if it means a loss, may be the only viable strategy. Liquidating or selling the unit as an operating entity may be the solution if the corporation finds itself in a weak competitive position or the industry is extremely unattractive to corporate management. Because the cause of nearly every

---

[7]As listed in D. E. Hussey, *Corporate Planning Theory and Practice,* 2nd ed. (New York: Pergamon Press, 1982), p. 146.

divestiture situation can be traced back to a management error,[8] divestiture may be an answer to continuing managerial errors. The sell-off situation in economic terms is one where the costs of being part of the parent exceed the benefits.

A re-evaluation of a corporation's operational philosophy and overall business strategy—whether this re-evaluation is voluntary or forced on the company by the economy—may result in divestiture plans to reduce losses and to concentrate on successful business units. The resulting fractional divestiture reviews may be directed to segments that don't appear to fit into the total corporate portfolio. These divestiture candidates are units with no hope of recovery in the present parent corporation.

The development of a divestment strategy is formalized when a situation arises that cannot be solved by continuing to operate the particular business unit. Corporate segment reporting, both internal and external, can focus attention on activities that are not up to corporate standards. Initiative can be taken to perform divestment reviews in periodic corporate planning exercises that spotlight company trouble spots. The resulting reviews frequently have given divestment analysis an air of respectability.[9]

The separation or other divestment preparations may require some further investment; advertising, price, distribution, and geographic expenditures may make the offered property more attractive. Although excessive additional investment may reduce the return on the sale, little expenditure may limit the number of potential buyers or reduce the purchase price. Either the seller or the buyer can adjust the purchase price for a variety of reasons, including synergistic effects of complementary product lines, sales patterns, or distribution facilities.

Other costs of divestment may include:

- Disposal costs of specialized assets.
- Costs of breaking long-term supplier and labor contracts.
- Costs associated with losing customers for other corporate products.
- Costs from plummeting worker morale in the remaining corporate segments.

Management has to ask questions concerning the interrelationships between the divested activity and other corporate activities. Would a divestment impair the viability of the remaining segments of the

---

[8]According to G. Bing, *Corporate Divestment* (Houston: Gulf Publishing, 1978), pp. 3–4.

[9]Some excellent studies of divestiture strategy are provided in D. A. Aaker, *Developing Business Strategies* (New York: John Wiley & Sons, 1984); R. H. Hayes, "New Emphasis on Divestment Opportunities," *Harvard Business Review,* July-August 1972, pp. 55–64; and *Mergers and Acquisitions,* ed. M. Keenan and L. J. White (Lexington, Mass.: Lexington Books, 1982).

company? Would lower sales volumes result in uneconomic production runs of the company's other lines? How dependent are the marketing and distribution systems on the sales volume of the divested operations? An obvious but frequently overlooked consideration is that "the components must be ones which can logically be separated from other parts of the property."[10]

As one student of divestiture observed:

> Top management will probably be concerned primarily with the effects of disposal on the remaining organization rather than with the mathematics of alternative investment possibilities for the capital involved.[11]

The conception of a divestment strategy often begins with a listing of the reasons for possible divestiture. They may include:

- Unsatisfactory profit performance as determined by corporate management.
- A desire to improve a current or future cash flow position.
- Avoidance of a future major capital investment requirement.
- Debt reduction for the corporate entity.
- A desire to reduce business risk, including the failure (either present or anticipated) of a particular business area.
- High cost and badly located operations.
- A desire for diversification which is currently hampered by being in a particular business.
- Lack of fit with the company's perception of what it should be doing or activities that are not in harmony with the rest of the corporation.
- Lack of top management knowledge in a narrow line of business.
- Personality conflicts among management.
- Receipt of an attractive offer.
- Government decree to divest.

Table 1 summarizes the reasons for divestiture that were enumerated by managers in one study.

GUIDELINES FOR DIVESTITURE

With the foregoing considerations in mind, internal management guidelines for divestment should be developed. Management must remember that:

---

[10]A. Bettauer, "Strategy for Disvestment," *Harvard Business Review*, March-April 1967, p. 119.

[11]Bettauer (note 10), p. 117.

TABLE 1 Reasons Managers Give for Divesting a Segment of Their Business

	Frequently %	*Occasionally* %	*Total* %
Poor performance	40	20	26
Changes in plans	30	19	23
Excessive resource needs	14	22	19
Constraints in operations	9	17	15
Source of fund	7	12	10
Antitrust	0	10	7
Total	100	100	100

Source: L. Vignola, Jr., *Strategic Divestment* (New York: Amacon, 1974), p. 18.

- The sum of a division's parts may be greater in value than the whole division.
- Simple components of a division may be sold more easily than the whole complex division itself.
- The disposal of a corporate division is a major marketing operation.
- Planning should include an evaluation from the viewpoint of potential buyers.
- A spin-off should be considered if the division has sufficient size and potential to be a publicly owned company.

SPIN-OFFS

One divestment strategy that has increased in popularity is to spin off a subsidiary as an independent corporation. How can management decide whether to sell or spin off a divested segment? One author suggests the following rule:

- **Sell** if the premium is positive and is judged to be the best obtainable.
- **Spin** off if the costs of being a part of the parent exceed the benefits and a desirable sale cannot be arranged.[12]

Voluntary spin-offs are generally healthier financially than are direct-sell divestments.[13] Involuntary spin-offs caused by federal or

[12]See T. H. Hopkins, *Mergers, Acquisitions, and Divestitures* (Homewood, Ill.: Dow Jones-Irwin, 1983), p. 120.

[13]This is the contention of R. J. Kudla and T. H. McInish, *Corporate Spin-Offs* (Westport, Conn.: Quorum, 1984), p. 7.

state regulatory agency complaints may or may not be beneficial to the stockholders.

Management may think that a spin-off operation will perform better independently than it did as a member of the parent organization because of the possibility of improved managerial decision making and incentives. Specialized management may deal with the very different business environments more effectively than did larger, more generalized organizational structure.

Investors may also value a spin-off division more highly than before because of the difficulty in valuing all of a diversified parent's lines of business. Approval by investors is necessary for future capital requirements.

LINKING INVESTMENT/DIVESTMENT STRATEGY TO MANUFACTURING AND ENGINEERING

An investment/divestment corporate strategy requires an implementation program if it is to be effective. Figure 2 illustrates the procedure suggested by W. E. Rothschild.[14]

Manufacturing

Defend via Promotion.   In the manufacturing area, Rothschild outlines two alternative responses for implementation. First, there is the *Defend via Promotion* procedure that is developed for large, corporate-owned manufacturing facilities with a nonspecialized series of products. Emphasis is on production load leveling a consistently high level of utilization. The facilities have a low to moderate level of flexibility based on capital-intensive rather than labor-intensive operations. Promotion of the product is designed to complement the production process. Production is expected to provide a sufficient product when promised, with the logistics capability of serving the created demand.

Growth via Revolutionary Design.   A second response is termed *Growth via Revolutionary Design.* The implementation technique is based on small manufacturing facilities located close to markets and customized to specific products. Flexibility of the operations is vital. "The company relies heavily on vendors because it does not want to overcommit or integrate operations too soon. The input to the manufac-

---

[14]In his *Strategic Alternatives* (New York: Amacon, 1979), pp. 184–88.

FIGURE 2 Linking Investment/Divestment Strategy to Manufacturing and Engineering

Investment / Divestment Strategy

Where, when, and why will the corporation invest or divest specific businesses?

Management Strategy

How will the corporation achieve the desired investment / divestment strategy?

What must each functional corporate component
do to effectively implement the chosen strategy?

Manufacturing   Engineering

Source: W. E. Rothschild, *Strategic Alternatives* (New York: Amacon, 1979), pp. 184–88.

turing system is more critical than the output because the product is unique. Complete control over logistics is not required.

When one of these two manufacturing implementation methods is chosen, divestment of existing operations may be required. As an initial preparation for divestiture, useful equipment, tools, and vehicles can be transferred from one unit to another to enhance divestment opportunities and strengthen remaining business units.

Engineering

Defend via Promotion.   Because engineering is a key factor in strategic implementation, Rothschild developed engineering responses similar to those he suggested for manufacturing. First the *Defend via Promotion* strategy assumes that basic and applied research and development are luxuries that the corporation cannot afford. What is needed is the ability to design or specify designs to maintain a competitive product. A philosophy that is most appropriate to this implementation is to quickly but carefully follow the competition. Leading in the business sense is not considered worth the effort. The corporation's reputation is one of a standardizer with sufficient quality to sustain the corporate image. Adopting or licensing the products of others will suffice because specialization is a luxury. Being exclusive and protective only add unnecessary costs.

Growth via Revolutionary Design.   With the second approach, *Growth via Revolutionary Design,* the corporation employs a full line of technical talent, beginning with basic research and development through applications, advanced engineering, and design engineering. The company attempts to be first with a concept—or at least first with a proven product or application. The product line must be differentiated or customized. Funding for engineering support must be sufficient for the company to move through the entire product life cycle. It is vital in such situations to have a proprietary and protected product position.

These two very different approaches affect the choice of business units available for divestment when general business profitability considerations indicate drastic remedies for the corporation.

The present business environment has made both divestiture and diversification acceptable business strategies. Public disclosure of segment operating results has helped force management to take action when a segment becomes unprofitable. Industry has responded by divesting undesirable segments. Other alternatives are available for unsuccessful operating divisions, but divestment is an important and viable alternative response.

A corporation may develop a divestment strategy to deal with this emotional subject. Management must consider the physical interrelationships of facilities, the interdependence of other corporate activities, and the costs of dissociating a business segment. Implementing a strategy has significant impacts on manufacturing and engineering.

Divestiture affects the entire corporation: production, distribution, marketing, engineering, and the public's perception of the corporation. One author put it this way: "Divestment is a public act and calls for a high degree of management courage."[15]

---

[15]Hussey (note 7), p. 147.

Divestiture: Antidote to Merger Mania

Clark E. Chastain

Corporate takeover mania appears to have become a permanent addition to the corporate landscape, not just a temporary blip as in the past.[1] While mergers and acquisitions seem to be common throughout U.S. industry, they have been particularly prevalent in several industries: oil; natural gas pipelines; media and publishing; airlines; banks; and advertising agencies. But acquisitions have a counterpoint—the divestiture of corporate units and assets. While not reported so widely on the front pages of newspapers, they are running at record levels. Corporate divestitures involving $1 million or more totaled 1,381 in 1986.[2]

Many corporate acquisitions don't succeed (sometimes two out of three fail), and divestitures often offer the most expedient and least costly way of fixing the failure. They tranquilize merger madness, usher in management sanity, and furnish a way out of corporate imbalance. They illustrate today's practice of asset management, a strategy that concentrates on efficiency and effectiveness. Divestiture is a chief tactic in corporate restructuring, the process that produces the lean, tough organization that has streamlined its resources, slashed its costs, ferreted out new markets, and conceived of and executed new strategies to reach those markets.

This article examines strategies for divesting subunits and other assets. It then discusses corporate restructuring and gives an example

---

Source: Reprinted from *Business Horizons* 30, no. 6, pp. 43–49. Copyright 1987 by the Foundation for the School of Business at Indiana University. Used with permission.

[1]Economic historians refer to three previous waves as follows: between 1893–1904 (horizontal mergers for monopoly), 1926–1930 (horizontal mergers that resulted in oligopolies), and 1955–1970 (conglomerates diversified their activities). See Tomislava Simic, ed., *Mergerstat Review* (Chicago: W. T. Grimm and Company, 1984).

[2]Data for 1986 supplied by *Mergers & Acquisitions Magazine, M & A Data Base.*

of the strategy. Methods of divesting business units are covered, and accounting concepts and divestiture techniques are presented. Finally, some of the tax considerations in divesting are outlined.

REASONS FOR DIVESTING

Unwise decisions in mergers or acquisitions lead to many divestitures. But once an unsound acquisition is made, the reasons for disposal become similar to those that apply to other undesirable organizational units that may have been built internally in the past years.

In reviewing its assets and their profit contributions, a corporation is likely to find some that are not sufficiently profitable. Management also may find that some assets do not fit with those used in its primary activities. In the words of Christensen et al., those assets that do not "build on what is unique to the particular situation" of a particular corporation should be eliminated.[3] If a company follows Alfred D. Chandler's theory that a company structures its resources so it can best accomplish its strategies, it will sell those assets that do not contribute.[4]

Changes in markets add to the risk that a particular business combination will not succeed. Conflict in business styles, which caused pharmaceutical companies to fail in cosmetics and perfume, or technological branching can destroy what were thought to be good fits. Prompt abandonment of poor performers, losers, and misfits avoids drains on other resources and keeps employee morale high.[5]

Corporate Restructuring

The almost universal strategy of streamlining (also known as restructuring, reorganization, retrenchment, or refocusing), which has dominated corporate activities since the 1980–82 recession, emphasizes divestiture. Cost cutting continues to rank as a priority strategy, as continued low inflation makes it difficult to raise revenues. To compete, indeed to survive, against fierce foreign competition and strong domes-

---

[3]For a basic discussion of strategy, see C. Roland Christensen, Norman A. Berg, Malcolm S. Salter, and Howard H. Stevenson, *Policy Formulation and Administration* (Homewood, Ill.: Richard D. Irwin, Inc., 1985), Chapter 1.

[4]Alfred D. Chandler, *Strategy and Structure* (Cambridge, Mass.: MIT Press, 1962).

[5]Arthur A. Thompson, Jr., and A. J. Strickland III, *Strategy and Policy: Concepts and Cases* (Dallas: Business Publications, Inc., 1978), p. 82.

tic rivalry, firms find it mandatory to pare costs. Real interest rates of 3 percent or more are high by traditional norms, so the cost of capital invested in assets remains high. The resulting lean, reduced-resource concern must frequently divest low-return assets to remain profitable. Deregulation in several industries since 1978 and economic troubles in industries such as steel and oil have stimulated corporate restructurings.

Often a divestiture has both an immediate, titanic effect on a firm's assets and a longer-run downward influence on earnings, thus significantly affecting its overall strategies. Wall Street frequently rewards the company that divests unprofitable, poorly managed, or unrelated units by raising its stock price.

Antitrust and Other Regulatory Restrictions

Current antitrust policy views an acquisition as an acceptable method of growth but, in protection of the public interest, prohibits those that tend to lessen competition or encourage monopolistic behavior.[6] The federal government or private competitors may challenge a merger under Section 7 of the Clayton Act, which is enforced by the Department of Justice (DOJ) and the Federal Trade Commission (FTC). The FTC also has jurisdiction over alleged unfair business practices. The Securities and Exchange Commission (SEC) oversees requirements for disclosure on tender offers. State laws also influence merger trends.

In addition, the attitude of the national administration toward corporate takeovers greatly affects how federal antitrust laws are applied. In 1986, the DOJ, following President Reagan's hands-off attitude, quickly ruled that General Electric's takeover of RCA Corporation and Burroughs' pursuit of Sperry presented no meaningful antitrust problems. Figure 1 shows how antitrust proceedings that deny certain acquisitions or force certain divestitures create acquisition candidates for other concerns. Mergers between weak firms usually are condoned to preserve the number of competitors in an industry. The DOJ and the FTC seek to determine the competitive impact of an acquisition on an industry or the relevant market. The agencies look at a potential combination's size and market power. Each firm's market share and the number of firms in a market are key variables. Possible mergers

---

[6]For further discussion see James W. Bradley and Donald H. Korn, *Acquisition and Corporate Development: A Contemporary Perspective for the Manager* (Lexington, Mass.: Lexington Books, 1981), Chapter 4.

FIGURE 1   Antitrust Divestitures

Divested Concern	Divested from	Acquirer or Potential New Owner
Avis	International Telephone and Telegraph (ITT)	Norton Simon
Peabody Coal	Kennecott Copper	Newmont Mining et al.
Grinnell Corp.	Grinnell Corp. et al.	ITT
Grinnell (Fire Protection business)	ITT	Tyco
Autolite		
Service Bureau Corp.	Ford Motor	Bendix Corp.
	International Business	Control Data Corp.*
Nuclear Chicago	Machines	
Rome Cable	Abbott Laboratories	G. D. Searle
	Alcoa	Cyprus Mines (now part of
Okonite		Std. Oil Co. Indiana)
	Kennecott Copper; LTV	LTV; public; ESOP

*In the out-of-court settlement of litigation between the companies.

Source: Adapted from James W. Bradley and Donald H. Korn, *Acquisition and Corporate Development: A Contemporary Perspective for the Manager* (Lexington, Mass: Lexington Books, 1981), Chapter 4, p. 79

having a substantial horizontal or vertical nature are usually challenged, and horizontal mergers between companies with high market shares are rarely approved.

Other Reasons for Divestitures

Other specific reasons for corporate divestitures vary. Low economic performance ranks high in importance. Any subsidiary, product line, division, or other component whose return on investment (ROI) is lower than the corporate norm is a candidate for divestiture. A common mistake in acquisitions is to overpay. Coupled with other problems, this often results in dismal earnings and a significantly depressed ROI. The strong emphasis on corporate focus has caused many corporations to sell subunits not clearly related to the rest of the company in production techniques or technology and markets. There is usually little management support for developing such unrelated units and maintaining their competitive position and profitability. Montgomery Ward (owned by Mobil Oil) and Wilson Sporting Goods (formerly held by Pepsi Cola) are illustrations.

The need for cash causes many firms to part with organizational elements, even profitable ones. Similarly, components sometimes are sold to reduce a high level of debt. Wickes has gone this route with Gamble-Skogmo. A divestiture often represents an antidote for acquisition mistakes.[7] Fluor Corporation, a construction firm, found it could not mesh management and corporate culture with St. Joe Minerals Corporation. Also, according to *Business Week*,[8] Fluor spent too little time investigating the potential acquisition.

A company's managers may believe they already are spread too thin for the number of units and resources that they currently own or control. Yet they may not want to add additional managers, diluting the power and control present executives hold. Thus, they may elect to divest some business units. Divestiture may also be the result of unhappiness among managers, employees, or stockholders of a subsidiary company with the present ownership, overall organizational structure, or corporate management. The subsidiary's managers may request a spin-off or a trade to another corporation it likes or arrange a leveraged buyout.

Gordon Bing lists 26 circumstances that cause owners of businesses, many independently owned, to sell. He emphasizes there usually are several in each case.[9] This also applies to smaller, privately owned companies whose owners wish to retire or move on to other interests.

RESTRUCTURING A CORPORATION

Corporate restructurings, which often lead to the disposal of some organizational segments occur frequently today. Companies that decide to restructure usually are experiencing lower income and cash flow than desired and may face serious changes in their markets. The restructuring process is a major strategic move that usually involves rearranging organizational units, managers, and employees in an attempt to better relate to new market developments and revised strategies.[10] Management usually seeks ways to employ its assets more effectively, and it may initiate cost-cutting moves to improve efficiency and profitability. In addition, it might restructure its capital structure, which might add more debt to the organization.

A proven and widely used approach in restructuring is to group organizational units around the strategic business unit (SBU). An SBU is considered a natural business unit. It is organized around a product or product line and often differs from divisional or other organization

---

[7]M. S. Salter and W. A. Weinhold, *Diversification Through Acquisitions: Strategies for Creating Economic Value* (New York: Free Press, 1979), examine at length the process of choosing compatible acquisitions. Unfortunately, the ease and risk associated with divesting an acquisition candidate is not considered.

[8]See *Business Week* (note 2), p. 92.

[9]Gordon Bing, *Corporate Acquisitions* (Houston: Gulf Publishing Co., 1980), pp. 7–9.

[10]See Chandler (note 4).

lines. In relating SBUs to profitable markets (a crucial task), management should ascertain which resources are needed and will contribute a desired level of return. Those units and assets that do not meet those criteria should be divested.

Strategic-planning systems focused on the SBUs may proceed in four steps.[11] The first is to gather facts, answering questions such as what are key characteristics of the market for each strategic business unit and what are its strengths and weaknesses. The second step is to analyze relevant facts for a SBU and develop its action plans. The third step links the SBU plans with corporate strategic plans, operating plans, and capital-expenditure budgets. In the fourth step, the results of the plan are monitored.

Tables 1 and 2 illustrate how the strategic process provides guidelines for divesting organizational components. The data are assumed for Flint Corporation (a hypothetical company), but the analysis is practical and useful. The corporation's major problem is that sales and income for strategic business unit C have been declining for a number of years. A primary goal of Flint Corporation is to earn 10 percent or more per year on the assets (ROA) employed. ROA for 1986 for business unit C is only 6.67 percent ($15 million on $225 million). When a significant decrease in sales was forecast for 1987, the firm decided that divestiture of C was the correct decision.

Assets, revenues, costs, investment, and employees have been computed for each SBU based on its market and profitability. In many companies this method poses a major measurement difficulty, because accounting systems are often structured along formal organizational lines. Note in Table 1 that the contribution margin is the key to a unit's desirability. Contribution margin is defined as sales less variable expenses (those deductions that change in proportion to changes in sales). Companies should work to increase sales volume in those units that have high contribution margins and considerable profits.[12]

A restructuring commonly involves a change in subunit boundaries and responsibilities. It may be associated with either acquisition or divestiture of corporate components, or both. Cost-cutting efforts are strong and pressure is applied for increased productivity, especially in a downside restructuring. Flint management should be euphoric in taking pride in their achievements, as reflected in Table 2. They decreased variable costs as a percentage of sales for business units A and B. Fixed expenses relative to sales also decreased in both units.

---

[11]Allen H. Seed III, "Strategic Planning: The Cutting Edge of Management Accounting," *Management Accounting,* May 1980, pp. 10–16.

[12]See Clark E. Chastain, "How Management Accountants Coped with the Recession," *Management Accounting,* January 1985, pp. 34–38; "Streamlining: Necessary Strategy for Licking a Profit Crunch," *Business Horizons,* March-April 1984, pp. 69–76.

TABLE 1 Accounting Data for Strategic Business Units, 1986 (figures in 000 except employees)

	Income Statement for 1986							
	A		*B*		*C*		*Total*	
Business Unit	*Amount*	*%*	*Amount*	*%*	*Amount*	*%*	*Amount*	*%*
Sales	$375,000	100%	$325,000	100%	$250,000	100%	$950,000	100.0
Less variable expenses	112,500	30	130,000	40	175,000	70	417,500	43.95
Contribution margin	$262,500	70%	$195,000	60%	$ 75,000	30%	$532,500	56.05%
Less fixed expenses	188,833		163,657		60,000		412,490	
Net income	$ 73,667		$ 31,343		$ 15,000		$120,010	
Other data:								
Assets employed	$337,500		$292,500		$225,000		$855,000	
Number of employees	3,381		3,250		2,813		9,444	
Capital expenditures	$ 34,320		$ 30,000		$ 19,110		$ 83,430	
Return on assets employed	21.8%		10.7%		6.67%		14.0%	

TABLE 2 Budgeted Accounting Data for Strategic Business Units, 1987 (figures in 000)

	Income Statement, Budgeted for 1986					
	A		*B*		*Total*	
Business Unit	*Amount*	*%*	*Amount*	*%*	*Amount*	*%*
Sales	$500,000	100%	$400,000	100%	$900,000	100.00%
Less variable expenses	140,000	28	156,000	39	296,000	32.89
Contribution margin	$360,000	72%	$244,000	61%	$604,000	67.11%
Less fixed expenses	220,000		190,000		410,000	
Net income	$140,000		$ 54,000		$194,000	
Other data:						
Assets employed	$371,250		$312,975		$684,225	
Number of employees	3,621		3,392		7,013	
Capital expenditures	$ 36,119		$ 31,117		$ 67,236	
Return on assets employed	37.7%		17.3%		28.4%	

And with the sale of unit C, profits increased by $73.9 million, or 61.7 percent, even with a $50 million decline in total sales. Many downside restructurings, of course, are not so successful.

In the typical downside restructuring, units that show falling sales also show declines in variable costs, and they may improve efficiency. Fixed costs are cut through terminating managers in manufacturing, selling, and administration; eliminating professionals and secretaries; negotiating salary reductions and freezing pay; selling planes, vacating luxurious offices, and eliminating executive cars, and decreasing travel, phone bills, conferences, and fringe benefits.[13]

Market strategies planned for 1987 promise substantial sales increases for the two business units retained by the Flint Corporation. Expected return on assets shows a significant increase. One other comment on the analysis is important. We have assumed that fixed expenses could be allocated accurately to each unit. In reality, accounting has to arbitrarily assign administrative, professional, service, and other costs of operating corporate headquarters to operating units. Income for each business unit is affected by these arbitrary actions.

A corporate divestiture may be largely an isolated event. But in many cases, especially where there are several within a short period, it may be associated with massive changes in overall company plans, goals, strategies, assets, and structure.[14]

METHODS OF DIVESTITURE[15]

A corporation typically uses one of three methods of divesting a component unit: outright sale, spin-off, or liquidation. Most companies prefer to sell a subsidiary's stock, although its assets may be sold instead. The sale of assets is simpler, because it avoids the problems of valuation of assets and settlement of liabilities (unless the sales agreement specifically mentions warranties by the seller).

An alternative arrangement is to sell the assets while retaining the corporate shell. The buyer often will pay more under this method, because he is assured that he will not later be charged with hidden liabilities that may arise.

The leveraged buyout, either to existing management, employees, or an investment group, is a common form of sale. Heavy debt is typically used, with the value of the subsidiary's assets and its earning power as collateral. The selling corporation may finance a significant portion of the sale by holding notes payable from the divested entity and/or common and preferred stock. Leveraged buyouts, with their heavy debt, pose significant risk; the seller should carefully assess whether the

---

[13]See Chastain, (note 12), p. 73.

[14]For the wide range in scope of corporate activities in strategic refocusing, see James K. Brown, *Refocusing the Company's Business* (The Conference Board, Inc., Report No. 873, 1985), p. 1–42.

[15]This section is based in part on Joseph M. Morris, *Acquisitions, Divestitures, and Corporate Joint Ventures* (New York: John Wiley & Sons, 1984), Chapter 7. He outlines and discusses such detailed topics as establishing an orderly organizational program for a divestiture and complete steps to follow. It is an excellent guide for officers and professionals who have the responsibility for divesting a unit.

business and its management can produce enough earnings and cash flow for both debt service and operations.[16]

The spin-off sets up the divested business as an independent corporation, and its capital stock usually is distributed to the parent company's existing shareholders. The critical test is how self-supporting the new company really is. If it is clearly independent, the parent is effectively freed from the spin-off's debt (including the balance sheet presentation) and from providing further capital. A spin-off may be structured as a tax-free exchange.

A considered spin-off by Borg-Warner of its marginally profitable York Air Conditioning subsidiary illustrates a number of these points.[17] The unit's profit in 1984 constituted about 2 percent of Borg-Warner's total income, but its debt of $60 million was about 17 percent of the corporation's total debt. The subsidiary's earnings fell because of the strong dollar; one-third of its sales is foreign, and much of that is in the Middle East, where income is dwindling.

As Borg-Warner could not find a buyer for York, it used the spin-off form of divestiture. It distributed shares of York stock to all Borg-Warner shareholders in proportion to their holdings.

As is the case with many divestitures, the newly created independent company prospered. York stock, which sold for $12 at the time of the spin-off, traded as high as $33.875 per share before the October drop in stock prices.

An optional spin-off treatment is to distribute the disposed units' assets to parent-company stockholders. The distribution may be proportionate, or it may be made only to certain stockholders who exchange stock equal to the fair value of the assets distributed.

In some cases, the owner may abandon or liquidate the fixed assets, intangibles, and real property of an unwanted business. The sale of individual assets may yield a greater amount than could be realized from the sale of the ongoing business. This may be preferable, even though its price as a going concern is higher, assuming the business is unprofitable and the seller has to take over its notes payable.

Pricing

Methods of pricing a divestiture run the gamut of those procedures available for an acquisition—discount of expected cash flows, price/earnings ratios, percentage of gross sales, value of the assets, the

---

[16]See "Leveraged Buyouts: There's Trouble in Paradise," *Business Week,* July 22, 1985, pp. 112–13.

[17]"Borg-Warner Corp. Says It May Spinoff Air Conditioning Unit," *The Wall Street Journal,* July 29, 1985, p. 5.

market value of the stock, and the arbitrary reliance on book value. Computing figures by as many methods as possible will expand the seller's knowledge of the value of the unit to be divested and potential markets, and assist it in the sale negotiations.

The privately owned company that includes significant personal assets of the owners may have to deviate from statistical or comparative computations, and accept values that accord with reality and the marketplace. Many departments can contribute to pricing a segment of a larger company. Accountants and finance personnel can list assets and assign estimated fair values; tax personnel can determine tax bases and tax liabilities or benefits associated with different prices and transaction structures; top executives and operations personnel familiar with the industry also may aid in the process.

An analysis of prices recently paid for companies in similar industries with comparable assets, sales, income, and growth patterns can help in the setting of a realistic price reasonable in the eyes of potential buyers, that is, if the seller wants a sale in a relatively short period. Buyers can be located through contacts with brokers, investment bankers, banks, lawyers, accountants, and other professionals. Advertisements placed in trade publications of industry associations and in classified-advertising sections of newspapers may help.

A business broker usually charges a fee based on a sliding scale for the size of the transaction and related to a percentage of the gross selling price. The buyer's capacity to manage the business effectively and his credit rating are important if the seller must hold promissory notes for part of the purchase price. To protect against default and the unattractive possibility of repossessing a deteriorated business, the seller may arrange for participation in the management.

The seller is concerned with receiving as much cash as possible at the time of sale and selling stock of the existing or newly organized corporation to clean up the financing. The tax structure of the sale, while important, may be subordinated to other factors. The seller may arrange transitional assistance—administrative, financial, systems, operations, or general management—for the buyer. Also, he should designate a responsible individual to take care of later questions about unresolved accounts receivable and unpaid bills, among others.

Accounting for Divestitures

Accounting for divestitures is governed primarily by Accounting Principles Board (APB) Opinion No. 30, "Reporting the Results of Operations: . . . ." which prescribes accounting recognition and special disclosures.[18] A major step in accounting for a divestiture is to determine if the divested unit should be classified as a segment of a business—a separate major product line or a class of customer. Separate presentation of operating results is required if the divested unit qualifies as a business segment. Paragraph 13 of Opinion 30 defines a segment of a business as follows:

> For purposes of this Opinion the term "segment of a business" refers to a component of an entity whose activities represent a separate major line of business or class of customer. A segment may be in the form of a subsidiary, a division, or a department, and in some cases a joint venture or other nonsubsidiary investee, provided that its assets, results of operations, and activities can be clearly distinguished, physically and operationally and for financial reporting operations, and activities of the entity.

For further elaboration of which divestitures constitute a segment of a business, see paragraph 13 of Opinion No. 30. In response to confusion among accountants and businesspeople, the American Institute of Certified Public Accountants issued a number of accounting interpretations of Opinion No. 30. Morris has summarized a number of examples cited by the APB, some of which are business segments and some of which are not.

Because divested units often have low or no profits, corporate executives frequently want the unit to qualify as a business segment. The separate presentation on the income statement leaves income from continuing operations at a higher level and presents a better picture of future results.

Income taxes must be computed separately for different parts of the income statement, such as income from continuing operations, income from discontinued operations, and gain or loss on disposal of a business segment. These captions are then reported net of tax, following intraperiod tax allocation.

Two dates are important in the accounting process. The *measurement date* is the date on which management commits itself to a formal plan for divesting a segment. The disposal date is the date the sale is closed or when operations cease. Income or loss is measured for the discontinued segment from the measurement date to the disposal date.

---

[18]The rest of the title is: ". . . .Reporting the Effects of Disposal of a Segment of a Business, and Extraordinary, Unusual and Infrequently Occurring Events and Transactions" (New York: AICPA, 1973).

Accounting for Income Taxes in a Divestiture

To compute the gain or loss on a divestiture, a company must compute and recognize the related income tax. These effects depend on the income taxes incurred in previous years. The accountant or tax expert will have to examine three interrelated factors.[19]

1. The structure of the sale and the nature of the assets sold to determine if income or loss is subject to ordinary tax rates or capital gains rates.
2. Calculations of recapture of depreciation, where applicable, must be made to determine how much of a gain is taxable at ordinary tax rates. When the recapture of investment credits is applicable, previous income tax expense must be adjusted.
3. Previously accumulated deferred tax balances for a divested unit should be reversed. The rates at which these taxes were provided may differ from the tax rates realized in divestment.

Corporate divestitures provide an antidote for merger mania. They not only support a psychological equilibrium; they also help firms maintain a desired level of resources, sales, earnings, and stock prices. They have become an important asset-management strategy, as businesses place added emphasis on efficiency and effectiveness. When a corporate component no longer contributes positively to revenues and profits, or does not fit the master plan of an organization, it should be divested. Frequent divestiture of corporate units, organizational restructurings, and major cost-cutting programs have been common since the 1980–82 recession and continue today as a low rate of inflation and merciless foreign and domestic competition characterize the economy. Business divestitures are expected to remain a major means of adjusting to continued high levels of mergers and acquisitions, shifts in goals and strategies, and changing economic conditions. They are the economy's quiet stabilizer.

---

[19]For further discussion and illustrations, see Joseph M. Morris, *op, cit.*, pp. 176–81.

From Warning to Crisis: A Turnaround Primer

P. Scott Scherrer

Long before a business fails, warning signals start flashing. But managers often don't notice the red lights, or even ignore them. When they finally do acknowledge something's amiss, some managers will treat the problem as a temporary phenomenon, putting out the fire but not remedying the hazard.

With a bit of education, however, managers can train themselves to perk up and recognize the bad signs, whether they are activated from within the organization or from the outside. Once managers learn the signals, they also can differentiate between the various stages of organizational decline. No matter what phase a company is in, managers need to act—fast.

Following is a turnaround primer that identifies warning signals, categorizes decline phases, and provides a framework to help managers reverse the direction of an organization that may well be on its way to hell in a handbasket.

INFLUENCING EXTERNALS

Many managers believe a downward trend will dissipate when bad news from the outside improves. The external elements that cause them trouble range from increased competition to legal/political vacillations (see Table I).

Among these external, uncontrollable elements are market changes, customer preference changes, foreign competition, capital market movements, legal precedents, and the political climate. Since all businesses in an industry are similarly affected by external elements, each business survives these changes only because of the ability of its

Source: Reprinted by permission of publisher, from *Management Review*, September/ 1988 © 1988. American Management Association, New York. All rights reserved.

TABLE I   Nine External Warning Signals

---

1. Economic growth activity gives management an indication of the economic climate and influences expansion plans.
2. Credit availability and money-market activity are barometers of trends in commercial and investment banking that will alter the cost of funds.
3. Capital market activity gives a clear signal to management of investor attitudes toward any given industry and the state of the business climate.
4. Business population characteristics show the numbers of businesses entering and exiting any given industry, signalling market expansion and contraction and the degree of competition within the industry.
5. Price-level changes indicate the rate of inflation and impact production considerations.
6. Changes in the competitive structure of the marketplace affect products, pricing, and marketing/distribution.
7. Breakthrough technology also causes changes in products, marketing/distribution, and production.
8. Cultural/social changes alter consumer preferences or the conditions under which a product can be sold.
9. Legal/political changes can adversely affect the marketplace or have an impact on the production, sale, and distribution of a product.

---

management. Some businesses come through external changes with increased market share and profitability; others fail.

A major problem with the uncontrollable elements is their interaction with each other. A cultural/social change, for example, can result in a legal/political change. This, in turn, can affect the economic environment, leading to a shift in technological developments. The rate of technological development affects the status of the competition, which in turn influences the cultural/social environment, and the circle is complete. What managers often do not realize is that they can create a similar chain reaction within their businesses to combat the external elements. Foresight and flexibility will help management safeguard against uncontrollable elements, using tactics such as promotion, education of the consumer, accelerated research and development, product improvements or elimination, changing expansion plans, changing markets, and changing channels of distribution.

Consider the tobacco companies. They have known for many years about the external changes taking place in their industry—most importantly, the discovery of smoking's serious health hazards. They have been affected by cultural/social and legal/political changes for the past several decades, and recently experienced severe tests in the court system. To offset declining product sales, they developed new products, such as smokeless tobaccos. They also invested in new businesses: RJR Nabisco, Miller Beer, and other consumer products companies that would use established channels of distribution to gain competitive advantage. The tobacco producers understood the early warning signals of the external, uncontrollable elements and acted to offset them. The ability to cope with external, uncontrollable elements requires that management plans for the unexpected and implements that plan when the unexpected occurs.

INTERNAL ELEMENTS

Only 20 percent of business failures are caused by external elements. The other 80 percent are the result of mishandled internal elements. Management is the force that drives the internal functions of finance, production, and marketing/distribution, and yet these elements are at the root of the majority of business failures.

When management does not recognize the internal signals of decline, it pretends that slowdowns are caused by external elements. A shortage of cash is often attributed to poor collections or lack of sales. In fact, the shortage of cash is usually a signal pointing to a deeper problem buried within the firm's management and accounting information systems. It may be that the firm is selling its products or services at a price that does not cover the variable costs of making the product or service. The firm may not have calculated contribution margins, actual product costs, and the direct cost of sales to determine the amount of profitability in the product or service.

Like external forces, the internal elements can interact with each other, and any one of the internal, controllable elements may spark a decline. Production techniques can become antiquated. Marketing/distribution can be in the wrong market with the wrong product. Finance can be unaware that the financial requirements of the other departments have changed. (Poor information flow between departments is another signal of decline.)

COPING WITH INTERNAL ELEMENTS

Management often does not use the managerial tools at its disposal to control internal forces. Many managers do not utilize cash projections, but are only aware of balance sheets and income statements. The heart of any company is the synergy developed between the efficient operations of its various departments. The pulse beat for that synergy is the financial statements. Businesses should run on budgets and cash projections. Budgets are the foundation of financial statements, which reflect the success or failure of the business. For many businesses, however, budgets are mystery stories couched in scenarios that allow managers to hedge their positions. Managers create budgets that cannot be wrong, and consequently they cannot be accurate.

Balance sheets may show adequate working capital even when a company is in decline. When the balance sheet is overly burdened with inventory and accounts receivable that are inaccurate, obsolete, or uncollectable, a company is in trouble. The manager should know the status of accounts receivable. If they are increasing on the financial statements, is it because sales are increasing or collections are slow? If inventory is increasing, is it because sales have decreased and production has not? Managers can reduce a firm's reliance on banks by increasing accounts receivable collections, reducing inventory, and paying accounts payable within the discount period to avoid penalties.

Internal elements require constant monitoring. Since management may be unable to understand the dynamic nature of the internal elements, it is not surprising that declines go unnoticed.

Management often doesn't understand its relationships with stakeholders—the people who work for, live near, invest in, or are affected by a company. Customer service, for example, is often a low priority. In most businesses, 80 percent of sales come from 20 percent of the customers. Often the cost of servicing a customer and the cost of a sale are unknown. Customers are not classified into categories to determine the most favorable customers to the business. Management may perceive that the best customers are those who order the most, although these may be the same people who pay the slowest. In many companies, channels of information—from customers, competition, employees, vendors, and other managers—are not open. Without this information, the business cannot adapt to change. Information and the ability to react to it are the most powerful weapons a business has against decline.

EARLY INTERNAL WARNING SIGNALS

Danger signals can be used by management to begin an internal corporate renewal. There are distinct phases of decline, and the danger signals vary within the stages (see Table II). Not all of the symptoms of decline will appear; there is sufficient cause to worry if some of them occur.

Also, internal warning signals take on different meaning depending on the company's growth rate. In stabilized companies, managers may continue to manage as if the growth will continue in the near future. When plans are not modified to address the new situation, the business courts trouble. Many companies religiously draft strategic plans. All too often, however, the plans are carved in granite and are not adaptable to changing situations. When shifts occur (internal, external, or

---

TABLE II   Common Danger Signals and the Stages When They Occur

---

Early Decline:
   Shortage of cash.
   Strained liquidity.
   Reduced working capital.
   Stretched accounts payable.
   Late accounts receivable.
   Reduction of ROI by 20 to 30%.
   Flat sales.
   Several quarters of losses.
   Increased employee absenteeism.
   Increased employee accidents.
   Increased customer complaints (product quality, delivery, back orders, stock-outs).
   Late financial and management information.

Mid-term decline:
   Increasing inventory.
   Decreasing sales.
   Decreasing margins.
   Increasing expenses.
   Increasing advances from banks.
   Additional requests for consideration from banks.
   Late and unreliable financial and management information.
   Eroding customer confidence.
   Accelerating accounts payable from vendors.
   Overdrafts at the bank.
   Delayed accounts receivable from opportunistic customers.
   Violation of loan covenants.
   Bank used to cover payroll.

Late decline:
   Little attention paid to decreasing profit.
   Staff is cut back without analyzing cause of problems.
   Overdrawn bank account substituted for a line of credit.
   Cash crisis.
   Accounts payable are 60 to 90 days late.
   Accounts receivable are more than 90 days late.
   Sales decline further.
   Employee morale is extremely low.
   Company credibility is eroding.
   Inventory turnover has decreased excessively.
   Supplier restrictions are initiated.
   Fewer reports to bank are submitted.
   Auditors qualify opinions.
   Checks bounce.
   Credit is offset.
   Accounts receivable continue to age.

TABLE II (concluded)

Margins decrease further.
Sales volume decreases further.
Uncollectable receivables increase.
No liquidity.
Working capital is depleted.
Lack of funds for payroll.
Ineffective management.
Attempts to convince lenders that company is viable and liquidation is not
   necessary.

Signals that can occur in any stage:
Decreased capital utilization.
Decreased market share in key product line(s).
Increased overhead costs.
Increased management and employee turnover.
Salaries and benefits growing faster than productivity and profits.
Increased management layers.
Losing market share to competition, which is not keeping up with
   marketplace changes.
Management in conflict with company goals and objectives.
Direction of management and company are different.
Sales forecasts predict company can sell its way out of difficulty.
Poor internal accounting.
Credit advances to customers who do not pay on time.
Nonseasonal borrowing.
Sudden overdrafts.
Increased trade inquiries.

---

both), the business is unable to cope with them, and instead continues to follow its strategic plan. Managers believe the strategic plan represents the very best of their creative abilities, and therefore are loathe to deviate from it. The strategic plan becomes part of the problem, rather than the solution.

FINANCIAL PREDICTORS

Many financial ratios are tip-offs to a downturn, but management often considers them accounting busy work and pays no heed. Five ratios useful throughout all phases of decline and the turnaround process are:

1. Working capital to total assets.
2. Retained earnings to total assets.
3. Earnings before interest and taxes (EBIT) to total assets.

4. Market value of equity to book value to total debt.
5. Sales to total assets.

These ratios are especially useful when they are used for at least three years. The business will begin to establish a pattern within the ratios, and deviations from the pattern can be corrected quickly. More mature businesses have long histories, and the ratios should have reached a point where they are consistent annually. A deviation is as good as a red flag.

The ratios noted by turnaround managers generate a picture of the company. They indicate the ability of the business to survive on its own. When they are extremely low, it is time to approach the bank for bridge capital. The bank will not be willing to have any further involvement unless the plan for the turnaround is valid and based on the business's actual ability to support itself after the turnaround.

DOUBLE DECLINE

Often a company suffers a decline thanks to a combination of internal and external elements. Some common signals when both forces are at work include:

- Management by exception rather than flexible planning.
- Delegation without inspection, control, feedback, or reinforcement.
- Vertical organization chart, with little if any interaction between departments.
- Managers with responsibility for more than five direct reports.
- Employees with more than one boss.
- Broken chain of command.
- Overreliance on management by objectives.
- Senior managers' abuse of perks.
- Marketing the wrong products.
- Marketing in the wrong markets.
- Inadequate research and development.
- Inappropriate channels of distribution.
- Unresponsive financial information systems.
- Loss of competitive advantage.
- Changing technology.
- Regulatory changes.
- Inadequate understanding of customers' needs.
- Allowing one department or business function to dominate and dictate the mission, goals, and objectives of the business.

Crazy Eddie, Inc. is an example of a company that has suffered from both internal and external problems. Internally, there were too many layers of management, excessive wages, corporate waste, cost over-runs, employee morale problems, and information-flow deficiencies. The company had almost every signal of decline.

Externally, new competitors entered the market. Since Crazy Eddie's had damaged its relationships with appliance suppliers, it could not receive the necessary merchandise to compete. The company is now undergoing a turnaround; part of the strategy is to cut costs and payroll by a minimum of $25 million. There is also a slump in the company's markets, so revenue has decreased. The internal elements were changed by laying off unnecessary managers, reducing wages, adding a profit-sharing plan, settling the lawsuits on corporate waste, reducing costs, and adding a computer system to prevent selling items below cost. The external elements are being addressed by rebuilding relationships with suppliers, banks, and consumers.

THE TURNAROUND PROCESS

Turnaround managers bring order to chaos, which usually means they must take control of every function in the business. They create budgets from the bottom up and strictly enforce accountability. They analyze products and markets to determine which have the most profitability. Those that generate losses are terminated quickly and permanently, regardless of the company's relationship with the customer or product. The turnaround manager cuts costs, increases the business's adaptability, and saves the profitable products and markets. Actual costs replace standard costing, and product contribution margins are used to determine which products contribute the most to the fixed costs of the business. Cash-flow reports are used continually; at first they may be used daily, then weekly, then monthly, and finally semiannually. The reports are used in developing the operating plan. The time line and the amount of cash flowing in will determine how the business can survive.

The classifications of customers and the aging of accounts receivable determine which customers are profitable. The business may have many customers with repeat orders, but they all may be delinquent in paying their accounts. The business cannot afford to carry them any longer. Reviewing accounts receivable is an essential task of turnaround managers. They decide which customers to keep and which to pursue for more business.

GET EVERYONE INVOLVED

Banks, vendors, customers, employees, boards of directors, and others affected by the decline of the business need to be made part of the solution. Banks and boards of directors are usually the parties that suggest the use of a turnaround manager. Normally, by the time they notice a problem exists, the situation is approaching crisis proportions. This is a common situation because bank executives and boards tend to be chiefly concerned with balance sheets and income statements-driven, despite the fact that healthy-looking balance sheets and income statements can disguise many problems. Bank managers and board members do not visit the business and review operations. They do not walk the plant floor and talk with employees. They do not review basic financial information, such as accounts receivable and payable. They only learn about employee morale, customer service, equipment condition, and other on-site situations from a report generated by management.

Trade vendors also need to be included in the situation. They are the business's lifeline to its supplies. When payments to them are delinquent, the business is in jeopardy of losing its supply line. Management may argue that it can find other suppliers, but unless the underlying problem causing delinquent payments is addressed, suppliers will evaporate along with the company's credit. New suppliers require credit references, and changing suppliers has substantial switching costs. The new supplier has to produce or acquire the supplies requested, schedule deliveries, and obtain payments. As the business adds new suppliers, the bank will receive credit report requests. This is another signal of decline.

Employee participation is essential in the turnaround process. Turnarounds often require asking for pay concessions. Hours on the job and working conditions may be affected. When employees are part of the restructuring plan, they tend to accept painful concessions with more ease. When the restructuring is complete, management should consider itself indebted to these people and should reward them financially.

SRC, a leveraged buyout from International Harvester, is an example of a turnaround where employee participation was the key ingredient for success. In 1979, the company was losing $2 million a year on sales of $26 million. In 1983, 13 employees of International Harvester bought SRC. They developed a detailed reporting system and a full-blown, daily cash-flow statement. In 1986, sales reached $42 million. Net operating income increased to 11 percent and the debt-to-equity ratio has been reduced from 89-to-1 to 5.1-to-1. The appraised value of a share in the company's stock ownership plan has increased from 10 cents to $8.45. Absenteeism and serious workplace accidents have almost disappeared. The company attributes the turnaround to allowing employees to reach their highest potential.

To facilitate a turnaround, union cooperation is essential. It also can greatly influence morale. A turnaround can be accomplished despite the unions, but may require drastic steps such as bankruptcy or massive layoffs. Concessions regarding pay rate, hours, working conditions, raises, vacations, accumulated sick leave, and benefits will be granted only when the union is convinced that the company can survive. That this is possible is indicated by the arrival of the turn-around manager and by the turnaround plan. The cooperation of the other stakeholders also places pressure on the union to cooperate.

Customers must also be taken into account during the turnaround, but businesses in decline tend to forsake customer service. Quality control diminishes, which causes more order returns. This adds expenses to an already strained financial condition. Orders are taken and delivery dates missed, causing loss of credibility with the customers. The inventory, which was a main part of the balance sheet, becomes obsolete and therefore not usable to meet the current demands of the customers. The end result is the loss of the customer base.

TYPES OF TURNAROUNDS AND STRATEGIES

A turnaround can take several forms. It can be *strategic* if the business needs to be redefined because of changing markets and products. In the General Nutrition turnaround, for example, the company moved away from its core of vitamins and specialty health foods to the much wider category of health in general. The stores needed items that would make people come to them rather than grocery stores. The company searched for new products and new lines. Brookstone, the specialty gadget store, inspired many of the changes made at General Nutrition. Prior to the turnaround, the stock had plummeted from a high of 29⅝ to a low of 3⅞.

An *operational* turnaround involves changing a business's operations, which could include cost-cutting, revenue generating, and asset reduction. In the case of General Nutrition, the turnaround was also focused on the operations of the business. (It is very common for turnarounds to be mounted on several fronts and combine stategies.) At General Nutrition the management team was strengthened and the company divided into three distinct segments: retailing, manufacturing, and specialty services.

Another example of an operational turnaround is Black and Decker. The company had more than 200 different motor sizes. It had split consumer and professional tools into two separate groups that seldom communicated with each other. This made it easy for the competition to find niches where Black and Decker did not make tools. To remedy the situation, the company organized plants around motor sizes, reduced product variations, and streamlined manufacturing. The number of plants was reduced from 25 to 19. Excess capacity utilization increased by 75 percent. In addition, the company began producing new products to meet consumer demand.

The *financial* turnaround restructures the financial operations of a business. The object is to utilize the financial strength of the business as an asset. ITT, for example, divested itself of 23 businesses for almost $1.5 billion and increased return on equity from 8 percent in 1979 to 12 percent in 1987. Management slashed expenses by abandoning its lavish lifestyle, renting out full floors at its Park Avenue headquarters, and cutting the workforce by two-thirds.

Each different type of turnaround may focus on a particular strategy. These include:

- *Revenue Generating.* Management tries to increase sales, advertising, and markets while decreasing prices.
- *Product/Markets Refocusing.* Managers analyze products and markets to determine their profitability. Customers are analyzed to determine the nature of their purchases, payment history, and ability to purchase more. Channels of distribution are analyzed to determine their effectiveness. Products are analyzed further to determine their saleability, contribution margins, actual cost of production, cost of sale, cost of distribution, manufacturing efficiency, inventory carrying costs, and cost of customer service. Businesses may have reached the limits of their growth in products and markets, in which case they need to analyze potential moves into other product and market areas.
- *Cost Cutting.* Managers reduce administrative costs, R&D, and marketing.
- *Asset Reduction.* Management removes unnecessary assets that usually look nice on the balance sheet but actually produce only costs of maintenance and no revenue stream.
- The combination of any of the above.

Using the correct strategy is part of the art of successfully turning around a company. As the turnaround progresses, the strategy may change. Cost cutting may be superseded by revenue generating, and so forth. Strategies may be combined and used in various sequences, but using an inappropriate strategy can be a terminal error. Here are four pointers to choosing the correct strategy:

- Mature businesses should use retrenchment and efficiency strategies, not product/marketing refocusing.
- Businesses with low capacity utilization should pursue cost-cutting strategies.
- Businesses with high capacity utilization should also pursue cost-cutting strategies.
- Businesses with high market share should pursue revenue-generating strategies and product/market refocusing.

The time frame for a turnaround varies depending upon the business, industry, market, severity of the crisis, cooperation of stakeholders, and turnaround manager. A business that has been in decline for several years cannot expect to be renewed quickly. Its reputation for low credibility will have permeated all of its stakeholders and will take some time to reverse. A business that recognizes signals of decline in the early stage can be renewed more quickly.

In general, turnarounds occur in five stages:

1. Evaluation of the situation, which can take from one week to three months.
2. Creating a plan, which can take from one to six months.
3. Implementation of the plan, which can take from six months to one year.
4. Stabilization of the business, which can take from six months to one year.
5. Return to growth of the business, which can take from one to two years.

Astute managers constantly monitor the health of their businesses and act on the warning signals. Often, managers can see the signals but need outside help to cure the problem. The need to address decline and failure is obvious. The waste of corporate assets and employees' talents that can stem from managerial ignorance can be astronomical. This waste can be minimized if management can notice and address decline in its early stages.

Customized Strategies for Service Sector Businesses

John A. Pearce II and Lanny Herron

There has been a longstanding perception that the planning problems that service sector firms face differ meaningfully from those of manufacturing companies (Fuchs, 1969). Yet, the exact nature of these differences is often elusive. Symptomatic of this problem has been the perpetuation of a myth that service industries have little in common with one another, thus necessitating that consultants develop unique approaches to service industry planning in order to ensure appropriately customized strategies for individual firms (Albrecht & Zemke, 1985).

However, a careful comparison of service with manufacturing firms and different service industries with one another suggests the possibility for developing analytical frameworks to aid consultants in their formulation of competitive strategies. This paper presents one such framework. It is intended to provide a basis for analysis that can be used in the identification and proper evaluation of competitive options particular to service industries. The importance of such an aid is that the competitive options available to service sector firms are quite often different from those available within goods-producing industries. For example, because of the intangibility and perishability of services, competitive strategies based on channels of distribution, push versus pull marketing, or brand identification are generally not open to service firms, but often can be replaced by strategies based on franchising, chain identification, or firm image (Berry, 1980; Blois, 1983; Carmen & Langeard, 1980; Lovelock, 1981; Rathmell, 1974; Zeithaml, Parasuraman & Berry, 1985).

The framework presents nine strategic options that are of specific relevance to service firms, and which encompass the major competitive methods available to any given service industry. It then proffers guidelines that consultants can employ in selecting favorable combinations of these options.

Source: John A. Pearce II and Lanny Herron, "Customized Strategies for Service Sector Businesses," *Consultation* 7, no. 3 (Fall 1988), pp. 135–52.

NINE STRATEGIC OPTIONS FOR SERVICE SECTOR FIRMS

The strategy of a business firm consists of the generalized guidelines it uses to compete in its industry (Pearce, 1981). Such guidelines permeate the thinking of the managers of the business and are pivotal in determining the options that managers will select as the basis of their business' operating plan. Obviously, the selection by a firm of its options and the nearly simultaneous determination of its strategy are keys to how successfully it will compete for profits in the marketplace.

Our experience suggests that the following list encompasses the major strategic options available to service firms. It differs from a set developed primarily for goods-producing industries by Porter (1980) because it takes into account the intangible nature of the service act. Nevertheless, his ideas support and have provided materials for this list.

1. *Focus.* The degree to which the firm narrowly concentrates its line of services, its targeted customer segments, and the geographic market it serves.
2. *Firm Image.* The degree to which management seeks to use the image of the firm itself as a sales tool in the marketplace.
3. *Chain Identification.* The extent to which a multi-location firm advertises so as to emphasize the entire chain or the affliction of all chain members as contrasted with having each location advertise as an individual unit with no regard to its chain affiliation.
4. *Franchising.* The extent to which a firm chooses to grow into multiple locations by franchising rather than by direct ownership.
5. *Service Quality.* The extent to which the firm competes by use of superior quality in terms of specifications, consistency, and features.
6. *Cost Position.* The extent to which the firm seeks to lower its costs without affecting its prices, service quality, or other competitive dimensions.
7. *Ancillary Services.* The degree to which the firm provides ancillary services along with its main services line.
8. *Low-Price Policy.* The extent to which the firm competes on the basis of its prices being low relative to the value it offers.
9. *Financial Leverage.* The amount of financial leverage the firm bears. This is a different type of strategic option than the other eight, but is included because of its consideration by Porter (1980).

It is a basic premise of this paper that the profit earned by a service firm will depend directly on the mix of strategies chosen from this list, and by how well it implements its choices.

WAYS TO DESCRIBE SERVICE FIRMS

In formulating a service firm strategy, consultants must choose from among the available strategic options, a single or combination option that will best match the specific characteristics of the firm to the opportunities in the competitive environment. The above nine options generally delimit all planners' choices of competitive weapons and thus, the more successful they are at crafting a combination suited to their firms' specific use, the more profitable the firms are likely to be. Therefore, the consultant benefits by understanding which characteristics of the firm are crucial to this choice and how each affects it.

The need to understand the specific character of a business gives rise to the need for a classification scheme for service firms that addresses both their internal and external characteristics. Two of the best partial approaches for classifying service businesses are those of Thomas (1978) who stressed internal characteristics based on the nature of the operational resources used in performing services, and of Lovelock (1983) who emphasized external factors based on a firm's customer interface characteristics. When combined, these approaches produce a basis for classification that is specific to service firms and that incorporates both key internal and external dimensions as follows:

1. *Classification by Internal Resource Base:* determined by the extent to which the firm's key resources are equipment or people based and by the skill levels required by those who are needed to maximize these resource advantages.
2. *Classification by Nature of Service Act:* reflects whether the service act involves tangible or intangible actions on people or things.
3. *Classification by Method of Service Delivery:* specifies if the customer comes to the service, if the service is delivered to the customer, or neither; and whether the delivery is single or multiple site.
4. *Classification by Customization and Judgment Involved:* determined by the extent of customization sought by the customer and by the level of judgment that customer contact personnel must exercise in assessing customer needs.
5. *Classification by Relationship with Customers:* reflects whether or not a membership relationship exists between the customer and the firm, and whether the delivery of the service involves continuous or discrete transactions.
6. *Classification by Nature of Supply versus Demand:* specifies whether the firm faces wide or narrow demand fluctuations with peak demands usually met or often exceeded.

The classification of a firm on each of these dimensions helps to clarify the differential advantage to be gained by the business from employing each of the nine competitive options, Thus, a matrix can be

FIGURE 1   Strategy Analysis Worksheet

Firm classifications

Competitive options	Internal resource base	Nature of service act	Method of service delivery	Customization and judgment	Relationship with customer	Nature of supply vs. demand
Focus						
Firm image						
Chain identification						
Franchising						
Service quality						
Cost position						
Ancillary services						
Low price policy						
Financial leverage						

formed, as shown in Figure 1, with the six company classifications on the horizontal axis and the nine competitive options on the vertical axis.

Each of the columns of this 9 x 6 matrix can be expanded to increase the specificity of the model with each new sub-column representing one of the possible categories of the main characteristic described by the original classification, as discussed in the next section.

CHOOSING STRATEGIC OPTIONS BASED ON SERVICE FIRM DESCRIPTIONS

The characteristics of any firm and its environment determine which competitive strategies are most favorable to it. Thus, it is important to understand how use of each of the nine competitive options may prove to be favorable or unfavorable to firms in each of the six firm classifications. We recommend that consultants become familiar with the following generalizations about the relationships between competitive options and the categories and variables used in each of the six service firm classifications:

Classification by Internal Resource Base

There are six major categories that classify a service firm according to the internal resources employed by it in the performance of its services (Thomas, 1978):

Automated Equipment-based.   This category contains those firms that perform their service with totally automated equipment, such as coin-operated laundromats. It favors both geographic focus and financial leverage due to the relatively high cost of capital involved. In addition, ease of control through automation as well as capital intensity enhances the value of franchising.

Equipment-based Monitored by Relatively Unskilled Operators. These firms use semi-automated equipment monitored by relatively unskilled operators to perform their services. Examples are motion picture theaters and tax processing. As with the completely automated type of service firms, this category leads to geographic focus, financial leverage, and franchising as desirable forms of competition.

Equipment-based Monitored by Relatively Skilled Operators. This category of firms sells services that are equipment-based but require highly skilled operators, as in the case of airlines and computer time-sharing companies. Due to the capital-intensive nature of these businesses, it is often desirable to compete with geographic or customer focus as well as with financial leverage. Franchising, however, will not be as desirable as in the other forms of capital-intensive firms because the need for highly skilled operators makes it difficult for individual franchised locations to obtain or train such operators. The skills of a firm's operators, though, give it the opportunity to compete on the basis of firm image, while the high cost of such operators presents the possibility of competing on the basis of cost. As in all operations with a high dependency on people, control of quality is difficult, making service quality a viable competitive option. In addition, the equipment-based nature of the industry tends to result in some standardization of the service among firms, which often leads to the desirability of a low price competitive option.

People-based with Unskilled Labor. These service firms are principally dependent on unskilled labor as service providers, as opposed to using equipment as the mainstay of their competitive base. They include security and janitoral services companies. Labor intensity can lead to the desirability of competing on quality while the ease of training the service providers lends itself to franchising. These firms are not capital intensive and competition using financial leverage will typically be unfavorable.

People-based with Skilled Labor. This category of firms is also labor-based but uses relatively skilled labor as service providers. Such firms as appliance repair shops and catering services fit here. As with other labor-based firms, quality is often an important competitive dimension while the financial structure of the business will probably be unfavorable to financial leverage because of lack of capital intensity.

People-based with Professionals. These firms are labor-based users of largely professional service providers. They include law firms, accountants, and management consultants. Such firms share the desirability of quality competition and the undesirability of financial leverage with other labor-based firms. However, many other strategic options come into favor with these firms because of the professional nature of the service-providers. Focus on the basis of product and customer may be desirable due to the high technical nature of the work, as may firm image. Cost position can be an important option due to the very high labor costs of professional service-providers. However, franchising will be an unfavorable option because of the difficulty of recruiting and training such labor, and the low price will be competitively unattractive since the customer's main choice criteria usually do not include price. Indeed, too low a price may even cause the customer to undervalue the service.

The first part of the matrix shown in Figure 2 summarizes the implications of these Internal Resource Base categories. If a particular category within this classification tends to be favorable for employing a particular competitive option, the cell was labeled F for favorable. Likewise—means the category tends to be neutral to the employment of that competitive option, and U means it is usually unfavorable to employing that option.

FIGURE 2 Detailed Firm Classifications with Favorableness of Competitive Options

Competitive options	Internal Resource Base						Nature of Service Act			
	Firm classifications						Firm classifications			
	Equipment-based			People-based						
	Automated	Monitored by relatively unskilled operators	Operated by unskilled operators	Unskilled labor	Skilled labor	Professionals	Automated	Monitored by relatively unskilled operators	Operated by unskilled operators	Unskilled labor
Focus	F	F	F	–	–	F	–	–	F	F
Firm image	–	–	F	–	–	F	F	–	F	F
Chain identification	–	–	–	–	–	–	–	–	–	F
Franchising	F	F	–	F	–	U	–	–	–	–
Service quality	–	–	F	F	F	F	–	–	–	F
Cost position	–	–	F	–	–	F	–	–	F	F
Ancillary services	–	–	–	–	–	–	–	–	F	F
Low-price policy	–	–	F	–	–	U	F	F	–	–
Financial leverage	F	F	F	U	U	U	–	–	–	–

F : Firms in this classification (column) will find it favorable to employ this competitive option (row).
– : Firms in this classification (column) will find it no advantage to employ this competitive option (row).
U : Firms in this classification (column) will find it unfavorable to employ this competitive option (row).

FIGURE 2 (continued)

Competitive options	Method of Service Delivery — Firm classifications						Customization and Judgment — Firm classifications			
	Customer to service – single-site	Customer to service – multi-site	Service to customer – single-site	Service to customer – multi-site	Neither – single-site	Neither – multi-site	High customization with high judgment	High customization with low judgment	Low customization with high judgment	Low customization with low judgment
Focus	–	F	–	F	–	F	F	F	–	–
Firm image	F	F	–	–	–	–	F	–	F	–
Chain identification	U	F	U	F	U	F	U	F	U	F
Franchising	U	F	U	F	U	F	–	F	–	F
Service quality	–	–	–	–	–	F	–	–	–	F
Cost position	–	F	–	F	F	–	–	F	–	F
Ancillary services	–	–	–	–	–	–	F	F	–	F
Low-price policy	–	–	–	–	–	–	U	U	F	F
Financial leverage	–	–	–	–	–	–	–	–	–	–

F : Firms in this classification (column) will find it favorable to employ this competitive option (row).
– : Firms in this classification (column) will find it no advantage to employ this competitive option (row).
U : Firms in this classification (column) will find it unfavorable to employ this competitive option (row).

FIGURE 2 (concluded)

Competitive options	Relationship with Customer — Firm classifications				Nature of Supply vs. Demand — Firm classifications			
	Membership relationship with continuous delivery	Membership relationship with discrete transactions	Membership relationship with continuous delivery	Membership relationship with discrete transactions	Wide demand fluctuations with peak usually met	Wide demand fluctuations with peak often exceeded	Narrow demand fluctuations with peak usually met	Narrow demand fluctuations with peak often exceeded
Focus	F	–	F	F	–	F	–	F
Firm image	F	F	–	–	–	–	–	–
Chain identification	F	F	–	–	–	–	–	–
Franchising	–	–	–	–	–	–	–	F
Service quality	F	F	–	–	–	–	–	–
Cost position	–	–	–	–	–	–	–	F
Ancillary services	F	F	–	–	–	–	–	–
Low-price policy	–	–	–	–	F	F	–	U
Financial leverage	–	–	?	–	F	–	–	F

F : Firms in this classification (column) will find it favorable to employ this competitive option (row).
– : Firms in this classification (column) will find it no advantage to employ this competitive option (row).
U : Firms in this classification (column) will find it unfavorable to employ this competitive option (row).

Classification by Nature of the Service Act

There are four major categories which classify service firms by the nature of the service they render (Lovelock, 1983). These categories are derived from studying two different aspects of the nature of the service: the degree of its intangibility (predicated on the tangibility of the object of the act), and whether the service action is rendered on people or on things.

Tangible Actions on People.   These are services directed at people's bodies. Such actions are considered to be more tangible than actions directed at people's minds because the object of the act is more tangible. Examples of firms that render these types of services are restaurants, beauty salons, airlines, and hospitals. Since these tangible services are directed at people's bodies, firm image is generally an important competitive option because people are very sensitive to their perception of that which affects them directly. Also, low price competition will usually be important to these firms because tangible actions are usually more easily measured and, therefore, compared on price than intangible ones.

Tangible Actions on Things.   Firms in this category provide services that are directed at goods and other physical possessions. Examples of this type of firm are trucking companies and yard services. Rendering this type of service generally makes it favorable for a firm to compete on the basis of low price because the ease of measuring tangible actions often leads to price comparisons.

Intangible Actions on People.   These firms offer services that are directed at people's minds (the objects of the act being intangible). Examples are educational institutions and radio broadcasting companies. Firm image will usually be an important competitive option for such firms because people are being affected directly. However, the intangibility of the action causes many other competitive options to become favorable as well. Focus on specific customers and subsets of services become important because intangibility lends itself to many fine distinctions, and ancillary services assume importance too because it is not always clear where the boundaries of such services stop. Finally, cost position becomes an important variable which can be approached creatively since the benefits of intangible services are often difficult to measure.

Intangible Actions on Things.   Firms classified as rendering these services are those which act on intangible assets. Such firms include banks, law firms, and insurance firms. This category of businesses has numerous favorable competitive options on which to draw. Due to the intangible nature of their services, focus, cost position, and ancillary services become important. Also, firm image and chain identification frequently have high value because the intangibility of the service gives rise to a marketing need to project a sense of permanence, stability, or institutional concreteness.

The second part of the matrix shown in Figure 2 summarizes this discussion of the classification by the Nature of the Service Act.

Classification by Method of Service Delivery

As shown in the third part of the matrix in Figure 2, six major categories can be used to classify the delivery methods of service firms (Lovelock, 1983). The firm may have one physical location or multiple sites, and the service may be rendered when the customer visits the firm's site, when the firm's representative visits the customer, or when no physical meeting ("neither") takes place as is the case in the delivery of a financial newsletter.

Customer Goes to a Single-sited Service Firm. Examples of such businesses are law firms, beauty salons, and restaurants. Whenever the customer goes to the service site, firm image in the form of physical surroundings becomes an important competitive option. Additionally, single-sited firms logically find franchising and chain identification to be unusable options unless they plan to expand into multi-sited organizations.

Customer Goes to a Multi-sited Service Firm. Examples of this type firm are fast food chains, airlines, and movie theater chains. Here again, firm image in the form of surroundings will be an important competitive consideration, and this time both franchising and chain identification will be simple because the firm is multi-sited. This multi-sited feature also enhances the appeal of two other competitive options: focus and cost position; the first because geographic focus becomes an option (single-sited firms usually have geographic focus as given and not as an option), the second because multiple sites tend to give operating leverage which leads to cost considerations.

Multi-sited Firm Comes to the Customer. Examples of such firms are trucking companies, national and regional real estate agencies, and multi-site computer maintenance services. As with any multi-sited organization, competition by chain identification and franchising both become promising considerations. Likewise, a multi-sited firm with a large geographic spread should consider niche strategies for geographic focus. Cost position also becomes an important possibility because multi-sited firms usually enjoy cost saving possibilities attributable to economics of scale.

Single-sited Firm Transacting at Arm's Length.   These firms include local radio stations and financial newsletters. Since the services are not produced under the customer's observation, manipulation of the physical production area in the interest of cost position becomes an important consideration. The condition of single-sitedness is unfavorable when the firm faces competition with strong franchising or chain identification qualities.

Multi-sited Firm Transacting at Arm's Length.   Examples of such firms are telephone companies and broadcasting networks. Once again, cost position is an important competitive consideration because of the customer's distance from the service production. Due to the multi-sited nature of these firms, chain identification, franchising, and geographic focus are also important considerations.

Classification by Customization and Judgment in Service Delivery

By combining the extent to which a firm's services are customized (high or low), and the extent to which customer-contact-personnel must exercise judgment in meeting the customer's needs (high or low), four meaningfully discriminating categories are possible (Lovelock, 1983):

High Customization Combined with High Judgment on the Part of Customer Contact Personnel.   Examples of firms in this category are legal firms, real estate agencies, and beauticians. The characteristic of high customization of a service is favorable to competing with focus and ancillary services, and unfavorable to competing with low price. Focus is important because it limits excessive customization. Ancillary services are important because high customization leaves the limits of the service ill-defined in the customer's mind, and opens the possibility of the profitable introduction of ancillaries. Low price can be very unfavorable since the degree of customization often makes it difficult to compare services from one firm to the next, and price can, therefore, become an indication of value in the customer's mind. On the other hand, using similar reasoning, chain identification is usually an unfavorable method of competition because a reputation for sound judgment is usually personified in the mind of the customer—a quality which a chain finds it difficult to acquire.

High Customization Combined with Low Judgment on the Part of Customer Contact Personnel.   Examples of such firms are telephone services, hotels and fine restaurants. Once again, focus and ancillary services are attractive bases of competition while low price is unattractive because of high customization costs. However, because of the low judgment required, firm reputation and hence firm image become less important. In contrast, chain identification is attractive because low judgment places an emphasis on standardization of the judgment. Likewise, franchising is promising because low judgment decisions are relatively easy to control, and easy control is a prerequisite of franchising.

Low Customization Combined with High Judgment on the Part of Customer Contact Personnel.   Examples of such firms are educational institutions and preventive health programs. As before, the high judgment and low customization both make firm image promising as a competitive option but chain identification unattractive. In addition, the low customization tends to make low price important because a standardization service is easy for the customer to compare and thus leads to price competition (as the case with commodity prices among goods producers).

Low Customization Combined with Low Judgment on the Part of Customer Contact Personnel.   Examples are public transportation, routine appliance repair, and spectator sports organizations. Since this category contains standardization of both service and the judgment involved in providing it, the favorable competitive dimensions become those involved with standardization: chain identification, franchising, service quality, cost position, and low price.

The fourth part of the matrix shown in Figure 2 summarizes the discussion of Customization and Judgment.

Classification by Relationship with Customers

Lovelock (1983) and Mills and Margulies (1980) suggest that valuable insights can be gained by combining "formality" of the relationship (membership or no formal relationship) and the nature of the delivery service (continuous delivery or discrete transactions). The four categories that result are as follows:

Member Relationship Combined with Continuous Delivery of Service.   Due to the membership type of relationship that firms such as insurance companies, local telephone companies, and banks have with their customers, obtaining "members" becomes very important.

This leads to firm image and chain identification both being attractive competitive options since the customer needs to identify with the firm before they are likely to commit to a repetitive (membership) relationship. It is also important to retain customers once they have become members. This causes service quality to become an important competitive option because, although there is an inertia which causes membership relations to be maintained, customer irritation owing to poor service is the factor most likely to overcome that inertia. Since the member is somewhat captive by virtue of that inertia, the potential is great for successful competition based on an offering of ancillary services. The continuous delivery of the service in this category leads also to competition by focus on product type because of the difficulty of offering a wide variety of continuously offered services. (See the fifth part of the matrix in Figure 2).

Member Relationship Combined with Discrete Transactions. The membership relationship in such firms as long-distance telephone companies, brokerage firms, and firms offering season tickets favors options of firm image, chain identification, service quality, and ancillary services, as in the case of membership relationship combined with continuous transactions.

No Formal Relationship Combined with Continuous Delivery of Service.   Examples of this type of firm are radio and television stations. The continuous delivery causes focus to be an attractive competitive option since continuously offered services are very difficult to render when the variety offered is wide.

No Formal Relationship Combined with Discrete Transactions. Examples of this type firm are car rentals, pay phones, and mail service. This particular firm characteristic does not lend itself to assisting in the choice of competitive strategies. Firms in this category must look to their categories in the other five service firm classifications for guidance.

Classification by Nature of Supply versus Demand

The nature of the supply and the demand faced by service firms gives rise to another four-category classification (Lovelock, 1983). These are combinations of whether a demand on the firm fluctuates over a wide or narrow range, versus whether its supply is usually adequate or not adequate to meet peak demands (see the sixth and last part of the matrix in Figure 2).

Wide Demand Fluctuations with Peak Usually Met.   Generally such businesses as electrical utilities, telephone service, and hospital emergency units incur high fixed costs to maintain the capacity to meet their peak demands. Thus, financial leverage is usually an attractive competitive option. In addition, the need to manage demand gives rise to low price being a promising option when reduced low prices at certain times can help to manage demand.

Wide Demand Fluctuations with Peak Often Exceeded. Examples of such firms are tax preparation, hotels, airlines, and theaters. These firms will share low price as a favorable option with the category above. In addition they can often manage demand by focusing on various target customer groups.

Narrow Demand Fluctuations with Peak Usually Met. Examples of firms falling into this category are legal firms, banks, and insurance companies. These firms are neutral to all of the strategic competitive options.

Narrow Demand Fluctuations with Peak Often Exceeded. Such firms consist of those in the previous category but which have insufficient capacity for their base level of business. These firms have a need to manage the demand versus their growth rate. Low price is unfavorable to them since they are often pressured to raise prices, but focus is a favorable way to manage their demand. These firms also need to investigate growth, so cost position, financial leverage, and franchising all become favorable considerations.

APPLYING THE MODEL

The matrix in Figure 2 is a tool that can be used by consultants as part of their process in determining the optimal strategy combinations for service firms, as described below. Each of the cells in Figure 2 has a recommended rating as either F, —, or U, corresponding to whether the particular strategy option is favorable, neutral, or unfavorable for inclusion in a competitive plan for a firm in the category shown at the top of the matrix.

In developing a plan for a particular service firm, consultants can begin by analyzing the company in terms of the six generic service classifications (these are shown across the top of Figure 1, which can be used as a worksheet). These same six classifications are broken into categories in Figure 2, with a group of columns under each classification. Only six of the 28 columns in the 9 x 28 matrix of Figure 2 will apply to a specific firm analysis—one column under each of the six firm classifications. For a particular firm, the consultant would identify which category best describes the firm within each classification. These categories determine which six columns from Figure 2 will be used in evaluating strategy options for this firm. The worksheet (Figure 1) is completed by transferring the entries (F, —, or U) for each cell in these six columns from Figure 2 to the worksheet. The resulting 9 x 6 matrix provides a summary judgment of the relative merit of each of the nine competitive strategy options for this firm.

The entries in the worksheet matrix can be combined into a relative numerical score by assigning numerical values to F, —, and U (we recommend the values of 1, 0, and −1, respectively) and summing the scores for each row to calculate the relative score for each strategy option. With the values of 1, 0, and −1, each strategy (row) will have a resultant score between −6 and 6. This score will indicate the relative favorableness of using the particular strategy option, with 6 being highly favorable, 0 being neutral, and −6 being highly unfavorable.

A Law Firm Example

In order to better understand the application of the model, it will help to consider an analysis of a general law firm.

The first step is to analyze the firm in terms of the six generic service firm classifications to identify which category best describes the firm within each classification.

1. *Classification by Internal Resource Base.* Studying the options in the first part of the matrix of Figure 2, it is apparent that a general law firm is "People-based with Professionals" because it is labor intensive and because the main service givers and customer contact people are professional attorneys.
2. *Classification by Nature of Service Act.* Looking at the second part of the matrix in Figure 2, the category that best fits this firm is "Intangible Actions on Things" since law firms perform services directed at intangible assets.
3. *Classifications by Method of Service Delivery.* For this third classification, the category that best fits a law firm is "Customer Goes to Single-Sited Service Firm" because such a firm normally has only one location and the client goes to visit the lawyer in order to obtain services.
4. *Classification by Customization and Judgment Involved.* The fourth part of the matrix in Figure 2 shows that the category of "High Customization Combined with High Judgment on the Part of Customer Contact Personnel" best fits this firm since every legal case is different and attorneys must exercise the high levels of judgment.

5. *Classification by Relationship with Customers.* Of the choices offered in the fifth part of the matrix in Figure 2, the one which best fits this firm is "Membership Relationship Combined with Discrete Transactions." This is because the client-attorney relationship is normally a lasting one (membership) that is dormant except during periods of activity specifically requested by the client.

6. *Classification by Nature of Supply versus Demand.* The sixth part of the matrix in Figure 2 leads to the labeling of this firm as "Narrow Demand Fluctuations with Peak Usually Met." This is because there are typically no seasonal or other calendar-related patterns in legal work, and client loads tend to average out. When they do not (e.g., real estate closings in summer, tax return preparations in the spring), the attorneys within the firm are able to spread the workload by helping each other.

RESULTS

Having determined the individual categories within the six generic service firm classifications, it is now possible to prepare the matrix in Figure 3 as an aid in determining the optimal strategy for this firm. This is done by taking the column from Figure 2 corresponding to each of the six individual categories determined above and duplicating it in the appropriate column in Figure 3. Then, the comparative scores for each competitive option (shown in the right column of Figure 3) are calculated, giving the following results: Focus = 3, Firm Image = 5, Chain Indentification = 0, Franchising = −2, Service Quality = 2, Cost Position = 2, Ancillary Services = 3, Low Price = −2, and Financial Leverage = −1.

A discussion of each of these competitive options would be instructive for a law firm client:

Firm Image. This strategy has the most favorable indicator, and also has high intuitive appeal based on the view that the image of a law firm will be a very important factor in its competitive arsenal.

Focus. This competitive possibility is next in favorable strength. Investigation of each of the three characteristics that impact favorably on it (see Figure 3) leads to consideration of focus in the product area. Perhaps the law firm should focus by specializing in estates and trusts, or in tax law. If the market is not broad enough for the entire firm to specialize, the individual attorneys might consider doing so.

Ancillary Services. This strategic option is equally favorable to the option of Focus due to the intangible nature of the service, the

FIGURE 3   Strategy Analysis Example for a Law Firm

Firm classifications

Row scores

Competitive options		Internal resource base	Nature of service act	Method of service delivery	Custom-ization and judgment	Relation-ship with customer	Nature of supply versus demand	Row scores
	Focus	F (+1)	F (+1)	—	F (+1)	—	—	+3
	Firm image	F (+1)	F (+1)	F (+1)	F (+1)	F (+1)	—	+5
	Chain identification	—	F (+1)	U (−1)	U (−1)	F (+1)	—	0
	Franchising	U (−1)	—	U (−1)	—	—	—	−2
	Service quality	F (+1)	—	—	—	F (+1)	—	+2
	Cost position	F (+1)	F (+1)	—	—	—	—	+2
	Ancillary services	—	F (+1)	—	F (+1)	F (+1)	—	+3
	Low-price policy	U (−1)	—	—	U (−1)	—	—	−2
	Financial leverage	U (−1)	—	—	—	—	—	−1

high customization and judgment, and the membership relation with the customers. There are ancillary services that can be provided by this type firm such as providing trustees for their customers. However, the Code of Professional Responsibility is a consideration for law firms, which may make it difficult to offer ancillary services, whereas other types of service firms with these same characteristics may more readily do so. This raises an important caution which managers should consider when using the matrix model. Although the model is meant to highlight those elements of competitive strategy that may be favorably exercised by a firm, it certainly does not encompass every eventuality relevant to every service sector firm. As such, the model should be used as a guide to idea generation and not as a final prescription to be followed uncritically.

Service Quality. Emphasizing this competitive option is attractive because of the professional base and membership relationship. It is certainly important to this firm and in fact should positively affect the firm's image.

Cost Position. With a score of $+2$, this is an important area for potential study for two reasons. First, the labor intensive, professional work force generates high marginal costs. Second, the service action on intangible assets indicates that the customer will not be needed physically for much of the process, thus leaving open the door to delegate that part of the process to less costly paralegals, legal secretaries, and computer operations.

CAUTIONS AND ENCOURAGEMENTS

The model developed in this paper has broad applicability for consultants of service firms in their decision making on competitive options. It is a guide to productive idea generation and it provides a powerful, fundamental way to think about service firm opportunities and constraints.

The ease with which the model can be used, coupled with the strength of the rationale that relates service firm characteristics to strategic options, provides the true power of the model. However, the shortcomings as well as the advantages of the model are illustrated by the law firm example. Firms have individual peculiarities that bear on the appropriate design of their competitive strategies. Such peculiarities must be overlaid on any model.

In addition, because the model is intended to overview general conditions affecting most of the firms in an industry, users will find themselves gravitating toward traditional views of both problems and solutions. For example, the law firm matrix as constructed in Figure 3 fails to encourage such innovative options as the franchising of legal assistance. Thus, an unquestioning acceptance of the model's generalizations could lead to narrow, misleading, or incorrect recommendations or managerial action. To avoid such problems, strategic decision makers must be willing to openly question the favorableness of each of the model's cells. Though the ratings as shown may well reflect conventional wisdom, they tend not to be anticipatory of future conditions. Nevertheless, as a framework for consultants to use in systematically analyzing their perspectives on service firm planning, and for helping to customize product-market strategies for service sector businesses, the model provides a defensible and experience reinforcing decision aid.

REFERENCES

Albrecht, K., & Zemke, R. (1985). *Service America.* Homewood, IL: Dow Jones-Irwin.

Berry, L. (1980, May-June). Services marketing is different. *Business, 30,* 24–29.

Blois, K. (1983). The structure of service firms and their marketing policies. *Strategic Management Journal, 4,* 251–261.

Carmen, J. & Langeard, E. (1980). Growth strategies of service firms, *Strategic Management Journal, 1,* 7–22.

Fuchs, V. (1969). *Production and productivity in the service industries.* New York: National Bureau of Economic Research, Inc.

Lovelock, C. (1981). Why marketing management needs to be different for services. In J. H. Donnelly & W. R. George (Eds.), *Marketing of Services,* Chicago, IL: American Marketing.

Lovelock, C. (1983, Summer). Classifying services to gain strategic marketing insight. *Journal of Marketing, 47,* 9–20.

Mills, P., & Margulies, M. (1980). Toward a core typology of service organizations. *Academy of Management Review, 5,* 255–265.

Pearce, J. (1981, Fall). An executive level perspective on the strategic management process. *California Management Review, 29,* 39–48.

Porter, M. (1980). *Competitive strategy.* New York: The Free Press.

Rathmell, J. (1974). *Marketing in the services section.* Cambridge, MA: Winthrop Publishing.

Thomas, D. (1978, July-August). Strategy is different in service businesses. *Harvard Business Review, 56,* 158–165.

Zeithaml, V., Parasuraman, A., & Berry, L. (1985, Spring). Problems and strategies in services marketing. *Journal of Marketing, 49,* 33–46.

PART IV

Strategy Implementation

This final selection of articles examines what is commonly called the *action phase* of the strategic management process: implementation of the chosen strategy. The six readings begin with a reading that details the major steps that managers should take in order to translate a newly formulated plan into action, followed in article 25 by a discussion of ways to overcome the difficulties commonly encountered in operationalizing a company's strategic plans.

The focus of the readings then shifts to two articles that deal specifically with the broad and critically important issues involved in implementing a strategy. The initial focus is on eight principles that lead to the implementation of an effective strategic management system. The topic of strategic control is considered next, with attention directed to the systemic, behavioral, and political factors that act as barriers to the strategy implementation process.

The final two articles in the book investigate two special interest topics. In the first reading, the volatile nature of industry growth is explored with special attention to its effects on strategy implementation. In the second reading, the authors report on the findings from a survey of 100 small business executives who were asked to evaluate their needs for planning assistance from consultants and advisers. Their responses, and their evaluation of the value to be gained from employing outsiders, make for an interesting comparison with the strategic planning and management needs of large firm executives.

Abstracts

FIVE STEPS TO STRATEGIC ACTION

Strategic planning tools have developed enormously over the past 20 years. Unfortunately, the tools for implementing strategies have not developed as quickly as the tools used for planning. Despite recent attention to the problems of strategy implementation, three critical questions remain unanswered. How can executives more effectively implement chosen strategies? How can the planning process be managed to ensure that the resultant strategies are realistic? How can we reconcile the static academic dogma, "First formulate strategy, then implement it," with the dynamic reality of managerial work?

This article proposes that approaches to strategy implementation can be categorized into five basic descriptions: the commander approach where the chief executive officer (CEO) formulates strategy first then instructs others on how to implement it; the organizational change approach where the CEO implements developed strategy through such steps as reorganizing company structure; the collaborative approach where the CEO includes all key personnel in strategy formulation; the cultural approach where input by middle- to lower-level employees is sought; and the crescive approach where the CEO addresses strategy planning and implementation simultaneously.

These five approaches to developing and implementing strategy represent a range of techniques. The choice of method should depend on the size of the company, degree of diversification, degree of geographical dispersion, stability of the business environment, and the managerial style currently embodied in the company's culture.

PROBLEMS ENCOUNTERED IN OPERATIONALIZING A COMPANY'S STRATEGIC PLANS

An organization's long-range plans are sometimes coupled directly and specifically with its current operating budgets, while in other cases the two planning processes are almost completely unrelated. The purpose of this article is to discuss the existence and importance of certain planning practices which have been found to weaken the planning process, and to ascertain whether these practices are correlated with the presence of requisite characteristics of the plans.

A strategic plan which is too precise or too inward-directed does not provide sufficient latitude to profit managers, while one which is too general does not provide sufficient information to guide a profit manager in the more detailed planning responsibilities. Weak planning may or may not produce weak plans, but even strong plans which are insufficiently communicated are difficult to implement.

Through these relationships the authors provide insight into the process of implementing strategic plans and the extent to which perceived problems exist in the implementation process. While certain attributes of a strategic plan such as lack of accuracy, inconsistency in objectives, and even inadequate rewards for efforts expended in planning may have an effect on the translation of strategic plans into current budgets, a sound system of communications may be sufficient to overcome these perceived weaknesses.

HOW TO IMPLEMENT STRATEGIC PLANS

It is axiomatic that the best strategic plans are worthless if the organization cannot implement and react effectively to them. This article discusses eight principles that govern the successful practice of strategic management:

1. The chief executive officer must be determined to see that the indicated decisions are made and then executed.
2. The firm must be properly organized so that strategic management can indeed be practiced.
3. The strategic plans must possess credibility.
4. The functional action plans developed must support the strategy.
5. Corporate resource allocations must be realistic with respect to the strategic plans and must also support corporate goals.
6. The organizational culture of the business unit, especially the psychology of its general manager, must be compatible with its strategy.
7. To deal with the strategy deviations, the firm must have a good monitoring and early warning system.
8. Rewards must be provided for the operating managers who are successful in implementing the strategy.

Without a strategic management system, the strategic plans are not likely to be implemented. Professional planners have an important role in implementing each of the eight principles but this role does not include substituting them for line management.

CONSIDERATIONS IN IMPLEMENTING STRATEGIC CONTROL

As a subject for research, strategic planning continues to attract broad attention. Oddly, however, strategic control has not received comparable scrutiny. This article presents some empirical results from a recent survey study on strategic control which reveals problems that managers perceive in the design and implementation of effective strategic control systems. In attempting to explore implementational consequences associated with pursuing a strategic control approach, three general sets of issues emerge which may make it difficult to implement effective strategic control.

First, a number of dysfunctional factors apparently play significant roles. Barriers in the strategy implementation process derive from systematic issues, such as striving for more consistent design of an integrated planning and control system, from behavioral factors that impose constraints on the ways a strategic control system might function, and from political factors representing potential barriers to effective implementation that arise from how coalitions within the firm react to control. Second, there is a relatively widespread acceptance of the need to tailor the strategic control dimension to the type of strategy at hand and also to have a budget that reflects this fact. Finally, widespread perceptual differences between planners and controllers regarding strategic control processes, task delineation, and cooperation between the two functions imply that planners and controllers are not sufficiently pulling in the same direction. Rather than facilitating strategy implementation, these two staff cultures may represent a barrier to successful implementation.

GROWTH INDUSTRIES: HERE TODAY, GONE TOMORROW

Many investors mistakenly believe that today's growth industries will continue into the indefinite future. The reality is that most rapidly growing industries neither continue their extraordinary growth for an extended period nor offer easily penetrable, profitable markets. Competition is strong, and products and markets change rapidly. One of the factors in the continued success of perennial top performers is the recognition that today's growth markets are not necessarily the markets to be in tomorrow. These companies continually position themselves to move into new areas of promise, a move that entails both benefits and costs.

This article provides a realistic and flexible implementation plan for companies wanting to move into a growth posture. The steps in this process include evaluating the industry, identifying market opportunities, obtaining a competitive position, developing an implementation plan, and integrating the growth plan with the company's overall strategic plan.

Two lessons can be learned from high-performing companies in any manufacturing industry. Strategic planners must find a niche in which they have a marketplace and adjust their product mix to meet these changes, not look for ways to protect the current product mix.

SMALL MANUFACTURERS—WHEN GOING OUTSIDE MAKES SENSE

This article describes the needs and use of outside assistance in strategic planning by small businesses executives. A survey of 100 small manufacturing firms' CEOs shows that small firms which incorporated outsider services in strategic planning and decision making outperformed similar sized firms that did not. The general areas of possible assistance that are explored in the article include strategic planning, computer systems, financial and accounting activities, personnel and productivity, insurance, cost reduction techniques, growth, and frequency activities.

Responding executives evaluated 12 sources of outside assistance in terms of their range of services, level of expertise, and hourly cost. CPA firms and management consultants were found to be the most favorably perceived sources of outsiders. In a related finding, the executives strongly desired to work with separate specialists on separate decision areas.

The specific strategic activities in which the small business CEOs found outside assistance to be most valuable were tax return preparation, tax planning, pension plans and profit sharing, identification and measurement of new markets, risk avoidance, motivational studies, market research, employee benefit analysis, investment tax credit studies, and selecting computer systems.

Five Steps to
Strategic Action

David R. Brodwin and L. J. Bourgeois III

Strategic planning tools have developed enormously over the past 20 years. Such techniques as the growth/share matrix and the experience curve are in widespread use, and other planning techniques allow the manager to evaluate the impact of alternative strategies on the stock price of the corporation. Management consulting firms offer strategic planning on a commodity basis, and any new M.B.A. comes equipped with at least one method for developing such plans.

Unfortunately, the tools for implementing strategies have not developed as quickly as the tools we use for planning. The result of this discrepancy—failed plans and abandoned planning efforts—is all too visible:

> A major diversified manufacturer concluded that a steady stream of new products was the most important factor in improving the stock price, yet the performance measures and management reports imposed on the division heads stress quarterly profit. As a result, division managers don't make the long-term investment required for successful new product development.

> A leading consumer goods company committed itself to strategic planning and built a staff of over thirty planners, many with MBAs and experience in consulting firms. Unfortunately, the expected benefits of planning failed to materialize; in less than two years, the department was disbanded and planning responsibility returned to the operating units.

Recently, business writers have begun to pay more attention to the problems of strategy implementation. Corporate culture is now widely acknowledged as an important force in the success or failure of business ventures; studies of Japanese management practices point out the effectiveness of participative methods in securing wholehearted commitment to new strategies at all levels of the organization.

Despite this interest, three critical questions remain unanswered:

Source: © 1984 by the Regents of the University of California. Reprinted/Condensed from the *California Management Review* 26, no. 3, pp. 176–90. By permission of The Regents.

- How can executives be more effective in putting chosen strategies into action?
- How can the planning process be managed so that the strategies which emerge are realistic, not only in terms of the marketplace, but also in terms of the politics, culture, and competence of the organization?
- Research shows that managers do not analyze opportunities exhaustively before taking action: rather, they shape strategy through a continuing stream of individual decisions and actions. How can we reconcile the static academic dogma, "First formulate strategy, then implement it," with the dynamic reality of managerial work?

To shed some light on these questions, we studied management practice at a number of companies. We have found that their approaches to strategy implementation can be categorized into one of five basic descriptions. In each one, the chief executive officer plays a somewhat different role and uses distinctive methods for developing and implementing strategies. The approaches differ in a number of other dimensions as well (see Chart 1). We have given each description a title to distinguish its main characteristics.

The first two descriptions represent traditional approaches to implementation. Here the CEO formulates strategy first, and then thinks about implementation later.

1. **The Commander Approach.** The CEO concentrates on formulating the strategy, applying rigorous logic and analysis. He either develops the strategy himself or supervises a team of planners. Once he's satisfied that he has the "best" strategy, he passes it along to those who are instructed to "make it happen."
2. **The Organizational Change Approach.** Once a strategy has been developed, the executive puts it into effect by taking such steps as reorganizing the company structure, changing incentive compensation schemes, or hiring personnel.

The next two approaches involve more recent attempts to enhance implementation by broadening the bases of participation in the planning process:

3. **The Collaborative Approach.** Rather than develop the strategy in a vacuum, the CEO enlists the help of his senior managers during the planning process in order to assure that all the key players will back the final plan.
4. **The Cultural Approach.** This is an extension of the collaborative model to involve people at middle and sometimes lower levels of the organization. It seeks to implement strategy through the development of a corporate culture throughout the organization.

CHART 1 Comparison of Five Approaches

Factor	Approach				
	Commander	Change	Collaborative	Cultural	Crescive
How are goals set? Where in the organization (top or bottom) are the strategic goals established?	Dictated from top	Dictated from top	Negotiated among top team	Embodied in culture	Stated loosely from top; refined from bottom
What signifies success? What signifies a successful outcome to the strategic planning/implementation process?	A good plan, as judged on economic criteria	Organization and structure which fit the strategy	An acceptable plan with broad top management support	An army of busy implementers	Sound strategies with champions behind them
What factors are considered? What are the kinds of factors or types of rationality used in developing a strategy for resolving conflicts between alternative proposed strategies?	Economic	Economic, political	Economic, social, political	Economic, social	Economic, social, political, behavioral
What is the typical level of organization-wide effort required?					
during the Planning phase	Low	Low	High	High	High
during the Implementation phase	N/A	High	Low	Low	Low
How stringent are the requirements placed on the CEO in order for the approach to succeed?					
Required CEO knowledge. To what extent must the CEO be able to maintain personal awareness of all significant strategic opportunities or threats?	High	High	Moderate	Low	Low
Required CEO power. To what extent must the CEO have the power to impose a detailed implementation plan on the organization?	High	High	Moderate	Moderate	Moderate

The final approach begins to answer some of the questions posed above, by taking advantage of managers' natural inclinations to develop opportunities as they are encountered. While it has not been widely recognized or studied up to now, we think it may represent the next major advancement in the art of strategic management.

5. **The Crescive Approach.** In this approach, the CEO addresses strategy planning and implementation simultaneously. He is not interested in strategizing alone, or even in leading others through a protracted planning process. Rather, he tries, through his statements and actions, to guide his managers into coming forward as champions of sound strategies. (Since this involves "growing" strategies from within the firm, our label comes from the Latin *crescere*, to grow.)

In these five approaches we see a trend toward the CEO playing an increasingly indirect and more subtle role in strategy development. We question the recentralization of strategy-making at headquarters, a trend documented (and encouraged) by some recent writers. We think, at least for some firms, that this might be a mistake.

Our Approach

For clarity, we have reduced the five approaches to their essential elements. This may border on caricature; the Commander Approach, in particular, can be applied with much more subtlety than we have indicated here. Our intent here is not to denigrate any approach but—by exaggerating the differences between approaches—to better identify and analyze the assumptions on which they rest. (To highlight the differences in abbreviated form, Table 1 summarizes the five approaches, showing for each the form of the strategic management question and the CEO's role.)

THE COMMANDER APPROACH

The Scenario

You are the chief executive officer of a large industrial corporation. After six months of study, your consultant hands you a report detailing which businesses the firm should be in and how it should compete in each area. You have studied the report and it supports your own calculations. Now you call all your top managers into a conference room, present the strategy, tell them to implement it, and await the results.

TABLE 1 The Five Approaches in Brief

Approach	The CEO's Strategic Question	CEO's Role
Commander	"How do I formulate the optimum strategy?"	Rational actor
Change	"I have a strategy in mind; now how do I implement it?"	Architect
Collaborative	"How do I involve top management to get commitment to strategies from the start?"	Coordinator
Cultural	"How do I involve the whole organization in implementation?"	Coach
Crescive	"How do I encourage managers to come forward as champions of sound strategies?"	Premise-setter and judge

The Approach

The Commander Approach addresses the traditional strategic management question of "How can I, as a general manager, develop a strategy for my business which will guide day-to-day decisions in support of my longer-term objectives?" The Commander Approach typically employs such tools as experience curves, growth/share matrices, PIMS studies, and industry and competitive analyses.

Strengths and Limitations

In the right company, the Commander Approach will help the executive make difficult day-to-day decisions from a strategic perspective. However, the following conditions must exist for the approach to succeed:

- The CEO must wield enough power to command implementation; or, the strategy must pose little threat to the current management, otherwise implementation will be resisted.
- Accurate and timely information must be available and the environment must be stable enough to allow it to be assimilated.
- The strategist (if different from the CEO) should be insulated from personal biases and political influences which may affect the content of the plan.

An additional drawback of the Commander Approach is that it can sap motivation. People on the firing line tend to withhold strategic alternatives which they think have little chance of acceptance.[1] If the CEO creates the belief that the only acceptable strategies are those developed at the top, he may find himself faced with an extremely unmotivated, un-innovative group of employees.

Why This Approach Persists

In light of the limitations of the Commander Approach in its pure form, why is it still prevalent in business schools and among consultants? Several factors account for its popularity. First, despite its drawbacks, it offers a valuable perspective to the chief executive. Second, by dividing the strategic management task into two stages—"thinking" and "doing"—the general manager reduces the number of factors he must consider simultaneously. Third, it fits the predisposition common in younger managers toward dealing with the quantitative and objective elements of a situation, rather than with more subjective and behavioral considerations. Finally, the separation between the planner/manager as a thinker and everyone else as a doer fits the view of the boss as an all-powerful hero, shaping the destiny of thousands with his decisions. This somewhat macho view naturally appeals to many aspiring managers.

THE ORGANIZATIONAL CHANGE APPROACH

The Scenario

After receiving your planning group's strategic recommendations, you have reviewed them and have made your strategy decisions. Now you plan modifications to the organization which will support the success of the plan. This includes a new organization structure, personnel changes, new information systems, and revisions to the compensation scheme.

The Approach

The Organizational Change Approach extends the Commander Approach by addressing the question "I have a strategy—now how do I get my organization to implement it?" This approach starts where the Commander Approach ends: with implementation. It assumes that the economic tools described above for strategy formulation have been mastered and adds to the tool kit several behavioral science techniques—including: the use of structure and staffing to focus attention on the firm's new priorities; revising planning and control systems; and other organizational change techniques. The role of the CEO is that of an architect, designing administrative systems to push his recalcitrant company towards new goals.

Structure and Staffing

Perhaps the most obvious tool for strategy implementation is to reorganize or to shift personnel in order to lead the firm in the desired direction. The logic behind this approach is that the organization structure should foster the skill-set and outlook needed for the strategy to succeed. For example, a strategy calling for worldwide coordination of manufacturing in order to capture cost efficiencies demands a functional organization for production, while a strategy calling for coordination of marketing (e.g., Procter & Gamble) calls for a product-oriented organization.

Planning and Control Systems

Planning systems governing capital and operating budgets can be adjusted to encourage decisions consistent with the strategy. For example, if the firm's strategy calls for investing in some businesses while harvesting others, it would be folly to rely on a capital budgeting system which arbitrarily approves every project with a return above a given hurdle rate.

Information systems should translate the strategy into meaningful short-term milestones, so that the progress according to the strategy can be monitored. The key to effective use of information systems in implementing a strategy lies in modern database technology. With traditional systems it was possible to summarize data in only one dimension, usually the line reporting structure. With a database approach, it is possible to track the strategy from multiple perspectives—e.g., division, geography, product line, and type of expense.

The power of such an information system is enhanced considerably when integrated with incentive compensation. Unfortunately, in many cases it isn't possible to translate strategic goals into the clearcut terms needed to support an effective incentive compensation system. At a minimum, however, the general manager must insure that current compensation arrangements don't create an incentive in opposition to the substance of the strategic plan.

Cultural Adaptation

To implement strategy more effectively, the manager can rely on techniques discovered by third world development agencies.[2] These techniques for introducing change in an organization include such fundamentals as: using demonstrations rather than words to communicate the desired new activities; focusing early efforts on the needs that are already recognized as important by most of the organization; and having solutions presented by persons who have high credibility in the organization. These techniques apply equally to the corporate world. For example, the successful introduction of a new technology in one geographic division (a "demonstration") makes it easier to subsequently obtain organization-wide adoption particularly if the test division shows a significant performance gain.

Strengths and Limitations

With a set of powerful implementation tools at his disposal, the executive using the Change Approach can carry out more difficult plans than would be possible without them. Thus, in a very practical sense, this approach will be more effective than the pure Commander Approach in many organizations.

However, tacking "implementation" unto "strategy" doesn't solve most of the problems encountered with the first approach: i.e., the Change Approach doesn't help the CEO and planning staff stay abreast of rapidly changing business conditions; it doesn't deal with situations where politics and personal agendas discourage objectivity among the planners; and, since it still calls for imposing the strategy in top-down fashion, it doesn't resolve the motivational problems created by the first approach.

Finally, this approach can backfire in uncertain or rapidly changing business conditions. The general manager trades off important strategic flexibility by manipulating the systems and structures of the organizations in support of a particular strategy. Some of these systems, particularly incentive compensation, take a long time to design and install. Should a change in the environment require a new strategy, it may be very difficult to change the firm's course, since all the "levers" controlling the firm have been set firmly in support of the now-obsolete game plan.

THE COLLABORATIVE APPROACH

The Scenario

With key executives and division managers, you embark on a week-long planning retreat. Each participant presents his own ideas of where the firm should head. Extensive discussions follow, until the group reaches a consensus around the firm's longer-range mission and near-term strategy. Upon returning to their respective offices, each participant charges ahead in the agreed-upon direction.

The Approach

The Collaborative Approach extends strategic decision-making to the organization's top management team in answer to the question "How can I get my top management team to help develop and commit to a good set of goals and strategies?"

In this approach, the CEO employs group dynamics and "brainstorming" techniques to get managers with differing points of view to contribute to the strategic planning process in order to extract whatever "group wisdom" is inherent in these multiple perspectives. The role of the CEO is that of coordinator, ensuring that all good ideas are entertained.

A number of corporations use some type of collaborative approach. General Motors formed "business teams" in 1980 which consisted of managers from different functional areas. The role of the team was simply to bring different points of view on whatever strategic—usually product-focused—problem was identified. Exxon's major strategic decisions are made by its management committee, which is comprised of all of Exxon's inside directors and is chaired by the board chairman. Every committee member serves as "contact executive" for the line managers of one or more of Exxon's 13 affiliates and subsidiaries.

Strengths and Limitations

The Collaborative Approach overcomes two key limitations inherent in the previous two. By capturing information carried by executives closer to operations, and by engaging several brains at once, it increases the quality and timeliness of the information incorporated in the plan. And, to the extent that participation breeds commitment among the deciders, it improves the probability of successful implementation.

However, what the Collaborative Approach gains in team commitment it may lose in economic rationality. In this approach, strategy is a negotiated outcome among players with different points of view and, possibly, different goals. The negotiated aspect of the process brings with it several risks—that the strategy will be more conservative and less visionary than one developed by a single person or staff team; that the decision-making group may block out bad news, leading to the disorder known variously as "marketing myopia" or "groupthink"; and that gaming or fief-building tendencies on the part of senior managers may prevent a consensus from emerging.

A more fundamental criticism of the Collaborative Approach is that it is not "real" collective decision-making from an organizational standpoint because the managers—the organizational elite—cannot or will not give up centralized control. In effect, this approach preserves the artificial distinction between thinkers and doers and fails to draw upon the full human potential within and throughout the organization. It is the plumbing of this potential that forms the basis of our fourth approach.

THE CULTURAL APPROACH

The Scenario

Having formulated both a competitive strategy and a long-term "vision" for your company (either alone or with the collaboration of your senior managers), you proceed to inculcate your entire organization with this vision by molding the organization's culture in such a way that *all* organization members participate in making decisions that will perpetuate the vision. You draft and publish a company creed and song, and create other symbols which, when absorbed by both workers and managers, will ensure singleness of purpose and unity in action.

The Approach

The Cultural Approach extends the Collaborative Approach to lower levels in the organization as an answer to the strategic management question "How can I get my whole organization committed to our goals and strategies?"

In this approach, the CEO guides his organization by communicating and instilling his vision of the overarching mission for the firm, and then allowing each individual to design his own work activities in concert with that mission. So, once the game plan is set, the CEO plays the role of coach in giving general direction, but encourages individual decision-making to determine the operating details of executing the plan.

To a large extent, the Cultural Approach represents the latest wave of management techniques promulgated to (and, in some cases, enthusiastically adopted by) American managers seeking the panacea to our recent economic woes in the face of successful Japanese competition.

The implementation tools used in building a strong corporate culture range from such simple notions as publishing a company creed and singing a company song to much more complex techniques. These more complex—and usually effective—techniques involve implementing strategy by employing the concept of "third-order control."

Since implementation involves controlling the behavior of others, we can think of three levels of control. First-order control involves direct supervision. Second-order control involves using rules, procedures, and organization structure to guide the behavior of others (as in the Organizational Change Approach described above). Third-order control is a much more subtle—and potentially more powerful—means of influencing behavior through shaping the norms, values, symbols, and beliefs that managers and employees use in making day-to-day decisions.

The key distinction between managers using the Cultural Approach and those simply engaged in "participative management," is that these executives understand that corporate culture should serve as the handmaiden to corporate strategy, rather than proselytize "power equalization" and the like for its own sake.

The Cultural Approach begins to break down the barriers between "thinkers" and "doers." Examples of the successful application of this model are numerous. Hewlett-Packard is a much-heralded example of a company where the employees share a strong awareness of the corporate mission. They all know that the "HP way" encourages product innovation at every level and at every bench. Matsushita starts each day at 8:00 A.M. with 87,000 employees singing the company song and reciting its code of values.

Strengths and Limitations

Once a corporate culture that supports the firm's goals is established, the chief executive's implementation task is 90 percent done. With a cadre of committed managers and workers, the organization can more or less put itself on "automatic pilot" with new strategic thrusts being assimilated and implemented at lower levels.

The most visible cost of this system also yields its primary strength. The consensus decision-making and other culture-inculcating activities consume enormous amounts of time, but the pay-off can be speedy execution and reduced gamesmanship among managers. As Wiliam

Coates, executive vice president of the Westinghouse construction group, described it, "We spend a lot of time trying to get a consensus, but once you get it, the implementation is instantaneous. We don't have to fight any negative feelings."[3]

Based on our assessment of the nature of companies which are generally held up as examples of this approach, it appears that the cultural approach works best where the organization has sufficient resources to absorb the cost of building and maintaining the value system. The example firms, Hewlett-Packard, IBM, Matsushita, and Intel, are high-growth firms. Intel, for example, "promised not to fire any permanent employee whose job was eliminated. The company's phenomenal sales growth, 29.3% in 1980, helps absorb everyone who wants to stay."[4]

The Cultural Method has several limitations. For one, it only works with informed and intelligent people (note that most of the examples are firms in high technology industries). Second, it consumes enormous amounts of time to install. Third, it can foster such a strong sense of organizational identity among employees that it becomes almost a handicap—that is, it can be difficult to have outsiders at top levels because the executives won't accept the infusion of alien blood.

In addition, companies with excessively strong cultures will often suppress deviance, impede attempts to change, and tend to foster homogeneity and inbreeding.[5] The intolerance of deviance can be a problem when innovation is critical to strategic success. But a strong culture will reject inconsistency.

To handle this conformist tendency, companies such as IBM, Xerox and GM have separated their ongoing research units and their new product development efforts, sometimes placing them in physical locations far enough away to shield them from the corporation's culture.

Homogeneity can stifle creativity, encouraging non-conformists to leave for more accepting pastures and thereby robbing the firm of its innovative talent. The strongest criticism of the Cultural Approach is that it has such an overwhelming doctrinal air about it. It smacks of faddism and may really be just another variant of the CEO-centered approaches (i.e., Commander and Organizational Change Approaches). As such, it runs the risk of maintaining the wall between "thinkers" and "doers."

Preserving that thinker/doer distinction may be the Cultural Approach's main appeal. It affords executives an illusion of control. But holding tight the reins of control (a natural tendency in turbulent times) may result in some lost opportunities—opportunities encountered by line managers in their day-to-day routines.

The next section outlines how some firms capitalize on these opportunities.

THE CRESCIVE APPROACH

The Scenario

As a general manager, you have just received a proposal to pursue continued development of a new product. You evaluate the report, deflate some overly optimistic figures, and consider the manager's track record. The product offers attractive profit potential and seems to fit the general direction you envision for the firm, so you approve the proposal.

The Approach

The Crescive Approach addresses some of the limitations ascribed to the previous approaches by posing the CEO's question as follows: "How can I encourage my managers to develop, champion, and implement sound strategies?"

The Crescive Approach differs from others in several respects. First, instead of strategy being delivered downward by top management or a planning department, it moves upward from the "doers" (salespeople, engineers, production workers) and lower middle-level managers. Second, "strategy" becomes the sum of all the individual proposals that surface throughout the year. Third, the top management team shapes the employees' premises—that is, their notions of what would constitute supportable strategic projects. Fourth, the chief executive functions more as a judge, evaluating the proposals that reach his desk, than as a master strategist.

The Plight of the Chief Executive

At first, the Crescive Approach may sound too risky. After all, it calls for the chief executive to relinquish a lot of control over the strategy-making process, seemingly leaving to chance the major decisions which determine the long-term competitive strength of the company.

To understand the forces which underlie the emergence of the crescive approach, it is necessary to take a fresh look at the task facing the chief executive of large diversified corporations. The CEO faces an unusual dilemma. He is ultimately responsible for the corporation and its divisions, but the size and complexity of the business make it impossible for him to know and understand all the strategic and operating situations facing these divisions.[6] Therefore, if he is to exploit the fact that they can see strategic opportunities which he cannot, he must give up some control over it in order to foster strategic opportunism and achievement. However, this places his career (if not his personal wealth) in the hands of others. How can he manage this?

To answer this question, let's consider five aspects of the strategic management problem:

1. *The chief executive cannot monitor all significant opportunities and threats.* If the company is highly diversified, it is impossible for senior management to stay abreast of developments in all of the firm's different industries. Similarly, if an industry is shifting very quickly (e.g., personal computers), information collected at lower levels often becomes stale before it can be assimilated, summarized, and passed up the ranks. Even in more stable industries, the time required to process information upward through many management levels can mean that decisions are being based on outdated information.

   As a result, in many cases the CEO must abandon the effort to plan centrally. Instead, an incentive scheme or "free-market" environment is established to encourage operating managers to make decisions that will further the long-range interests of the company.

2. *The power of the chief executive is limited.* The chief executive typically enjoys substantial power derived from the ability to bestow rewards, allocate resources, and reduce the uncertainty for members of the organization. Thus, to an extent, the executive can impose his or her will on other members of the organization.

   However, the chief executive is not omnipotent. Employees can always leave the firm, and key managers wield control over information and important client relationships. As a result, the CEO must often compromise on programs he wishes to implement.

   Research indicates that new projects led by managers who were coerced into the leadership role fail, regardless of the intrinsic merit of the proposal. In contrast, a second-best strategy championed by a capable and determined advocate may be far more worthwhile than the optimum strategy with only lukewarm support.

3. *Few executives have the freedom to plan.* Although it is often said that one of the most important jobs of an executive is to engage in thoughtful planning, research shows that few executives actually set aside time to plan. Most spend the majority of their work days attending to short-range problems.[7]

   Thus, any realistic approach to strategic planning must recognize that executives simply don't plan much. They are bombarded constantly by requests from subordinates. So they shape the company's future more through their day-to-day decisions—encouraging some projects and discouraging others—than by sweeping policy statements or written plans. This process has been described as "logical incrementalism" because it can be a rational process that proceeds in small steps rather than by long leaps.[8]

4. *Tight control systems hinder the planning process.* In formulating strategies, top managers rely heavily on subordinates for up-to-date information, strategic recommendations, and approval of the operating goals.

The CEO's dependence on his subordinate managers creates a thorny control problem. In essence, if managers know they'll be accountable for plans they formulate or the information they provide, they have an incentive to bias their estimates of their division's performance. A branch of decision science called "agency theory" suggests how this situation should be handled. First, if the CEO wants his managers to deliver unbiased estimates, he cannot hold them tightly accountable for the successful implementation of each strategic proposal. Without such accountability, he can place great emphasis on commitment as a force for getting things done.

Second, in order to assess the true ability and motivation of any subordinate, the CEO must observe him over a long period of time on a number of different projects. Occasional failures should be expected, tolerated, and not penalized.

One means to promote the ongoing flow of strategic information is to establish a special venture capital fund to take advantage of promising ideas that arise after the strategic and operating plans have been completed. Like the IBM "Fellows" or the Texas Instruments "Idea" programs, this approach allows opportunities to be seized and developed by their champions at the time they are perceived.

5. *Strategies are produced by groups, not individuals.* Strategies are rarely created by single individuals. They are usually developed by groups of people, and they incorporate different perspectives on the business. The problem with group decisions is that groups tend to avoid uncertainty and to smooth over conflicts prematurely.

To reduce the distortions that can result from group decision-making, the CEO can concentrate on three tools: first, encouraging an atmosphere that tolerates expression of different opinions; second, using organization development techniques (such as group dynamics exercises) to reduce individual defensiveness and to increase the receptivity of the group to discrepant data; and third, establish separate planning groups at the corporate level and the line organization.

The Responsibilities of the Chief Executive

The Crescive Approach for strategic management suggests some generalizations concerning how the chief executive of the large divisionalized firm should help the organization generate and implement sound strategies. The recommendation consists of the following four elements:

- Maintain the openness of the organization to new and discrepant information. This can be done through careful use of staff, external consultants, and market research, and through judicious hiring and rotation policies.
- Articulate a general strategy to guide the firm's growth. This should delineate corporate priorities and shape the premises by which managers at all levels decide which strategic opportunities to pursue.
- Manipulate systems and structures to encourage bottom-up strategy formulation. Critical to this goal is the availability of seed funding for good ideas, unencumbered by bureaucratic approval cycles; tolerance for the inevitable failures when a strong effort has been made; and favorable publicity for the innovators.
- Use the "logical incrementalist" manner described by James Brian Quinn,[9] to select from among the strategies which emerge.

One of the most important and potentially elusive of these methods is the process of shaping managers' decision-making premises. The CEO can shape these premises in at least three ways. First, the CEO can emphasize a particular theme or strategic thrust ("We are in the information business") to direct strategic thinking. Second, the planning methodology endorsed by the CEO can be communicated to affect the way managers view the business. Third, the organizational structure can indicate the dimensions on which strategies should focus. A firm with a product-divisional structure will probably encourage managers to generate strategies for domination in certain product categories, whereas a firm organized around geographical territories will probably evoke strategies to secure maximum penetration of all products in particular regions.

CONCLUSION

These five approaches to developing and implementing strategy represent a range of techniques. Through extensive interviews, most managers indicated to us that one of these five approaches predominates in their company, although often one or two of the other approaches may also play a limited role.

The choice of method should depend on the size of the company, the degree of diversification, the degree of geographical dispersion, the stability of the business environment, and, finally, the managerial style currently embodied in the company's culture. Our research suggests that the Commander, Change, and Collaborative Approaches can be effective for smaller companies and firms in stable industries while the Cultural and Crescive alternatives are used by more complex corporations.

In the few cases where two different approaches played equally strong roles in the same company, an explanation could be found in the history and makeup of the company. For example, one company we studied was active in two distinct industries: its aerospace divisions, based in California, used a crescive strategic management process, while its automotive operation, headquartered in the Midwest, used a planning system incorporating elements of both the Commander and the Organizational Change Approaches.

Business strategy was once a science of classification: divide the businesses into four piles; get rid of some and nurture others. Now it has become a much more subtle enterprise. Considerations of motivation and the politics of organizations are inescapable. Culture is discovered to have a decisive effect, a finding that should shock no one. It becomes impossible to separate the underlying economic merits of strategy from the drive and dedication of the person who proposes it.

Clearly this situation calls for new approaches. While many observers of the business scene have embraced solutions from overseas, a few companies have been quietly developing a more practical approach. This approach recognizes the need for sound analysis without overlooking the importance of motivation. It acknowledges the chief executive's responsibility for strategy but recognizes his dependence on the eyes, ears, brains, and hands of others in the firm. This approach is crescive management.

REFERENCES

1. Eugene E. Carter, "The Behavioral Theory of the Firm and Top-Level Corporate Decisions." *Administrative Science Quarterly* 16, no. 4 (1971):413–28.
2. Conrad M. Arensburg and Arthur H. Niehoff, *Introducing Social Change,* 2nd ed. (Chicago: Aldine, 1971).
3. Jeremy Main. "Westinghouse's Cultural Revolution. "*Fortune,* June 15, 1981, pp. 74–93.
4. Jeremy Main, "How to Battle Your Own Bureaucracy." *Fortune,* June 29, 1981.
5. William G. Ouchi, *Theory Z: How American Business Can Meet the Japanese Challenge,* (Reading, MA: Addison-Wesley, 1981).
6. Norman Berg, "Strategic Planning in Conglomerate Companies," *Harvard Business Review* (May/June 1965), pp. 79–91.

7. Henry Mintzberg, "The Manager's Job: Folklore and Fact," *Harvard Business Review* (July/August 1975), pp. 49–61.
8. James Brian Quinn, "Strategic Change: 'Logical Incrementalism'," *Sloan Management Review*, Vol. 20, No. 1 (Fall 1978): 7–21.
9. Ibid.

Problems Encountered in Operationalizing a Company's Strategic Plans

Robert E. Seiler and Kamal E. Said

An organization's long-range plans are sometimes coupled directly and specifically with its current operating budgets, while in other cases the two planning processes are almost completely unrelated. Where the coupling is direct the first year of a 5-year long-range plan can be identical to the current year's budget. This type of planning system insures that deliberate attention is given to moving toward the long-range position, but is also confining and tends to reduce the long-range plan to an exercise in forecasting instead of strategy-building. Several current state-of-the-art studies have indicated that a number of organizations in the U.S. employ totally uncoupled planning systems, and others are fully integrated; most companies fall somewhere between the two extremes.

The purpose of this article is to determine the existence and importance of certain planning practices which have been found to weaken the planning process, and to ascertain whether these practices are correlated with the presence of certain requisite characteristics of the plans themselves. Through these relationships the authors hope to provide additional insight into the process of implementing strategic plans and the extent to which perceived problems exist in the implementation process.

INHERENT LINKAGE PROBLEMS

There are several inherent differences between a strategic planning process and an organization's short-term operational plans which make the coupling of the two a difficult and somewhat complex management

Source: Robert E. Seiler and Kamal E. Said, "Problems Encountered in Operationalizing a Company's Strategic Plans," *Managerial Planning* 31, no. 4 (January-February 1983), pp. 16–20.

art. Strategic planning is the process of positioning the organization so that future prospects are maximized while future risks are minimized. Peter Drucker described this not as a process of making decisions about the future but as the futurity of present decisions. To sidestep the problem of a precise definition, let us for the moment accept an operational definition of strategic planning as the identification of choices concerning possible future positions in which the organization may find itself, and their evaluation such that one possible position is selected over the others. Current operating budgets must then be prepared which move the organization more in the direction of the preferred position than toward any of the other possibilities.

The above simplified definition is used to provide a base for discussing the differences which are inherent between the strategic planning process and the operational budgeting process. Those who formulate strategic plans and those in another echelon who must implement them and translate them into specific action have inherently differing postures. These unavoidable organizational differences give the two planning processes different dimensions in at least four areas:

1. Different planning premises.
2. Dissimilar planning biases.
3. Perceptions of inequitable personal rewards.
4. Communication difficulties.

Differing planning premises exist because the strategic planners must by the very nature of their task assume an outward look, while operational budgets require a more inward perspective. The long-range planner must scan the external environment as far into the future as possible, looking for signs of potential problems and for the optimal organizational response to those problems. The profit manager who must prepare an operating plan, on the other hand, must look more toward the inside of the organization. He must watch costs and volumes, personnel and processes, and must maintain internal balance between an almost infinite array of changing variables. If the operational budget has too much latitude the process of implementing the organization's long-range plans will be weakened, while too much authoritarian control over the operational budget will likely produce long-range plans which are not sufficiently visionary. Constructing a planning system which permits the outward look of the strategic planner and the more inward look of those who must implement the long-range plans is a balancing act which requires constant attention.

Dissimilar planning biases exist at the strategic and the operational level because of the innate human tendency to become identified with our own creations. Planners may be objective at the beginning of the process, but by the time their plans are ready for communication they become advocates of their creations and press for their adoption and implementation. Suggestions from profit managers who have operational budgeting responsibilities are not given as much attention or weighted as heavily as they might have been earlier in the strategic planning process, and the participation by persons other than the long-range planning group may become pseudo or cosmetic. The strategic plans in turn receive less than enthusiastic adoption by operating executives, and the coupling process is undermined.

Inadequate rewards for concentrated effort in attempting to implement the strategic plans are inevitable results of the inability to measure an individual's performance by matching actual events against the strategic plan. The time frame for strategic planning is just too long to permit effective matching of one's strategic planning ability with the actual movement of the organization toward the desired long-range position.

There is considerable evidence of profit managers opting for a current choice of action which is in the overall sense less desirable but which is more evident on current operating financial statements. Real difficulties exist in maintaining sufficient enthusiasm for selecting the best long-range course of action when the impacts on the company cannot be measured except in very long time frames, and even then only in a relatively obscure way.

Communication problems cause frayed coupling between strategic and operational plans as the result of a variety of factors. Semantics can always be a problem, but communication of ideas and underlying reasoning tends to compound the communication of strategic plans. Meetings and discussions instead of written documents help eliminate some communication problems, but both strategic planners and profit managers have limited time for meetings. In addition, the lack of full written communication destroys the ability to match actual events with plans made at an earlier date. As discussed later, communications problems may be the most significant of these four problem areas.

TRANSLATING STRATEGIC INTO OPERATING PLANS

How effectively can a long-range strategic plan be translated into a short-range specific operating budget? The problems just discussed indicate that the translation is less than a certainty and this research study confirmed that condition. Only one-half (49%) of the profit managers contacted in this study indicated that the strategic plan was directly applicable in the preparation of the annual operating budget.

Information utilized in this study was obtained from data gathered from profit managers of 68 large industrial corporations, all listed in the *Fortune* 500. A total of 143 individuals provided the data included in the analysis, all from profit managers with heavy budget responsibility. The profit managers were requested to express their opinions about their company's long-range planning process and about selected characteristics of the plans as communicated to them. Data were also gathered concerning the problems these profit managers encountered in coupling the long-range plans to their current operating budgets. The Planning Executives Institute assisted in the data gathering process by making the original contact with the participating companies.[1] Only personnel from companies with formal strategic planning processes were asked to participate.

Table 1 reports the results of the question which asked profit managers of the 68 companies to indicate the degree of applicability of their company's strategic plans in the formulation of the annual operational budget. A relatively small percentage, approximately 14% found the long-range plan directly applicable, and 37% found the long-range plan only generally applicable. The conclusion is clear that strategic plans do have an impact on how most profit managers establish their operating budgets, but there appears to be considerable spread in the extent of applicability.

STRATEGIC PLANNING PRACTICES

The profit managers were asked to indicate the existence and relative importance of certain planning practices which have been identified in prior studies as the most significant. George Steiner in his landmark writings on strategic planning listed a number of problem areas and identified those listed in Table 2 as the most important and the most prevalent. The 143 profit managers evaluated each of the six planning practices using a 1 through 5 scale, where 1 is *never existing* and 5 is *always existing* in their companies. The profit managers felt that performance evaluation problems existed most frequently, followed by weak communication and insufficient planning goals. Delegation of the planning function was a clear last place.

Since 2.5 is the average of the five possible ratings, the only one of the six practices which had a score *above* the mean was the failure to encourage long-range planning by rewarding divisional managers solely on the basis of short-run performance measures. This planning practice appears to exist most frequently, while the least frequently encountered problem area appears to be the practice of delegating the planning function. The other four problem areas, i.e., communication in the form of providing guidance, development of goals, negating plans by using intuitive decisions, and inadequate review of plans are closely bunched at the center of the rank ordering.

TABLE 1   Applicability of Strategic Plans to Operating Budgets
(N = 143 profit managers)

	Number of Respondents	Percent
Direct Application: The data for the first year of the long-range plan are sufficiently specific and comprehensive and are used as a basis for the numbers in the current operating budget.	72	49.4
General Application: The data in the first year of the long-range plan are general in nature and are used to establish guidelines and assumptions for the annual operating budget.	53	36.3
Limited Application: 1. The content of the long-range plan is specific in nature but has a limited scope and is applicable to only a portion of the items in the current operating budget.	10	6.8
2. The content of the long-range plan has a broad scope but is vague in nature and is used in a limited fashion to formulate guidelines for the current operating budget.	6	4.1
No Application: The long-range plan is not used in constructing the annual budget.	5	3.4
	146	100.0%

ATTRIBUTES OF STRATEGIC PLANS

The profit managers were asked to provide information concerning the existence and importance of six attributes of their company's long-range plans, as these attributes relate to the application of the strategic plan to their annual operational budget. These attributes are those of relevance, consistency, usefulness for coordination efforts, specificity, usefulness in performance evaluation, and accuracy. The participants in the study were asked to give their perceptions of these strategic plan attributes on a 1 through 5 scale, with 1 representing a "low" or "inadequate" rating and 5 a "high" or "adequate" rating. Table 3 reflects the results of the rankings.

Since 2.5 is the average of the 1 through 5 scale, none of the plan attributes was assessed as generally inadequate (less than 2.5) but a

TABLE 2   Relative Significance of Six Strategic Planning Weaknesses
            (N = 143 profit managers)

	Average Score (on 1 through 5 basis)	*Rank (1 = most significant)*
Top management fails to encourage long-range planning by rewarding divisional managers solely on the basis of short-run performance measures.	2.7	1
Top management and/or the planning staff fails to give departments and divisions sufficient information and guidance.	2.3	2
Top management fails to develop goals suitable for long-range plans.	2.3	3
Top management rejects the formal planning mechanism by making intuitive decisions which conflict with the formal plan.	2.2	4
Top management fails to adequately review plans with department or divisional heads.	2.1	5
Top management assumes that it can delegate the planning function to a planner.	1.8	6

significant gap between the top four and the bottom two attributes does exist. The accuracy of the strategic plan was assessed as the least adequate feature, preceeded slightly by the usefulness of the plans for performance evaluation. Since neither of these is generally considered necessary for a sound strategic planning process, their positioning at the bottom of the list is not surprising.

PLANNING PRACTICES CORRELATED WITH PLAN ATTRIBUTES

One of the primary objectives of this study was to determine which of the six attributes of strategic plans (shown in Table 3) were most closely associated with the six strategic planning practices (shown in Table 2). The resulting correlation coefficients for the planning practices and the plan attributes are shown in Table 4. Note that every

TABLE 3   Attributes of Strategic Plans as They Relate to Current Operating Budgets (N = 143 profit managers)

	Average Score (1 through 5 basis)	Rank (1 = most significant)
Long-range plans are **relevant** to the process of budget preparation.	3.9	1
Long-range plans are **internally consistent** in developing business objectives.	3.9	2
Long-range plans are **useful in coordinating** business activities.	3.9	3
Long-range plans are **sufficiently specific** to be of assistance in preparing annual budgets.	3.8	4
Long-range plans are **useful in evaluating performance**.	3.3	5
Long-range plans are sufficiently **accurate** in projecting future events.	3.1	6

coefficient in the table is negative, indicating the increasing degrees of weakness in the planning activity produce a decreased perceived applicability of the plan to the preparation of operating budgets, For example, the $-.329$*** coefficient in the lower right corner of the table indicates that the failure to review strategic plans adequately with profit managers is highly correlated with lesser degrees of usefulness of the strategic plan in the preparation of the operating budget. The *** notation indicates that there is only a one-out-of-a-thousand probability that a correlation this large could be produced by pure chance.

The two planning practices which relate to *communications* appear at the bottom of the table and have the largest and most statistically significant correlations with the six planning practices. These coefficients are shown in Table 4 inside the box made with *dotted lines* at the bottom of the table. In similar manner, the two plan characteristics of *usefulness* (at the right of the table) appear to be the most highly correlated with all six of the planning practices. These are shown at the right of the table inside the box with *dashed lines*. These high correlations indicate that as the planning practices (which are stated in negative fashion) grow more pronounced, the profit managers perceive that the usefulness of the plans for both performance evaluation and coordination decrease.

TABLE 4   Correlation Coefficients of Planning Practices and Plan Attributes
(N = 143 profit managers)

Planning Practices		Plan Attributes					
	Sufficiently Specific	Relevant to Operating Budgets	Accurate in Projecting Future Events	Consistent with Long-Range Objectives	Useful in Evaluating Performance	Usefulness in Coordinating Activities
Planning Premises						
1. Top management fails to develop goals suitable for long-range plans.	−.053	−.035	−.164*	−.211**	−.139*	−.271***
Planning Biases						
2. Top management rejects the formal planning mechanism by making intuitive decisions which conflict with the plan.	−.168*	−.147*	−.147*	−.127	−.193**	−.173*
3. Top management assumes that it can delegate the planning function to a planner.	−.122	−.114	−.087	−.127	−.180*	−.213**
Perceptions of Rewards for Planning						
4. Top management fails to encourage long-range planning by rewarding divisional managers solely on the basis of short-run performance.	−.126	−.153*	−.182*	−.136	−.255**	−.1.71*
Communications of Plans						
5. Top management and/or the planning staff fails to give departments and divisions sufficient information and guidance.	−.125	−.180*	−.250**	−.387***	−.265***	−.363***
6. Top management fails to adequately review plans with departmental or divisional management.	−.283***	−.259**	−.155*	−.230**	−.269***	−.329***

* P <.05
** P <.01
*** P <.001

Two significant conclusions may be drawn from these correlations. One is that when communication problems are perceived by profit managers to be of significance the strategic plans themselves are considered to have less accuracy, relevance, specificity, and usefulness for preparation of the operating budget. The chances that this situation could, in turn, lead to a weak or insufficient coupling of the strategic plan to the

How to Implement Strategic Plans

Don Collier

In this column, I will discuss the principles involved in getting strategic plans implemented and what the professional planner's role should be vis-à-vis these principles. I will also give examples of how these principles are applied in practice. My comments will apply especially to decentralized multibusiness companies; but the principles should be generally applicable.

A fundamental principle is that in order to get strategic plans implemented, the organization must practice strategic *management*. The best strategic plans in the world are worthless if the organization cannot effectively react to them. Flowing from this fundamental principle are a series of principles that one must follow to successfully practice strategic management.

1. The chief executive officer must be committed to see that the indicated decisions are made and carried out.
2. The company must be properly organized to practice strategic management.
3. The strategic plans must be credible.
4. The functional action plans must support the strategy.
5. The corporate resource allocations must support the corporate goals and be realistic with respect to the strategic plans.
6. The business unit's organizational culture, and especially the psychology of its general manager, must be compatible with its strategy.
7. The corporation must have a good monitoring and "early warning" system for strategy deviations.
8. The operating managers must be rewarded for their success in implementing the strategy.

Source: Don Collier, "How to Implement Strategic Plans," *The Journal of Business Strategy*, 4, no. 3 (1984), pp. 92–96.

A COMMITTED CEO

It is not enough that the chief executive officer be committed to strategic planning. He must also be committed to strategic management, which is a much more active role. What this means is that he must make and carry out the corporate decisions that are indicated by the strategic plans.

In the context of the decentralized multibusiness corporation (and it doesn't have to be a large one) that we are using as a model, these decisions are usually resource allocation decisions. In such a company, the corporate strategy is usually a portfolio strategy. The CEO must be prepared to make allocation decisions, both to his existing portfolio of business and to the acquisition of businesses he wishes to add to the portfolio.

In addition to the corporate resource allocations, the CEO must lend the weight of his office to ensuring that the operating organization makes and implements the decisions that flow from the corporate strategic decisions. What this means is he must insist that the line managers, not the planners, make the strategic plans for their organizations. If you want real commitment to carrying out a strategic plan (which only the line organization can do), the line managers have to get their hands dirty so that it becomes their plan, not the planner's plan.

The professional planner's role with respect to this principle is to see that the plans and the analyses of the plans clearly set forth the decisions to be made and the likely consequences of the alternatives that the decisionmaker has.

A PROPERLY ORGANIZED COMPANY

Strategic management requires that there be organizational units to which resources can be allocated and which have the capability of carrying out a strategy once agreed to. Thus, this involves more than looking at the growth rate of served markets and the organization's shares of these markets.

Exhibit 1 shows an example of a deversified multibusiness company organized properly to carry out strategic management. The strategic business units are integrated profit centers. All of the functions (manufacturing, engineering, sales, etc.) are under the control of a general manager. These units should have one or more compatible served markets and one or more identifiable competitors.

It is important that these business units' product-market segments be carefully chosen so that a unified strategy for each unit can be devel-

EXHIBIT 1   Typical Organizational Structure

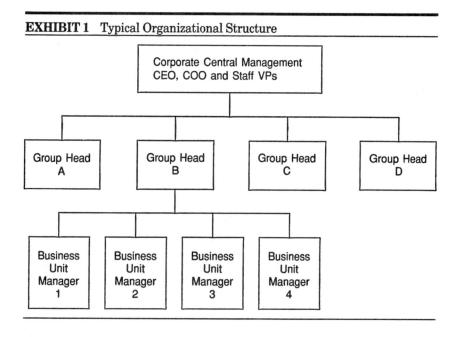

oped. Trying to carry out incompatible strategies—for instance, trying to be the low-cost producer in one market while at the same time producing a custom-engineered product for another—in the same organization usually results in inferior performance in both markets. At the same time, the organization must be able to stand on its own feet so that the allocations to it do not affect or are not affected by another strategic business unit.

The next level up, the group heads, are important in diversified companies, especially ones that have a large number of strategic business units. The group heads can challenge and refine the strategies of the business units from a substantive standpoint, asking such questions as "Do you really think you can take two points of market share away from Acme Ash Can when they've just opened a new plant?" These group heads also supervise the implementation of the agreed-upon strategies. It is impractical for the central management to get into the details of all but a few key business unit strategies in a typical multibusiness diversified company.

The planners can assist in this very important step of properly defining the business units by pointing out the problems of incompatible strategies in the same organization or business that are not truly separable for corporate allocation purposes. However, the final authority to make these definition decisions should be left to the line organizations, since they have to live with the decisions that have been made.

CREDIBLE PLANS

Here, we have a major role for the professional planners. It is up to them to see that technology compatible with the organizational culture is available to permit the line organization to make and assess good business unit strategic plans. Good strategic plans are difficult to develop because, in contrast to operational plans, they frequently involve a change in direction. Making technology available involves developing the planning system, conducting seminars on how to apply it, and coaching the line management on its use. In short, the planners should develop a good planning system and maintain its integrity. A good planning system and properly trained managers should lead to the production of credible plans.

A credible plan involves an accurate analysis of the strengths and the weaknesses of the organization versus the needs of the customers in the served markets and the competitors for these customers. It should be based on sound assumptions with respect to the trends in the needs, the environment, and the competitors' future actions. The plan should embody realistic expectations of what is possible and propose innovative strategies that will lead to *defensible* competitive positions. Finally, the plan should recognize contingencies that could negate the strategies and have good responses prepared for these contingencies.

SUPPORTIVE FUNCTIONAL ACTION PLANS

The action plans of the various functions within the business unit—manufacturing, marketing, R&D, etc.—should be driven by its strategy and not vice versa. For instance, if the strategy is to gain market share by means of superior products, there should be a R&D program to develop them, a manufacturing program to produce them—properly timed with respect to the R&D program—and a marketing program to introduce the resulting new products to the customers.

However, the chosen strategy must reflect the "state of the art" in the various functions versus the unit's competitors, both actual and potential ones. It also must reflect the capability of the various functions to respond to the customer's changing needs.

Both the general manager who is developing his strategy and his group head who is assessing it should be aware of the sensitivity of the strategy to the success or failure of the various functional action plans. In other words, how serious is a miss in the timing or the degree of accomplishment of *their* goals to the success of the overall strategy?

All of this requires good communication between the various functional heads and with their general manager, and between the general manager and his group head. The planner's role here is to catalyze these communications by making sure the right questions are raised.

REALISTIC RESOURCE ALLOCATIONS

In our model company, the role of the corporate central managers is to allocate the resources the stockholders have put at their disposal in such a way as to maximize the total return (price + yield) to the stockholder in proper short- and long-term balance. To do this requires sound and mature executive judgment. There is no substitute for such judgment.

The role of the professional planner in the resource allocation step is to increase the focus and objectivity of the information and discussions on which these judgments are based.

The resource allocations must not only support the corporate goals but must be realistic in terms of the probabilities of the success or failure of the individual unit strategic plans on which each resource allocation is based. There is a quote from Damon Runyon that applies here: "The race is not always to the swift nor the battle to the strong—but that's the way to bet."

CULTURALLY COMPATIBLE STRATEGIES

An important and not widely recognized (until after the fact) cause of failure is trying to carry out a strategy that is not compatible with the business unit's culture—especially the psychology of its general manager. There is nothing more frustrating to a general manager with an "invest and grow" psychology than to be put in charge of the unit that should be carrying out a "harvest" strategy. This manager will always be looking for opportunities to "turn the unit around." In most cases, this will result in an erratic strategy. Conversely, a hard-nosed, harvest-type manager will be too risk-adverse to grasp the opportunities that an "invest and grow" unit should be looking at.

A general manager will usually build an organization compatible with his psychology. But this takes time. Therefore, be especially sensitive to this when making transfers or new appointments of general managers. The role for the planner at the next level up in the organization from the unit in question is to make sure his line manager, who is making the personnel decision or the allocation decision, is aware of this problem.

GOOD STRATEGY MONITORING SYSTEM

Strategy is not a goal but a journey. A strategic plan is a road map. As in any journey, if you want to get to the destination (goal) efficiently, you should check your actual position versus the map at key junctures. You should also be monitoring to determine whether the "road conditions" have changed enough that a detour is in order.

The implementation of the strategies of the limited number of business units that have a major impact upon the corporate performance should be monitored by the CEO through the chief operating officer. The strategy implementation of the other units should be monitored by the appropriate line officer at the organizational level one up from the action. The role of the professional planner is to: (1) devise a good monitoring system; (2) develop aids that make it easy for the line managers to use the system; and (3) "nag" the organization into having the discipline to use the system on a continuing and appropriately frequent basis.

At Borg-Warner, the strategy implementation of the limited number of units that should be monitored by the CEO is done through a strategic issue system. During the annual resource allocation procedure, the planners at the corporate level identify as "critical" about twenty to thirty of the 100 SBU plans that are submitted. A critical SBU is one whose impact—positive or negative—on the corporation's overall performance or resource requirement is important or where there is a serious question about its strategy. The corporate central management selects ten or twelve of these critical SBU plans to be made strategic issues.

For the limited number of SBUs that have been made strategic issues, corporate management withholds allocation judgment until it is given a detailed presentation of the strategy by the appropriate management. Following this presentation and dicussion, the corporate central management decides whether to accept or modify the strategy and makes a capital allocation appropriate to that decision. This decision goes back to the affected management both verbally and in writing, together with the reasons therefor. Both this response and the original strategic issue report outlining the questions that the CEO would like addressed in the presentation are made by the planners for approval by the CEO.

Following the strategy response by the corporate central management to the affected SBU, the chief operating officer is given a set of questions to raise at his regular quarterly operating reviews to test whether the strategy is being implemented in the way the central corporate response is directed. These questions are prepared by the corporate planning staff. If the answers indicate that the strategy is being implemented in line with the response, no action is required on the part of the CEO. If the answers indicate a deviation is occurring, the COO brings this to the attention of the CEO if, in the COO's judgment, the deviation cannot be corrected. At that point, the CEO decides whether to permit the deviation, change the allocation, or call for a new presentation of strategy to be followed with a new decision. The quarterly checking continues until the strategy outlined in the response is fully implemented.

COMPENSATION LINKED TO STRATEGY

As with most things in life, you get what you pay for. So, if you want operating managers to develop good strategy and successfully implement it, you should pay them for doing just that. The loudest message that the manager hears is what the company pays him for.

A straightforward vehicle to accomplish this pay linkage to strategy is through the manager's annual bonus based on a management by objectives (MBO) system. The trick is to relate the objectives to the strategy implementation expected in the first year of the strategic plan. This assumes that the planning system cycles each year. The management objectives must be a mixture of financial and nonfinancial goals since much strategy is expressed in nonfinancial terms, e.g., market share, quality improvement, new product development, etc.

In the negotiations that take place between the group head and the SBU general managers to set MBO goals, objectives that most quantitatively and sensitively measure the implementation are selected and weighted according to their relative importance. The negotiators then set a reasonable range of accomplishment for those objectives and relate the degree of accomplishment to the number of bonus points that will be awarded. The total weighted numbers of bonus points then determines the share of the company's bonus pot that the manager will get.

The SBU general manager's bonus is usually determined 20 percent according to the corporation's overall performance and 80 percent according to his unit's performance. The functional managers' bonuses are determined 20 percent by the corporation performance, 40 percent by their unit's performance and 40 percent by the department's performance that they head. In this way the managers are encouraged to be team players as well as to focus on making their own goals.

A recognition that strategies have different risks—for instance, invest and grow versus a harvest strategy—can be taken into account by varying the ratio of bonus to salary in the total compensation of the manager. Here it is important to set the total compensation equal for competent performance by both types of managers. However, an invest and grow manager will have a higher proportion of bonus to base salary in his total compensation so that if he does better than competent, he will make more money than the harvester who makes the same level of accomplishment with respect to his goals. However, if he does less well than competent, he will make less money than the comparably performing harvest manager. This procedure avoids making second-class citizens out of managers who are carrying out a harvest strategy.

The role of the planners here is to provide a "laundry list" of suggested objectives related to the strategy of the unit in question, together with suggested weights and levels of accomplishment. This provides an initial list from which the negotiators can choose in arriving at their final agreements on the goals to be incorporated in the MBO "contracts."

CONCLUSION

These eight principles lead to well-working strategic management system:

1. A committed CEO.
2. A properly organized company.
3. Credible plans.
4. Supportive functional action plans.
5. Realistic resource allocations.
6. Culturally compatible strategies.
7. A good strategy monitoring system.
8. Compensation linked to strategy.

Without a strategic management system, the strategic plans are not likely to be implemented. The professional planner has an important role in implementing each of the eight principles, but this role does not include substituting him for line management.

Considerations in Implementing Strategic Control

Peter Lorange and Declan Murphy

As a subject for research, strategic planning continues to attract broad attention. Objective setting, the design of strategic programs, and plan-budget interfaces have all received extensive treatment in the literature. Oddly, however, strategic control has not received comparable scrutiny. This relative dearth of attention is all the more curious given current research interest in methods for improving the implementation of strategic planning systems.

This article will present some empirical results from a recent survey study on strategic control. The approach here is diagnostic. It is our hope that a systematic discussion of some of the pressing problems that managers perceive in the design and implementation of effective strategic control systems will suggest new avenues for future research.

STUDY OBJECTIVES AND RESEARCH DESIGN

The primary objectives of this survey study were: (1) to gather information on barriers to effective strategic control in large, multidivisional U.S. corporations; (2) to ascertain whether certain normative assumptions regarding the design of strategic control systems had a basis in practice; (3) to document any perceptual differences between planners and controllers on the worth of current strategic control systems; and (4) to gauge the adequacy of task delineation and job coordination between controllers and planners in the area of strategic control.

To meet these objectives, a structured interview agenda was designed. This agenda was administered over the telephone to one

Source: Peter Lorange and Declan Murphy, "Considerations in Implementing Strategic Control," *The Journal of Business Strategy* 4, no. 4 (1984), pp. 27–35.

corporate-level planner and one corporate-level controller in each of twenty-five *Fortune* 500 firms. A desire to secure a system designer's perspective on strategic control issues governed the selection of this sample. While it would have been optimal to study the perceptions of the users of these systems, difficulties in identifying a stratified set of line managers while maintaining a relatively simple research design restricted inquiry to the system designers alone.

The interview agenda consisted of both qualitative and quantitative questions that addressed issues of strategic control across three levels of the firm at which strategy may be set: the business-element level, the business-family level, and the corporate/portfolio level.[11] The qualitative questions were intended to allow the interviewees to expatiate upon the problems and obstacles they routinely encountered in the implementation of strategic control systems. Several of the qualitative questions also sought to address the extent to which firms employed specific system design features that might be appropriate for effective strategic control systems, e.g., clear linkage between the strategic plan and the budget, and separate categorization of strategic and operating expenditures within the overall corporate budget. The qualitative questions were thus meant primarily to address research objectives 1 and 2, listed above.

The quantitative questions focused on research objectives 3 and 4. Some of these questions employed a five-point ordinal Likert scale to measure the perceived worth of in-place strategic control systems. Another set of quantitative questions drew upon the same methodology to measure the relative success firms have had in designing strategic control systems that preclude jurisdictional disputes between planners and controllers.

As indicated above, these issues were studied across the levels of the firm at which strategy is formulated and implemented, for it was hypothesized that barriers of effective strategic control might differ across these levels. The quantitative results across *functions* were also examined. Perceptual discontinuity and/or "turf fights" between planners and controllers not only imply potential trouble for the strategic control system; they may also bespeak a fundamental dysfunctionality in the overall management system of the firm.

Of the fifty executives contacted, thirty-nine offered to cooperate (twenty-four planners and fifteen controllers). Of the thirty-nine respondents, eighteen represented nine matched pairs from the same companies. This relatively high response rate can be interpreted as an indication of the level of interest management practitioners have in these issues. Each interview lasted approximately one hour and opened with several qualitative questions to set an appropriate context for the quantitative questions that followed.

EXHIBIT 1   Four Dimensional Inputs in the Strategic Control Process

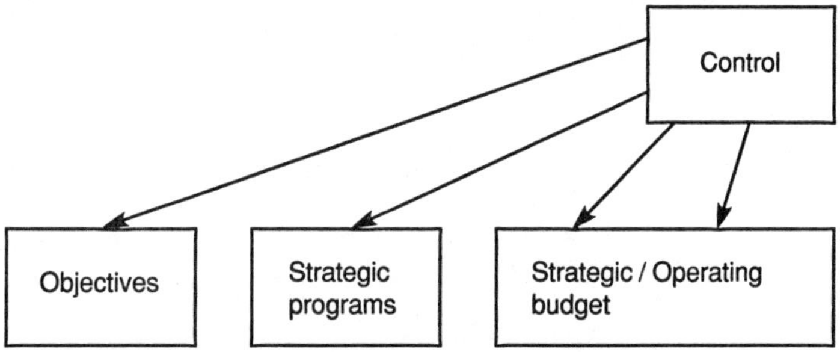

SOURCE: P. Lorange, *Corporate Planning: An Executive Viewpoint* (Englewood Cliffs, N.J.: Prentice Hall, Inc., 1980).

Exhibit 1 portrays the strategic control process as it functions at each strategic level. A detailed conceptual framework for a strategic control system is described elsewhere.[12,13] The general purpose of the research reported in this article is to shed light on the plausibility of this conceptual scheme.

BARRIERS TO STRATEGIC CONTROL

The qualitative questions yielded a number of diagnostic insights into the kinds of barriers that can cause a strategic control system to malfunction. These barriers are grouped into three classes: systemic, behavioral, and political.[2]

Systemic Barriers

Certain barriers to effective strategic control may stem from deficiencies in the design of the control system itself or from the organization's inability to manage the system once it is in place. Given the complexity of such a system, it is hardly surprising that the design and linking of the various parts of the system together in a consistent manner can be very challenging. With the passing of time, incremental changes affecting parts of the system may also result in inconsistencies.

With regard to system design, several respondents said that their firms were experiencing difficulties with the definition of adequate performance measurements for strategic control. Interestingly, the tailoring of such measurements to the requirements of individual businesses was *not* the problem. The issue, as these executives saw it, lay in the inability of their firms to agree upon a common unit of measure that would permit meaningful comparison of performance between businesses. To illustrate, a chemical industry executive said:

> We have two major problems with our control system. First, it is difficult to get results that are consistent and comparable across units. Second, it is equally difficult to isolate a standard against which to control. For example, how do you know if the ROI achieved in a particular business is good or bad? Against what standard can you judge that?

An oil industry executive voiced similar concerns, stating that "there is no common unit of measure between our businesses. Exploration and Production differs drastically from Marketing where share of market is the key measure." Lack of such universally applicable control measures certainly complicates the exercise of "top down," corporate-level control of business elements and families. Indeed, another oil industry executive believes that "the major problem at the business-element level is to fine-tune the right mix between the top-down vs. bottom-up components of the control system."

Given the value of the strategic control task as delineated in Exhibit 1, one would expect that while the critical underlying environmental assumptions that affect each business might differ from case to case, the measures for budgetary performance would be more standard. Thus, "upgrading" from a more conventional control system to a strategic one implies adding unique business-specific information for each business, i.e., going beyond a relatively few uniform measures to include more tailored, business-contingent measures. The requirement that top management know its businesses is thus a critical one. There will probably also be real limits to the number of businesses top management can know intimately enough for true strategic control. The survey sample, as noted above, consisted of corporate-level planners and controllers. This observed preoccupation with universally applicable control measures may reflect a concern that the corporate suite is too far removed from particular product/market combinations to exercise meaningful top-down control.

Excessive complexity of the control system was another problem the survey respondents repeatedly cited. A control system, for example, that requires reams of paperwork may function too slowly to be useful given the speed with which the environment changes. Furthermore, with all the variables to monitor, all the manifold interactions required to interpret control signals, and all the delicate organizational interrelationships to consider, the process can easily become too cumbersome. Loss of relevance and timeliness may result. A controller at a major consumer products company stated that "understanding the environment is a big problem. It changes so fast, especially at the business element level, that you get stale information and hence unreliable forecasts."

Similarly, the head planner at a major integrated oil company explained that "we don't get data fast enough—it's 30 to 40 days behind the events. We are working to improve this, but I wonder if it will be worth all the paperwork." This last point is particularly interesting, for this firm apparently believes it can improve the speed and timeliness of its control system by *increasing* the paperwork involved. In other words: Can the limitations upon the speed and timeliness of the control process be alleviated through systemic design improvements? While this remedy has been the prevalent approach, a more balanced emphasis on behavioral, political, *and* systemic bottlenecks is normally needed to improve systemic capacity.

As already noted, another system design problem that can hamper meaningful strategic control involves cognitive capacity. Can the members of the organization meaningfully reconcile such a diversity of variables? Can the diverse, sophisticated, and perhaps overabundant information be sufficiently assimilated by management to permit good decisionmaking? An executive at a major automobile manufacturer stated that "our management control system may provide information that is too sophisticated for our top management to utilize effectively. Traditionally, our top management has not been all that attuned to strategic issues."

In interpreting this and similar statements, one should keep in mind that strategic control requires the executive to *reconcile* the several types of feedback information for each particular business, i.e., to carry out a *multidimensional* interpretation of a business' performance. This can be seen in Exhibit 1, where four types of feedback control information have to be "blended together" and interpreted in context. Information volume and overload can become a major problem. It can result in the misinterpretation of strategic control signals, a tendency to react to signals out of context, and a management team that is afraid to innovate.[1] Moreover, the control system can easily become too large and unwieldy.

A third system design issue that stems from the complexity of the strategic control system concerns the extensive time and effort that the organization must invest to *learn* how to use such a complex system. It may simply take a very long time for the organization to feel comfortable with it, and the strategic control effort in this interim period will necessarily suffer.[15] Similarly, to have the strategic control process undergo major modifications at later stages may prove difficult, since it would require reexperience of the same diseconomies.[14]

In this context, the controller in a large electronics company explained that "we can't afford to have managers operate in too many new systems. They have to have time to manage. It takes two to three years to institutionalize each major change. That's time away from management."

What can be done to cope with the inherent systemic problems identified in the previous paragraphs? Above all, it is critical to keep the strategic control process as simple as the external environment will permit. Consequently, the task of analyzing the environment itself must be done carefully to develop robust measures that can serve as useful, early-warning signals of major changes that might affect the business. This must be done for each business. Considerable environmental and strategy analysis are needed for proper tailoring of the strategic control system. This will also be critical if executives are to be able to *interpret* the control signals. Possibly, many of the interview quotes indicate that insufficient emphasis has been placed on the integrated system design.

Thus far, the systemic problems that derive from faulty design of the control process have been discussed. Another set of systemic problems can arise from inadequate management of in-place control systems. For example, long-term strategic goals handed down from the corporate level sometimes conflict with short-term control targets at the business-element level. As one oil industry executive explained:

> Targets at the business element level are set on a quantitative basis. Personnel know their financial goals, but qualitative goals are not transmitted down to this level. Qualitative goals sometimes conflict with the unique settings of individual business units. For example, we recently shut down one of our European refineries. This necessitated a larger crew for our other European refinery when we had a qualitative goal of reducing manpower for both.

An auto industry respondent noted similar problems:

> Short-term goals and strategic goals sometimes conflict here. We had a strategic goal of improving our technical inventiveness. In many cases that is simply a function of hiring more engineers. But such hiring conflicts with the short-term objective of reducing the size of our workforce.

Such inconsistency reflects insufficient coordination and communication between the various management levels involved in setting control targets. Moreover, it suggests the need for a more formalized integrative mechanism to review control targets for consistency across the strategic levels of the firm. Such a mechanism can often remain elusive, however, especially in the context of a highly diversified conglomerate where the corporate level is often unaware of what goes on below the business family level. The vertical interdependencies in a hierarchical management system must, however, be understood.[13,16] The role of "slack" as a strategic parameter that can lessen the severity of interdependence between strategies that derives from hierarchical interrelationships is probably critical in this respect.[9,10] This issue, however, has not been addressed in this research.

Behavioral Barriers

Behavioral problems can also complicate the implementation of effective strategic control. These difficulties often stem from an inability to dispense with the habit of thinking that an executive's functional background, education, and training and/or the corporate culture have molded the executive over many years. These characteristics, however, may be dysfunctional in a strategic control context. The difficulties may also stem from cognitive limits to managers' basic intellectual capacity. A statement from the controller of a major midwestern manufacturing company illustrates this point:

> Managers who have been with a cash cow for 15 years don't like to think of it as a cash cow. For them, it is still a growth business. This attitude is especially characteristic of engineers who often don't want to let a business die gradually but want to "fix" it. This creates real problems of a behavioral nature for *ad hoc* strategy modification at lower levels since the control data is self-reported and managers will try to hide data that confirms the cash cow position of their product. Corporate must therefore get involved when a manager wants to change his objectives.

In this case, the executives involved have invested so much time and effort in a particular product that the "sunk costs" now prevent them from critically reexamining its life-cycle position. The executives in question are probably *not* trying deliberately to recast the data. Rather, they simply cannot see the control signals through any other lenses than their own. Such "entrapment" makes it impossible for the executive involved to respond, or even comprehend, the signals that the strategic control system is providing.[4] Vested interests and sunk costs typify the entrapments that can adversely affect the utility of strategic control. Unrealistic, wishful thinking may be the result.

Another closely related type of entrapment is the fear of "losing face" or being proved wrong. For an executive who has spearheaded and sponsored a particular strategy, it may be difficult to face up to the realization of error.[3] Thus, the gatekeeper for a particular strategy may become a filter who subsequently screens out conflicting control signals. Entrapment of this kind can also adversely affect top management's willingness to overcome the inertia that hinders disposition of a business that no longer accords with the overall corporate portfolio strategy.

Behaviorally defective responses to strategic control signals also surfaced in an interview conducted with the planner at a large high-tech electronics concern. He explained:

> Our CEOs have all been engineers who like to roll up their sleeves and get involved in the middle of projects where they don't understand the markets. Unfortunately, our control system has provided them with signals that cue

this type of behavior. We need to change the type of information the system generates as one step toward the solving of this problem.

Here, the "hands on" engineering training of the top management precipitated a misuse of the strategic control system to the detriment of realism: Top management may have allowed their own biases and preconceptions to affect their better judgment. "Uninteresting" data are conveniently ignored.

Effective response to control signals in this type of setting would require top management to depart from the very type of behavior that may have earned them entrance to the executive suite in the first place.

A similar type of problem emerged in a conversation with the head planner of a large heavy equipment manufacturer:

> One of our problems is that our SBUs don't coincide with the way history organized the company. Our plants, not our SBUs, are the profit centers. This complicates the planner's task enormously since data collection and cost allocation are extraordinarily difficult tasks. The bean counter mentality of our controller's people makes it difficult for them to think in terms of SBUs.

Here, too, the traditional behavior required for success in the control function is incompatible with the management of the strategic aspects of the control system. While this quote also indicates that there may be systemic problems when the strategic structure differs from the operating structure, the *behavioral* impacts of being asked to control along dimensions that differ from the formal operating structure seem particularly striking. This may go totally against the grain of many executives who have been taught that control should follow strict authority lines. Strong behavioral barriers prevent many managers from accepting the concept that real responsibility should be higher than formal authority.[16]

The difficulty involved in abandoning familiar thought patterns and acquired behaviors should thus not be underestimated. As an oil industry respondent put in, "In the oil industry, the external environment is critical and we don't assess it well. We tend to look backward to give us confidence rather than forward to the future where the environment is so uncertain." Accustomed patterns of thought can be very comforting, especially in an industry where the environment is capable of producing sudden, unpleasant surprises. Thus, the strong cultural traditions of particular businesses often make it difficult for executives to reassess current events. There is an abundance of illustrative examples and "war stories" on this theme.

What can be done to counteract the dysfunctional effects of such entrapments? A first step in restoring effective strategic control is the creation of a broader and more explicit awareness of these issues in the organization. Executive development, career planning, and job reassignment can probably contribute effectively in this context.[6] Another step is to "institutionalize" the strategic control process, i.e., make the process more explicit. Such a tactic requires designating the specific variables to be monitored *beforehand* and seeking organizational agreement on the critical environmental assumptions. It also calls for a delineation of *who* is to monitor *what* and a specification of the frequency and mode of reporting. While again a major feature of such an approach will be more explicit environmental strategic analysis, an element that is possibly even more critical is to emphasize the need to develop interactive and iterative procedures for the *line* managers, so that *they* can delineate the critical environmental issues and agree on how these should be handled. A good strategic planning process should facilitate this. Strategic control is probably much more easily realizable in contexts where a strong planning process exists. An important benefit of this clarification process is thus the legitimization of the strategic control process as a vehicle for interaction within the organization. This will allow for an agreement among key managers to track critical issues systemically over time. Through these "routines," critical issues can be brought up early and as a matter of normal procedure, given that organizational agreement now exists to consider such issues.

Political Barriers

The achievement of strategic progress in an organization does, of course, depend on management's ability to create a sufficiently broad sense of agreement regarding basic direction, as well as on their ability to allocate the resources needed to get there. Indeed, a primary purpose of the planning process is to create agreement among coalitions of member groups regarding a direction that is acceptable to all.[7] As such, the process should function as a useful vehicle for the creation of acceptance and commitment as discussed previously. It goes without saying that such a strategy must be "politically" acceptable for the various power groups and coalitions that can be found in an organization.[5] The strategic control process may call for changes in the basic strategic agenda. These are changes that typically will also affect the internal power groups and that might even be seen as potentially disruptive of the relative power of coalitions. Resistance may result.

One indication of this can be seen in a reluctance to share information. In some organizations, for example, controllers may dislike sharing some of their traditional prerogatives with the planning unit. Consider the following statement by an oil industry planner: "Our problems between the planner's and controller's offices stem from the fact that planning is relatively new here, and the controllers resent the power of the new kid on the block."

Such problems can be greatly exacerbated if planners and controllers define their relationship in an adversarial way. There was, for example, one firm in the sample where relations between the planner's and controller's offices were uniformly difficult. It is indicative that the planner defined his corporate role in the strategic control process by stating that "my job is to make sure that the accountants don't produce any wrong numbers. I must curb the facile use and nature of the numbers they generate. This leads to problems with the controller's function."

Similarly, some controllers saw their role as that of the corporate critic and saw their colleagues in planning as poor quantitative analysts. Several firms said that the problems they experienced between these two functions were so severe that they were only able to solve them through some type of system suboptimization. The planner of a consumer products company explained that "our controllers don't think strategically. We have good relations with them but only because we have given up trying to induce them to think strategically. In this sense, we have abdicated our responsibilities."

Or, consider the following statement by the controller of a major chemical company:

> We solved the conflict between the planner and controller through a kind of system suboptimization. We rotate the planner and the controller out of their jobs very regularly. We also keep the groups around them smaller than they perhaps ought to be. This kind of approach leads to system inefficiency, but it did curb the confrontation.

A clear definition of responsibilities can help to ameliorate such problems, but the real solution probably lies in the negotiation of roles on the basis of a common interest in the long-term success of the firm. It is a task of top management to assess the extent to which such friction exists between the planning and control functions. Given that this is likely to be highly dysfunctional for the firm, top management should intervene to prevent such situations. One approach that was followed by several of the firms in the sample was to have *both* the planning and the control functions report to a common senior staff executive.

Another set of political barriers to strategic control results from the unwillingness of lower-level managers, who often control the relevant data, to report unfavorable results to top management. A planner of an integrated oil company, for example, stated that "our big problem at the corporate level is that control information at this level derives from the divisions, and the divisions won't reveal detrimental information about themselves."

Interorganizational trust is a key ingredient in the creation of a viable control atmosphere. The strategic control system will suffer in direct proportion to the extent that it is associated with job insecurity, scapegoating, or categorization of line executives as "winners" or "losers." Similarly, strategic control will benefit from a shared perception that it can safeguard the long-run viability of the firm and, thereby, of its employees as well.

The preceding classification of barriers to strategic control into systemic, behavioral, and political categories implies that firms should adopt a multi-perspective approach to the removal of these barriers. Systemic problems often have their roots in underlying behavioral and/ or political problems and the multidimensional nature of the issues involved demands multidimensional solutions.

THE TAILORING OF THE CONTROL PROCESSES

The qualitative questions addressed to the respondents also attempted to test the validity of certain normative hypotheses made regarding the optimal design of strategic control systems. One such hypothesis concerned the need for tailoring the control system itself according to the type and maturity of the business under consideration. What might be a valid control measurement for one type of business might be inappropriate for another type. For a new start-up business, for example, more emphasis might be placed on controlling market share indicators than would be the case for mature businesses where control of efficiency and profitability might be relatively more important. Under this hypothesis, therefore, management should focus its control approach on a few critical issue factors, tailormade for the particular strategy. Slightly over half of the sample (twenty out of thirty-eight respondents) stated that they did indeed attempt to tailor the control system in this way. Many respondents who answered in the negative claimed it was sufficient to tailor the substantive targets for the phenomena being controlled alone.

On another issue, the respondents were asked whether they felt there was a sufficiently close relationship between the strategic plan and the budget. According to the hypothesis, the budget should be the "action plan" for the implementation of the overall strategy. Lack of a clear linkage would therefore raise questions regarding the effectiveness of strategy implementation.[8,11] About 75 percent of the sample (thirty out of thirty-eight respondents) said they were satisfied with the linkage as it existed. Of the remainder, several stated that they felt that this was indeed a problem that needed to be addressed. Most of these respondents indicated that there was a need, in particular, to identify more clearly which organizational entities would be responsible for the various implementational tasks and to earmark budgetary resources for this in such specific terms that the implementation tasks in fact would become doable.

A question related to the above attempted to discover how many of the firms in the sample broke out strategic expenditures separately from operating expenditures in the budgets of their operating units. The assumption here was that a rational delineation of expenditures along these lines would help managers to keep their strategic goals in view, and would make it more difficult for them to succumb to the ever-present temptation to divert resources away from long-term projects to fight short-term operating fires.[8] Again, slightly over half of the respondents (twenty out of thirty-eight respondents) stated that this crucial distinction was formally enshrined in their budgets. Several of the capital-intensive firms in the sample (for example, those in the oil industry) said that they used their capital budgets as proxies for strategic budgets—a predictable and plausible response pattern for this type of firm. Curiously, however, none of the participating chemical companies used their capital budgets for this purpose.

QUANTITATIVE RESULTS

Two different sets of quantitative questions were posed to the respondents. The first set of questions asked them to rate on a five-point ordinal Lickert scale their overall level of satisfaction with their in-place strategic control systems as it was perceived to function at the business-element, business-family, and corporate/portfolio levels. The second set of questions asked them to rate their overall level of satisfaction with the task delineation and job coordination between the planners' and controllers' functions, again at each of the three strategy levels of the firm. The responses were analyzed across the two functions to see if there were any major perceptual differences between planners and controllers on these issues. The responses, by level, are printed in Exhibits 2–7.

Looking first at the question of general satisfaction with in-place strategic control systems across the strategy levels of the firm (Exhibits 2, 4, and 6), there is a small increase in the level of above-average satisfaction, ascending from the business-element level to the business-family level, and up to the corporate level. Even though this result may reflect the fact that the respondents were corporate-level executives who may feel more comfortable with the systems they know best, i.e., the strategic control system at the corporate level, it may also reflect a time problem in meaningfully implementing decentralized strategic control. Such a problem will, of course, limit an organization's ability to implement highly diversified, complex strategies.

With regard to the question on the delineation between controllers and planners regarding their perceptions about the quality of strategic control across the strategy levels of the firm, relatively higher levels of

EXHIBIT 2   Degree of Satisfaction with the Strategic Control System—The Business-Element Level

Organizational entity \ Degree of satisfaction	Low 1	2	3	4	High 5
Controller	0	1	5	6	2
Planner	0	4	10	9	0
Combined sample	0	5	15	15	2

EXHIBIT 3   Strategic Control—The Business-Element Level

Organizational entity \ Degree of satisfaction	Low 1	2	3	4	High 5
Controller	0	2	1	11	0
Planner	1	3	2	15	2
Combined sample	1	5	3	26	2

EXHIBIT 4   Degree of Satisfaction with the Strategic Control System—The Business-Family Level

Organizational entity \ Degree of satisfaction	Low 1	2	3	4	High 5
Controller	0	1	4	8	1
Planner	0	1	9	9	0
Combined sample	0	2	13	17	1

above-average satisfaction for the controllers relative to those of the planners are evident, particularly at the business-element and corporate levels. There is, however, a somewhat lower level of satisfaction for the controllers relative to that of the planners at the business-family level. This result was unexpected in several respects. First, given

EXHIBIT 5   Degree of Cooperation between Controller and Planner on Strategic Control—The Business-Family Level

Organizational entity / Degree of satisfaction	Low 1	2	3	4	High 5
Controller	0	2	2	9	1
Planner	0	3	8	9	0
Combined sample	0	5	10	18	1

EXHIBIT 6   Degree of Satisfaction with the Strategic Control System—The Corporate Level

Organizational entity / Degree of satisfaction	Low 1	2	3	4	High 5
Controller	0	2	2	9	1
Planner	1	3	9	9	1
Combined sample	1	5	11	18	2

EXHIBIT 7   Degree of Cooperation between Controller and Planner on Strategic Control—The Corporate Level

Organizational entity / Degree of satisfaction	Low 1	2	3	4	High 5
Controller	0	1	0	12	1
Planner	1	1	4	15	3
Combined sample	1	2	4	27	4

that the controllers tend to have the direct charter for the design and execution of control processes and activities, it may be that this group is more satisfied with its own task fulfillment than the planners. This lack of perceived agreement may also reflect complacency and a lack of realism on the part of the controllers. Second, the complexity of the strategic control task at the business-family level—for example, monitoring for synergies between business elements—may render the control task more difficult in this type of setting.

Turning again to the perceptional differences, which indicate that controllers are more satisfied than planners with their in-place strategic control systems at each of the three levels of the firm, this finding may reflect a certain "pride of authorship" reaction by the controllers, who are usually primarily responsible for the design and implementation of these systems. Planners, who are usually more frequent "users" of these systems may not be quite as sanguine about them as controllers.

Satisfaction with task delineation and job coordination between planners and controllers was also generally higher for controllers across the three levels of strategy of the firm, as can be seen from Exhibits 3, 5, and 7. However, both planners and controllers were less happy with the way they were interacting at the business-family level. Here, it was particularly clear that the planners were much more negative than the controllers. The level of satisfaction of both groups with task delineation at the corporate level was generally high. In many firms, a highly interactive personal relationship between the head planner and corporate controller may account for this result.

The small size of the survey sample suggests that the above results should be interpreted with caution. The chi-square test, for example, revealed a significant difference between planners and controllers only for Exhibit 7. These distributions have been presented only to suggest trends and not to offer any comprehensive test of hypotheses. Thus, the physical proximity between the planners and the controller that typically can be found in a corporate headquarters may facilitate a shared perception of satisfactory working relationships. At the lower levels of the firm there may be more of a "distance" between planners and controllers, leading to less satisfaction with working relationships.

CONCLUSIONS

We have attempted to explore implementational consequences associated with pursuing a strategic control approach. Three general sets of issues emerge which may make it difficult to implement effective strategic control.

First, a number of dysfunctional factors apparently play significant roles. Some of these derive from systemic issues, such as striving for more consistent design of an integrated planning and control system.

Other issues stem from behavioral factors that impose constraints on the ways a strategic control system might function; cognitive biases and skill limitations are good examples. Finally, there were political factors representing potential barriers to effective implementation that arise from how coalitions within the firm react to control.

Second, there seems to be relatively widespread, although not universal, acceptance of the need to tailor the strategic control dimension to the type of strategy at hand and also to have a strategic budget dimension reflecting this in the overall budget.

Third, we found widespread perceptual differences between planners and controllers regarding how the strategic control processes were functioning as well as how the task delineation and cooperation between the two functions were working out. Given that *both* planners and controllers are supposed to be key catalysts impacting the implementation of the firm's strategies through the *same* administrative system, these perceptional differences are troublesome. They may imply that planners and controllers are *not* sufficiently pulling in the same direction. Rather than facilitating strategy implementation, these two staff cultures may represent a barrier to successful implementation.

REFERENCES

1. R. L. Ackoff, "Management Misinformation Systems," *Management Science,* Vol. 14, No. 4, 1967.
2. G. T. Allison, *Essence of Decision* (Boston: Little, Brown and Co., 1971).
3. J. Bower, *Managing the Resource Allocation Process* (Boston: Harvard Business School, Division of Research, 1971).
4. J. Brockner, M. C. Shaw, and J. Z. Rubin "Factors Affecting Withdrawal From Escalating Conflict: Quitting Before It Is Too Late," *Journal of Experimental Psychology,* Vol. 15, 1979.
5. G. Donaldson and J. Lorsch, *Decision Making at the Top* (New York: Basic Books, 1983).
6. A. Edstrom and P. Lorange, "Matching Strategy and Human Resources in Multinational Corporations," *Journal of International Business Studies,* Vol. 15, No. 2, 1984.
7. R. E. Freeman, *Strategic Management: A Stakeholder Approach* (Marshfield, Mass.: Pitman Publishing, Inc., 1984).
8. P. E. Haggerty, "The Corporation and Innovation," *Strategic Management Journal,* Vol. 2, No. 2, 1981.
9. D. Jemison, "Contributions of Administrative Behavior to Strategic Management," *Academy of Management Review,* Vol. 6, No. 4, 1981.
10. D. Jemison, "The Implementation of an Integrative Approach to Strategic Management Research," *Academy of Management Review,* Vol. 6, No. 4, 1981.
11. P. Lorange, *Corporate Planning: An Executive Viewpoint* (Englewood Cliffs, N.J.: Prentice-Hall, Inc., 1980).

12. P. Lorange, "Strategic Control: Some Issues in Making It Operationally More Useful," in R. Lamb, ed., *Latest Advances in Strategic Management* (Englewood Cliffs, N.J.: Prentice-Hall, Inc., 1984).
13. P. Lorange, "Monitoring of Strategic Progress and Ad Hoc Strategic Modification," in G. John, *New Perspectives on Strategic Management* (Greenwich, Conn.: JAI Press, Inc., 1984).
14. P. Lorange and R. F. Vancil, *Strategic Planning Systems* (Englewood Cliffs, N.J.: Prentice-Hall Inc., 1977).
15. W. H. Newman, *Constructive Control* (Englewood Cliffs, N.J.: Prentice-Hall, Inc., 1975).
16. R. F. Vancil, *Decentralization: Managing Ambiguity by Design* (Homewood, Ill.: Dow Jones-Irwin, 1980).

Growth Industries: Here Today, Gone Tomorrow

Clair Starry and Nick McGaughey

Many investors mistakenly believe that today's growth industries will continue their rapid growth into the indefinite future. Many also assume that entering a growth industry essentially guarantees easy access to large, growing, and profitable markets. The reality is that most rapidly growing industries (those with 20 percent or higher annual increases in sales) neither continue their extraordinary growth for an extended period nor offer easily penetrable, profitable markets. Competition is strong, and products and markets change rapidly. Late entrants into growth industries often make costly mistakes, because industry sales are not growing fast enough to accommodate all of the expansion plans. Naturally, industry profits fall.

The video-game industry is a prime example. In the early 1980s this industry flourished, and profitability was high. Demand became saturated, and no new applications appeared. Consumers grew disinterested; both sales and profits plummeted. Although this example is extreme, the same pattern has emerged in other high-growth industries.

But despite the fact that industries grow and decline, some companies are perennial top performers. One of the factors in their continued success is the recognition that today's growth markets are not necessarily the markets to be in tomorrow. These companies continually position themselves to move into new areas of promise.

What can we learn from recent experiences that will help a manufacturing company position itself in growth industries? What are the growth areas for manufacturing in the next ten years? How can a company move into growth industries profitably? This article will attempt to answer these questions.

Source: Reprinted from *Business Horizons* 31, no. 4. Copyright 1988 by the Foundation for the School of Business at Indiana University. Used with permission.

LESSONS FROM THE PAST

A decade ago, energy industries and supporting manufacturers and services dominated the list of growth industries. Financial and service industries experienced rapid growth in the early to mid-1980s, in part because of deregulation. More recently, retail and consumer industries have become the most rapidly growing industries.

Electronics and computers, despite their glamour, are not among the ten fastest-growing industries. In fact, few manufacturing industries are high-growth industries. Prices decline as technology improves (yielding a lower growth in dollar sales than in unit output), and consumers now are consuming greater amounts of services.

Their purchases account for about two-thirds of U.S. gross national product.

An analysis of those manufacturing industries that experience fast growth yields important information about their characteristics.

- Those manufacturing industries that are very profitable tend to be ones that experience above-average growth; produce high-technology equipment, such as computers or electronics; appeal to a consumer fad or trend, such as sport/aerobic shoes; or take advantage of a market aberration, such as oilfield drilling equipment in the 1970s. In most instances, the underlying factor does not persist for long and industry growth falls.
- Profitability tends to decline as the industry matures. In Table 1, five-year growth rates and returns on equity (ROEs) are given for the computer and electronics-equipment industries. Industry profitability declines as new (including foreign) entrants increase industry competition.
- Debt-to-equity ratios are low during the growth phase. Use of venture capital, investment by major companies looking for new opportunities, and self-investment by entrepreneurs reduce the amount of debt financing needed by these industries. Risks are also higher, and

Table 1　Growth Rates and Returns on Equity

	1974–78	*1977–81*	*1980–84*	*1982–86*
Computers				
Sales growth rate	14.5%	23.0%	18.2%	14.6%
ROE	17.7%	19.0%	17.4%	13.1%
Electronic Equipment				
Sales growth rate	12.8%	17.9%	14.9%	12.1%
ROE	19.4%	19.1%	17.9%	7.8%

investors want to be able to capture some of the gains if the endeavor succeeds. As an industry matures, risks decline and debt financing is used more extensively.

- Cash flow tends to be a problem, because growth requires cash to pay for investment, employees, production, new facilities, and so forth. Even though the balance sheet and income statement look good, a company may have a significant cash flow problem that can impede its growth prospects.

- As shown in Table 2, few manufacturing industries are included in the list of top-growth industries for each of four 5-year periods. The shift in growth industries from energy to finance and from services to consumer products and services is apparent. Manufacturing industries and companies that are good performers follow that shift. Mining and drilling equipment made the list for the first two periods because of the spate of drilling activity that followed the energy crisis. That industry is now experiencing poor growth. Computers made the list for the second and third periods but fell off the list during the 1982–1986 period (ranking 14th), as did telecommunications equipment (ranking 18th). The only manufacturing industry on the 1982–1986 list is recreational vehicles, the result of a short-term shift in market demand.

Company-Level Analysis

Most but not all high-performing companies are in growth industries. Table 3 shows the distribution of the 25 best public companies in 5-year sales growth and 5-year ROE by the level of their respective industry's growth. Although manufacturing industries are not well represented among the high-growth industries, many manufacturing companies are among the high-performing companies as measured by growth in sales or ROE. Of the 25 fastest-growing companies in the 5-year period ending in 1986, 11 were manufacturing companies; of the 25 most profitable companies (highest ROE), nine were manufacturing companies. There companies are shown in Table 4.

Not all manufacturing companies in high-growth industries are highly profitable or rapidly growing. For example, many computer companies, some well established and some new entrants, failed to take advantage of the rapid growth in personal-computer sales. Some of the larger, more established companies did not obtain sufficient market share in the mainframe market and could not find a suitable niche in the emerging microcomputer market. Several of the larger companies tried to be all things to all people and could not. Other companies, Osborne for example, could not compete with IBM once that company entered the personal-computer market.

TABLE 2 Fastest Growing Industries by Time Period: 1974–1986

	5-Year ROE	12-Month ROE	5-Year Sales	12-Month Sales	5-Year EPS	12-Month EPS	Debt/ Equity	Net Profit Margin
1982–1986:								
Health care services	24.7	11.4	32.5	19.2	24.4	-10.8	157.9	4.3
Recreational vehicles	18.5	8.5	28.0	-2.8	20.5	-24.8	8.9	3.1
Thrift institutions	15.8	17.9	23.8	9.5	NM	27.4	106.1	5.4
Brokerage houses	19.4	18.5	23.5	17.9	-5.9	11.3	57.9	3.8
Retailer— miscellaneous	18.8	14.7	22.0	12.9	17.9	2.3	34.3	2.8
Leisure—toys & electronics	33.4	7.2	21.6	-4.1	NM	-33.9	112.9	1.4
Retailers—catalog showroom	10.0	def	20.1	-1.8	-14.3	P-D	99.8	def
Retailers— convenience stores	16.3	10.8	19.3	-0.7	11.3	-18.9	125.7	1.4
Life and health insurance	13.1	14.3	17.3	12.9	10.1	54.2	15.2	5.8
Retailers—apparel	18.3	13.9	15.2	10.2	10.8	19.9	36.6	3.2
Retailers—discount & variety	17.2	13.9	14.9	14.4	26.7	-7.3	62.4	1.8
Banks—Southeast	16.6	17.5	14.7	6.9	15.9	11.7	27.6	9.1
1980–1984								
Health care—hospital management	22.9	18.2	39.8	11.5	29.1	18.2	1.4	7.6
Trading companies	25.5	10.3	31.1	8.5	24.1	-51.8	0.4	4.5
Banks—Southwest	17.9	12.0	26.6	19.8	12.4	-8.5	0.3	7.5
Leisure—toys & electronics	39.6	-1.1	24.4	10.9	NM	P-D	0.3	2.9
Telecommunications manufacturing	19.7	8.1	23.0	20.6	15.7	13.9	0.3	4.6
Thrift institutions	4.1	9.9	22.8	30.6	NM	9.1	0.2	5.1
Banks—Northeast	15.1	15.5	21.7	22.9	14.1	2.4	0.3	7.9
Retailers—catalog showroom	14.8	8.2	21.3	15.2	-4.5	-5.2	0.7	1.8
Banks—Southeast	16.9	18.4	21.0	18.3	15.1	15.7	0.3	8.5
Services—industrial	20.8	18.5	19.3	15.8	12.0	8.3	0.3	5.3
Computers	17.4	12.9	18.2	15.1	3.1	28.0	0.3	5.6
Banks—Midwest	12.3	11.7	17.5	11.1	0.5	7.5	0.2	6.3
1977–1981								
Brokerage	13.8	17.6	30.8		11.3		0.5	4.5
Mining and drilling equipment	21.7	25.1	27.1		24.4		0.3	10.5
Office services	25.1	19.1	24.3		24.8		0.2	3.9

TABLE 2   *(concluded)*

	5-Year ROE	12-Month ROE	5-Year Sales	12-Month Sales	5-Year EPS	12-Month EPS	Debt/ Equity	Net Profit Margin
Natural gas pipeline & distributors	18.3	22.4	23.8		13.1		0.5	5.4
Computers	19.0	13.7	23.0		21.3		0.2	6.3
Natural gas producers	18.3	21.1	23.0		12.7		0.7	5.0
Domestic oils	20.2	18.1	22.9		16.7		0.5	4.4
Retailers—drug chains	19.1	18.6	20.3		18.6		0.6	2.4
Electric utilities— West	11.2	13.3	20.3		1.2		0.9	10.9
Health care	19.2	19.2	20.2		21.8		0.2	6.3
Thrift institutions	11.8	def	19.8		10.0		0.5	def
1974–1978								
Food service	23.6	15.0	27.9		26.1		0.8	4.8
Other oil & gas	16.1	14.5	24.3		18.9		0.5	7.3
Mining & drilling equipment	18.2	18.7	21.3		30.6		0.3	3.9
Electric utilities— Southeast	11.7	13.2	20.1		3.2		1.0	8.4
International oils	15.1	13.1	19.9		10.7		0.3	5.3
Health care products & services	15.7	17.7	19.8		17.5		0.4	4.8
Coal	18.9	1.0	19.7		23.0		0.3	10.1
New York banks	12.0	11.7	19.4		6.1		0.5	3.6
Natural gas pipelines & distributors	17.1	15.8	19.2		12.7		0.8	7.9
Electric utilities— Southwest	13.3	13.7	18.9		4.4			
Heavy construction contractors	18.5	14.0	18.0		32.5		0.4	2.5
Electric utilities— West	11.3	10.8	17.6		1.8		1.0	11.7

All figures are percentages.
def: deficit
NM: not meaningful
P-D: profit to deficit

Source: Forbes, various issues.

Well-run companies in moderate- or low-growth manufacturing industries can be top performers, too. For example, Levi Strauss and Nike are two profitable and growing companies in the apparel indus-

TABLE 3 Distribution of Fastest Growing and Most Profitable Publicly Held Companies by Industry Growth: 1982–1986

| | *Industry Growth* | | |
	High Growth (above 10.5% per year)	*Medium Growth (from 5% to 10.5% per year)*	*Low Growth (below 5% per year)*
Top 25 companies by 5-year sales growth	17	7	1
Top 25 companies by 5-year ROE growth	14	9	2

Source: Forbes, January 12, 1987; and SRI International

try. These companies have been able to identify niches that fit the changing lifestyles of American and foreign consumers. Other companies in moderate- to poorly performing industries that made the list of top companies from 1982–1986 are James River of Virginia (forest products), Jefferson Smurfit (packaging), and ConAgra (branded foods).

Two lessons can be learned from high-performing companies in any manufacturing industry. You must find a niche in which you have a comparative advantage (marketability, cost, resources, or management acumen), and you must recognize changes in the marketplace and adjust your product mix to meet these changes, not look for ways to protect the current product mix.

PROSPECTS FOR THE FUTURE

The manufacturing industries that will be on top over the next 10 years will be those that fit the changing demands of consumers, business, and government. To identify those industries we evaluated not only the outlook for the U.S. and world economies, but also the ability of businesses to develop new technologies and apply them to new markets.

The move toward services by consumers, governments, and businesses will lead to growth in the manufacturing of equipment to support those services—from computers to telecommunications equipment, from health and diagnostic equipment to automated office equipment and workstations. These industries are already near the top and will probably stay there a while longer, but over time they will be replaced by a new breed of growth industries. Some of these are discussed below.

TABLE 4 Fastest Growing and Most Profitable Manufacturing Companies by 5-year Period

Company	Industry	Qualified by ROE/Growth	Period In Which Company Was Top Performer			
			1974–78	1977–81	1980–84	1982–86
Lockheed	Aerospace	ROE	X	X	X	X
Levi Strauss	Apparel	ROE	X			X
Liz Claiborne	Apparel	Both				
NIKE	Apparel	Both		X	X	X
Emerson Radio	Appliances	Growth				X
Allegheny Beverage	Beverages	Growth			X	
ConAgra	Branded foods	Both				X
International Minerals and Chemicals	Chemicals	ROE	X			
Apple Computer	Computers	Both			X	X
Data General	Computers	Growth	X	X		
Digital Equipment	Computers	Growth	X			
Intergraph	Computers	Both				X
Prime Computer	Computers	Both			X	
SCI Systems	Computers	Growth				X
Storage Technology	Computers	Growth		X		
Wang Laboratories	Computers	Growth		X	X	
Avon Products	Cosmetics	ROE	X			
American Home Products	Drugs	ROE	X			X
SmithKline	Drugs	ROW		X		
Intel	Electronics	Both	X			
National Semiconductor	Electronics	ROE	X			
Schlumberger	Electronics	ROE	X	X		
Tandy	Electronics	ROE	X	X	X	X
Teledyne	Electronics	ROE	X	X		
James River of VA	Forest products	Growth		X	X	X
Savin	Office equipment	Both		X		
GEO International	Oil equipment	ROE		X		
L B Foster	Oil equipment	ROE		X		
Jefferson Smurfit	Packaging	Both			X	
M/A-Com	Telecommunications	Both			X	
Rolm	Telecommunications	Both			X	
TIE/Communications		Growth			X	
Coleco Industries	Toys/electronics	Both			X	X
Hasbro	Toy/electronics	Growth				X
Mattel	Toys/electronics	ROE	X			

Note: Growth indicates an increase in sales over the preceding 5-year period. ROE indicates a return on equity over the preceding 5-year period.

Source: *Forbes*, various issues.

Automation. The spread of information technology to all business sectors and to the consumer. The current growth of the computer industry parallels in some ways that experienced by the petrochemical industry. After an initial spurt of growth, strong growth has continued as new applications are found in several areas. Profitability falls, however. Specific areas in the computer/electronic-equipment areas that should grow rapidly are:

- Software/expert systems—the need to use available computing capacity and enhance the ability of professionals to work with computers.
- Intelligent workstations for financial institutions, brokers, traders, retail establishments, and others.
- Robotics—replacing labor with equipment in warehousing, manufacturing, distribution, transportation, and so forth.
- CAD/CAM, CIM—linking the design, operations, and engineering functions together.
- VLIC and VHSIC chips—rapid increases in technology and demands for greater computing power in smaller machines are leading to the development of bigger and better integrated circuits. Military applications will be especially important in VHSIC production. Even though costs are rapidly declining for these chips, the industry should continue to grow, reaching the $50–$60 billion sales level by the mid-1990s.

Biotechnology. Using genetic engineering to increase productivity in agriculture, pharmaceuticals, waste disposal, and elsewhere. This industry is expected to grow from essentially zero sales to over $10 billion annually by 1995.

Composites and Other New Materials. These lightweight, better-performing materials have already been used for transportation and defense applications. As their prices fall and quality (compared to metals and other construction materials) improves, they will be replacing many of the materials currently used in manufacturing and construction.

Defense. Various programs, including the Strategic Defense Initiative, will require large-scale R&D efforts in aerospace, laser, supercomputer, and related industries with heavy defense applications.

Health Equipment. As health care continues to remain at or near the top of growth industries, the demand for health products, especially diagnostic equipment and monitoring devices, will be strong.

Industrial Security.   The security industry, formerly labor-intensive, is becoming electronics-intensive. Security monitoring devices and other equipment have experienced very rapid growth. This growth should continue as the need for security increases and the ability of computer and information technology to perform in the security field grows.

Packaging Equipment.   More and more products are moving into world markets. Many of these products have not had to be transported long distances and experience extreme changes in climate before. Packaging improvements are required, and so is the equipment to support these improvements.

Security and Labor-Saving Devices for the Home.   Female labor-force participation rates are forecast to top 70 percent by the mid-1990s. The need for security to protect one's valuables and for labor-saving devices that reduce time spent on household chores will continue to increase. The spread of computer technology to these areas should result in some new niches in the consumer-product markets.

Superconductivity.   A concept that has moved to the forefront of R&D efforts for many companies in the last year. This technology offers the ability to transport electricity with almost no energy loss. If superconductive materials can be found, many new applications for the electrical-utility industry will emerge.

These areas are not the only ones a manufacturing company should consider as it plans for the next ten years. They do, however, point to areas in which growth will be rapid and the need for innovative companies to identify and exploit market niches is strong.

MOVING TO A GROWTH POSTURE

Once a company has identified the industries and niches that form the best fits, the difficult task of moving into them remains. A successful move requires that earnings per share grow and investors receive higher returns.

The move entails both benefits and costs. Because growth industries are expanding rapidly, new customers and needs are emerging. Many other companies are probably entering the industry, though, and technology is probably changing rapidly. A company that wants to enter a growth industry needs an implementation plan—one that is realistic, flexible, and suited to the resources available.

Step 1: Industry Evaluation

The first step in developing an effective business plan is to thoroughly understand the industry being considered: the reasons for its growth; current and potential competition; the outlook for continued growth; customers and customer requirements; expected investment in plant, equipment, labor force, and research and development. Of particular importance is the identification of specific niches within the industry that are of interest to the investigating company. These niches are the ones that should be further evaluated.

Step 2: Market Opportunity Identification

The next step is to develop a tailored list of market opportunities that match a company's current competitive strengths. The success factors for operating in the targeted areas are compared to a company's strengths to determine if the company should consider the specific area.

Step 3: Competitive Positioning

For those niches selected, the company must decide how to obtain a competitive position. This process is specifically linked to the current strengths of the company and its existing methods of manufacturing, distribution, sales, and so forth. Weaknesses are identified, and ways to mitigate them pursued.

Step 4: Implementation Plan Development

The target areas are selected and an implementation plan is written. It includes a list of the resources needed to enter the market (facilities, labor, financing, management, customers, and so forth); the timing of production and product introduction; cash flow and financial statements; contingencies for unforeseen problems; and ways to meet the competition. The ability of the new products to be manufactured and sold using existing facilities and distribution channels is also evaluated. If entirely new facilities or channels are needed, managers must be trained or hired to handle these new functions.

Step 5: Integration with Corporate Plan

The move to the new market area should be considered part of a company's overall strategic plan. It should represent a direction for the company that will enhance its overall earnings per share and shareholder value. Moving to a growth industry without such integration can result in substantial losses.

Growth industries are out there. Just because they're here today, however, doesn't mean they'll be here tomorrow. And a company that identifies and moves into one thinking it will grow indefinitely is in for an unpleasant, and maybe a fatal, surprise. The consistently high-performing companies are those that identify growth markets, get into them early, and move on before the markets stop growing.

Small Manufacturers—When Going outside Makes Sense

Richard B. Robinson and Patricia P. Mc Dougall

Strategic planning has become a fact of life for almost all businesses, large and small. Although studies examining the value of such planning activities have resulted in contradictory evidence, the benefits of strategic planning have generally been accepted by the business community.

But how does strategic planning differ between large and small business firms? Are the planning needs (both process and content) of small firms similar to those of the large, multibusiness firms from which most planning research has been derived? Tentatively, the answer appears to be no. Strategic planning in small firms focuses on short time horizons, is informal, deemphasizes mission and goal identification, and incorporates the use of *outsiders*—advisers who are not company employees.[1] In fact, the practice of using outsiders appears to be particularly important in improving the effectiveness of small firms. For example, one researcher found that small firms that incorporated a significant outsider involvement in their decision making significantly outperformed similar firms that did not.[2]

While the value of outsiders should come as no surprise to practicing outsiders—management consultants, public accountants, attorneys, for example—small firm owner/managers have seemingly ignored this resource. One study found that *money* had a lot to do with this state of affairs.[3] Essentially, owner/managers *perceived* outsider costs to be prohibitive—often without ever checking to confirm such costs. Others have found owner/managers unsure of what services an outsider can offer and are suspicious of any outsider's expertise.[4]

This orientation appears to be changing, however. Virtually all the Big Eight and major regional accounting firms have set up small business service components in their practice. This component has been a

---

Source: Richard B. Robinson and Patricia P. Mc Dougall, "Small Manufacturers When Going Outside Makes Sense," *Business* 39, no. 1 (January-March 1989; Georgia State University Business Press), pp. 48–53.

major basis for CPA growth in the 1980s, and major CPA firms have detected a greater receptivity to outsiders on the part of small firms. In an *Inc* magazine survey of its readership, 84% of the responding small firm executives had *no* finance background—indicating a definite need for an outside financial management adviser.[5]

Most research to date on outsider-based planning in small firms has focused on the use of such an approach or what would generally be called process-related issues. Surprisingly, little, if any, research has been directed toward identifying the needs for outsider assistance as perceived by the small firm executive. This issue provides the main focus for this article.

WHERE CONSULTANTS ARE NEEDED

This section (Phase I of this study) summarizes the responses and focuses on the eight functional areas of possible need for outside assistance. Particular attention will be given to those firms (within each functional area) that indicated the greatest receptivity to the use of outside consultants.

Strategic Planning and General Long-Term Management Decisions

Market research received the most interest, with 31% of the respondents indicating a strong interest in receiving assistance. Over half the CEOs indicated they would seek this service either annually or semiannually. The results were mixed regarding how much company management would be willing to pay for this service, with 42% in the $500 to $2,000 range and 42% in the above $10,000 range. There was only moderate interest in receiving outside assistance for the four other items in this category: long-term planning, research into competitors, plant/office site location, transportation network analysis.

Computer Systems

Selection of a computer system received the most interest; 25% of the respondents indicated significant interest. This figure seems low and may be influenced by the size of the firms responding. There is a high probability that many had recently been through the system selection process, The majority of respondents indicated that this activity was needed every three to five years. This may be a function of changing technology as well as growth requirements. Responses indicated that

37.5% of these companies would pay from $500 to $2,000 for such advice, while 25% would pay over $10,000.

Use of outside assistance in the selection and training of data processing personnel was of little interest, with 68% indicating no interest. In fact, answers indicated that outside assistance in evaluating present systems was not important.

Financial Activities and Controls

As might be expected, tax return preparation generated heavy interest, with 80% expressing need for outside assistance; 36% indicated they would pay $500 to $2,000 annually; 54% indicated they would pay over $2,000 annually. A close second to tax return preparation was tax planning, with 70% indicating heavy demand for annual tax planning services. The flat rate the respondents were willing to pay ranged from below $2,000 (60%) to over $2,000 (40%).

In a similar study, respondents to *Inc* magazine's readership survey listed tax return preparation as the service for which they most frequently used outsiders.[6] *Inc* found an inverse relationship between demand for outsider return preparation and sales.

Of those surveyed, 26% indicated heavy interest in outsider-generated investment tax credit studies. However, 80% of the respondents felt that this service would be a part of their tax planning activity.

Financing Activities

Although this category included five financing activities, only 5% of the executives indicated *any* interest in outside assistance with a specific activity. This is somewhat surprising since many consultants to small, growth-oriented manufacturers consider this their bread-and-butter area.[7]

It may be that CEOs perceive that performance of these activities does not require significantly high levels of expertise and that paying an outside consultant may not be particularly cost effective.

Personnel and Productivity

Pension plan and profit-sharing activity led in this category with 47% of the respondents indicating significant interest in outside assistance. The frequency with which this activity is addressed ranges from 56% who are interested on either a semiannual or annual basis to the remaining 44% who showed interest on a less frequent basis. Of particular interest to management consultants, 33% of those answering this survey chose motivation studies as a significant area for using outside consultants. Furthermore, 76% felt they would need such assistance on an annual basis. Surprisingly, respondents were unwilling to indicate the dollar value they placed on such a service. Employee benefit analysis also interested many respondents, with 30% indicating heavy demand for outside assistance, 26% expressing moderate demand, and 83% expecting to pay under $2,000 per year for this type of assistance.

Growth

Identification and measurement of new market areas is the clear leader in this grouping of activities with 42% of those responding showing strong interest in enlisting outside consultants to perform this service. These executives indicated that they devote considerable attention to new markets, with 78% indicating at least annual interest. However, the majority of respondents failed to indicate the cost they associate with this activity. While 26% indicated significant interest in outside assistance with new product development, 86% wished to have this service annually. Again, those responding were unwilling to indicate the cost they associate with such a service.

Cost Reduction Techniques

Surprisingly, small manufacturing executives did not indicate a significant demand for outside assistance in this category. While energy efficiency audits were of some interest (25% of the respondents placed strong emphasis on outside assistance), there was little interest in outside assistance for inventory planning/control, freight alternative audits, maintenance cost control.

Insurance

Risk avoidance attracted significant interest; 25% of those responding indicated a heavy demand for outside assistance; 90% said they would require the service at least every two years. Again, the majority of these executives did not indicate the value they would associate with such a service.

Product/service liability received moderate interest (33%). This activity would be sought on an annual basis by 69% of those interested.

Frequency Activities

The majority of these activities received little to no interest, indicating that because of their frequent nature, the firm must employ internal staffs to control them. The respondents did indicate some interest in receiving outside assistance with operating budgets—24% reported strong interest; 43% indicated they spend between zero and nine hours per month in the operating budget activity.

METHODOLOGY AND SAMPLE

This study sought to answer the following questions:

1. What is the relative importance of outsider assistance to CEOs of small manufacturing firms (50–500 employees) when confronting 48 specific decision areas?
2. What is the CEO perception of the range and level of expertise and costs associated with various types of outsiders?

A comprehensive questionnaire (see Exhibit 1) was sent to a random sample of 100 senior executives of small manufacturers (50–500 employees and less than $45 million in annual sales) in South Carolina. Thirty-two usable responses were received for a 16% response rate. The questionnaire asked the executives to rate the *importance* of outside assistance on each of the 48 decision areas as well as the *frequency of need* for such assistance and the *dollar value* associated with it. The 48 items were divided into nine functional categories. Finally, the questionnaire asked CEOs to evaluate several sources of such assistance.

The low response rate was addressed in three ways:

- Responding firms were compared to the overall sample in terms of size and industry type. No significant differences in the two groups in terms of size distribution and industry types were found.
- Fifteen nonresponding firms were randomly selected and called to find reasons for not responding. "Didn't have the time" (67%) and "Company policy not to respond to surveys" (33%) were the reasons offered by these firms.
- Results of this study were compared with a similar, confidential proprietary study conducted by a branch office of Ernst & Whinney and found to be very similar.

Exhibit 2 summarizes the demographic characteristics of the respondents.

EXHIBIT 1   Consulting Services Questionnaire

The questionnaire was eight pages long counting a cover letter. The format for asking about each decision area was as follows:

Column 1	Column 2	Column 3	Column 4
Please indicate relative importance you place on outside assistance.	Infrequent or nonrecurring activities	Estimated frequency of need. (Check one.)	Dollar value you would place on each activity. (Rate or flat fee.)

Example

Not at all	Not very	Somewhat	Very	Extremely	Please respond based on these items	Semiannual	Annual	Every 1–2 years	Every 3–5 years	Every 6+ years	
1	2	3	4	5	a. Plant site location analysis						$ _____

The following categories and items (within each category) were included in the questionnaire:

I. Strategic planning and general long-term management decisions.
  a. Long-term planning and guidance.
  b. Market research.
  c. Research into competition.
  d. Plant/office site location analysis.
  e. Transportation network analysis.

II. Computer systems
  a. Evaluation of present system and system design.
  b. Aid in selecting a computer system.
  c. Selecting and training data processing personnel.
  d. An evaluation of available service bureaus and what they offer.

III. Financial activities and control
  a. Evaluation and development of accounting controls and systems.
  b. Records retention guidelines.
  c. Depreciation policy alternatives.
  d. Records storage evaluation/ recommendations.
  e. Tax return preparation.
  f. Tax planning.
  g. Investment tax credit.
  h. Capital budgeting.
  i. Financial analysis—How does firm compare with others in the industry? What will your banker look for?
  j. Forecasting and financial modeling.

EXHIBIT 1 (concluded)

IV. Financing activities
   a. Banking and trade credit relationships—How to establish and maintain a relationship for financing growth.
   b. Factoring versus maintaining accounts receivable.
   c. Venture capital—How to obtain it.
   d. Financial planning for growth—How to finance.
   e. Small Business Administration—What is available, at what cost, and how to apply.
V. Personnel and productivity
   a. Productivity measurement.
   b. Office and plant layout efficiency.
   c. Assembly line balancing.
   d. Stress management—How to deal with it.
   e. Time management.
   f. Employee benefit analysis—Local trends and wage levels.
   g. Motivation studies—How to increase productivity and reduce turnover.
   h. Pension plans and profit sharing.
VI. Growth
   a. Identifying merger or acquisition candidates.
   b. New product development.
   c. Data interpretation—What information is important to your firm.
   d. Identification and measurement of new markets.
   e. Product life cycle—Competitive position analysis and implications for future growth.
VII. Cost reduction techniques
   a. Inventory planning and control.
   b. Energy alternative audits.
   c. Freight alternative audits.
   d. Fleet maintenance.
VIII. Insurance
   a. Risk management audits.
   b. Insurance premium audits.
   c. Product/service liability.

EVALUATING OUTSIDER SOURCES

The second section of the questionnaire (Phase II of the survey) asked responding executives to evaluate 12 outsider sources in terms of the likelihood of providing a broad range of these services, probable level of expertise, and likely hourly cost. Exhibit 3 provides a description of the question format and reports the responses for each outsider organization.

Likelihood of Providing a Broad Range of Consulting Services

Management consultants (47.4%) and Big Eight CPA firms (44.4%) were perceived to be the most likely providers of a broad range of consulting services. They were followed by a second group composed of universities, regional CPA firms, and interstate banks.

EXHIBIT 2 Respondent Characteristics

Area	*Percent of Respondents*
Major market areas:	
Local	5.26%
Entire state	10.53
Southeast	15.79
National	57.90
International	10.53
Ownership:	
Publicly held	31.58%
Privately held	57.90
Annual sales:	

Sales (in millions of dollars)	*Percent of Respondents*
$2–$3	10.52%
$3–$5	5.26
$5–$7	5.26
$7–$10	10.52
$10–$20	15.79
$20–$30	15.79
$30–$40	31.57

Probable Level of Expertise

Similarly, Big Eight CPA firms and management consultants were ranked highest in level of perceived expertise. They were followed by regional CPA firms. Quite noticeable is the perceived *lack* of expertise in organizations commonly thought of as key outsiders for small firms: local banks, local CPAs, SBAs, SBDCs, insurance companies, and—to a lesser extent—universities.

Likely Hourly Costs

Again, Big Eight CPA firms and management consultants received a pattern of response clearly different from the other outsider organizations. Three out of four respondents expect the cost of these services to exceed $50 per hour. It is clear that executives of small manufacturers expect the cost to rise along with perceived expertise and range of services. An hourly rate between $36 to $50 was the most commonly predicted for other types of consultants.

The responses to Phase II suggest Big Eight CPA firms and management consultants generally are the most favorably perceived sources of

EXHIBIT 3 Last Page of the Survey Questionnaire

Numerous types of organizations are seeking to provide such services on a "one-stop" basis to small and medium-sized businesses. The next questions seek to gauge your perception of this development.

1. Several organizations are listed below and blanks are included for you to add to that list. To the right of this list are three columns in which you are asked to indicate (a) how likely a broad range of such services would come from each organization; (b) your opinion of the level of expertise you would expect to be associated with that range of services; and (c) the cost you would expect each to ask.

Organization Which Might Offer Services	Likelihood of Providing a Broad Range of Services (circle one for each organization)				Probable Level of Expertise (Circle one for each organization)				Likely Hourly Cost (check one for each organization)			
	Defi-nitely Not	Un-likely	Pos-sible	Most Likely	Poor	Ade-quate	Above Average	High	$20 or Less	$21 to $35	$26 to $50	Above $50
Statewide bank	25.0%	40.0%	25.0%	10.0%	23.5%	53.0%	23.5%	—	10.0%	26.7%	13.3%	—
Interstate bank	5.7	33.3	33.3	27.7	27.8	16.7	38.9	16.6%	31.3	25.0	43.7	—
Brokerage firm	11.8	64.7	17.6	5.9	40.0	40.0	20.0	—	30.7	15.4	38.5	15.4%
Investment banker	17.6	35.3	35.3	11.8	33.3	6.7	46.7	13.3	7.7	7.7	53.8	30.8
Local CPA firm	11.8	35.3	41.2	11.7	13.3	60.0	20.0	6.7	7.1	28.6	42.9	21.4
Regional CPA firm	5.6	22.2	50.0	22.2	5.9	23.5	58.8	11.8	—	13.3	53.3	33.3
Big-Eight CPA firm	—	11.1	44.4	44.4	5.9	17.6	41.2	35.3	—	6.7	20.0	73.3
Management consultants	—	21.1	31.6	47.4	5.9	23.5	41.2	29.4	—	12.5	12.5	75.0
University	—	31.6	36.8	31.6	5.6	50.0	11.1	33.3	—	26.7	60.0	13.3
SBA (Small Business Administration)	23.5	17.6	47.1	11.8	43.8	43.8	12.4	—	38.5	46.2	15.3	—
SBDC (Small Business Development Center)	23.5	35.3	29.4	11.8	31.3	62.5	6.2	—	46.2	46.2	7.7	—
Large insurance company	17.6	47.1	35.3	—	31.3	62.5	6.2	—	23.1	38.5	30.8	7.6
Others:												

EXHIBIT 4   One-Stop versus Multiple Sources

Considering the decision-making *practices in your firm* and the future use of "outsiders" for assistance, what is your preference for a "one-stop" source versus numerous outside sources? Please check below:

Prefer "one-stop" source		Neutral			Prefer several out- sider specialists
7.1%	7.1%	28.6%	21.4%	35.7%	

---

outsiders. However, this does not mean they have a strong corner on the consulting market. When asked to identify their preference for "one stop" versus "multiple" sources of outside consultants, the executives in this study expressed a strong preference for multiple sources (see Exhibit 4). So while they think highly of Big Eight CPAs and management consultants, executives of small manufacturing firms want to keep their options on sources of outside consultants rather broad.

CONCLUSIONS

The following ten activities stood out as decision areas in which executives in small manufacturing firms desired outside assistance (the percentage of interested firms is in parentheses):

- Tax return preparation (80%).
- Tax planning (70%).
- Pension plans and profit sharing (47%).
- Identification/measurement of new markets (42%).
- Risk avoidance (35%).
- Motivational studies (33%).
- Market research (31%).
- Employee benefit analysis (30%).
- Investment tax credit studies (26%).
- Selecting computer systems (25%).

While they perceive Big Eight firms and management consultants to be the best (and costliest) source of such assistance, these executives strongly desire to work with separate specialists on separate decision areas.

The favorable perception for management consultants is encouraging for interested academic consultants. However, the negative perception of university sources, coupled with a low perceived hourly rate, suggests the academic-based consultant must carefully market his or her credentials.

A big question remains in the perceived cost area. Our survey had "above $50" as a top category in Phase I. In retrospect, it should have been higher to better gauge price sensitivity. On the other hand, executives clearly differentiated the value of different sources in a manner consistent with current conditions. And following earlier outsider research, it appears small manufacturers are seriously incorporating (or considering the need to incorporate) outsiders into their planning/decision making in at least ten key decision areas.

NOTES

1. R. B. Robinson, "Forecasting and Small Business: A study of the Strategic Planning Process," *Journal of Small Business Management* 11, No. 1 (1979): 19–27; R. B. Judy, "When Is Small Large Enough?" Paper presented at the 1982 Academy of Management Annual Meeting, New York; R. B. Robinson, "The Importance of 'Outsiders' in Small Firm Strategic Planning." *Academy of Management Journal* 25, No. 3 (1982): 80–89.
2. Robinson, "Importance of 'Outsiders'," 80–89.
3. H. S. Kreutzman and J. N. Samaras, "Can Small Businesses Use Consultants?" *Harvard Business Review* (May/June 1960): 38, 57–64.
4. D. L. Sexton and P. M. Van Auben, "Prevalence of Strategic Planning in Small Business," *Journal of Small Business Management* 20, No. 3 (1982), 20–26.
5. *Inc.* "You and Your Accountant," March 1982, 81–90.
6. Ibid., 81–90.
7. Judy, "When Is Small."